BRITAIN IN THE WORLD ECONOMY
SINCE 1880

A Social and Economic History of England/Twentieth-Century Britain

Edited by Asa Briggs

Anglo-Saxon England the Norman Conquest (2nd Edition)
  H. R. Loyn

Medieval England: Rural Society and Economic Change 1086–1348
  E. Miller and J. Hatcher

Medieval England: Towns, Commerce and Crafts, 1086–1348
  E. Miller and J. Hatcher

The Age of Plunder 1500–1547 W. G. Hoskins

The Age of Elizabeth 1547–1603 (2nd Edition) D. M. Palliser

*England's Apprenticeship 1603–1763 Charles Wilson

The Vital Century: England's Economy 1714–1815 John Rule

Albion's People: English Society, 1714–1815 John Rule

*The Rise of Industrial Society in England 1815–1885
  S. G. Checkland

Britain in the World Economy since 1880 B. W. E. Alford

* Not currently available

BRITAIN IN THE WORLD ECONOMY SINCE 1880

B. W. E. Alford

LONGMAN
London and New York

Longman Group Limited
Longman House, Burnt Mill,
Harlow, Essex CM20 2JE, England
and Associated Companies throughout the world.

Published in the United States of America
by Longman Publishing, New York

First published 1996

ISBN 0 582 48675 0 CSD
ISBN 0 582 48676 9 PPR

British Library Cataloguing-in-Publication Data

A catalogue record for this book is
available from the British Library

Library of Congress Cataloging-in-Publication Data

Alford, B. W. E.
    Britain in the world economy since 1880 / B.W.E. Alford.
        p. cm. – (Social and economic history of England)
    Includes bibliographical references and index.
    ISBN 0-582-48675-0 (case). – ISBN 0-582-48676-9 (pbk.)
        1. Great Britain–Economic conditions–19th century. 3. Great
Britain–Economic conditions–20th century. 2. Great Britain–
Commerce–History. 4. Economic history. 5. International trade.
I. Title. II. Series.
HC255.A72 1996
330.941–dc20   95-5930
                                                                    CIP

Set by 7B in 10/12pt Baskerville
Produced by Longman Singapore Publishers (Pte) Ltd.
Printed in Singapore

Contents

List of Tables and Figures

CHAPTER 3

CHAPTER 4

CHAPTER 5

CHAPTER 6

CHAPTER 7

CHAPTER 8

CHAPTER 9

CHAPTER 10

List of Abbreviations

AACP	Anglo-American Council on Productivity
CAP	Common Agricultural Policy of the European Community
ECU	European Currency Unit
EEC	European Economic Community
EPU	European Payments Union
ERM	Exchange Rate Mechanism
ERP	European Recovery Programme
GATT	General Agreement on Tariffs and Trade
IMF	International Monetary Fund
IRC	Industrial Reorganization Corporation
MITI	Ministry of International Trade and Industry (Japan)
NEDC	National Economic Development Council
OECD	Organization for Economic Cooperation and Development
OEEC	Organization for European Economic Cooperation
OPEC	Organization of Petroleum Exporting Countries
SDR	Special Drawing Rights

Preface

The changing role, and diminishing influence, of Britain in the international economy during the past century is the central concern of this book. Within this focus a number of themes are examined in detail, including the relationship between Empire and economy, the pattern and nature of British trade, overseas investment, international financial policy, industrial competitiveness and the relationship between economic policy and performance. The analysis is set within a comparative international framework and particular attention is paid to the Western European nations, the USA and Japan. The period encompasses two world wars and their impact on Britain's position in the world economy is assessed.

This study does not purport to offer a comprehensive economic and social history of Britain. The approach is not, however, narrowly economic, and one of the major conclusions of the analysis is that the explanation of Britain's economic performance is to be found in a wide range of political, social and cultural, as well as economic, conditions. In those places where theoretical and technical issues have to be addressed, every effort has been made to make the discussion 'user-friendly'. In range and coverage, the statistical tables should prove particularly useful to students and the general reader interested in the period.

In a study of this kind I have drawn on the work of many scholars whom it is not possible to acknowledge, though my large debt to them is obvious. The footnotes provide detailed references to those sources I have found most useful as well as suggestions for further reading. For this reason it is not thought necessary to provide a collected bibliography.

I should like to thank the staffs of the University of Bristol Library and the Public Record Office.

I have accumulated many debts to colleagues at Bristol and

elsewhere. In particular, I received encouragement from the late William Ashworth and constructive criticism, advice and help from my colleagues Rodney Lowe, Roger Middleton and Philip Richardson. Anne Griffiths has my special thanks, not only for having converted my manuscript into typescript but also for her continuing patience and support. Andrew MacLennan has been an indulgent editor during the years that this book has been promised. Like many of the issues covered by this book, my debt to Valerie Alford is unquantifiable.

13 June, 1995

The reader should note that in the references, the place of publication is London unless otherwise stated.

The publishers would like to thank the following for granting permission to reproduce textual material: Liverpool University Press for figure 2.1; Routledge (Unwin Hyman 1978) for table 2.12; Routledge (Allen and Unwin 1984) for table 3.4; Routledge for tables 6.3, 6.6 and 7.8; Methuen & Co for table 6.4; Dr John Wells, Dr R. E. Rowthorn and Cambridge University Press for tables 7.3, 7.4, 7.7, 8.2, 9.2, 9.3 and 9.4; the National Institute Economic Review for tables 8.4 and 10.9; Blackwell Publishers for tables 2.14 and 10.6.

To the memory of
Winifred and Ernest Alford

Introduction

From being the world's top nation in the 1880s Britain now has fallen back to its pre-imperial status of an offshore island of a powerful continent. The emergence of the USA and Russia as superpowers and the economic recovery of Western Europe and Japan after the Second World War left Britain stranded at the head of a rapidly diminishing empire. But British imperialism had not been sustained by economic and military hegemony alone. It rested on elements of economic and military strength in combination with an imperial idea, which centred on a belief in the innate superiority and civilizing power of British (and more particularly English) liberal, Christian values.[1] This ideology contained large ingredients of hypocrisy and self-delusion, which proved treacherous in the longer run. It was impossible to insist on the values of individualism and parliamentary institutions without conceding self-determination to empire countries. For all this, it by no means follows that the loss of empire inevitably carried with it Britain's relative economic decline.

A country's economic performance is commonly judged in comparative international terms. Success in these stakes is not the preserve of large nations, as the examples of Switzerland and Belgium testify. Yet in the latter half of the twentieth century Britain has experienced growing difficulty in maintaining a place among the major world economies. It is, of course, important to remember that quantifiable economic performance is not the sum total of welfare, and this fact can be no more obvious than for the period covered by this book, which includes two world wars. And in making international comparisons in the chapters which follow, it

1. An interesting analysis is provided by J. M. Mackenzie, *Propaganda and Empire: The Manipulation of British Public Opinion 1880–1960* (Manchester, 1984).

1

will be necessary to consider to what extent Britain surrendered measurable income for welfare in other forms. This is an acutely difficult problem, however, since it involves all the imprecision of qualitative judgement together with the problems of balancing the claims of various sections of the community against one another, within a framework of changing levels of expectations.

It remains the case, nevertheless, that for much of the period covered by this study there has been a wide and increasing concern in Britain over the failure to match economic expectations with performance. In the interwar years the general consciousness of economic failure was sharpened by the experience of high levels of unemployment, though this was modified to the extent that in the 1930s the economic depression was international in its effects and Britain did not seem to be failing unduly. In the second half of the twentieth century the country's relative economic decline in the world has been felt much more acutely – to such an extent that it has been popularly diagnosed as the manifestation of the 'British disease'. Whether this disease is as country-specific as this implies and, indeed, whether it is real or imagined, are important questions which this book seeks to answer.

Much of the literature on which this study is based reflects the major influence that economic theory has had on historical analysis, particularly on work published since the Second World War. But whilst the application of economic theory has contributed a great deal to historical understanding, it has been mainly in terms of the proximate causes of economic outcomes. Thus, for example, it has focused on levels of investment, exchange rate policies, fiscal regimes. It has provided little by way of explanation of the underlying causes of economic change and development. This is not something that results simply from inadequate and inaccurate data and from the fact that the operations of many economic agents are unquantifiable, important though these things are. It is the consequence of two, more fundamental problems.

The first problem stems directly from the inherent limitations of neo-classical economics, which is the dominant orthodoxy of modern economic theory. It is a system of analysis in which, in basic terms, the point of departure is where resources and technology are given. Economists then set out to explore the market which allocates resources. It is a strange world peopled by individual maximizers, homogeneous factors of production and representative firms, and it is subject to such conditions as equilibrium, constrained optimization and transactions costs. It is a world in which there are few recognizable institutions and in which normal time does not operate; a world in which changes in conditions are measured by comparative static analysis, by intervals of rational time. In other words, neo-classical economics operates in the realm of possible worlds in contrast to what is commonly understood as the reality of the present and the past. Thus the contribution of counter-factual models in historical analysis can be revealing in terms of what might have been, but they are treacherous guides to understanding what actually happened.

The second problem arises from the fact that proximate economic causes are not necessarily economic in origin. For example, whilst it may be the case that Britain's economic performance has suffered from too low a level of industrial investment, it is not immediately clear why this should have been so. Unless the historian adopts a Marxist view of the world, so that everything has an economic explanation, the reason for poor investment performance may be found among a whole range of political, social and cultural conditions and motivations. The policy implications are equally important, in the sense that the identification of the proximate cause of an economic problem does not automatically lead to the prescription for its cure. By the same token, the fact that historians have the advantage of hindsight does not enable them to select the appropriate economic model to provide the sought-for explanation. Moreover, economic changes, especially those measured as aggregates, are frequently the result of several causes operating in conjunction.

To recognize these limitations is not to argue that economic analysis should be ignored as irrelevant, but that it should be seen as part of the hybrid nature of historical analysis and explanation. 'Hypothesis and abstraction are essential tools but not the goal of explanation ... [and] must not be a substitute for missing or awkward evidence just because it is simpler to analyse'.[2] In the chapters which follow, the attempt has been made to set the more theoretical analyses within a broader framework of historiography. And whilst heavy reliance has been placed on statistical data in the service of both illustration and explanation, in most cases the aim is to show that there are no neat quantitative answers to the historical questions that are raised.

It is not claimed that this study offers a complete explanation of

2. W. Ashworth, 'The Newest and Truest Economic History?', *Economic History Review*, 35 (1982), pp. 440–1.

Britain's economic odyssey during the past century. Moreover, important parts of the story are missing and await detailed investigation. Nevertheless, the broad conclusion which is drawn from the available evidence is that the relative international economic decline that Britain has experienced during the period as whole, and especially since the Second World War, amounts to a failure of economic performance. It has not been the result of a process at work among Western European countries and Japan of economic catch-up and forging ahead from low starting points; a process which cannot ultimately be to Britain's disadvantage since by its very nature Britain will in turn come to benefit from it as a follower economy. To the contrary, the evidence points strongly to fundamental failings in the nature and operation of British society and economy that have resulted in a widening gap between economic expectations and performance.

CHAPTER ONE
The Challenge to Late Victorian Apogee

ECONOMY AND SOCIETY

The economic ascendancy that Britain had achieved over the world economy by 1880 was the outcome of a cumulative process extending over the previous two centuries. At its core were the dynamics of industrialization. To what extent this growth stemmed from revolutionary changes in economic development in the mid-eighteenth century or from evolutionary changes extending over a longer period is still a matter of dispute.[1] But it is clear that during the nineteenth century growth rates were low by modern standards. Britain can be characterized as a two per cent economy. More detailed figures are provided in Table 1.1. Translated into GDP per worker the rate fluctuated around 1 per cent per year.

For all their apparent precision these statistics provide no more than crude orders of magnitude because of the far from perfect data from which they have been constructed. The main features of economic growth are reasonably clear, however. Not only was it moderate, it was fairly evenly distributed over all sectors of the economy and, it should be noted, services maintained its important role, albeit in changing form. Coketown and Mr. Gradgrind, brought to public consciousness by Dickens, by no means wholly typified the economy at any stage in the nineteenth century. The worlds of *Middlemarch* and *Cranford* were equally the reality. Some

---

1. For a useful survey of the debate on the industrial revolution see P. Hudson, *The Industrial Revolution* (1992). See also J. Hoppitt, 'Counting the Industrial Revolution', *Economic History Review*, 43 (1990), pp. 173–93; J. Mokyr, 'The Industrial Revolution and the New Economic History', in Mokyr (ed.), *The Economics of the Industrial Revolution* (1985). In many respects the best analysis remains D. C. Coleman, 'Industrial Growth and Industrial Revolutions', *Economica*, 89 (1956), pp. 1–22.

Table 1.1 United Kingdom: average annual rates of growth of GDP, 1820–1913

	(*Constant prices*)	
	I	*II*
1820–1870	2.0	–
1856–1913	–	1.9
1882–1913	1.8	1.8
1856–1873	–	2.2
1873–1882	1.9	1.8
1882–1899	2.2	2.2
1899–1913	1.3	1.4

Sources: I Maddison (1991), Tables A5, A6, 207, 210–11; II Mitchell (1988), 836.

indication of the nature of economic society is given by the fact that the 1871 census was the first to register a decline in the agricultural workforce. But with a labour force of 3 million, agriculture still remained the single largest occupation and it accounted for 22 per cent of the working population. Equally significant was the continued rise in the number employed in domestic service. At 1.85 million it amounted to 12.3 per cent of the workforce in 1881. But industrialization and industrialism were the new forces with which the old order had to come to terms.[2]

Britain's leading world position in 1880 was universally recognized though it was not conceived of in the kind of quantitative measures which are nowadays an essential part of the vernacular of political economy. In economic matters, as in much else, the Victorians thought in terms of progress and expansion. Economic growth did not have the meaning now attached to it, but steady growth was, in effect, fully in accord with Victorian values. In common form these values were popularized by Samuel Smiles in his best-selling book *Thrift*, which extolled the virtue of regular saving and the power of compound interest.[3] This rhythm of economic progress was in harmony with the expansion of the Empire. British imperialism was a process of accumulation. It is true

2. Although superseded in some respects, H. M. Lynd, *England in the Eighteen Eighties* (Oxford, 1945) still offers an outstanding interpretation of the period.
3. A. Briggs, *Victorian People* (1955), Chapter 5.

Table 1.2 Indicators of Britain's position in the world economy, c.1870/80

	Index: GDP per head 1870	Index: GDP per man hour 1870	Share of world exports 1870[a](%)	Share of world manufactured exports 1880 (%)	Share of world manufactured output 1880 (%)
UK	100	100	30.0	41.4	22.9
Belgium	80	79	4.0		1.8
France	60	54	17.0	22.2	7.8
Germany	50	48	13.0	19.3	8.5
Italy	46	39	6.0		2.5
Japan	24	18	0.4		2.4
Netherlands	79	85	1.6		
Sweden	50	45	1.3		0.8
Switzerland	70	60	1.9		0.8
USA	86	96	12.0	2.8	14.7

[a] Total for 16 major countries. Merchandize Exports.

Sources: Bairoch (1982), 296; Maddison (1991), 6–7, 53, 324; Saul (1965), 12.

that imperial rivalry among the Great Powers at the end of the century became a vigorous affair, and that between 1870 and 1914 the British Empire increased in area by nearly two and a half times, but in economic terms this was expansion at the margin since the old territories remained dominant in imperial trade and finance. And the new acquisitions owed much to the simple extension and consolidation of existing territorial advantage and to the habitual exercise of diplomatic skills.[4]

Victorians and Victorian values are, nevertheless, concepts easily open to historical misrepresentation. They can be used to convey a sense of coherence and consistency that is alien to reality. The society of the time has been aptly described as 'ramshackle and amorphous' because of the continuous cross currents of change and conflict within it.[5] A Victorian, so defined, did not become

4. There is a huge literature but useful surveys are P. J. Cain, *Economic Foundations of British Imperialism* (1980); P. J. Cain and A. G. Hopkins, *British Imperialism: Innovation and Expansion 1688–1914* (1993); D. K. Fieldhouse, *Economics and Empire, 1880–1914* (1973); R. Owen and B. Sutcliffe (eds), *Studies in the Theory of Imperialism* (1972); B. Porter, *The Lion's Share, A Short History of British Imperialism* (1975).

5. José Harris, *Private Lives, Public Spirit: A Social History of Britain, 1870–1914* (1993), p. 8.

overnight the quite different person of an Edwardian simply because one monarch succeeded another. Such a transformation would truly reflect a monarchy of awesome power. And the society of which these individuals were a part is difficult to define because its boundaries were fluid. These boundaries could extend beyond the frontiers of the nation state to incorporate, for example, imperial links or foreign ethnic ties. There are, in other words, various levels at which society may be perceived, each layer involving sets of relationships in turn interlinked with other layers.[6]

The analysis of political, and more particularly in this context, economic power, is similarly vulnerable to undue historical simplification. For example, Marx, an eminent Victorian no less, reduced the complexities of social relationships to subservience to the dominant and unifying power of capitalist exploitation. Whilst Marxian analysis finds little favour among historians nowadays, the idea within it of the power of an elite group to manipulate the economy to its own ends still holds strong appeal. The most important recent version takes the historical form of so-called gentlemanly capitalism.[7] This creature will be examined in more detail later (Chapter 3) but in essence it embodied 'a complex of economic, social and political influences' centred on the City of London, of such power that it controlled much of the economic life of the nation and directed it to its own ends. One of the problems with such historical characterizations is that, even when economic power can be identified and its exercise documented, the outcome is not a foregone conclusion. Historical actors, no less than those of the present day, operated within a world of imperfect knowledge in which the outcome of their actions was frequently unintended and consequently not in their self-interest.

The economic divisions in society in the late nineteenth century were thus complex and changing. What might appear to be precise definitions of occupations in census returns cover wide variations in practice, and these variations increased over time. Whilst it is essential to recognize this fact it is, however, impossible and unnecessary in this context to provide a comprehensive analysis of late Victorian society. For present purposes, a broad brush will be applied to paint contrasts between the gainers and losers from late-nineteenth-century British prosperity.

6. A study of particular aspects of this general issue is provided by D. Feldman, *Englishmen and Jews: Social Relations and Political Culture, 1840–1914* (1994).

7. Cain and Hopkins, *British Imperialism*.

During the latter half of the Victorian period prosperity spread to the mass of the people and covered a rise in population from 23 million in 1861 to 30 million by 1881. Whilst the richest 4 per cent of income receivers swallowed up nearly half the total income in 1880, absolute real incomes had risen for nearly all.[8] Between 1861 and 1881 average real wages rose by 37 per cent. In large part this was the result of Britain's ability to reap the comparative advantage of exporting manufactured goods and financial and commercial services in return for imports of increasingly cheap grain from North and South America, in particular. Over the 1880s real wages rose by a further 19 per cent.[9] And to the flow of cheap foreign grain was added a growing amount of chilled meat from the southern hemisphere transported in the new technology of refrigerated ships. Even among wage-earners, however, these gains were not distributed evenly. There were significant occupational and regional differences; moreover, the available statistics probably overstate the gains since they do not adequately take account of the 'reserve army' of the underemployed and those in low-paid service occupations. At the extreme, income per head in London was between two and four times the level in Wales. Nevertheless, the gains for all regions were substantial.[10]

The working class contained many elements. There was obviously a broad distinction between urban and rural workers. But within each of these categories the divisions were multifarious. The elite was made up of artisans: those who practised a particular manual skill. In terms of income they sometimes ranked higher than those immediately above them in the social scale, and they created their own distinctive culture which, by the 1880s, contained many elements of aspiration to middle-class status. Their major concern was to maintain their position within a plentifully supplied labour market and the obvious way in which to do this was through exclusive craft unions that placed great emphasis on forms of apprenticeship, demarcation rules and wage differentials. These

8. A. L. Bowley, *The Change in the Distribution of National Income, 1880–1913* (Oxford, 1920), p. 16.

9. B. R. Mitchell, *British Historical Statistics* (Cambridge, 1988), pp. 149–50. See also C. Feinstein, 'What Really Happened to Real Wages? Trends in wages, prices, and productivity in the United Kingdom, 1880–1913', *Economic History Review*, 43 (1990), pp. 329–55 and *idem.*, 'New Estimates of Average Earnings in the United Kingdom, 1880–1913', *Economic History Review, loc. cit.*, pp. 595–632.

10. C. H. Lee, *The British Economy since 1700: A Macroeconomic Perspective* (Cambridge, 1986), p. 131. E. H. Hunt, 'Industrialization and Regional Inequality: Wages in Britain', *Journal of Economic History*, 46 (1986), pp. 935–66.

practices were reinforced by a commitment to self-help, self-improvement and, above all, to self-esteem. Welfare schemes, social clubs and intermarriage were important means through which this artisan culture was expressed and sustained.[11] Those unable to defend themselves in this way were the unskilled and, to a lesser extent, the semi-skilled.

The rate of growth of the population of working age peaked in the last two decades of the century and exceeded the rate of growth of total population.

Table 1.3 Growth of total population and working population in the UK, 1871–1911 (% per year)

	Population	*Working population*
1871–1881	1.0	0.7
1881–1891	0.8	1.0
1891–1901	1.0	1.2
1901–1911	0.8	0.9

Source: Matthews, Feinstein and Odling-Smee (1982), 52.

In such conditions underemployment was a more important feature of the labour market than unemployment. The biggest reservoir of underemployed workers was in the service sector and this is a major reason why calculations of occupational change are difficult to interpret. Large towns and, in particular, the London of Charles Booth's famous survey – *Life and Labour in London* – were the places in which could be found the major part of what Marx called 'the reserve army of labour'.[12] The pressure of underemployment was also reflected in the large numbers of

11. See G. Crossick, *An Artisan Elite in Victorian Society. Kentish London 1840–1880* (1978); and C. More, *Skill and the English Working Class* (1980). For a good survey of the class structure and a guide to the literature see A. J. Reid, *Social Classes and Social Relations in Britain, 1850–1914* (1992). The complexity of intra-class relationships is well brought out in M. Anderson, *Family Structure in Nineteenth Century Lancashire* (Cambridge, 1971).

12. A major study in this field is G. Stedman Jones, *Outcast London: a Study of the Relationship between Classes in Victorian Society* (Oxford, 1971). See also R. McKibben, *The Ideologies of Class. Social Relations in Britain 1888–1950* (Oxford, 1990), pp. 167–96.

abysmally paid domestic servants to be found in both town and country.

For the masses, cheap food was the main dividend from Britain's place in the world economy. For the middle and upper classes the dividends were received in the more usual form of returns on investments, professional fees, profits and rents. It is impossible to provide anything approaching precise measures of the incomes enjoyed by this group, but it is fairly certain that they grew in step with the general rise in national income, and this increase occurred in combination with a rise in the proportionate size of the group as a result of upward occupational mobility which became more marked from 1880 onwards. This pattern of income growth is corroborated by its consistency with the more reliable data available on the distribution of income in succeeding years.[13]

For the middle and professional classes rising real incomes supported higher standards of material comfort and greater social pretension.[14] The most obvious physical manifestations of this prosperity were the expanding suburbs of solid brick or stone villas within which the daily needs of the occupants were tended to by the growing army of domestic servants. It was the mahogany age: large quantities of heavily carved mahogany furniture were the mark of the material success of the middle classes and demonstrated their capacity to satisfy their demands by drawing on the resources of the far corners of the world. Employment in the professions was growing rapidly. The non-commissioned officers of the middle class were the clerks who worked in the counting houses and offices of industry, commerce and the professions. For most of them life was frequently a test of keeping up appearances, which meant distinguishing themselves from the ranks of shopkeepers, traders and lesser sorts who formed a kind of penumbra between the lower middle class and the working class.[15]

At the top of the social pyramid were the landed classes, the city merchants and leading industrialists. This last group was the

13. Bowley, *The Change in the Distribution of National Income*, p. 16. P. H. Lindert and J. G. Williamson, 'Reinterpreting Britain's Social Tables, 1688–1913', *Explorations in Economic History*, 20 (1983), pp. 94–109.

14. See for example J. A. Banks, *Prosperity and Parenthood. A Study of Family Planning among the Victorian Middle Classes* (1954); T. R. Gourvish, 'The Rise of the Professions', in T. R. Gourvish and A. O'Day (eds), *Later Victorian Britain* (1988), pp. 13–35; W. J. Reader, *Professional Men: The Rise of the Professional Class in Nineteenth Century England* (1966).

15. G. Crossick (ed.), *The Lower Middle Class in Britain, 1870–1914* (1978).

significant new element in the nineteenth century, though a number of historians have argued that landowners and merchants retained their economic as well as their political and social pre-eminence. Whilst the fortunes of individual landowners and city merchants altered in relation to the shifting sources of income and wealth during the century, evidence has been produced which suggests that their grasp on the nation's treasure held firm.[16] Landowners who relied heavily on agricultural rents for their income suffered relative if not absolute losses with the decline in agricultural prosperity in the last quarter of the century. But those with large urban estates and industrial interests such as the Duke of Westminster, the Duke of Bedford and the Marquis of Bute, became fabulously rich. This is an issue to which we shall return (in Chapter 3) since it bears directly on the nature of economic performance in the century before the First World War. Those of old wealth further embellished their fine houses and enhanced their style of living on their country estates, at their London houses and in their Continental playgrounds. They were aped by the *nouveaux riches* who commonly chose to build massive neo-Gothic country houses, mock castles in Scotland and maybe sought to establish themselves in London society through conspicuous consumption in modern Baroque mansions in the fashionable parts of town.[17]

16. See W. D. Rubenstein, *Men of Property: The Very Wealthy in Great Britain since the Industrial Revolution* (1981); *idem.*, *Wealth and Inequality in Britain* (1986). Valuable though these studies are they must be regarded as providing very broad measures. There are two major problems: Rubenstein's work is based on probate returns and before 1898 these included only personalty (personal effects, stocks and shares, bank credits and leaseholds) and not real property; estimates of wealth (on this limited basis) at death are only indirectly related to the amount of income disposed of during life. See N. J. Morgan and M. S. Moss, 'Listing the Wealthy in Scotland', *Bulletin of the Institute of Historical Research*, 59 (1986), pp. 189–95. One aspect of these problems has given rise to a detailed debate over the extent to which new wealth during this period was used to purchase land. The nature of the debate can be gathered from F. M. L. Thompson, 'Life after Death: How Successful Nineteenth-Century Businessmen Disposed of their Fortunes', *Economic History Review*, 43 (1990), pp. 40–61.

17. Examples are provided by F. M. L. Thompson, *English Landed Society in the Nineteenth Century* (1963), pp. 297*ff*. See also S. Chapman, 'Aristocracy and Meritocracy in Merchant Banking', *British Journal of Sociology*, 37 (1988), pp. 180–93 and J. Harris and P. Thane, 'British and European Bankers in Pre–1914 Europe', in P. Thane, G. Crossick and R. Floud (eds), *The Power of the Past* (1984), pp. 215–34.

INDUSTRY AND LABOUR

The advance of industrialization had depended on geographical and occupational mobility. These movements are, again, extremely difficult to measure because of the unreliability of the data. In particular, as noted earlier, there are enormous problems of definition of occupations and industries, and even within quite

Table 1.4 United Kingdom: distribution of the working population, selected years 1881–1911

	1881 (000's)	%	1891 (000's)	%	1901 (000's)	%	1911 (000's)	%
Industry								
Agriculture	2,790	18.5	2,560	15.4	2,360	12.6	2,340	11.5
Fishing	70	0.5	70	0.4	60	0.3	60	0.3
Mining & quarrying	680	4.5	840	5.0	1,020	5.5	1,290	6.3
Manufacturing	4,920	32.6	5,520	33.1	5,990	32.1	6,550	32.1
Building & contracting	830	5.5	840	5.0	1,090	5.8	1,030	5.1
Gas, electricity & water	40	0.3	60	0.4	100	0.5	120	0.6
Sub totals	9,330	61.9	9,890	59.3	10,620	56.8	11,390	55.9
Services								
Transport & communications	860	5.7	1,110	6.7	1,450	7.8	1,580	7.7
Distributive trades	1,300	8.6	1,640	9.8	1,990	10.7	2,460	12.1
Insurance, banking & finance	70	0.5	110	0.7	150	0.8	230	0.1
Public administration & defence:								
Central government	50	0.3	70	0.4	80	0.4	120	0.6
Local authorities	170	1.1	200	1.2	270	1.4	320	1.6
Defence	240	1.6	280	1.7	530	2.8	400	2.0
Professional services:								
Education	210	1.4	240	1.4	280	1.5	310	1.5
Medical & dental	80	0.5	100	0.6	120	0.6	150	0.7
Other	240	1.6	260	1.5	320	1.7	370	1.8
Miscellaneous services:								
Private & domestic	1,850	12.3	1,940	11.6	1,980	10.6	2,000	9.8
Catering, hotels, etc.	350	2.3	430	2.6	460	2.5	610	3.0
Other	320	2.1	390	2.3	430	2.3	450	2.2
Sub totals	5,740	38.0	6,770	40.5	8,060	43.1	9,000	43.1
Totals	15,070	100	16,660	100	18,680	100	20,390	100

Source: Mitchell (1988), 111, with corrections.

broad categories the decadal population censuses were far from consistent in this respect. In broad terms the major sectoral shifts during the latter part of the nineteenth century are shown in Table 1.4. The swing away from agriculture under the massive impact of imports of cheap grain is clear. The continued growth of services has already been noted. The major change in the Victorian period as a whole was an increase of nearly one million jobs in domestic service. Other services – insurance and the professions in particular – gained steadily and, moreover, the nature of these activities changed in line with the increase in scale and the growing international nature of Britain's economic development.[18]

Substantial though these changes were, it has been pointed out that they appear less impressive when translated into measures of structural change.

Table 1.5 Comparative growth rates of employment and structural change in Great Britain, 1851–1911 (% per year)

	Employment	*Structural change* [a]
1851–1861	1.16	1.08
1861–1871	1.23	1.31
1871–1881	0.70	0.84
1881–1891	1.31	0.90
1891–1901	1.17	1.29
1901–1911	1.17	0.86

[a] Structural change is measured as 'the sum of deviations of sectoral rates of growth from the total rate of growth, weighted by the size of the sector'.

Source: Lee (1986), 13.

The 1850s, 1860s and 1890s were the periods of most rapid shifts but even these fell below a rate of 2 per cent per year. In other words, the large changes in sectoral employment took place over a relatively long period of time. These calculations make no

18. For an excellent survey which covers this period see M. Anderson, 'The Social Implications of Demographic Change', in F. M. L. Thompson (ed.), *The Cambridge Social History of Britain 1750–1850. Vol. 2. People and Their Environment* (Cambridge, 1990), pp. 10–70.

allowance, of course, for what might have been large changes in the nature of occupations, especially through the application of new techniques, which retained the same census classification. But unless it can be shown that such changes were consistently rapid or that they occurred with particular intensity at certain times, it appears that the slow rate of economic growth was matched by, and was probably causally related to, the slow pace of structural change.

Table 1.6 Comparative growth of population and urbanization in England and Wales, 1851–1911

	Total population % per year	Urban population % per year	Urban total %
1851–1861	11.9	21.6	58.7
1861–1871	13.2	25.6	65.2
1871–1881	14.7	22.8	70.0
1881–1891	11.6	18.8	74.5
1891–1901	12.2	17.5	78.0
1901–1911	10.9	12.2	78.9

Source: Law (1967), 130.

A central part of population and occupational change was the growth of towns. In the present context two features are particularly important. First, throughout the nineteenth century urban growth was faster than population growth. Secondly, the highest rates of growth occurred up to the 1880s but thereafter the rate fell off quite sharply. According to the best estimates, between 1840 and 1900 60 per cent of urban growth was accounted for by natural increase and 40 per cent by immigration from rural areas.[19] In terms of regions, the increases relative to the overall growth of population were concentrated in the towns of the Northwest, Yorkshire/Humberside and, most significantly, in London and the Southeast which, depending on the extent of the area included, increased its share of the population of Great Britain from 17.9 (24.5) per cent in 1851 to 22.4 (28.4) per cent in 1901.[20]

19. D. E. Baines, *Migration in a Mature Economy: Emigration and Internal Migration in England and Wales, 1861–1900* (Cambridge, 1985), p. 219.
20. Lee, *The British Economy since 1700*, p. 127. The first figure in each case relates to the Home Counties and includes London, Middlesex, Kent, Surrey, Hertford and Essex. The figures in brackets include the remainder of the Southeast.

Urbanization on this scale meant that by the 1880s Britain was becoming a far more integrated economy than it was at the beginning of the Victorian era. What bound it together mainly was a highly developed rail transport system amounting at the end of the decade to 17,000 miles of track. For comparison, the much larger countries of France and Germany possessed 20,700 and 26,600 miles of track respectively by that date, and the huge empire of Austria Hungary had only 9,500 miles. Similar comparisons can be drawn in terms of urbanization though the figures must be taken as very approximate. In the 1880s, for example, between 50 per cent and 60 per cent of German population was urbanized and the corresponding range for France was between 30 per cent and 40 per cent.[21]

Yet, for all its close-knit nature, the British economy was made up of a number of distinctive regions and their distinctiveness was in most cases the consequence of their heavy reliance on one or two major industries or on a particular type of agriculture. It is important to note that these were interrelated, with political and social variations.[22] These regions ranged from Glasgow and the Clyde, with its concentration on shipbuilding and heavy engineering, to South Wales, the principality of anthracite and tinplate. Most concentrated of all was the Lancashire cotton industry which accounted for 26 per cent of the country's exports in 1880 and averaged 80 per cent of the world's exports of cotton goods. The Midland and London regions were to some degree the exceptions to the rule since their economies appeared more diversified because they contained a high proportion of small scale and workshop industries. Nevertheless, many of these were cognate manufacturing industries and London remained the largest manufacturing centre in the country. In the service sector London was highly concentrated and dominated the professional and commercial life of the country.[23]

When these economic features are combined with the political dominance of London, the political economy of Britain presents something of a unique picture in international terms in the late nineteenth century. To borrow from the jargon of business

21. R. Lawton and R. Lee (eds), *Urban Population Development in Western Europe from the Late Eighteenth to the Early Twentieth Century* (Liverpool, 1989), p. 4; C. Trebilcock, *The Industrialization of the Continental Powers 1780–1914* (1981), pp. 151–2.

22. An excellent regional study which illustrates this point is P. F. Clarke, *Lancaster and the New Liberalism* (Cambridge, 1971).

23. P. G. Hall, *The Industries of London since 1861* (1962); C. H. Lee, *British Regional Employment Statistics, 1841–1871* (Cambridge, 1979).

organization, Great Britain Limited might be described as a centralized, functionally departmentalized economy. By the standards of the time this was an up-to-date form of organization which in many respects appeared to be well ahead of its main industrial rivals.

POLITICAL ECONOMY

Whilst Samuel Smiles was preaching the fundamental virtues of thrift and sobriety, Marx was developing his theory of dialectical materialism which claimed to reveal the iron laws of history. In many obvious respects these would-be prophets were poles apart – self-improvement was the antithesis of the violence of the class struggle. Even so, they shared in the prevalent belief in progress, though for Marx this was to be achieved through conflict and struggle as the class-ridden society of the present gave birth to the classless utopia of the future. And both were stimulated by what they saw around them, particularly by what they perceived to be the value of labour and the power of capital accumulation. But for Marx, with his much greater intellectual sophistication than Smiles, the nature of capital incorporated class relationships and through these encompassed international trade and finance. So the question arises: was the economy of this period at the pinnacle of *laissez-faire* capitalist accumulation?

The practical approach to this question is to examine the record of savings and investment both at home and abroad.

Table 1.7 UK domestic and overseas capital formation, 1870–89 (% of GDP)

	Gross domestic capital formation	Overseas investment
1870–1879	10.2	4.8
1888–1889	8.3	5.0

Source: Mitchell (1988), 838, 871.

Table 1.8 UK comparative gross fixed non-residential capital formation, 1871–90 (% of GDP)

	UK	France	Japan	USA
1871–1880	7.5	9.0	–	11.5
1881–1890	5.9	10.4	8.9	12.2

Source: Maddison (1991), 41.

From Tables 1.7 and 1.8 it is clear that, by comparison with other countries, British levels of investment were not outstanding. What is even more striking is that within this comparatively modest investment performance a substantial proportion was devoted to foreign investment, a feature which Britain shared in common only with France among the Great Powers. This picture has to be qualified to the extent that there is not a directly proportionate relationship between the level of investment and the rate of economic growth. That rate depends on varying combinations of factors of production and the efficiency and intensity with which they are used. Nevertheless, levels of investment do reflect the nature and type of economic activity and it is the case, also, that there is a close relationship between increases in capital formation and higher rates of growth. By international standards, therefore, the late Victorians do not appear to have achieved outstanding levels of savings and capital accumulation.

The transfer of capital overseas was provided through the mechanism of the balance of payments. The UK share of exports of manufactured goods from the major economies in the early 1880s was approximately 41 per cent as compared with 22 per cent for France, 19 per cent for Germany and 3 per cent for the USA (Table 1.2). Despite this dominance the UK had a deficit on the balance of trade amounting to 23 per cent of the value of merchandise exports in the early 1880s. This deficit was more than balanced, however, by surpluses on services and property income from abroad, so that there was an overall surplus equivalent to 18 per cent of the value of merchandise exports. This balance was available for lending overseas on either a short or long-term basis. As a consequence, overseas investment income was already equal to one-fifth of merchandise exports by the 1880s and it was destined to become even higher (Chapter 3). On the one hand *rentier* income on this scale was the reward for prudent overseas investment over many years; on the other hand, increasing dependence on it reflected the faltering growth of the other sources of national income. To the extent that this dependence was the consequence of a low level of domestic investment, late Victorian capitalism showed at least the very early signs of senescence.

For Samuel Smiles *laissez-faire* in economic matters was a virtue which promoted enterprise, for Marx it was a necessary evil of capitalism. Whilst the period was by no means an age of pure *laissez-faire*, the fact that only 7.2 per cent of the national income passed through government hands in 1880 is a clear indication of the limited power of the government to influence the economy. Direct and indirect taxes were correspondingly low, and free trade was virtually achieved. It is true that legislation was introduced as time passed to deal with some of the problems and to curb some of the excesses created by an urban, industrial society; but much of this legislation was limited in compass and permissive in form. Economic liberalism was the order of the day. Like most historical labels, however, it is attached to a portmanteau of ideas and concepts, though common to all of them are notions of individualism and a wide measure of unregulated competition in all areas of human activity. These beliefs achieved ultimate, liturgical refinement in the form of classical economics of which John Stuart Mill was the late Victorian arch priest. For Mill and most of his fellow economists there was never any doubt that they were dealing with the principles and fundamental laws which governed the lives of individuals and, beyond them, of nations.[24]

Classical economists placed fundamental emphasis on the hidden hand of the market which was held to produce the optimum outcome of individual choices and actions, and thus maximized welfare. The philosophical overtones came through by much allusion to justice and a fair return. In its more extreme forms this view of the world even incorporated the Darwinian idea of the survival of the fittest: in this way self-improvement and market competition were neatly combined. Classical economists recognized, nevertheless, that theirs was, in many respects, an abstracted view of the world; but this abstraction was not seen as a

---

24. Invaluable surveys are provided by R. E. Backhouse, *Economists and the Economy* (1994) and M. Blaug, *Economic Theory in Retrospect* (Cambridge, 1978).

divorce from reality but as the distillation of essential truths or, more accurately, of the fundamental economic laws according to which the real world operated. With the major exception of Marx (whose credentials as a classical economist are nevertheless secure) these laws spelt harmony and not disharmony and their operation ensured the greater good consistent with natural inequalities between individuals. *Ex ante* prevention was, therefore, more important than *ex post* cure, since cure could only be achieved by allowing natural laws to reassert themselves.

The edifice of logic which was classical economics rested on such assumptions as economic rationality, perfect knowledge, infinite divisibility of factors of production and frictionless market adjustment, which were as unnatural and unreal then as they are now. But the appeal of economics then, as now, lay not in what it delivered in terms of prescription but in what it appeared to confirm in terms of popular belief. Classical economics provided a near-perfect fit for the popular belief in progress and the idea that prosperity stemmed from allowing free reign to individual choice and to the market. More than this, Britain's world role, including its power to enforce the *Pax Britannica*, demonstrated the universality of this version of economic liberalism.

Like all successful ideologies, economic liberalism contained elements of truth. The removal of restrictions on trade and the cumbersome system of indirect taxation had undoubtedly played a major part in promoting the success of Victorian enterprise. Moreover, classical economics was by no means concerned exclusively with deductive logic. Its development reflected major economic issues of the day, ranging from Ricardo's concern with the theory of rent in an economy dominated by landowners, to John Stuart Mill's refinement of the law of comparative cost, which sought to explain the relationship between industrial expansion and the potential gains from foreign trade.[25] The classical economists also recognized both the need for state provision of certain goods and services (public goods) which it was not in the interests of any individual or group to provide, and the need to regulate against monopoly and monopolistic practices. It was this sense of realism that gave classical economics its practical appeal and which ensured the elevation of economic liberalism from ideology to orthodoxy.

25. See R. E. Backhouse, *Economists and the Economy*, pp. 76 *ff.*

The manner in which major economic interests related to this dominant view gave Britain its distinctive form of political economy when compared with the other industrializing nations. In some ways the most surprising adjustment to the growth of industrialism had been made by the ruling landed class. The repeal of the Corn Laws in 1846 (and before that the passing of the great Reform Act of 1832) were an early acknowledgement of the shift of potential political power towards the growing urban middle class; a power that was realized with subsequent economic development and further constitutional change. The decline in agriculture was also an important part of this transformation.

The fortunes of industry conformed to the laws of classical economics. Under conditions of free trade Britain's comparative advantage lay in the production and export of manufactured goods, and in line with the law first defined by Engels, as real incomes rose consumers spent a smaller proportion of that income on basic necessities such as food. Taken together, these conditions required an adjustment in agricultural incomes in relation to the growth of incomes generally, which could only be achieved by a combination of contraction in the work force and an increase in productivity. As has been noted, however, the reduced condition of agriculture did not cause a matching reduction in the power and status of the traditional landed aristocracy because of the varied sources of the latter's income. Buoyed up by great wealth, this class was sustained to such an extent that the ultimate aspiration of many successful men of business was to attain admission to its ranks. By the 1880s for many of the great landowners agricultural estates were no longer their overriding source of income; but they remained the mark of supreme social achievement. In contrast, the gentry and lesser landowners suffered decline as a consequence of rapid changes in the nature of local government which gave increasing power to the urban middle class.[26]

The landed classes bolstered their position by means of the time-honoured method of the recruitment of wealth through

---

26. Agriculture's share of national income fell from approximately 20 per cent in 1850 to approximately 7 per cent by the end of the century. There is a vast literature on this subject but particularly useful are D. Cannadine, *The Decline and Fall of the British Aristocracy* (1990) and Thompson, *English Landed Society in the Nineteenth Century*. It may be questioned whether Cannadine overstates the decline of the aristocracy. For an accessible recent survey of the literature on the performance of British agriculture during this period see C. O'Grada, 'British Agriculture, 1860–1914', in R. Floud and D. McCloskey, *The Economic History of Britain since 1700. Vol. 2: 1860–1939* (Cambridge, 1994), pp. 145–72.

intermarriage, especially with families of city bankers and merchants. Recent research has indicated, moreover, that London bankers and merchants more than held their own among the ranks of the rich and wealthy, despite the rapid growth in industrial wealth in the nineteenth century.[27] Although Britain deservedly earned the epithet of 'workshop of the world', it drew much of its income from trade and finance. The institutions which handled this business were known collectively as the City. At the apex was the Bank of England and networked to it were a range of financial institutions – the Stock Exchange, Lloyds, merchant banks, commodity exchanges, acceptance houses, discount houses, clearing banks, trading houses, brokers and dealers of all kinds.[28] The nature and operation of this financial system will form a major theme of later analysis. For the moment, however, the focus is on what has been called 'the mind of the City', or, more prosaically, on the extent to which there was a collective view within the City as to its role in the economy and in the world at large.[29]

The City was private enterprise *par excellence*. The Bank of England, no less, was a private institution, though it was banker to the government. From the 1870s onwards, the Bank recognized that it stood in a particular relationship to the rest of the banking system and that this involved certain responsibilities for maintaining financial stability. This relationship was set out most elegantly in 1873 by the celebrated contemporary editor of the *Economist*, Walter Bagehot, in his now classic work, *Lombard Street*. The Bank's most important role was to act as lender in the last resort to the banking system. The price for this insurance was a premium rate of interest which became known as the bank rate. The system was by no means crisis-proof, as later events were to reveal. Moreover, the Bank acted independently of the government, and its governor and directors (the Court) were drawn exclusively from the leading financial institutions in the City. The overriding interest of members of the Court, in common with the other leading financiers and traders in the City, was the maintenance of London's dominant role in international trade and finance. Their potential power to pursue

27. See note 16.

28. See Y. Cassis, *City Bankers, 1830–1914* (Cambridge, 1994); S. Chapman, *The Rise of Merchant Banking* (1984); M. Collins, *Money and Banking in the UK A History* (1988); R. C. Michie, *The London and New York Stock Exchanges, 1850–1914* (1987); *idem, The City of London* (1991). The latter two works present the City in a favourable light.

29. The strongest claims in this respect are made by Cain and Hopkins, *British Imperialism: Innovation and Expansion*, see in particular pp. 125–31.

these self-interested aims through the institutional and social network of the City was enormous. This could well have consequences that far from matched the alleged ideal of Victorian liberalism, an issue that is examined in detail later (Chapter 3).

BUSINESSMEN AND INDUSTRY

For all the debate over whether there was an industrial revolution in the late eighteenth and early nineteenth centuries, the fact remains that British industrialization was in the main an eighteenth-century creation, not simply in the matter of inception, but also of the form and nature of industrial enterprises as well as the characteristics of those who ran them. 'If engineers were the devisors of the quintessential technology of the British industrial revolution, those who put the techniques into operation were often neither engineers nor patentees. Many were simply small businessmen with sharp eyes for the main chance. So far from being an homogeneous group of new men, the innovators *in toto* comprised a small number of pioneers, disposed to take risks on the promise of profit in the new device and a much larger number of imitators who followed in their footsteps'.[30] Small scale, profit-maximizing firms managed by practical men remained the dominant characteristic of British industry in the late nineteenth century. By 1907, the first year for which useful (though still very approximate) data are available, the hundred largest firms in manufacturing industry in the United Kingdom accounted for, at most, only 15 per cent of the net output of manufacturing.[31]

Over the nineteenth century firms had, of course, become bigger in order to match expanding markets and to incorporate new production techniques. But it was growth through existing forms and structures rather than through the introduction of new ones. By the 1880s this was beginning to show up more distinctly as the technical level of British industry began to fall behind international best practice.[32] These shortcomings were masked, however, by the

30. D. C. Coleman and C. MacLeod, 'Attitudes and New Techniques: British Businessmen, 1800–1950', *Economic History Review*, 39 (1986), p. 601.

31. L. Hannah, *The Rise of the Corporate Economy* (1983), p. 180 and *passim*.

32. The best analysis and survey of the relevant literature is provided by Coleman and MacLeod, 'Attitudes and New Techniques'. A defence of British industry's performance is offered by S. Pollard, *Britain's Prime and Britain's Decline. The British Economy 1870–1914* (1989), see in particular pp. 18–57, 260–71.

continuing importance of the staple industries – cotton textiles, iron and steel, shipbuilding and coal – which still found ready markets. The character of firms in these industries, and in British industry at large, was shaped by the men who ran them. They were, as one distinguished economic historian has described them, practical men: men who proceeded by means of experience and not by theory.[33] At all levels of business – production, selling and management organization – traditional methods were the measure of best practice. Changes were made because the possibilities of technical progress could not be totally ignored. But the pace of such adaptations was increasingly set by the competitive need to follow technical progress abroad rather than through the self-motivated pursuit of production opportunities arising from the discovery and application of new technology at home.

The rule of the practical man in British business, which was as true of the 1880s as of the 1780s, cannot be explained without reference to his counterpart, the gentleman amateur. The origins and odyssey of this business class are well chronicled. As the economy expanded many businessmen became prosperous, some became rich. But business success was by no means an end in itself. The aim of many men of business was to cross the social divide into the upper classes. Wealth could purchase the necessary accoutrements but the training was provided primarily by the rapidly burgeoning public schools and secondarily by the ancient universities of Oxford and Cambridge. The nature of this process of social aculturation has been the subject of much debate, but our concern is with the role of the gentleman, of the educated amateur, in British business in the 1880s.[34]

In later chapters the relationship between education, social class and economic performance will be examined more closely. For the moment, it can be observed that the ranks of gentlemen in industry were expanding in the late nineteenth century. The social division to which they adhered was externalized in the firm in the form of the boardroom: a sanctum to which only those who possessed the right social credentials were normally admitted. Business

33. D. C. Coleman, 'Gentlemen and Players', *Economic History Review*, 26, (1973), pp. 92–116.
34. The issues in this debate are surveyed in B. Collins and K. Robbins (eds), *British Culture and Economic Decline* (1990). See also F. M. L. Thompson, 'Life After Death' and W. D. Rubenstein, 'Gentlemen, Capitalism and British Industry, 1820–1914', *Past and Present*, 132 (1991), pp. 150–70 and 'Reply' by M. J. Daunton, *loc. cit.*, pp. 170–87.

organization thus reflected the broad features of the class system. The practical men ran things and the gentlemen directors decided business strategy with a strong emphasis on maintaining traditional methods and practices, and on ensuring a healthy flow of current income. There were exceptions to this pattern, but family ownership and short-term profit maximization were the predominant form and practice.

A number of commentators have, nevertheless, questioned why these gentlemen amateurs should have tended to curb the spirit of industrial enterprise, whereas their counterparts in City banks and finance houses were notably successful in the competitive world of international finance. This is an issue to which we shall return (Chapter 2) but, for the moment, it is important to recognize that, by its very nature, London's international financial business turned on short-term profit maximization. By contrast, industry was increasingly coming to depend on new, capital-intensive and science-based technologies requiring not only longer than customary time-horizons for the commitment of investment and the maximization of return, but also more specialized management and new forms of business organization.[35]

At this high point of Britain's world leadership doubts were being expressed about the capacity of the economy to sustain its economic progress, to such an extent that by the early 1880s there was growing concern among businessmen that the economy had entered a period of depression. Similar fears had emerged earlier in the area of agriculture, in which the effects of bad harvests in the early 1870s and growing foreign competition were plain for all to see. A Royal Commission had investigated the agricultural depression without coming to any clear conclusions, though the evidence it amassed did reveal marked variations in experience.[36] In general, arable farmers were faring far worse than dairy and livestock producers, thus reflecting foreign competition and changing levels of income and patterns of consumption. And the crucial fact was that landowners as a class continued to prosper because of their varied sources of income.[37]

35. *Cf.* D. C. Coleman, 'Failings and Achievements: Some British Businesses, 1910–80', *Business History*, 29 (1987), pp. 1–17.

36. The classic study remains T. W. Fletcher, 'The Great Depression of English Agriculture, 1873–96', *Economic History Review*, 13 (1961), pp. 417–32. See also O'Grada, 'British Agriculture, 1860–1914'.

37. F. M. L. Thompson, *English Landed Society*, pp. 292–326; D. N. Cannadine, *Lords and Landlords: The Aristocracy and the Towns 1774–1967* (Leicester, 1980).

The state of industry was a different matter. Falling prices, profits and rates of interest, combined with some sharp increases in unemployment in the late 1870s and early 1880s and sharp falls in the value of exports in the late 1870s and 1880s, were viewed with growing alarm. In what was becoming a time-honoured manner, a Royal Commission was set up to deliberate on the state of affairs. After calling leading businessmen and various experts (including the celebrated economist, Alfred Marshall) to give evidence before it, the Commission pronounced that industry and trade were fundamentally healthy though it drew attention to the fact that '... our position as the chief manufacturing nation of the world is not so undisputed as formerly, and ... foreign nations are beginning to compete with us successfully in many markets of which we formerly had a monopoly'.[38]

The report of the Commission touched on a range of factors which it judged to be causing difficulties for business – overproduction, reduction in the supply of gold, tariffs, foreign competition, labour regulations, superior foreign technical education – but at the same time it recognized that there was no falling off in the volume of trade or capital investment, and that wage earners had been gaining substantially from the fall in prices. The complex nature of the so-called 'Great Depression' has resulted in a variety of alternative explanations and an accompanying large literature. There is now general agreement among economic historians, however, that the term 'Great Depression' is a misnomer because the period was not one of depression in any unified sense. Trends in the major economic indicators can be traced back over longer periods and they do not move together, whilst the reduction in the supply of gold was more than compensated for by improvements in the efficiency and stability of the international monetary system. What is equally clear is that over the second half of the century there were substantial adjustments in cost/price ratios as a result of widespread gains in efficiency in the international economy.[39] The concern of the classical economists with the 'law of comparative advantage' was not merely an exercise in abstract logic; it reflected the real world. Enormous reductions in costs of transport by rail and sea both fed

38. *Final Report of the Royal Commission Appointed to Enquire Into the Depression of Trade and Industry*, BPP XXIII (C. 4893), 1886, paragraph 92.
39. S. B. Saul, *The Myth of the Great Depression 1873–1896* (1985). More detailed statistical evidence can be found in R. C. O. Matthews, C. H. Feinstein and J. C. Odling-Smee, *British Economic Growth 1856–1973* (Stanford, 1982).

through powerfully to the final prices of goods and services and made it possible to open up new highly productive areas of the world which were then able to supply the international marketplace with primary goods and raw materials in abundance.

These gains were largely the once-for-all outcome of the territorial expansion of the world economy. They were based on what might be termed extensive technology: the application of techniques in industry which rapidly increased the rate at which a limited range of raw materials could be processed to produce a flow of output of basic consumption and, to a lesser extent, capital goods; the parallel process for the agricultural and primary sectors was the application of methods which produced ever-increasing supplies to match industry's voracious appetite. When quantities and price changes were multiplied together the real gains to Britain amounted to a substantial increase in prosperity.

In important respects, therefore, the fears of contemporary businessmen were a case of mistaken identity. Yet contemporary business perceptions were by no means wholly mistaken. These real gains were occurring against a background of increasing competition faced by British industry. Those who sat on the Royal Commission were vaguely aware of this fact and sensed that domestic industry might not be adequately prepared to meet the foreign challenge. Nevertheless, they shared the belief of many of the witnesses who appeared before them that the real threat was unfair advantage, directly in the form of state assistance and indirectly in such forms as foreign tariffs and preferential taxes. This was another case of mistaken identity, as our analysis of the comparative performance of British industry in the world market in the chapters which follow will show.

BRITAIN IN AN INDUSTRIALIZING WORLD

A great deal of emphasis has been placed by historians on Britain being the first industrial nation. At the extreme the character of this early start was developed into a model by Rostow which, it was claimed, could be used to explain the pattern of the later industrialization of other nations.[40] According to this analysis, once countries had achieved the requisite preconditions – which included the abolition of archaic agricultural practices, the

40. W. W. Rostow, *The Stages of Economic Growth* (Cambridge, 1960).

provision of basic social overhead capital, the emergence of an entrepreneurial class and the existence of a value system favourable to economic progress – they were able to begin the process of economic growth and this process would occur in five stages. Hence the establishment of the necessary preconditions would be followed by the 'takeoff' which would in turn lead on to sustained economic growth, the drive to maturity and thence to the ultimate stage of high mass consumption. Each stage was defined in terms of measurable ranges of economic performance. The process is essentially a repeatable one over time and space or, as one historian has expressed it, was repeated 'from country to country lumbering through [a] pentametric rhythm'.[41] For all its early appeal, however, this model was soon exposed as not fitting the facts.[42] The preconditions for economic growth were shown to vary widely over time and space. What was a precondition in one case might well prove to be an obstacle to economic growth in another. More fundamentally, the model was essentially ahistorical because it did not take account of the accumulated experience of economic development: previous industrialization in open world economy was bound to effect the nature and scale of subsequent industrialization.

The stage model of economic growth was superseded by a far more sophisticated analysis by Gerschenkron whose central concept was that of economic backwardness.[43] It offered an analysis which has had a powerful influence on the study of comparative economic development. The longer a country delays industrialization, it is argued, the more economically backward it becomes in relation to those countries which have industrialized. In order to break into the process, a 'backward economy' has to find ways of overcoming this disadvantage by discovering substitutes for those factors which caused earlier industrializations. Thus, the industrialization of the major economies from the late eighteenth century to the late nineteenth century – from Britain to Russia – can be arranged on a time scale and each case of industrialization along this scale can be

41. A. Gerschenkron, *Economic Backwardness in Historical Perspective* (Harvard, 1962), p. 355.

42. A. K. Cairncross, *Factors in Economic Development* (1962), pp. 131–44; Gershenkron, *Economic Backwardness*, pp. 353–7; S. Kuznets, *Modern Economic Growth, Rate, Structure, and Speed* (1966). A number of critical pieces are included in W. W. Rostow (ed.), *The Economics of Take-Off Into Sustained Growth* (1963) – see especially the contribution by Kuznets, pp. 22–43.

43. A. Gerschenkron, *Economic Backwardness*.

characterized by the nature of the substitutes it incorporates. The later the industrialization the more accelerated it became and the greater its reliance on capital-intensive technology. Later still, industrialization required an increasing concentration of production and centralized direction. Hence the development ranged from *laissez-faire*, small-scale enterprise in Britain, through bank- and cartel-directed industry in Germany, zaibatsus in Japan to state capitalism in late Tsarist Russia.[44] In all cases, moreover, there was a matching ideology which became increasingly assertive in order to provide the necessary élan for big spurts of economic growth. *Laissez-faire* individualism was fine for Britain; the USA needed the added spur of the 'frontier'; Germany and Japan were driven by powerful nationalism; nothing short of Soviet communism could provide the final thrust for Russian industrialization.

The attraction of this typology has not, however, carried all before it. A number of economic historians have pointed to clear exceptions. Austria-Hungary, Italy and France are major cases in point.[45] The details cannot be considered here, but certain points bear directly on our general theme. Thus, one of the major criticisms which has been made is that those countries just listed industrialized during the second half of the nineteenth century without the aid of a 'great spurt'. They followed a pattern of uneven growth. Moreover, substitutes were not as clear cut either in form or operation as the typology claims. The alleged powerful and positive role of the banks in later industrialization, for example, has not been borne out by detailed investigation; somewhat surprisingly, banks exercised a risk-averse and retarding influence in some parts of German industry at the end of the century.[46]

44. A zaibatsu literally means a money group or plutocracy. They were, in effect, family-dominated banking and industrial conglomerates. The best introduction to modern Japanese economic history remains G. C. Allen, *A Short History of Modern Japan* (1972).

45. W. Ashworth, 'Typologies and Evidence: Has Nineteenth Century Europe a Guide to Economic Growth?', *Economic History Review*, 30 (1977), pp. 140–58; S. L. Barsby, 'Economic Backwardness and the Characteristics of Development', *Journal of Economic History*, 29 (1969), pp. 449–72; R. Cameron, 'A New View of European Industrialization', *Economic History Review*, 38 (1985), pp. 1–23. A detailed and useful bibliographical survey of the main literature is provided by P. K. O'Brien, 'Do We Have a Typology for the Study of European Industrialization in the XIXth Century?', *The Journal of European Economic History*, 15 (1986), pp. 291–333.

46. The literature is conveniently surveyed in Pollard, *Britain's Prime and Britain's Decline*, pp. 96–7. In essence, doubts as to the effectiveness of German banks were

Despite these qualifications to the typology of economic backwardness, however, it is still generally accepted that the basis of industrialization was changing fundamentally in the 1880s along broadly similar lines. There was growing reliance on science-based, capital-intensive industry – to such a degree that the period has often been referred to as that of the second industrial revolution. The chemical and electrical industries were central in this transformation. Other innovations pioneered in this period ranged from automobiles to mechanical typesetting. Even the staple industry of iron and steel was invaded by new science-based technology. Such changes have naturally raised the question: how well or badly did Britain – the first industrial nation – meet the challenge of the new technology? Depending on the answer given, the late Victorians and their Edwardian descendants are judged either guilty or innocent of the charge of having precipitated what developed into Britain's economic decline in the twentieth century.

Our analysis will seek to argue that this approach, even in a modified form, leads to a false perspective of Britain's comparative economic position in the late nineteenth-century. The main reasons for this claim must be outlined before the detailed evidence is examined in the chapters which follow. A basic reason concerns the heavy, and largely unavoidable, dependence which economic historians place on national income accounts. These data, the products of twentieth century concepts and research, have undoubtedly proved to be powerful tools of historical analysis. But they have major limitations to which, frequently, too little heed is paid. Most obviously, such estimates are subject to wide measures of error so that, given the marginal nature of percentage rates of economic growth, calculations of differences in growth rates between economies should not be taken at face value. Added to this, these accounts easily lend themselves to manipulation in ways which may purport to provide explanations of economic change, whereas, they can really do little more than provide a record of economic outcomes. For example, what for some countries might be represented as accelerated growth or 'big spurts' in comparison with Britain, may only in part represent a catching up; in part they

---

raised in some econometric studies. Despite valid criticisms of these methods the issue remains an open one. J. Edwards and K. Fischer, *Banks, Finance and Investment in Germany* (Cambridge, 1994). For a general survey see S. Pollard and D. Zeigler, 'Banking and Industrialization: Rondo Cameron Twenty Years on', in Y. Cassis (ed.), *Finance and Financiers in European History, 1880–1960* (Cambridge, 1992), pp. 17–36.

may be the measure of Britain's failure to keep up with the widening opportunities for faster economic growth.

Most significant in the present context is that, by definition, these accounts are defined in terms of national boundaries. The regulation of economic activity is, of course, very much a matter of national determination and the distribution of economic welfare is almost wholly so. But economic development occurs across national boundaries, over broad regions. These regions may be difficult to define with precision but they are recognizable. Such was the case in nineteenth-century Europe. Economic growth occurred as much through a process of diffusion as through more dramatic 'big spurts'. The outward-looking nature and interests of Britain in the 1880s have already been emphasized and it has been convincingly demonstrated that, within Europe, for the greater part of the nineteenth century there was a transnational region of economic development which stretched from Britain, across northern Europe and the Netherlands, through Prussia into northern Italy.[47]

The need to recognize transnational networks of economic development points to another limitation of the national approach. By focusing on differences between Britain, the USA, France, Germany, Austria-Hungary, Russia and Japan in the late nineteenth century, it is easy to undervalue their similarity. Whilst Russia was one of the poles of late development in the 1880s, even there the degree of economic backwardness was poles apart from the corresponding position of most Third World countries in the late twentieth century. Viewed over a longer time scale, the 'economic distances' between the major nations in the 1880s were considerably less than they are frequently represented as having been. In this perspective Britain's position in the world economy in the 1880s appears far less impressive than simple comparisons of income per head might suggest.

The proposition here is the obverse of the one which has been described. It is that economic backwardness does not condition the form of industrialization, rather it defines the scale of the challenge. The barriers facing Third World countries at the present time provide the clearest and most striking examples of this fact.

---

47. S. Pollard, 'Industrialization and the European Economy', *Economic History Review*, 26 (1973), pp. 636–48; *idem, Peaceful Conquest: The Industrialization of Europe 1760–1970* (Oxford, 1981). Pollard presents the case in the form that industralization in Europe was an integrated process. Whilst this overall approach is open to serious challenge (*cf.* Cameron, 'A New View of European Industrialization') the basic point remains.

The form of industrialization can vary contemporaneously between countries as has already been observed and it is determined by the nature of longer-term historical evolution. Thus, the involvement of the state and its associated bureaucracy in economic development was a long-established feature of the Prussian *cum* German nation from Frederick William I in the late eighteenth century, through the creation of the Zollverein in the 1840s to Bismarck's economic nationalism in the later nineteenth century; the traditional structure of Japanese society was highly suited to the managerial hierarchy of emerging corporate capitalism; how could the Russia of the Tsar (or Stalin) do other than adopt a highly centralized form of industrialization?[48] In short, those economies which grew rapidly in the late nineteenth century were able to do so not because they devised substitute conditions which enabled them to overcome backwardness, but mainly because the nature of new, science-based, capital-intensive technology was ideally suited to the particular character of their historical development.

British enterprise, it will be argued, did not decline during this period: it remained remarkably constant and inflexible. If the late Victorians and the Edwardians failed in their willingness to take risks and to change their economic practices, they did so because they were no better than their forefathers – not because they were worse. Britain was increasingly up against the test of superior economic performance. It is possible, of course, that to match the best demands of the new world economy, Britain would be required to achieve more than could be reasonably expected, given its resources. Added to this, a measure of relative decline was inevitable as other countries entered the process of industralialization. Thus, if Britain was beginning to experience flagging economic performance it might be seen rather as a natural condition than as evidence of culpable decline.

48. Perceptive studies in this vein are A. Gershenkron, *Europe in the Russian Mirror* (Cambridge, 1970); P. R. Gregory, *An Economic History of Russia from Emancipation to the First Five-Year Plan* (Princeton, 1994); M. Morishima, *Why Has Japan 'Succeeded'?* (Cambridge, 1982).

British Industry and World Trade, 1880–1914

Nineteenth-century Britain is often described as the workshop of the world. Between 40 per cent and 45 per cent of the world's exports of manufactured goods in the early 1880s were sent out from British factories and workshops and total exports amounted to 17 per cent of world trade. But this was only part of the picture. Britain was also the world's market place. As the centre of the world's financial and commodity markets it provided a wide range of profitable services, to such an extent that it was able to import a larger volume of goods and materials than it could afford to pay for by visible exports alone. This still left a surplus to be added to Britain's accumulating foreign investments. The multifarious nature of this activity was such that this chapter will focus on visible trade; the following chapter will complete the story by examining finance and services.

TRADE: PATTERN AND PERFORMANCE

Exports of goods and services accounted for, on average, 30 per cent of national income during the period 1880–1914. Merchandise exports, alone, were equivalent to 21 per cent of GDP in 1913. Detailed comparisons between Britain and other major economies are analysed below, but for the moment it can be noted that, for merchandise exports, the corresponding figure for Germany was 17.5 per cent and for the USA 6 per cent. The comparative scale of Britain's involvement in international trade is abundantly clear, therefore. But the central question concerns the nature of the relationship between foreign trade and domestic economic performance. To what extent was the one dependent on the other? Economic theory offers no guide to a ready answer. We shall begin, therefore, by examining the record in some detail in order to discover whether a clear pattern emerges. What is certain, however, is that the fortunes of British trade over the past hundred years have been the most sensitive indicator of the prosperity of the economy in general.

The composition of British trade in terms of exports is shown in Table 2.1.

Table 2.1 UK principal exports, 1881–1913: annual averages and percentages of total exports (current values; % shares)

	1881–90		1891–1910		1910–13	
	£m	%	£m	%	£m	%
Coal	11.6	5.0	15.6	6.5	35.6	9.4
Iron & steel	26.4	11.3	23.6	9.8	43.0	11.3
Machinery	12.5	5.3	16.4	6.8	26.9	7.1
Electrical goods			1.6	0.7	3.2	0.8
Motor vehicles			0.2	neg	2.1	0.6
Ships & boats			1.8	0.8	7.4	1.9
Non-ferrous metals & manus.	5.4	2.3	5.4	2.3	8.6	2.3
Cotton goods	73.5	31.4	66.7	27.8	97.7	25.7
Wool goods	23.6	10.1	21.2	8.8	25.6	6.7
Chemicals	10.7	4.6	11.8	4.9	16.5	4.3

Percentages do not total to 100 because of rounding. Re-exports are excluded.

Source: Mitchell (1988), 453, 483.

Two factors stand out. First, there was a heavy reliance on a limited range of staple manufactures, in particular cotton textiles and iron and steel. Secondly, coal exports grew rapidly. In terms of weight, coal exports increased fourfold during the period or the equivalent of 4.4 per cent per annum.

As the centre of the world's commodity markets Britain also attracted a significant re-export trade. The main commodities are shown in Table 2.2 and a comparison of these figures with those for total imports reveals that in most cases the proportionate relationship is substantial and in no case is it insignificant.

Table 2.2 UK principal re-exports, 1881–1913: annual averages as a share of imports (current values)

	1881–90		1891–1900		1901–13	
	£m	% of imports	£m	% of imports	£m	% of imports
Coffee	3.1	76.0	2.1	60.0	1.7	65.4
Tea	2.1	19.8	1.5	14.6	2.1	19.4
Raw cotton	5.2	12.1	4.2	12.0	8.9	15.0
Raw wool	14.6	56.0	12.8	49.8	12.4	42.9
Hides, skins & furs	2.8	43.0	3.9	57.4	6.0	58.3
Non-ferrous metals & manus.	2.9	33.7	2.9	26.6	6.3	29.6
Rubber	1.3	48.0	2.7	58.7	8.5	66.9
Petroleum	–	–	0.1	2.9	0.2	3.2

Source: Mitchell (1988), 475–6, 478–9, 487.

The main categories of exports and imports are shown in Table 2.3.

Table 2.3 UK main categories of imports and exports by share, 1881–1913 (current values)

	Foodstuffs and livestock		Raw materials and mainly unmanufactured goods		Finished manufactures	
	%		%		%	
	Imports	Exports	Imports	Exports	Imports	Exports
1881–90	42.5	5.1	41.8	11.4	15.8	83.5
1890–1901	43.2	5.2	36.8	13.9	19.9	80.6
1901–11	40.0	6.0	35.1	12.6	24.6	79.7

Source: Mitchell (1988), 456–7. Slight adjustments have been made to the basic data to take account of changes in the coverage of statistics in 1899. Re-exports are excluded from exports.

Within the main categories the major items are shown in Table 2.4.

Table 2.4 UK principal imports, 1881–1913: annual averages and percentage share of total imports (current values)

	1881–90		1891–1900		1901–13	
	£m	%	£m	%	£m	%
Grain & flour	54.1	13.7	55.6	12.1	70.1	11.3
Sugar	20.3	5.1	18.8	4.2	20.1	3.2
Tea	10.6	2.7	10.3	2.2	10.8	1.7
Meat & animals	25.4	6.4	36.3	8.1	50.2	8.1
Butter & margarine	12.1	3.1	17.5	3.9	25.2	4.1
Timber	16.2	4.1	20.3	4.6	26.2	4.2
Raw cotton	42.3	10.7	34.9	7.8	59.3	9.6
Raw wool	26.0	6.6	25.7	5.6	28.9	4.7
Silk yarn & goods	11.3	2.9	14.7	3.2	13.4	2.2
Tobacco	3.2	0.8	4.0	0.9	5.1	0.8
Oils, oil seed, gums, resins, tallow	15.7	4.0	15.6	3.5	23.7	3.8
Iron & steel	4.1	1.0	4.1	0.9	9.2	1.4
Hides, skins & furs	6.5	1.6	6.8	1.5	10.3	1.7
Rubber	2.7	0.7	4.6	1.0	12.7	2.1
Non-ferrous metals & manus.	8.6	2.2	10.9	2.4	21.3	3.4
Petroleum	2.2	0.6	3.4	0.8	6.2	1.0
Machinery	–	–	1.3	0.3	5.1	0.8

Source: Mitchell (1988), 453, 475–6, 478–9.

Likewise the major sources of imports are well known: the United States supplied vast quantities of cereals, meat and cotton, as well as large amounts of lumber and minerals; from India came, in order of importance at the turn of the century, tea, jute, wheat and raw cotton; Australia and South Africa became significant sources of wool and meat; Canada not only supplied large quantities of grain but substantial quantities of timber and flour. Imports of manufactured goods included a wide range of both consumer and capital goods. Germany, in particular, steadily increased its importance in British trade through this sector. Indeed, the most noticeable general feature in this respect is the rapid rate at which manufactures as a group was increasing its share of imports from 1880 onwards. When these figures are placed alongside those for UK exports of coal, they present a somewhat unexpected pattern for the workshop of the world.

The predominance of certain bulk commodities must not be allowed to obscure the equal importance of the multifarious essential supplies drawn from all quarters of the globe. The monetary value of tin from Bolivia and the Far East or of copper from Spain could not match that of imports of chilled meat and grain from the *latifundia* of South America or that of tea from the plantations of the sub-continent; but without base metals such as these, large sections of British industry would have ground to a standstill.

The broad geographical distribution of Britain's foreign trade has been analysed by Capie.

Table 2.5 Distribution of British overseas trade, 1870 and 1914

	1870	*1914*
Imports from:		
Foreign	78.6	73.0
Empire	21.4	27.0
Exports to:		
Foreign	77.3	65.1
Empire	22.7	34.9

Source: Capie (1983), 13. Includes re-exports.

The swing to the Empire is clear, though this has to be balanced by the fact that the area of the Empire grew substantially and, more importantly, its population virtually doubled during the period. A more detailed breakdown of figures shows the stability of the group of Britain's major trading partners, though there was some change in relative positions and there was a noticeable shift away from France and the USA.

Table 2.6 Annual average shares of various countries in UK trade, 1880–1914 (%)

	1880–89	1890–99	1900–9	1910–14
British exports to:				
Australia	7.3	6.2	5.6	0.6
Canada	3.3	2.6	3.4	4.5
India	11.0	10.2	10.2	10.9
New Zealand	1.3	1.4	1.8	2.0
South Africa	2.1	3.8	5.0	3.8
France	8.7	7.2	6.5	6.7
Germany	9.9	10.7	10.2	9.7
United States	12.9	12.5	11.2	11.4
British imports from:				
Australia	5.0	5.1	4.5	5.3
Canada	2.8	3.6	4.4	4.0
India	8.6	6.5	5.9	6.5
New Zealand	1.4	1.9	2.4	2.9
South Africa	1.4	2.5	1.2	1.5
France	10.0	10.9	8.7	6.0
Germany	6.3	6.2	7.4	9.1
USA	23.1	23.9	22.4	18.4

Sources: Capie (1983), 16; Mitchell (1988), 453, 510–11 for additional data. Exports include re-exports.

One further measure is needed to complete the broad picture of UK trade, namely, trade balances. As has already been noted, total deficits outweighed surpluses by a significant margin. Between 1900 and 1906 the gap averaged the equivalent of 44 per cent of exports, and although it dropped to 25 per cent between 1907 and 1913 it was obviously still large. Nevertheless, within the limits of the returns from exports Britain was able to settle its debts on a multilateral basis. Probably the best known arrangement was the triangular one that allowed the UK to settle part of its large deficit with the USA through the surpluses it earned with tropical countries (especially India) with whom the USA, in turn, had deficits.

Table 2.7 Mean trade balances for principal deficits and surpluses: annual averages, 1904–13

Country	£'000s
USA	–71,325
Russia	–17,018
France	–13,469
Denmark	–13,415
Argentina	–12,466
North Africa	–9,874
Germany	–9,536
Spain	–8,560
New Zealand	–7,943
Canada	–6,450
Australia	–4,350
Netherlands	+194
Italy	+6,818
China	+7,150
Japan	+7,530
India	+9,926
Southern Africa	+10,896

Source: Capie (1983), 23.

An attempt to explain the disproportionate growth in Empire trade will be made later in this chapter. It should be noted, however, that the answer is not to be found in terms of the direct exercise of imperial power. Throughout the period the Empire was a free trade area. The prices received by Empire producers matched those ruling on international markets. And Australia, Canada, South Africa and New Zealand were major countries in imperial trade which were emerging into virtually independent states during the period of trade expansion – in part because of it. India, it is true, is a more complicated case that will have to be considered more fully later. But even here the question has to be posed, as it has to be for the Empire in general: was the alternative to trade with Britain simply one of less trade? Without doubt, less trade would have meant less welfare for Empire countries in total; and in those countries where the welfare gains were distributed very unequally, this was far more the result of endemic social relationships which in many respects were an extension of the class system at home, than a consequence of imperialism in itself. The fundamental economic fact was that an open Empire was an essential part of the dynamics of world trade and, in particular, of Britain's need for multilateral settlements.

British trade meant British shipping. In 1880 this vast merchant

Figure 2.1 World pattern of payments settlements in 1910 (£m)

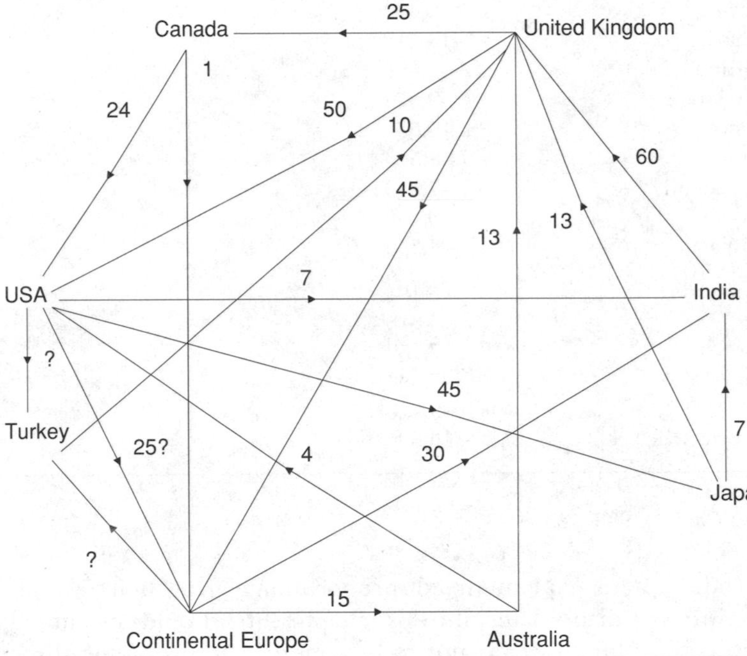

Source : Saul (1960), 58

fleet amounted to 6.5 million net tons which was the equivalent of 40 per cent of the world total, when allowance is made for the higher proportion of steam ships it contained in relation to other countries. It not only had the capacity to carry goods to and from home ports but also to supply services through charter and tramp ships to foreign trade. Great steam ship companies such as the Ocean Steamship Company founded by Alfred Holt in Liverpool in 1866 became known throughout the world.[1] They and their foreign

1. See for example M. Falkus, *The Blue Funnel Legend: A History of the Ocean Steam Ship Company, 1865–1973* (1990); F. E. Hyde and J. R. Harris, *Blue Funnel: A History of Alfred Holt & Co., 1865–1914* (Liverpool, 1956); F. E. Hyde, *Cunard and the North Atlantic, 1840–1973. A History of Shipping and Financial Management* (1975).

agents were part of an expanding and intricate network of commercial activity linked by the cable telegraph that girdled the globe.

Table 2.8 Average rates of growth of the volume of exports for selected countries, 1880–1913 (% year)

	UK	Belgium	France	Germany	Switzerland	USA	World
1880–89	3.1	4.2	2.4	2.6	–	1.0	3.4[a]
1890–99	1.2	2.2	2.0	3.9	–	6.3	2.4[b]
1900–13	4.2	4.9	3.8	6.4	5.2	2.5	4.1
1880–13	2.9	3.8	2.7	4.9	–	3.4	3.4

[a] 1881–90. [b] 1890–1900.

Source: Maddison (1991), 312–14.

World trade grew more rapidly than British trade over the period as a whole. Among the large economies the USA and Germany achieved particularly high rates of growth, whilst Belgium and Switzerland are prime examples of what could be achieved by small nations. Correspondingly, there were major changes in national shares of world trade. For the UK the outcome was a marked decline in its relative standing. Whether this represented a degree of failure or whether it should be regarded as a natural and direct consequence of world economic expansion is the issue on which the analysis will now focus.

Table 2.9 Shares of world trade, selected countries and years, 1880–1913 (%)

(a) Merchandise exports

	1885	1900	1913
UK	16.7	15.0	13.9
Belgium	3.7	3.9	3.9
France	9.6	8.4	7.2
Germany	11.0	11.6	13.1
Switzerland	2.1	1.7	1.4
USA	11.2	15.0	12.9

(b) Exports of manufactured goods

	1880	1899	1913
UK	41.4	32.5	29.9
France	22.2	15.8	12.9
Germany	19.3	92.2	26.4
USA	2.8	11.2	12.6

Sources: (a) Maddison (1962), 212. There are a number of estimates available but the figures above are broadly representative.
(b) Pollard (1989), 15. Pollard uses a range of estimates but the ones above are broadly representative.

TRADE AS AN ENGINE OF GROWTH

There have been numerous attempts to explain the relationship between trade and economic growth. The idea of trade as an 'engine of growth' has provided the basis for the best known analysis of international expansion before 1914, and it provides a useful starting point for examining the major theoretical issues that underlie our historical analysis.[2] In broad terms, the international exchange of primary commodities for manufactured and semi-manufactured goods is held to be the mechanism for the complementary nature of economic development within a physically expanding international economy, as new territories were opened up. Resources of capital and labour were thus drawn into new sectors and activities, yielding economies of scale and facilitating gains from comparative advantage in the process of international trade. Crucial to this system of complementary economic development was the maintenance of a broad balance between the suppliers of basic commodities and the producers of manufactured goods. This relationship depended crucially on the extensive nature of technical change, which provided the means for increasing and then transforming flows of raw materials through rapidly expanding production into basic manufactured goods. Consequently, net value added in this process amounted to a small and fairly constant

2. The major formulation of this analysis is R. Nurkse, *Patterns of Trade and Development* (Oxford, 1961). Also helpful though it focuses mainly on a more recent period is R. A. Batchelor, R. L. Major and A. D. Margon, *Industrialization and the Basis for Trade* (Cambridge, 1980).

proportion of the final price of the goods produced, and thus a balance was maintained between the growth of incomes of primary producers and manufacturers.

Cotton, wool, silk, lumber, various minerals, corn, meat: these were the commodities which linked the emerging economies of North and South America, India and Oceania to the industrial countries of Europe and, pre-eminently, to Great Britain. But there was still substantial cross trade in primaries.

Table 2.10 Commodity structure of world trade in 1913 (%)

| Food | Raw materials | | Total primary products | Manufactures |
	Agricultural	Mineral		
27.0	22.7	14.0	63.7	36.7

Source: Lamartine Yates (1959), 44.

This pattern of trade conformed to the orthodoxy of free trade. Seemingly, all could be explained in terms of the law of comparative advantage, whereby each country specialized in the production of those goods and commodities for which its resources of land, labour and capital were most suited. The monetary gains from trade were transmitted through the autonomous operation of the international gold standard. But the logic of this system could be demonstrated only if a sufficient number of assumptions were made about the nature of the economic world, to make it the unreal world of perfect competition – the world of perfect knowledge, frictionless movement of factors of production and instantaneous adjustment of costs and prices.[3]

It is possible to argue, nevertheless, that for a world which very roughly approximated to these conditions some assessment of trading relationships and performance can be made in terms of comparative advantage. Even so there remains a fundamental problem with the (essentially Ricardian) theory outlined, namely, that it is abstract to the extent that it does not define the sources of comparative advantage. Subsequent theories have endeavoured to overcome this problem by identifying these sources as being

3. D. P. O'Brien, *The Classical Economists* (Oxford, 1975), especially Chapter 7.

basically four in number.[4] First, there are climatic and natural advantages, and Ricardian analysis was by implication based on these. Secondly, advantages can arise from the possession of scarce resources, and these are not fixed for all time but can emerge as production possibilities change. The identification of this source amounts to an important refinement of the basic Ricardian analysis. Thirdly, there are differences in technology which arise through the complexities which determine the rate and diffusion of technical change in one country as compared with another. And finally, there are differences in the prices of factors of production, the most obvious being the effect on wage costs of changes in the quantity and quality of the labour supply.

Whilst it is clear that gains can accrue through the possession of one or more of these advantages, in practical terms their definition does not automatically make for clear, unambiguous analysis. It is, in fact, extremely difficult to identify these conditions; they are hard to measure, particularly in the case of relative factor costs. Also, it is frequently impossible to know to what extent the failure to exploit an advantage results from a failure of perception on the part of the economic actors involved, though this in itself becomes an element in comparative advantage. Over and above this there is the question of how markets are to be defined and how they relate to one another. Within national economies there can be substantial regional variations. This was certainly the case in the nineteenth century and the most obvious manifestation of this condition was differences in wage rates for a given occupation.[5] Hence, comparative advantages may generate intra-regional trade that cuts across international trade as might be predicted on the basis of national, aggregate data. And this is further complicated by the distance between markets which is a function of time and transport costs. These costs fell sharply over the latter half of the nineteenth century, for example, and consequently this had a strong, dynamic effect on comparative advantages.[6] The ambiguity and indeterminate nature of comparative advantage should thus be clear.

4. An excellent survey of economic theory is provided by R. Backhouse, *A History of Modern Economic Analysis* (1985).
5. E. H. Hunt, *Regional Wage Variations in Britain, 1850–1914* (Oxford, 1973); *idem*, 'Industrialization and Regional Inequality: Wages in Britain', *Journal of Economic History*, 46 (1986), pp. 935 66.
6. The outstanding book in this field is W. A. Lewis, *Growth and Fluctuations, 1870–1913* (1978), especially pp. 158–92.

As the international economy expanded its complexity increased. Within individual countries the process of industrialization was more in accordance with the ideas of economic nationalism than with the principles of perfect competition, one sign of which was the spread of tariffs among the major European countries, beginning with Germany in 1879 and culminating in a spate of tariff legislation in the 1890s. In 1892 the French raised protection of their industry and agriculture to its highest level with the famous Méline tariff. Perhaps more surprising was the introduction of protection by the USA with the McKinley tariff of 1890, followed by the Dingley tariff in 1897.

Protectionism can be seen as contributing to a reduction of world trade from the level it would have achieved under freer conditions, simply because it interfered with the efficient flow of factors of production between alternative uses. But such a view is essentially short term and takes no account of the conditions for longer-term economic growth. Whilst trade barriers may be purely restrictive and bolster the inefficient use of resources, under fixed exchange rates they may alternatively provide the means whereby industries can overcome short-term disadvantages and develop to a position where they can compete effectively in international markets. Nor is this simply an argument in terms of 'infant industries'. It includes, also, those industries which need to match rapid changes in technology. In other words, international competition takes place in the context of economic change over real time and not under conditions of *ceteris paribus* and abstract periods of time (rational time) within which the law of comparative costs is defined. Similarly, adjustments between sectors within economies and within the international framework do not occur automatically and instantaneously through the market; they are mediated through institutions in a discrete and unpredictable manner. At all events, during this period the evidence indicates clearly that the overall protective effect of tariffs was minimal.[7]

Part of the case for trade as an engine of growth in the late nineteenth century turns on the economies of scale which the increased production for export markets made possible. Even here, the picture is far from clear cut. In terms of production economies of scale, the maximum gains may well have been achieved at levels of demand within the capacity of the domestic market and,

7. F. H. Capie, 'Tariff Protection and Economic Performance in the Nineteenth Century', in J. Black and L. A. Winters (eds), *Policy and Performance in International Trade* (1983), pp. 1–24.

therefore, it is the productivity achieved at that level which then underpins export competitiveness. There are, moreover, economies of scale in terms of marketing and finance and these could well lead to monopolistic forms of organization. Such features were becoming more pronounced in Britain and the other major economies during the period, especially in certain industries (such as iron and steel, chemicals and heavy engineering) that figured large in the rapidly growing sectors of international trade.

The ultimate aim of trade is to secure gains in welfare. Indeed, the reason why the theory of international trade was a central part of classical economics was because it was seen as completing the process whereby the market maximized total welfare for all those participating in it. Modern analysis is more conflicting. On the one hand, emphasis is placed on the demand side and the manner in which trade is part of a virtuous circle in which the gains from trade feed into the process of economic growth. On the other hand, supply-side theories emphasize the limited gains from trade because, it is argued, they are once-for-all-gains. In the short run they may stimulate growth but in the longer run an economy can grow no faster than its domestic resources allow and this fact will determine the level of economic growth.[8] Whilst demand-side theory still clearly begs the question of the dynamic role of foreign trade as against domestic factors, the supply-side theories depend on very tight and unrealistic assumptions. Continuous short-term gains may well be achievable because comparative advantage may change in relation to new opportunities for economic growth, particularly as a consequence of new techniques. Quite apart from this, what are defined as short-term gains may well accrue over quite long periods, as appears to have been the case in the late nineteenth century. And it is this kind of gain that is important in evaluating the effects of trade on a particular economy.

It is important, furthermore, to avoid the pitfall of assuming that those economies which enjoy comparative advantage in high productivity sectors necessarily gain more from trade than those which are forced to concentrate on low productivity activities. What determines the gain from trade depends on what happens to relative prices in international markets and on whether high productivity sectors (or countries) are forced by competition to pass on the benefits of that greater efficiency to customers in other

8. Backhouse, *A History of Modern Economic Analysis*; Batchelor *et al, Industriali-zation and the Basis for Trade.*

countries, through the terms of trade – in other words, through lower prices. And as well as its problematic nature, the measurement of gains from trade in terms of comparative advantage is narrow in conception. Gains calculated in terms of direct income may be at the expense of costs imposed elsewhere; there may, in other words, be a problem of externalities. For example, the growth promoted through trade may be at the cost of urban slums and environmental pollution.

In sum, whilst the concept of comparative advantage offers a broad basis for the analysis of the relationship between British trade and growth in the period between 1880 and 1914, it does not provide a sharply defined framework from which clear results can be obtained. With this limitation firmly in mind we must now examine the relationship between British trade and economic performance.

TRADE AND COMPARATIVE ADVANTAGE

There is general agreement that the growth of the economy slowed during the forty years leading up to the First World War. But the margin of error in the available statistics has, not surprisingly, provided ample opportunity for the exercise of much ingenuity in defining significant turning points. The two years most canvassed are 1870 and 1899. The significance of these dates is that, depending on which is chosen, the charge of failure falls upon the late Victorians or on the Edwardians. There is, however, a fair measure of artificiality in this debate since, as has been noted, it is fanciful to claim that the character of the nation changes according to the rhythm of dynastic succession. What appear to be the best estimates available indicate that British economic performance was weakening during the whole period with an acceleration in this decline around the turn of the century, though it was less marked than some earlier figures have indicated.[9] (See Table 1.1.)

Much of the argument about British industrial performance has turned on the analysis of factor costs, based mainly on a comparison between Britain and the USA. According to the leading proponents, the British economy was using its resources in the late

9. C. H. Feinstein, 'What Really Happened to Real Wages? Trends in Wages, Prices, and Productivity in the United Kingdom, 1880–1913', *Economic History Review*, 43 (1990), pp. 595–632.

Table 2.11 Average annual growth rates of GDP per worker-year in the United Kingdom compared with six other industrial countries, 1873–1913

	1873–99	*1899–1913*
UK	1.2	0.5
USA	1.9	1.3
Sweden	1.5	2.1
France	1.3	1.6
Germany	1.5	1.5
Italy	0.3	2.5
Japan	1.1	1.8

Sources: Matthews, Feinstein and Odling-Smee (1982), 31. In relation to the sources listed there some revisions have subsequently been made, but they do not seriously affect the overall picture. See Feinstein (1990a).

nineteenth century in something approaching the optimum manner and this involved the choice of techniques in manufacturing industry which, because of relative factor prices, were more labour intensive in the UK than in the USA. There is the further implication that this allocation of resources meant that near maximum comparative advantage was being gained from international trade. Any failure in performance is thus judged to have occurred after the turn of the century.[10]

These claims and the method of assessment on which they are based have attracted a great deal of criticism. A number of critics have pointed to the unrealistic assumptions on which the analysis is based, namely, a neo-classical equilibrium model of the economy which assumes constant returns to scale and full employment. The latter condition is especially bizarre in an economy characterized by

10. This debate is an outstanding example of how the recycling of historical statistics is subject to rapid degeneration. The basic treatises are H. J. Habakkuk, *American and British Technology in the Nineteenth Century* (Cambridge, 1962); D. N. McCloskey, 'Did Victorian Britain Fail?', *Economic History Review*, 23 (1970), pp. 446–59; *idem* (ed.), *Essays on a Mature Economy* (1971); *idem, Enterprise and Trade in Victorian Britain: Essays in Historical Economics* (1981). J. Foreman-Peck (ed.), *New Perspectives on the Late Victorian Economy: Essays in Quantitative Economic History, 1860–1914* (Cambridge, 1991). Most of the additional literature is cited in the last two works.

a wide margin of underemployment. And whilst throughout the period Britain was losing population through emigration, these losses were well outstripped by natural increase. The heaviest net emigrations occurred in the 1880s (820,000) and the 1900s (720,000) but, even then, the corresponding natural increases were five and three times these numbers.[11] It is important to note, moreover, that fluctuations in emigration flows did not occur in accordance with upswings and downswings in the domestic economy or conform to a pattern of sectoral labour markets. In other words, the source of emigration was not rural Britain, with the destination alternating cyclically between the rapidly growing towns at home and centres of economic growth abroad, predominantly in North America and the Antipodes: emigrants came mainly from urban centres and were broadly representative of the population as a whole.[12] The explanation of emigration thus involves complex relationships, but its general nature is fully consistent with persistent underemployment in the economy.

The most fundamental criticism of the relative factor costs model focuses on the assumption that technology is homogeneous across national boundaries.[13] If this were so, then it can be convincingly demonstrated that even though relative factor costs differ between two economies the most economic use of resources may still require that the same technology is adopted. In the specific cases of Britain and the USA, industrial wages in the former in the late nineteenth century were much lower than the corresponding rates in the latter so that labour costs *relative* to capital costs were lower in Britain than in the USA. Thus, it is argued, Britain was optimizing resources by employing relatively labour-intensive techniques in comparison with the USA. The difficulty with this argument is that it ignores the possibility that the gain in physical output from employing the more capital-intensive technique in Britain might have more than compensated for using less of the cheaper labour, when this gain was translated into unit costs of output. In other words, relative labour and capital costs have to be interpreted in relation to alternative production possibilities and not in isolation.

11. D. Baines, 'Population, Migration and Regional Development, 1870–1939', in R. Floud and D. McCloskey, *The Economic History of Britain. Volume 2: 1860–1939* (Cambridge, 1994), pp. 30, 45.

12. D. E. Baines, *Migration in a Mature Economy. Emigration and Internal Migration in England and Wales, 1861–1900* (Cambridge, 1985).

13. It is nothing short of an elegant *coup de grâce*. Lewis, *Growth and Fluctuations*, pp. 123–5.

Plausible assumptions as to relative capital and labour costs indicate that Britain should have adopted more capital-intensive techniques in a range of industries. The question thus arises: why did Britain fail to do so on anything like the scale that occurred in the United States? Even more strongly, why did Britain fail to match Germany in this respect, where the relativity of wages in comparison with the USA was even lower than in the case of the United Kingdom? At one level, the answer must be that technology was not homogenous across national boundaries, which means that a given capital-intensive technique in Britain did not yield the same level of physical output as in the United States. The deeper problem is to explain why this was so, and this lies at the heart of the relationship between British industrial and trading performance.

In broader terms, growth in trade in the international economy during the late nineteenth century did owe much to the largely unhampered operation of comparative advantage. The enormous increase in the supply of primary products and raw materials together with a substantial fall in their prices was central to the process.

Table 2.12 International primary product prices, 1881–1913 (1913 = 100)

Year	Index	Year	Index	Year	Index
1881	96.4	1891	84.3	1901	83.1
1882	96.0	1892	81.3	1902	82.6
1883	94.8	1893	80.4	1903	82.6
1884	87.8	1894	73.9	1904	83.8
1885	83.7	1895	73.0	1905	86.3
1886	81.1	1896	71.4	1906	91.5
1887	80.1	1897	72.5	1907	95.1
1888	81.9	1898	74.8	1908	87.6
1889	83.3	1899	79.7	1909	88.7
1890	83.9	1900	87.8	1910	93.0
				1911	94.7
				1912	99.7
				1913	100.0

Source: Lewis (1978), 280–1.

These gains were reflected in the terms of trade which moved strongly in Britain's favour.

Table 2.13 UK terms of trade, annual averages, 1880–1913 (1880 = 100)

1880–85	99.5
1885–90	104.6
1890–95	109.2
1895–1900	112.2
1900–05	115.1
1905–10	112.3
1910–19	113.8

Source: Mitchell (1988), 526–7.

Producers of primary goods and raw materials were not, however, losers from trade, since not only was their absolute level of trade rising but also the prices they received for their products were not falling in direct proportion to the prices of manufactured goods. This was because the movement in the terms of trade was largely determined by lower transport costs, particularly by lower freight rates for shipping, which were mainly captured by the industrializing countries.[14] A broad measure of an individual country's gain is provided by the income terms of trade: quantity and value changes are combined by multiplying the change in the index of the volume of exports over a given period by the corresponding change in the net barter terms of trade, which is the ratio between the weighted average prices of exports and imports. This gives a total gain for the UK of 78 per cent during the period 1880–1913, or on average a rate of growth of just over 3 per cent per year.

The pattern and composition of trade which lay behind these trends has already been analysed. If it is assumed that those goods which a country exports will tend to be those in which it enjoys comparative advantages, it is possible to apply a crude test – known as revealed comparative advantage – to measure the nature of those advantages. When this is done for the United Kingdom it confirms what is fairly apparent from simply looking at the goods exported: comparative advantage lay in those goods which were produced by unskilled-labour-intensive methods and which were dependent on

14. Lewis, *Growth and Fluctuations*, pp. 167–76.

plentiful supplies of raw material imports.[15] The clearest contrast is with the United States for which comparative advantage lay in human-capital-intensive commodities. And, significantly, Germany and France can be shown to have had a pattern of trade which was nearer that of the United States than of Britain.

Revealed comparative advantage is, however, a measure of outcome, not an explanation of it. The truth is that comparative advantage is not God-given as part of the state of nature. Even climatic advantages have to be perceived and turned to advantage. Thus the combination of climate and soil which exists in Burgundy had to be discovered, and the knowledge and skills to exploit it had to be devised, before that region could yield the nectar for which it has become renowned. The capacity to recognize and create advantages is what determines the quantifiable revealed outcome. It is on this non-quantifiable basis, therefore, that an economy's performance has to be judged.

There is one further general and related point to be borne in mind. The slow growth of an economy (which may in turn lead to slow growth in exports) may not be solely the outcome of inefficiency or the failure to achieve a high rate of technical change. To some degree it may reflect the pattern of domestic demand which places high preferences on those goods and services in which, by their very nature, it is not possible to achieve high rates of output growth. For example, the very uneven distribution of income may well lead to a correspondingly disproportionate demand for highly labour-intensive personal services in which productivity is low. Moreover, in late nineteenth century Britain, substantial investments were made in social overhead capital – in sanitation, water supply, urban transport and urban improvement – which yielded low rates of return over long periods, including the benefits they produced for the general health of the population and the labour force.[16] Even so, this pattern of investment in Britain has to be seen in the context of low absolute levels of capital accumulation. Social improvement was not obviously at the expense of the crowding out of industrial investment.

15. N. F. R. Crafts, 'Revealed Comparative Advantage in Manufacturing, 1899–1950', *Journal of European Economic History*, 18 (1989), pp. 127–37; *idem* and M. Thomas, 'Comparative Advantage in UK Manufacturing Trade, 1910–1935', *Economic Journal*, 96 (1986), pp. 629–45.

16. W. Ashworth, 'The Late Victorian Economy', *Economica*, 33 (1966), pp. 17–33.

Slow-growing, labour-intensive manufacturing industry and trade performance were thus directly related. This can be further illustrated by apportioning British exports according to whether they were in the fast- or slow-growing sectors of world trade.

Table 2.14 Shares of trade in manufactures grouped by rates of growth in 1899 and 1913 (% shares)

		Expanding	*Stable*	*Declining*
1989	United Kingdom	17.7	18.6	62.9
	USA	23.4	54.1	21.7
	Germany	11.2	45.8	42.5
	France	5.8	31.0	62.8
1913	United Kingdom	21.3	13.3	65.4
	USA	34.1	38.3	38.2
	Germany	28.5	33.3	38.2
	France	14.3	26.0	59.7

Source: Saul (1965), 15.

The most significant feature of this division is the marked trend towards the slow-growing sectors. And this trend was correlated with the steady rise in the proportion of exports going to the Empire, a rise from 23 per cent in 1870 to 35 per cent by 1914.

It has proved tempting to some historians to interpret this evidence as proof that intensifying competition from Germany, the USA and Japan caused Britain to turn increasingly to the exploitation of her formal and informal empires.[17] The latter is defined as comprising those countries – especially those of South America – which Britain had drawn into her economic orbit, particularly through their reliance on British capital, without establishing formal political control over them.[18] Whether one

17. For two major examples that place a somewhat different interpretation on these trends than the one above, see P. J. Cain and A. G. Hopkins, *British Imperialism: Innovation and Expansion 1688–1914* (1993), pp. 161–73 and E. J. Hobsbawm, *The Age of Empire 1875–1914* (1987), pp. 34–55.

18. The classic article in this context is J. Gallagher and R. E. Robinson, 'The Imperialism of Free Trade', *Economic History Review*, 6 (1953) pp. 1–15. See also D. K. Fieldhouse, *Economics and Empire, 1880–1914* (1973).

accepts the notion of informal empire or not, such an interpretation of British trade patterns is somewhat facile. It fails to comprehend how the system of international trade operated to match mutual self-interest. The fact, for example, that Britain settled a significant part of her deficit with Europe and the USA through India suited Europe and the USA, which needed supplies from India and the Far East, and it suited India and the Far East as it enabled them to finance necessary supplies of manufactures and capital from Great Britain. Such arrangements were possible so long as Britain's industrial competitors had the need to pay for their imports from the Empire and other countries by direct exports, and so long as those countries themselves had not developed to the point at which they could produce their own substitutes for imports from Britain. As later events were to prove (Chapter 5) Britain was not so much exploiting her imperial advantage as being driven along by the tide of international commerce generated by the growing force of Germany and the United States in the production of new ranges of capital and consumer goods. And when, in the years between the world wars, countries within the Empire decided to adjust matters more to their own interests, it was clear that there was little Britain could do about it.

This analysis is, of course, in terms of the overall pattern of trade. In reality, this pattern was the outcome of innumerable decisions made by manufacturers and traders who were not conditioned by some kind of imperial pheromone. Imperial markets obviously had their attractions, but why they and not others were sought, and why certain types of goods and not others were exported, requires explanation which goes beyond the formalism of trade and Empire. If Britain had changed the pattern of industrial production so that there would have been a decline in imports of manufactured goods, there is no obvious reason why displaced traders from Germany and the United States, for example, would have sought refuge in British empire markets at the expense of traditional British exporters. These markets were not a soft option: their main demands were for low technology manufactured goods in which the United Kingdom had a comparative advantage, albeit of a residual nature.

BUSINESS ORGANIZATION AND INDUSTRIAL PERFORMANCE

The alleged shortcomings and failures of British industry in the late nineteenth and early twentieth centuries are the subject of major and continuing debate in economic history that cannot be covered here in detail. As has been indicated, our concern is with the relationship between Britain's industrial performance and her international economic standing, and the best way of focusing more sharply on this issue is through examination of industry's technical performance which was the lynch-pin of international comparative advantage.

Technical change is largely the outcome of decision-making within individual firms. The list of failures to match best practice in the latter part of the nineteenth century has steadily lengthened as a result of the investigations of business historians. It is unnecessary to describe these findings in other than broad outline, but the indictment they present is a formidable one. In textiles, the woollen industry was failing to match foreign standards from the 1860s onwards, and a little later Lancashire cotton failed to adopt ring-spinning and automatic looms. Iron and steel progressively fell behind best international practice from the 1860s. By 1913 coal was one of Britain's major export industries, yet only 8 per cent of its output was mechanically cut. In the multifarious engineering industry many unfavourable comparisons can be made between British and foreign producers. And so the list can be extended down to the smaller industries such as tin-plate and watch-making and to newly emerging industries of which chemicals and electricity were critical examples. The catalogue of evidence and, indeed, of contemporary complaint about the technical shortcomings of British industry is long and compelling.[19]

There is the danger, of course, that this form of chimney counting can easily result in a biased charge against British industry. There were, after all, many cases of technical advance, ranging from those which were a response to foreign challenges to those which originated from within Britain. Among the former were examples in footwear, bicycles, printing, machine tools and motor vehicles. Among the latter were numbered Wills in cigarettes,

---

19. Useful surveys are provided by D. C. Coleman and C. MacLeod, 'Attitudes to New Techniques: British Businessmen, 1800–1950', *Economic History Review*, 39 (1986), pp. 588–611, and S. Pollard, *Britain's Prime and Britain's Decline. The British Economy 1870–1914* (1989), pp. 18–57. The conclusions that Pollard draws from the evidence are counter to those above.

Courtaulds in man-made fibres and BP and Anglo-Dutch Shell in oil.[20] Among the older industries shipbuilding retained its dominant position. Whilst its share of world production had fallen from a peak of 80 per cent in the 1890s, it still produced 60 per cent of total tonnage in the years immediately before the war; and if subsidized foreign production is discounted, the industry's share had not fallen. British shipyards still relied heavily on craft skills and traditional methods that remained competitive so long as demand was not standardized. But even here there were signs that things were changing and that British builders were not moving into the production of more cost-effective oil-fired ships driven by diesel or turbine engines[21]. Even if they had shown more initiative in this direction it is difficult to see how it could have developed very far, since their main customers, British ship-owners, showed little interest in modernizing their fleets in this way.[22] More generally, the additional line of defence, that even in those industries where the latest techniques were not being used, businessmen were behaving rationally in terms of relative costs and returns from alternative processes of production, has already been discounted. It can be added that, apart from its inherent shortcomings, factor cost analysis is essentially static. It fails to explain the dynamics of technical change. As the leading historian of technology puts it: '*Today's* factor substitution possibilities are made possible by *yesterday's* technological innovations'.[23]

20. For specific studies see B. W. E. Alford, *W. D. & H. O. Wills and the Development of the UK Tobacco Industry, 1786–1965* (1973); D. C. Coleman, *Courtaulds. An Economic and Social History* (Oxford, 1969); R. Henriques, *Marcus Samuel: First Viscount Bearsted and Founder of 'Shell' Transport and Trading Company, 1853–1927* (1960). And for the diverse nature of the engineering industry see A. E. Harrison, 'The Competitiveness of the British Cycle Industry, 1890–1914', *Economic History Review*, 22 (1969), pp. 287–303 and S. B. Saul, 'The Market and the Development of the Mechanical Engineering Industries in Britain, 1860–1914', *Economic History Review*, 20 (1967), pp. 111–30.

21. S. Pollard, *Britain's Prime and Britain's Decline*, pp. 23–5. Despite recognizing the weaknesses of the industry Pollard suggests that caution (backwardness) in the short term might have given shipbuilders the advantage in the long run of being able 'to pick the new methods like ripe plums when they began to pay off'. The subsequent history of the industry hardly supports this view. See E. H. Lorenz, *Economic Decline in Britain. The Shipbuilding Industry, 1890–1970* (Oxford, 1991) and A. Slaven, 'Growth and Stagnation in British/Scottish Shipbuilding, 1913–1977', in J. Kusse and A. Slaven (eds), *Proceedings of the SSRC Conference on Scottish and Scandinavian Shipbuilding* (Gothenberg, 1980), pp. 18–54.

22. S. G. Sturmey, *British Shipping and World Competition* (1962).

23. N. Rosenberg, *Perspectives on Technology* (Cambridge, 1976), p. 253 and *passim* for an excellent and stimulating examination of issues in this field.

The test of technical performance thus comes down to one of balance between successes and failures, though not in the simple form of machine counting. It is a matter of a combination of different weights of individual industries within the economy and the extent to which best practice is achieved within each. In short, the issue is one of technical diffusion. But diffusion is far more easily defined than measured. Much evidence exists for the period under examination but still it is not enough to provide anywhere near precise answers for particular industries or sectors. We are driven, therefore, to apply the general test of industrial performance as measured by aggregate growth rates and the rate of growth of productivity. It has already been shown (Chapter 1) that on these counts late Victorian British industry cannot be judged favourably.

The nature of this assessment introduces a complication, however. The focus is on technical change, whereas these measures of performance are the result of a number of elements, some of which operate independently of technical change and some of which act directly to hinder it. But this limitation is not as serious as might first appear. First, technical change is a major determinant of economic performance on any measure. Secondly, technical change must not be conceived of in narrow 'nuts and bolts' terms. It includes managerial practices and business structure and organization, as well as investment in plant and machinery. Thirdly, those influences which act directly on the pace of technical change cannot be ignored. They are part and parcel of the underlying explanation of it and must form part of our analysis.

The 'machinery question' cast a long shadow over the nineteenth century and beyond. It covered well-documented, and often bitter, disputes between employers and workers. According to inclination, such disputes are commonly represented either as reactions of bloody-minded and conservative workers to new methods of production, or as the result of capitalist employers' determination to deskill the labour force in order to maintain tight control over the work process as the means of extracting a maximum rate of profit.[24] There is, however, evidence to support

24. S. Tolliday and J. Zeitlin (eds), *The Power to Manage? Employers and Industrial Relations in Comparative-Historical Perspective* (1991); J. Zeitlin, 'Industrial Structure, Employer Strategy, and Job Control in Britain, 1880–1920', in W. J. Mommsen and H. G. Husung (eds), *The Development of Trade Unionism in Great Britain and Germany, 1880–1914* (1985) pp. 325–37. For a more theoretical approach see A. L. Friedman, *Industry and Labour. Class Struggle at Work and Monopoly Capitalism* (1977). And for critical analysis of the neo-marxist viewpoint see J. Wood (ed.), *The Degradation of Work? Skill, Deskilling and the Labour Process* (1982).

another alternative; namely, that employers and workers shared the belief that technical change inevitably reduced the demand for labour. Hence, the interests of employers intent on a quiet life and those of employees acutely concerned for job security met in an unconscious alliance that, ultimately, served the interests of neither party. Short-termism, to cite a more modern concept, was endemic to both sides of British industry.[25]

British businessmen of this period have been characterized as gentlemen and players. Overall direction and control was exercised by the former, who subscribed to the cult of the amateur, whilst the day-to-day running of affairs was entrusted to men of practical experience. Professionalism was disdained. But not all businessmen conformed to this pattern. Exceptions, such as Lever, Lipton, Cadbury, Newnes, Courtauld, Dunlop, Crossfield and Parsons have duly been extolled as shining examples of late-Victorian enterprise.[26] Yet it is the collectivity which finally matters. And judged *ex post*, there is much evidence to suggest that businessmen of the late Victorian and Edwardian period failed to make the grade when measured against their German and American counterparts. Yet this kind of *ex post* damnation takes no account of *ex ante* conditions and expectations. Nor does it tell us directly how much blame for flagging industrial performance should be apportioned to the ranks of businessmen.

Victorian and Edwardian businessmen were no more economically rational, in the sense that neo-classical economics assumed, than businessmen of our own time. But those of the earlier generations were more strongly influenced by Britain's international economic power and by her world role than are businessmen of the late twentieth century. It was part of a general sense of superiority which, in its most refined form, was transmitted through the burgeoning public schools of the period. A liberal education for a civilized and civilizing English gentleman was the hallmark; though paradoxically these ideas and ideals were imparted in the semi-barbarous organization which constituted the English public school. The most exotic flowering of these principles was to be found in the pro-consul environments of the Empire. But its more common manifestation was the cult of the gentleman and the amateur. In such an atmosphere, applied scientific and

25. Coleman and MacCleod, 'Attitudes to New Techniques', p. 608.
26. For a classic statement, see C. Wilson, 'Economy and Society in Late Victorian Britain', *Economic History Review*, 18 (1965), pp. 183–98.

technical education did not easily flourish and it certainly did not attract high esteem.[27]

This influence is, nevertheless, more easily identified than it is quantified. A number of economic historians have challenged the importance of public school education as an influence on business performance. In one case it has been argued that the proportion of industrialists in the late nineteenth century who had been to public school was a pronounced minority. It is further claimed, somewhat oddly, that public schools did not contribute to an anti-business culture because there was no significant falling-off in the proportion of public school leavers entering business during the period and that a substantial number of sons followed in their fathers' footsteps.[28] As to the content of education, there have been attempts to show that whilst scientific and technical education in Britain was not nationally structured as in Germany, the range of its provision was by no means as relatively backward as has been frequently alleged. Added to which, the dead weight of the classics appears to have borne as heavily and for as long on German education as it did on British.[29]

Whilst the businessman was as much a figure of ridicule and derision in, say, German and American as in English literature, the similarities in other and more important respects are far less marked.[30] Thus, comparative syllabus counting is misplaced. What is far more important was the ethos of the institutions in which education took place. The public schools and the ancient universities of Britain had no counterparts in Germany. Their social and cultural divisiveness is much attested to, even by those who seek

27. D. C. Coleman, 'Gentlemen and Players', *Economic History Review*, 26 (1973), pp. 92–116.

28. H. Berghoff, 'Public Schools and the Decline of the British Economy, 1870–1914', *Past and Present*, 129 (1990), pp. 148–67.

29. H. James, 'The German Experience and the Myth of British Cultural Exceptionalism', in B. Collins and K. Robbins (eds), *British Culture and Economic Decline* (1990), pp. 91–128. Useful for the information it contains but the economic argument it advances is somewhat question-begging – see, in particular, the concluding comments, p. 124. Pollard, *Britain's Prime and Britain's Decline*, pp. 115–213 likewise emphasizes the similarities between the content of British and German education.

30. James, 'The German Experience', pp. 95–106; B. Collins, 'American Enterprise and the British Comparison', in Collins and Robbins, *British Culture and Economic Decline*, pp. 159 *ff.*; N. McKendrick, ' "Gentlemen and Players" Revisited: The Gentlemanly Ideal, The Business Ideal and the Professional Ideal in English Literary Culture', in N. McKendrick and R. B. Outhwaite, *Business Life and Public Policy* (Cambridge, 1986), pp. 98–136.

to play down their educational influence. Put another way, precisely what subjects were studied may not, in themselves, have been of direct economic importance, but in Britain it mattered a great deal where those subjects were studied.[31] Furthermore, unlike the elite universities in the USA at the turn of the century, Oxford and Cambridge did not develop centres for business training in the professional sense of the term. The first business schools in Britain did not appear until half a century later.[32]

These educational institutions did not so much contribute to an anti-business culture as foster a particular kind of business culture. Manufacturing industry was, after all, a major source of income and fortune. Industry was socially acceptable provided it recruited to its managerial ranks in the same fashion as to an officer corps and provided its operations at the highest level were directed from behind the lines. Industry was nevertheless still widely viewed as an inferior form of business life: the superior form existed in the upper reaches of banking, finance and commodity trading (Chapter 3). Occupational analyses of public school leavers and their fathers are, in this respect, beside the point. Whilst there may be a fair match between fathers in business and their sons who followed them, it is putting the cart before the horse to conclude that, because the public school ethos did not lead its cadets away from business life, this was to the advantage of business. It was they who brought that ethos into the boardroom with serious consequences for management structure and business organization, as many business historians have demonstrated. What some of the recent investigations into the social origins of late nineteenth century business do reveal, however, is that the public school influence on business attitudes and practices was increasing at that time and that its largest effects were set to occur in the decades and century which followed.[33]

There is the danger, of course, that the characterization of late Victorian and Edwardian businessmen in general relies too heavily on evidence drawn from a limited range of well-known firms that have been the subject of detailed investigation. But to the extent

31. Good illustrations of this are provided by Cain and Hopkins, *British Imperialism: Innovation and Expansion*, pp. 123, 124, 132, 134.
32. In the USA business schools were founded at Wharton in 1881, Chicago in 1889 and Harvard in 1908.
33. Berghoff, 'Public Schools and the Decline of the Economy', in my view incorrectly emphasizes the former point and, correspondingly, pays insufficient attention to the latter and more important outcome of his investigation.

that these firms were atypical it was because in most cases they were among the most successful of their day and, therefore, if there is bias, it strengthens the case with respect to the remainder.[34] Moreover, prosoprographical analysis that has penetrated lower down the scale of business enterprise reveals similar and related patterns of behaviour to those outlined. British businessmen were noticeably Anglocentric in their education and experience, an attitude which expanding imperialism reinforced. Their German counterparts, by contrast, tended to spend part of their early careers abroad, which gave them not only a wider experience of markets, technology and commercial practices than would otherwise have been the case, but also made them aware of the need to adjust their methods to match these conditions when seeking foreign sales. Not least, they understood the value of being able to conduct business in the customer's own language.[35]

Similar patterns can be discerned in the public life of businessmen. Whilst the movement of wealthy businessmen into the ranks of large landowners and the haemorrhage of capital from industry to the land may not have occurred on the scale that was once thought, there is still much evidence of successful businessmen aping the style of the upper classes, and with this went a strong sense of the need to engage in public duties. The social standing of businessmen was bound up with the extent to which they involved themselves in local political, educational, charitable, cultural and religious activities. Once again the contrast with

34. The amount of literature generated by the debate on entrepreneurship during this period has now reached library proportions. A wide-ranging survey of the literature is provided by P. L. Payne, 'Entrepreneurship and British Economic Decline', in Collins and Robbins, *British Culture and Economic Decline* pp. 25–58. Payne on balance gives entrepreneurs the benefit of the doubt but draws attention to the more complex problem of the failure of entrepreneurship, implying that this is made up of elements which involve relationships between the individual firm and the market and institutional structures within which they operated. On this theme see B. W. E. Alford, 'Entrepreneurship, Business Performance and Industrial Development', *Business History*, 19 (1977), pp. 116–33.

35. H. Berghoff and R. Möller, 'Tired Pioneers and Dynamic Newcomers? A Comparative Essay on English and German Entrepreneurial History, 1870–1914', *Economic History Review*, 47 (1994), pp. 262–87. An important example of the different attitudes among European businessmen towards the need for education and vocational experience abroad is provided by A. Heerding, *The History of N. V. Philips' Gloeilampen Fabrieken, Volume 1, The Origin of the Dutch Incandescent Lamp Industry* (Cambridge, 1986), pp. 62 *ff.* Somewhat ironically Gerard Philips gained an important part of his technical education at the University of Glasgow under Professor A. Jamieson, an expert in marine lighting.

German businessmen is clear. They did far less of these things and had 'considerably more time and energy for a single-minded pursuit of economic ambitions than their English competitors, who felt obliged to take over a multitude of public duties'.[36] It might be claimed that, although they were unlike their German counterparts, successful British businessmen had much more in common with American industrialists who displayed a strong taste for conspicuous consumption. But this is to ignore the quite different nature of social values between the two countries, epitomized by the absence of a traditional ruling class in the USA. It was the difference between wealth and social position.

The hierarchical and restricted nature of the higher reaches of educational and professional training were paralleled by traditional forms of training among skilled workers. Apprenticeship systems produced skilled craftsmen but this form of training was rooted in traditional methods and practices which became an increasing barrier to technical change, especially where it involved the replacement of labour-intensive by capital-intensive methods.[37] Such patterns of training were reflected in the structure of labour organization in which the primary interest of unions of craft and skilled workers was to maintain established demarcations and differentials between themselves and the mass of the labour force. These interests coalesced as part of the ruling orthodoxy on universal education. It was, as Tawney expressed it, an orthodoxy which decreed that for the masses educational provision should be sufficient to enable a worker to understand an order but not sufficient for him to question it. Maybe there was an element of exaggeration in this view, but what it did not exaggerate was that education in the fullest sense, and regardless of its content, was seen as a prerogative of social class and not as an essential investment for a modern industrialized society.

Superficially, British industrial organization does not appear to have been lagging in the late nineteenth century. Indeed, the reverse seems to be the case with the formation of large companies – the so-called amalgamation movement – which placed Britain

36. Berghoff and Möller, 'Tired Pioneers', p. 283.
37. A wide range of evidence covering the period from 1850–1939 is provided in H. F. Gospel (ed.), *Industrial Training and Technological Innovation: a Comparative and Historical Study* (1991); P. Summerfield and E. J. Evans (eds), *Technical Education and the State since 1850: Historical and Contemporary Perspectives* (Manchester, 1990). A more focused study is R. R. Locke, *The End of Practical Man: Entrepreneurship and Higher Education in Germany, France and Great Britain* (Greenwich, Connecticut, 1984).

ahead of continental rivals and more in line with the USA in terms of the share of output of manufacturing industry accounted for by large firms. The fifty largest companies in the UK in 1905 ranged from Imperial Tobacco with an issued capital of £17.5 million, Watney Coombe, Read (£15 million) and J. & P. Coates (£11.2 million) down to Waterlow & Sons (£1.4 million), Tootal, Broadhurst, Lea (£1.3 million) and Nobel Explosives (£1.3 million). Brewers, textile manufacturers, shipbuilders and metal manufacturers figured most prominently in the list.[38] These companies had established reputations throughout the world for goods made in Britain.

But appearances are deceptive. Many of these company formations occurred as defensive alliances in basic industries – such as iron and steel and shipbuilding – where trading and market conditions were becoming increasingly tight; others were in basic consumer industries – such as brewing and tobacco – serving low-income mass markets.[39] Special conditions both facilitated and placed a premium on amalgamation. In brewing, new licensing laws offered major advantages to those firms that could acquire a long string of tied public houses. And in both brewing and tobacco the large amounts of capital needed to finance the excise duty acted as a barrier to the entry of new firms once the big firms were established. The largest amalgamations in iron and steel were in the armaments industry, namely, Vickers, Son & Maxim, Armstrong-Whitworth and Cammell Laird. The ability of these firms to supply weapons of ever-increasing complexity to the British government enabled them to secure strong monopolistic advantages. Moreover, these amalgamated companies adopted federal forms of organization which allowed existing business structures and management practices to remain largely undisturbed. In many of the new companies, management deteriorated from the inefficient to the chaotic. The Calico Printers' Association, established in 1899, was characterized in 1907 as 'a study in disorganisation' and its 'form of administration resembled the crude democratic expedient of government by mass-meeting'.[40] If this was by no means the rule, it is still difficult to find evidence of best practice management among these leading companies. Lever Brothers is perhaps such an

38. L. Hannah, *The Rise of the Corporate Economy* (1983), pp. 187–8.
39. P. L. Payne, 'The Emergence of the Large-Scale Company in Great Britain', *Economic History Review*, 20, (1967), pp. 519–42.
40. Payne, 'The Emergence of the Large-Scale Company', p. 528.

example, though even here William Lever's dominance in the firm created big problems for the future.[41] More typical, probably, is J. B. Dunlop, who was very successful in building up a multinational tyre company yet squandered some of his gains through poor management.[42]

The amalgamation movement, as it became known, was accompanied by attendant company promoters and downright speculators, but in the main companies experienced little difficulty in raising capital. A major reason for this was that in many cases the process involved transforming private family firms into public companies by capitalizing the good will in the firm and issuing this to the family as ordinary shares, and then offering the remainder of the capital as fixed interest stock to the public. In this way, family control was maintained whilst additional capital was made available either for retention in the business or for distribution to meet family demands.[43] Correspondingly, it is easy to see how this form of company promotion was not conducive to changes in management practices.

For all these shortcomings it is important to recognize that the hundred largest firms in manufacturing accounted for only 15 per cent of total output in 1905. There were, moreover, large private firms such as Harland & Wolf in shipbuilding, Crosse & Blackwell in food, and Pilkingtons in glass, that were at the forefront of their industries and well managed by the standards of the time.[44] In the iron and steel industry, the existence of family firms that were small by international standards can be explained in terms of the varied foreign markets that they served, in contrast to the large mass domestic markets on which US and German steelworks based their production. In the electrical engineering industry there was, again, a variety of experience. Britain was a world leader in cable manufacture but fell behind in traction, heavy machinery, electric

41. C. Wilson, *The History of Unilever: A Study in Economic Growth and Social Change. Volume I* (1994), pp. 257–8, 269–70, and more generally pp. 243–312.

42. G. Jones, 'The Growth and Performance of British Multinational Firms Before 1939: The Case of Dunlop', *Economic History Review,* 37 (1984), pp. 35–53.

43. The classic but unpublished study is J. R. Jeffreys, *Trends in Business Organisation in Great Britain since 1856,* London Ph.D. thesis 1938. The thesis has been reproduced by Arno Press, New York, 1977. An example of how capital values were increased in this way is provided by Alford, *W. D. & H. O. Wills,* pp. 183–6, though in this case the family was so rich and the management sufficiently competent that the wider family absorbed all the fixed interest capital. The basic reason for incorporation in this case was the need to provide for family succession.

44. An excellent study of such a firm is T. C. Barker, *The Glassmakers. Pilkingtons: The Rise of an International Company 1826–1876* (1977).

lamps and telephones. But in an increasingly competitive world, it was the balance of performance that mattered. In the British economy this balance was shifting in the wrong direction in the years leading up to 1914. Too many large and small firms were alike in their increasingly backward management practices and their failure to adopt new techniques and seek out new markets than was good for the longer-term competitive health of the economy.

By contrast, in the USA corporate growth was increasingly the outcome of a new type of business organization in which professional management was at the core. Business diplomacy through an established social network rather than aggressive company formation was the order of the day in Britain. The degree of concentration in manufacturing in the other major economies was less than in Britain and the USA, though large companies existed in rapidly growing industry in the form of cartels in Germany or zaibatsus in Japan, for example.[45] And their organization and management were more closely matched to the needs of modern technology. Even family firms appear to have followed this pattern to a significantly greater extent than their British counterparts. The firms of Krupp and Siemens in Germany are leading cases of family firms which prospered on the basis of applying new science and new methods. Such examples show, moreover, that backward business practices are not a necessary consequence of the form of company ownership, but that they have much to do with business attitudes formed within a wider cultural and institutional context.[46]

Adaptability was uniquely important for Britain since long-established methods which had served well enough in the past needed to be changed. The consequences of an 'early start' can easily be explained away by the self-adjusting market mechanisms of neo-classical economic models, but in the real world such smooth adjustments are a fantasy. Even so, the shortcomings of business-

45. A large amount of information on business organization in the USA, Britain and Germany during this period is collected in A. D. Chandler, Jnr., *Scale and Scope. The Dynamics of Industrial Capitalism* (1990); W. M. Frewin, *The Japanese Enterprise System: Competitive Strategies and Co-operative Structures* (Oxford, 1992).

46. J. Kocka, 'Enterprise and Managers in German Industrialization' in P. Mathias and M. M. Postan (eds), *The Cambridge Economic History of Europe, Volume VII, The Industrial Economies . . . Part I* (Cambridge, 1978), pp. 180–230; *idem*, 'Family and Bureaucracy in German Industrial Management, 1850–1914; *Business History Review*, 45 (1971), pp. 133–56; P. L. Payne, 'Family Business in Britain: An Historical and Analytical Survey', in A. Okochi and S. Yasuoka, *Family Business in the Era of Industrial Growth* (Tokyo, 1984), pp. 171–206.

men in traditional industries are one thing: but what of the opportunities in new industries which new entrepreneurs might have grasped? More generally, were there obvious limits to what individual businessmen could be expected to achieve? These are very difficult questions to answer but there are two areas which are of particular relevance in this connection: the role of the banks and government policy on trade and market competition.

The issue of bank/industry relations turns on the short time horizons to which the banking system had accustomed itself during the nineteenth century and on its major concern with international business through the London money market.[47] In fact, the latter reinforced the former, which originated early in the century as a consequence of the failure of large numbers of country banks that had been tied to particular industries and localities. There followed a series of legislative acts leading to the emergence of joint stock, branch banking, which concentrated on cheque-clearing business and on short-term lending to the money market. Separated from the clearing banks were merchant banks which were engaged in company promotion and international lending. Thus, it is argued, British industry was handicapped in the process of modernization, involving more capital-intensive technical change, through the lack of access to finance.

An immediate problem with this argument is that of weighing factors of supply and demand. Whilst the limited extent of long-term funds actually supplied to industry by banks is clearly recorded, it is by no means equally clear whether this outcome was the result of restrictiveness on the part of banks or of lack of demand on the part of industry.[48] The fact that interest rates were low during the period and that capital was fairly easily raised from the public for large-scale amalgamations, might suggest the latter; but it could equally have been the outcome of a slack market for finance because industry was deterred by known banking practice, which included the reluctance of banks and finance houses to underwrite the issue of capital in new types of business enterprise.[49] What does seem likely – but is heartily challenged nevertheless – is

47. M. Collins, *Money and Banking in the UK. A History* (1988).

48. F. Capie and M. Collins, *Have the Banks Failed British Industry?* (1992); M. Collins, *Banks and Industrial Finance in Britain 1800–1939* (1991). These present a view that justifies the passive role of banks in this respect. For a more general treatment, see P. L. Cottrell, *Industrial Finance 1830–1914* (1980).

49. And, of course, historical data of actual rates tell us nothing about the marginal rate.

that there was a bias in information in the capital market in favour of overseas investment that made it difficult for new firms to raise money from the public.[50] Yet when all is said, even if finance had been more easily available would firms have been able to make effective use of it?

The thrust of our analysis has been that, within the international arena, British industry was failing to match the pace of technical change. To do so required company reorganization of a kind that involved substantial injections of capital. The renewal of short-term overdraft facilities to firms in established industries did not amount to the provision of long-term finance in the manner required, as some economic historians have implied. The intention behind this lending was one of providing stop-gap finance, not of achieving structural change. It is, however, in the new sectors of industry that the more critical issue arises, though there is always the problem of the extent to which new industries developed from the stems of older ones. Chemicals, electrical engineering and motor vehicles are major examples of new, largely independent business opportunities. By contrast, developments within metal manufacture, artificial fibres and marine engineering occurred within well-established industries. To the extent that these older industries produced stunted development – and this was not true in all cases, as the example of Courtaulds in artificial fibres shows – it was a reflection on British industry rather than a necessary condition, as the growth of these industries in other countries demonstrates. For both categories, however, strong international comparisons can be drawn in relation to the provision of capital and finance. In the USA such developments were associated with investment banking and company promotion, in Germany with the formation of bank-financed cartels and in Japan with the growth of financial conglomerates. Of course, the question arises as to whether the role of banks in industry was a permissive rather than a causal element in overcoming economic backwardness in the manner that Gerschenkron has described.[51] Yet even if they were largely supportive, the important fact is that in other countries they existed to perform that role. The absence of such institutions in Britain does at least lend some support to the view that although the

---

50. This aspect is covered in detail in Chapter 3.
51. R. Cameron (ed.), *Financing Industrialization*, 2 Vols. (Cheltenham, 1992). A wide-ranging collection covering the major economies. The editor emphasizes the permissive role of banks. The best individual study is *idem., France and the Economic Development of Europe, 1800–1914* (Princeton, 1961).

banking system may not have acted as a direct drag on industrial change, it did not provide a financial framework that was conducive to the kind of business reorganization that was increasingly necessary for efficient economic performance, even allowing for the fact that the initiative for change had to come from business itself.

As for government policy on trade and market competition, the principles of economic liberalism during this period have already been examined (Chapter 1). Its most important practical manifestation was the policy of free trade. In considering whether this policy had serious and damaging consequences for British industry, a comparison of trade policies between Britain on the one hand and the United States, Germany, Japan and France on the other, would seem to offer a *prima facie* case for protection. However, detailed analysis has shown that in all these cases the *effective* rate of tariff protection, as opposed to the *nominal* rate, was very modest between 1880 and 1914, even when it was a response to industrial demands or to political pressure groups rather than a means for raising government revenue.[52] The competitiveness of foreign producers was thus substantially based on comparative advantage. Put another way, they did not need trade protection; though this leaves open the issue, to which we shall return, of whether some degree of protection was afforded by other means. For Britain, by contrast, the case for protection might be made on the grounds that it would have provided the means for creating the conditions for industrial reorganization. As always, however, this possibility involves the assumption that the opportunities thus created would have been taken up by the industries concerned.[53]

Protection had considerable support among industrialists, the clearest evidence of which was provided by the tariff reform movement that originated in the 1880s.[54] The movement was at its

52. Capie, 'Tariff Protection and Economic Performance in the Nineteenth Century'; S. B. Saul, *Studies in British Overseas Trade 1870–1914* (Liverpool, 1960), pp. 134–65. See p. 140 for an explanation of nominal and effective tariffs.

53. On plausible assumptions, and allowing for all the imprecision of counter-factual calculations, the probable loss from switching to free trade was negligible up to the 1880s – D. N. McCloskey, 'Magnanimous Albion: Free Trade and British National Income, 1841–81', *Explorations in Economic History*, 17 (1980), pp. 303–20. Given that Britain's imports were predominantly food and raw materials this conclusion is hardly surprising. The critical issue arises during the period 1880–1914.

54. This issue has provoked as much division historiographically as it did historically. Interesting analyses are provided by Cain and Hopkins, *British Imperialism: Innovation and Expansion*, pp. 202–25 and by Pollard, *Britain's Prime and Britain's Decline*, pp. 235–44.

height between 1895, when Joseph Chamberlain became colonial secretary, and the 1906 general election when it was rejected by the electorate.[55] Manufacturers joining the ranks included those of iron and steel, chemicals, textiles (though only parts of the cotton industry), glass and tobacco. Against them, certain industries remained firm supporters of free trade as they were dependent on large export markets – shipbuilding, coal and sections of cotton textiles being the most important. Such a division of interests runs counter to those who claim that industry as a whole was swinging behind City financial interests in support of free trade imperialism.[56] At all events, the movement for tariff reform failed to win over voters in 1906 because of popular concern over cheap food, high-Tory resistance to what was incorrectly seen as a shift in the balance of power away from London and the City to provincial industries, and the diverse nature of industrial interests.

In itself, the failure to introduce trade protection probably did not represent a lost opportunity, given the limited responsive capabilities of British industry. It did, however, mark the beginning of a much more fundamental weakness in the political economy of the nation that, it will be argued, was to grow in proportion to Britain's problems in the world economy in the twentieth century. It was the failure to develop a relationship between the state and industry which matched the needs of technological change within an increasingly outdated industrial structure. Of particular interest and importance in this respect was government policy towards the so-called network industries, which included railways, gas, water, urban transport, telegraphs, telephones, electricity generation and electricity supply.[57] The railway system, for example, had for long suffered from the ambivalence of policy that attempted to reconcile the irreconcilable principles of *laissez-faire* and state regulation. The result, by 1900, was a railway network suffering from over-capitalization and excessive competition. Its productivity was declining and its record of innovation, especially in electric

55. Much alarmist contemporary opinion was raised by E. E. Williams, *Made in Germany* (1896) and F. A. MacKenzie, *The American Invaders* (1902) but their practical effect was not significant.

56. *Cf.* Cain and Hopkins, *British Imperialism: Innovation and Expansion*, who attempt to square the diverse nature of the interests involved in the contemporary political debate with their own organizing concept of 'gentlemanly capitalism'. But see M. J. Daunton, 'Gentlemanly Capitalism and British Industry, 1820–1914', *Past and Present*, 122 (1989), pp. 119–58.

57. J. Foreman-Peck and R. Millward (eds), *Public and Private Ownership of British Industry, 1820–1990* (Oxford, 1994).

traction, was falling significantly below international best practice. In many ways, the standard set by railway policy was matched by that regulating the other network industries: 'what seems distinctive about the British approach in these years is the lack of consensus and consultation which led to frequent national policy changes and contributed to poor business performance'.[58] As well as restrictive regulations in this field, well-established Crown agencies and the vested interests of municipal companies posed formidable barriers to change.

A particular feature was the manner in which the business organizations, built upon the early forms of technology in these industries, were bound up in a web of legislation that subsequently became the barrier to restructuring and reorganization made necessary by advances in technology. The electricity supply industry is a case *par excellence.*[59] These industries were, furthermore, both part of and crucial to the effective development of new science-based technologies in industry generally. And evidence on comparative international performance adds weight to the charge that Britain was failing to make the grade in them. Its competitors possessed a source of comparative advantage, in their forms of government which permitted more efficient national systems, that set them more in tune with modern economic needs. It was Britain, above all among the industrial countries, that needed to develop substitutes to overcome its growing economic backwardness.

OUTCOME AND PROSPECT

Did the changes in British trade performance between 1880 and 1914 amount to a serious case of failure to match the standards of its competitors or were they mainly relative adjustments as part of a process of catching up by the newly emergent industrial nations? Clearly some diminution in Britain's world position was inevitable. And on the face of it that reduction does not seem seriously out of line with the growth in world production and income. In 1913 Britain's share of world trade was on a par with that of Germany, just ahead of that of the United States and nearly double that of France. Yet these statistics do not capture the qualitative and

58. Foreman-Peck and Millward, *Public and Private Ownership of British Industry*, p. 112.
59. L. Hannah, *Electricity Before Nationalization* (1979).

dynamic nature of trade. In these respects it has been shown that Britain's comparative position was worsening, though in judging it there is the difficulty of balancing the short against the longer run.

Coal is a particularly interesting case in point. Exports boomed during the period and brought good returns. But this was comparative advantage based on a heavily localized, labour-intensive industry with an unimpressive productivity record and, as it proved, limited future prospects.[60] A similar case could be made in respect of cotton textiles.[61] Long-term adjustments for industries such as these present no problems to those who believe in the simplifications of neo-classical market mechanisms; but in the real world the situation is much different. The capacity for adaptability and change in the face of changing market conditions and technological possibilities is the outcome of a combination of luck and judgement. Our analysis suggests that within the competitive international market, Britain was beginning to suffer from bad luck and poor judgement. The charge of failure made against late Victorian and Edwardian businessmen and the financial and government institutions within which they operated must be modified to the extent that in each case their quality was no worse during this period than it had been during the earlier part of the century. The fact is that it needed to be different in order to match the requirements of new, science-based technology on which modern industry was increasingly based. Failure to achieve this change was turning economic maturity into economic senescence. As to the specific question raised at the outset of this chapter, the balance of evidence points strongly to Britain's weakening performance in world trade stemming from growing weaknesses in industry at home.

60. R. Church, 'Production, Employment and Labour Productivity in the British Coalfields, 1880–1913: Some Reinterpretations', *Business History*, 31 (1989), pp. 6–27, argues, in line with his earlier work, that the productivity performance of the industry between 1880 and 1914 was better than has been commonly argued; but this appears to be mainly a matter of degree. See *idem*, *The History of the British Coal Industry. Volume 2: 1830–1913. Victorian Pre-eminence* (Oxford, 1986), p. 477.

61. Not surprisingly a subject that has generated a huge literature. The main issues are dealt with from different standpoints by W. Lazonick, 'The Cotton Industry' in B. Elbaum and W. Lazonick (eds), *The Decline of the British Economy* (Oxford, 1986), pp. 18–50 and L. Sandberg, *Lancashire in Decline: A Study of Entrepreneurship, Technology and International Trade* (Columbus, Ohio, 1974).

CHAPTER THREE

Finance and Empire, *1880–1914*

Britain was the centre of international finance and capital in the late nineteenth century. The Bank of England both symbolized this power and was at the hub of the system. The Bank was, moreover, a private institution and the influence that it exercised was seen as the outcome of the natural processes of the market. To what extent belief accorded with reality and to what extent the status of the Bank represented the broader ascendancy of finance over industry in the domestic economy are fundamental issues to be examined.

THE GOLD STANDARD

The mechanism of international finance was the gold standard (otherwise known as the price-specie flow mechanism), which contemporaries judged to be a fundamental part of the natural economic law. Countries on the gold standard each valued their unit of currency in terms of a standard quantity of gold and thus fixed their international exchange rate. The rules required that there had to be free movement of gold, the domestic money supply had to vary directly in relation to a country's gold reserve and any disequilibrium in the balance of payments had to be corrected through price adjustments consequent upon the money-supply effect of the movement of gold. A balance of payments deficit, for example, would cause gold to flow out, which in turn would reduce the money base and the domestic money supply, cause prices to fall and interest rates to rise. The economy would thus become more price-competitive internationally and this would be further aided by the obverse effects of the inflow of gold into economies in trade surplus. This implied that the basic adjustments would be achieved through changes in the levels of income and employment.

Underlying this belief in a self-adjusting mechanism was a whole range of assumptions which added up to a neo-classical world of perfect competition – a world of frictionless and continuous market adjustment under conditions of perfect information. The real world was, of course, very different. For example, relative elasticities of demand for internationally traded goods might result in very large changes in prices having a small effect on quantities demanded, with the consequence that balance of payments adjustments through falling prices would not be achieved. Multiplier and accelerator effects could then come into play and disequilibrium would intensify. Similar frictions and maladjustments could occur on the supply side, especially if there existed monopolistic conditions in industrial structures and factor markets.

Such deficiencies of analysis have long since given rise to alternative theories of balance of payments adjustment under a regime of fixed exchange rates. A brief excursion through alternative theories is important for two reasons. First, a satisfactory understanding of the nature of the pre-First World War international financial system can only be gained against a framework of possible theoretical explanations. Secondly, however unreal the assumptions and beliefs of economic actors were about the gold standard, the actions flowing from those beliefs had decidedly real effects.

Quite apart from the inherent flaws in the pure theory of the gold standard, there are clearly problems connected with variations in the money supply and international capital flows. It is not hard to demonstrate that under a formal gold standard monetary authorities could not and did not necessarily attempt to achieve regulation of the money supply in line with gold reserves. Levels of credit were manipulated by banks and by governments to satisfy other needs. Even if the intentions of the central monetary authorities were in line with the formal requirements of the system, the speed of their reactions might be too delayed to have the required effect.[1] And a further complication arises when account is taken of possible changes in the velocity of circulation of the money supply. Some economists claim that the velocity is fairly stable over time whilst others argue that it can alter rapidly and easily offset

---

1. A good survey of the gold standard in theory and practice in the nineteenth century is provided by B. J. Eichengreen, *Golden Fetters: The Gold Standard and the Great Depression, 1919–1939* (Oxford, 1992); also *idem.*, 'The Gold Standard Since Alec Ford', in S. N. Broadberry and N. F. R. Crafts (eds), *Britain in the International Economy* (Cambridge, 1992), pp. 49–79.

changes in the money supply manipulated by the monetary authorities.[2]

The international movement of capital under the price-specie flow mechanism is assumed to be independently determined and interactive with trade flows. Thus a country in surplus may, in effect, use the surplus to finance overseas lending and thus avoid the need for the transfer of bullion. The essential requirement for such an adjustment is a completely multilateral system of financial settlements. But the exogenity of capital movements and the existence of lags and friction in the system (not least because trade creditors are by no means the same individuals as overseas investors) can produce disequilibrium.

The major alternative theory to the price-specie flow model, under fixed rates of exchange, is the monetary theory of the balance of payments. This assumes that capital flows are endogenous and that balance of payments equilibrium should be seen in terms of the *stock* of money instead of as the outcome of *flows* of trade and capital. The residents of a given country will thus choose to hold a given stock of money and the balance of payments must adjust to these claims. The movement of gold thus becomes the result of the adjustment process instead of the cause of it. If a country demands more money than the balance of payments can supply at the existing stock of domestic gold, more gold must be imported.[3] Put simply, the difference between the two theories is that the former assumes that changes in the money supply can have real effects on the economy whereas the latter assumes that the money supply is neutral over the longer run.

2. The velocity of circulation measures the number of times each money unit is used to purchase each year's output of final goods and services. For example, if final output is £200 billion and the money supply (in all forms) is £10 billion the velocity of circulation is 20. Monetarists hold that the ratio is fairly stable and alters only slowly over time, otherwise they could not argue that there is a direct link between the money supply and prices and between the growth in the money supply and rate of inflation. By contrast, Keynesian economists argue that the velocity of circulation can change rapidly, offsetting any changes in the money supply. The unsuccessful attempts at monetary control under Mrs Thatcher would suggest that Keynesians are the more likely to be correct.

3. In other words, more money will be demanded if the level of output rises, and the balance of payments on current account will tend to improve, thus attracting the necessary gold. The check to excessive increases in the money supply occurs when the rate of growth of the national money supply significantly exceeds the international rate, thus causing an outflow of speculative gold which reduces the monetary base and sets in motion corresponding upward adjustments in interest rates.

A third line of theory derives from Keynesian economics. Here the automatic mechanism is specified in terms of income adjustments in the domestic economy assisted by flows of capital which are, therefore, endogenously determined. In this way, swings in the balance of payments tend to be compensated for by short-term capital movements (hot money) and variations in the level of employment, thus obviating the need for major changes in the stock of gold. It was this view of the operation of the gold standard that caused Keynes to become strongly opposed to it in the 1930s because of the high levels of unemployment to which it was assumed to give rise. There are further variations on these main themes but what they all have in common is the notion that there was a high (or complete) degree of automatic adjustment in the system, even if this had to be trimmed on occasion by central bank action. The adjustment was in terms of compensating flows of gold, capital and money supply.[4]

The testing of alternative theories of balance of payments adjustment requires data to be internationally comprehensive and accurate to a degree which it is impossible to achieve. The problem is even more fundamental, however. Even if such data were available the theories are untestable. The real world of trade and finance does not have a number of fixed points at which everything is in equilibrium so that subsequent disturbances can be measured from a firm point. The system is one of continuous adjustment, co-determined by a number of variables as far as the naked cyc of the economist can see. Thus, it has as yet proved impossible to demonstrate that a particular variable, or set of variables, is at least consistent with one or other of these alternative explanations.[5] Above all, it is clear that disequilibrium within the system of international finance could and did exist for considerable periods of time. Equally clear is the fact that before 1914 the system did not collapse into crisis. How, then, was such stability maintained?

An immediate response is that the strict rules of the gold standard were not obeyed. Gold did not flow in anything like the volume that would have been required to balance the books of

4. A useful survey of these alternatives (in addition to those indicated in note 1) is given by I. M. Drummond, *The Gold Standard and the International Monetary System 1900–1939* (1987).

5. The monetary theory of the balance of payments is logically flawed, however, since it assumes perfectly integrated financial and commodity markets. See J. Foreman-Peck, *A History of the World Economy. International Economic Relations since 1850* (1983), pp. 180–1.

Britain in the World Economy since 1880

deficit economies. Until 1900 an important element in this process of adjustment was the Bank of England's influence on international settlements through the London money market. Some two-thirds of the bills of exchange which financed international trade were handled in London. Through a system of acceptance and discount houses, bills (which were usually of 30 or 90 days' maturity) could be converted into cash by traders. The credit which the bill brokers used to finance their operations was supplied on very short term by the clearing banks. The Bank of England could expand or contract the credit base of clearing banks through open-market operations which affected the size of their reserves. This device was operated in combination with the rate of interest which the Bank charged for loans to its customers. Thus, for example, by selling government bonds the Bank could withdraw cash from the banking system and hence its reserves, and the corresponding tendency for bond prices to fall would reinforce the higher rate of interest imposed by the Bank. Commercial banks would restrict funds to acceptance and discount houses which in turn would be forced to borrow from the Bank of England at the higher rate of interest, which became known as the bank rate. The reverse policies would have the opposite effect of expanding credit. In this way the Bank protected its own gold reserve and provided credit to the system (at a price), and in this way obviated the need for gold movements.[6]

The Bank of England remained a private institution throughout this period. It competed with other banks for business, and this major element of self-interest has been the subject of criticism by some economic historians, on the grounds that it resulted in a significantly less than optimum domestic monetary policy.[7] The Bank's concern to protect its gold reserve – which was small in relation to its sphere and scale of operations – led to numerous changes in interest rates which are held to have been destabilizing to the domestic economy. Against this view it can be argued that within a system of fixed, gold-based exchange rates, there was every reason for the major central bank to give close attention to the state of its gold reserves. Moreover, there is substantial evidence that the Bank increasingly recognized its primary responsibilities in

6. M. Collins, *Money and Banking in the UK. A History* (1988); R. C. Michie, *The City of London: Continuity and Change, 1850–1990* (1992); W. H. Scammel, *The London Discount Market* (New York, 1968).

7. For a somewhat ambivalent discussion of the role of the Bank, which also provides a comprehensive survey of the literature, see P. J. Cain and A. G. Hopkins, *British Imperialism: Innovation and Expansion 1688–1914* (1993), pp. 143–58.

international finance and for maintaining the stability of the domestic banking system.[8] Nevertheless, it is questionable whether the Bank behaved consistently in certain notable financial crises, including the Baring crisis of 1890 which is considered in detail later. And whether it would act as lender in the last resort clearly depended on private considerations rather than on a judgement of what was for the public good, however defined.

Another major element in the stability of the system was central bank cooperation. Whilst the modes of operation and financial objectives of other central financial institutions undoubtedly differed from those of the Bank of England, they had a shared, basic interest in maintaining the gold value of their currencies. Beyond this, the volume of British trade was such as to maintain a flow of sterling throughout the system which effectively made sterling the reserve currency of international finance. Sterling was as good as gold, not simply because of its inherent strength but also because countries holding sterling reserves had a vested interest in ensuring that their actions did not place undue short-term pressures on sterling.

As has been seen (Chapter 2) the surplus on invisible trade was sufficient to finance the persistent deficit on the balance of trade and still leave ample funds to sustain an increasing flow of overseas investment. This flow was made up of a combination of short- and long-term capital; in certain cases the former eventually became the basis for the latter. Together these flows facilitated balance of payments adjustments within the fixed exchange rate system. On the available evidence it would appear that the short-term capital position of Britain was strong and was bolstered by exchange reserves held in sterling by foreign countries, to which reference has been made. Such flexibility was especially important to those economies entering the process of economic development through the periphery of international trade, by supplying food and raw materials to the already industrializing nations. Argentina is a case in point. Its ability to remain more or less on the gold standard depended on the flexibility of its financial and capital relations with

8. The classic analysis of the Bank's role was provided by W. Bagehot, *Lombard Street* (1973); see also R. S. Sayers, *Central Banking After Bagehot* (Oxford, 1957). *Cf.* Cain and Hopkins, *British Imperialism: Innovation and Expansion, loc. cit.*, who present the Bank as primarily part of the 'City' interest, and who tend to confuse the reasons for its actions with their validity in terms of national economic interests. How differently could the Bank have behaved?

Britain.[9] Thus Britain's strength as an international creditor in the 1880s and the 1890s reduces the issue of whether capital flows were exogenously or endogenously determined to something of a theoretical nicety. For all practical purposes, full understanding of the process by contemporaries did not matter since it did not fail.

A third important element in maintaining the viability of the system was that pressures which arose initially from disequilibria in trade flows tended to be self-compensating. In general terms, this was because such movements occurred against a trend of growth in trade and income in the world economy. Short-term accommodation was usually sufficiently effective, therefore. Trade fluctuations were, moreover, dispersed throughout the system and were not highly synchronized, which again eased the process of adjustment. More intricately, the trading systems of the major economies were not totally bi-modal; in particular, alterations in the level of stocks (inventories) could provide compensating adjustments for fluctuations in trade balances. There was one further element of flexibility, namely, that provided by domestic banking. In so far as external conditions required adjustments to the domestic money supply, at least part could be met by commercial banks within normal discretionary limits without any effect on the central bank. Once again, the trend of income growth facilitated such operations.

This capacity for adjustment and international cooperation was the reality behind the formal gold standard. The strength and operation of the four major elements described varied in relation to one another during the period, depending on the source and nature of short-term disturbances to the system. It is for this reason that flows of foreign investment do not conform to the neat patterns predicted by theoretical models based on highly aggregated data. What, according to these models, appear as perverse movements that can perhaps be explained away in terms of leads and lags are, in fact, no more nor less than the very elements of flexibility within the system. And the Bank of England's role was far from being all-powerful; but it was the central institutional focus of the system. Another aspect of this reality was that the gold standard in which contemporaries had such faith was never put to the test.

Fixed exchange rates did impose adjustments on an economy through employment and income effects which the population at large, and organized labour in particular, might not be willing to

9. A. G. Ford, *The Gold Standard 1880–1914: Britain and Argentina* (Oxford, 1962).

accept. Before 1914 there was, however, no serious challenge of this kind in Britain. In general, adjustments of this nature were tolerated and tolerable because the power of effective opposition did not exist and because the upward, if modest, trend of growth in the economy meant that they were experienced within a broader framework of rising incomes and expectations.

To this point the analysis has focused on the period up to 1900 because until that time the position of Britain in international finance remained substantially unaltered. Thereafter it began to change. At the level of overseas investment things altered only to the extent that the volume of capital flowing abroad increased, the nature and extent of which will be considered shortly. Britain's trading position changed substantially, however. The sharp rise in the volume of world trade and the increased share of it accounted for by other major economies, significantly altered Britain's relative position. The US dollar, the German mark and the French franc were strong currencies by 1900 and were becoming increasingly important in multilateral financial settlement and capital movements. The pound sterling had never been, in modern parlance, a master currency; but it had clearly been the top currency, reaching its zenith in the 1880s.[10] Thereafter its relative power steadily declined. That it remained central to the system of international settlements right up to the First World War, there can be no doubt. But its centrality became increasingly pivotal in nature; it operated at the point of balance between the other strong currencies. Sterling was thus placed in such a position that if one or more of these forces went markedly out of control, it did not possess sufficient strength to enable it to restore the balance. Harbingers of this fate appeared in the form of a sterling crisis in 1906 and a banking panic in the USA in 1907. Both events reflected the growing scale of the US economy within the world economy and its huge need for monetary gold, whilst at the same time its limited dependence on the international economy (which accounted for only 3 per cent of its national income) meant that the US financial authorities did not set their sights in accordance with international needs. Furthermore, the USA did not possess a central bank until 1913.[11]

10. An excellent study in this context is S. Strange, *Sterling and British Policy* (1971), especially pp. 1–40.
11. The financial crisis of 1907 was solved through the cooperation of major private bankers under the lead of J. Pierpont Morgan, but it set in train a course of events that led to the establishment of the Federal Reserve System in 1913.

In these circumstances sterling was, in part, acquiring a proxy role, representing the strength of other currencies trading internationally in London as the financial centre of the world economy. These underlying changes were not, however, matched by changes in attitudes or understanding among those responsible for operating the system. In the financial sphere as in other areas of life, the decade before the First World War was imbued with much illusion.

OVERSEAS INVESTMENT

The free flow of capital was a marked feature of the pre-World War international economy. The market was dominated by Britain both directly in terms of capital supply and indirectly through housing the major institutions concerned with international capital transactions.

Figure 3.1 Net UK foreign investment: nominal price series (1873 = 100), and as a percentage of GDP, 1870–1913

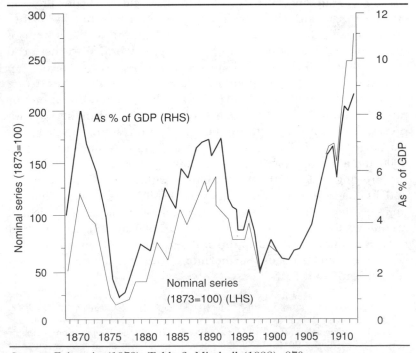

Sources: Feinstein (1972), Table 3; Mitchell (1988), 870.

The volume of British foreign investment fluctuated quite sharply around an upward trend. Net foreign investment rose from the equivalent of 67 per cent of gross domestic fixed investment in the 1880s to the equivalent of 90 per cent in the decade leading up to the First World War. The income it generated as a share of gross national income rose correspondingly from 6 per cent to 8 per cent. For much of the period, however, less was invested abroad than was being received in dividends, interest and repayments. This is an aspect which will be considered more fully later.

Overseas investment is not easily quantified. There are three main methods of calculation, each of which throws a different light on the process of accumulation. First, it is possible to cumulate the value of all overseas issues during the period.[12] The results provide a useful analysis of the distribution of investment both geographically and by type. There are, however, obvious problems: it is not always easy to distinguish between nominal capital and the amounts actually called up; no account is taken of subsequent market transactions, including losses and the redemption of loans; and valuations are historical – at the time of issue – and not current market values. To some extent these problems can be discounted. Hence, these estimates are strongest when used to analyse the flow of lending and borrowing, and the surge of investment in the latter years of the period minimizes cumulative error. But the problems of double counting as loans were renewed by means of new issues and the repayment of loans remains. In sum, the results are subject to a significant margin of error.

Table 3.1 Foreign investments of the leading countries in 1914 (£m)

		% of total
United Kingdom	4,115	44.0
France	1,860	19.9
Germany	1,193	12.8
United States	720	7.7
Others	1,460	15.6

Source: Woodruff (1966), 150. The original gives the figures in dollars and these have been converted by the appropriate exchange rate.

12. M. Simon, 'The Pattern of New British Portfolio Investment, 1865–1914', in A. R. Hall, *The Export of Capital From Britain 1870–1914* (1968), pp. 15–44; M. Edelstein, *Overseas Investment in the Age of High Imperialism: The United Kingdom, 1850–1914* (New York, 1982).

The distribution of investment was the outcome of opportunity. Thus European, and to some extent North American, investment was at the height of fashion before 1880. In the 1880s the spotlight was on South America and Australia, before it swung to South Africa and then back again to Latin America and Canada. The contrast between Britain and the other major European investors by 1913 – France and Germany – is noteworthy. British investment was multilateral in the sense that it flowed throughout the world, facilitating the increased flow of raw materials and primary products and, indirectly much more than directly, opening up markets for British manufactured goods. Investment by France and Germany was related much more directly to their industrial development in terms of markets, and it was heavily concentrated in Central and Eastern Europe and in Russia, amounting to about 50 per cent in each case.[13] The United States was beginning to emerge as a source of international capital, but before the First World War its activities were largely confined to Central and South America.

Table 3.2 Geographical distribution of British overseas portfolio investments in 1914 (% shares)

	Empire	Foreign
Asia	10.8	3.5
Australasia	11.1	–
North America	13.7	20.1
Latin America/Caribbean	–	20.1
Africa	10.8	1.2
Europe	–	5.8
Other	0.9	2.1
Total	47.3	52.8

Sources: Feis (1930), 23; Pollard (1989), 60. Pollard provides a number of alternative estimates but the variations are, not surprisingly, small since the calculations are based on a broadly common data set.

The second method of calculating overseas investment is by adding up the net flows of funds available as shown in the balance

13. An outstanding study is R. Cameron, *France and the Economic Development of Europe, 1800–1914* (Princeton, 1961).

of payments.[14] Problems concerning the accuracy of data, double counting and changes in the value of assets over time, remain. But this method does reveal the manner in which the economy financed overseas investment. In particular, it shows that from 1870 onwards the returns from overseas investments were, on average, greater than the amounts of new foreign investment and, hence, the extent to which Britain had come to depend on the invisible sector for its overseas income.

The third form of estimate is based on capitalizing the annual income from overseas investment.[15] Once again accuracy is a problem since the calculations depend on the effective coverage of dividend coupons received by a large number of individuals. For the bench mark year of 1914 the total value of British overseas portfolio investment is given as approximately £3,500m., at which level it is much in line with the results obtained by the other two methods of calculation. This figure, however, has been vigorously challenged as a substantial overestimate, on the grounds that the basic data are inaccurate and that they make no allowance for the redemption of loans and the operation of secondary markets. The latter objection has been considered above in terms of the surge of investment in the decade, or so, before 1914. As to the former, it loses much of its force when it is shown that the estimate for 1914 squares quite well with more firmly based estimates for the post-1918 period. In other words, whilst it would be foolish to deny that estimates of British overseas investment for this period can be anything other than very rough approximations, it would seem that the more extreme errors tend to be self-cancelling.[16]

Confidence in these estimates of total holdings is strengthened by the fact that in addition to portfolio investments there was an outward flow of direct investment by companies and individuals. In the days of no exchange controls the extent of this accumulation is exceedingly difficult to determine. Until recently, authorities accepted a contemporary estimate (that was little more than a guess) that put the figure at approximately £500 million in 1914.

14. A. H. Imlah, *Economic Elements in the Pax Britannica. Studies in British Foreign Trade in the Nineteenth Century* (Cambridge, Mass., 1958).

15. The classic articles are G. Paish, 'Great Britain's Capital Investment in Other Lands', *Journal of the Royal Statistical Society*, 72 (1909), pp. 465–95; *idem.*, 'Great Britain's Capital Investments in Individual Colonial and Foreign Countries', *Journal of the Royal Statistical Society*, 74 (1911), pp. 167–200.

16. This issue is surveyed by C. Feinstein, 'Britain's Overseas Investments in 1913', *Economic History Review*, 43 (1990), pp. 288–95.

Table 3.3 Distribution of new British portfolio investment by sector, 1909–13 (% share)

Agriculture	5.6
Mining	9.3
Manufacture	4.8
Transportation	46.6
Utilities	6.4
Public works	17.3
Other, including defence	10.0
Total	100.0

Source: Pollard (1989), 60. These estimates are based on the earlier work of Matthew Simon *loc.cit.* Pollard provides an alternative estimate derived from L. E. Davis and R. A. Huttenback *Mammon and the Pursuit of Empire* (Cambridge, 1986), p. 59. However, since its publication the coverage and methods of estimation of the latter have been subject to considerable criticism. In any event, the differences between the two estimates are not generally large given the unavoidable margin of error in the basic data.

Recent and current research, based on individual company records, indicates that the amount was somewhat larger.[17] If so, then the long accepted gross amount of £4,000 million for both portfo' o and direct British overseas investment in 1914 would seem to be well within reasonable bounds.

Overseas investment was part of the complex nexus of financial operations conducted by the institutions that made up the City. The role of the Bank of England and its relationship to the domestic banking system has already been commented on. Likewise, the importance of London as the centre of world commodity markets formed part of the story of British trade (Chapter 2). Other types of banking institution must be considered briefly, however, since their operations had an important bearing on Britain's position in the world economy.

17. S. Pollard, *Britain's Prime and Britain's Decline. The British Economy 1870–1914* (1989), pp. 63, 102 covers the evidence. See more generally pp. 58–114, for his discussion of overseas investment based on an exhaustive survey of the literature. His interpretation differs somewhat from the one above. M. Wilkins, 'The Free-Standing Company, 1870–1914: An Important Type of British Foreign Direct Investment', *Economic History Review*, 51 (1988), pp. 259–82 collects together useful information of direct investment, though the concept of the free-standing company appears somewhat contrived.

The numbers and types of private banks operating in London are shown in Table 3.4.

Table 3.4 Number and types of private banks in London, selected years 1885–1915

Type	1885	1895	1904–5	1914–15
'Merchants'	25	55	56	68
Agency houses	6	17	20	17
Core merchant banks	31	72	76	85
Army and Navy agents	4	7	6	5
Foreign banks	10	15	17	15
Merchant banks – broad definition	14	22	23	20
Total merchant banks	45	94	99	105
Discount agents	17	18	23	20
Deposit banks	23	14	7	6
Miscellaneous	8	11	5	6
Closed down	0	0	2	2
Grand Total	93	137	136	139

Source: Chapman (1984), 58. The definition of a merchant bank is not precise. Hence the distinction in the table above between core and broad.

Foremost were the merchant banks. But as the table indicates, they were by no means a homogeneous group. They ranged from general 'merchants' involved in the finance of trade to more specialist houses concentrating on the issue of foreign loans to the public, the acceptance of bills of exchange and arbitrage dealings in financial markets. The acceptance business was a system whereby a merchant bank would guarantee a bill of exchange drawn in favour of a trader and payable at some date hence for a consideration based on its face value, thus enabling the trader to exchange the bill immediately for cash at a discount house or to use it as a negotiable instrument. The discount houses financed themselves by borrowing from the deposit banks on shorter terms than they advanced cash against bills, an arrangement that made the finance of foreign trade sensitive to Bank of England operations in the way described earlier. The international standing of a merchant bank was a direct indication of the quality of a bill of exchange and was correspondingly reflected in the rates of discount that were applied.

Rothschild, Stern, Seligman, Baring, Morgan: these were among the names of leading merchant banks with world-wide reputations. They had built up intricate and seemingly mysterious networks through which they received commercial and financial information from around the globe. The Rothschilds were renowned for their lucrative contacts with royal houses across Europe which were constantly in need of loans; the house of Morgan, because of its US origins, built up a powerful position in Anglo-American financial operations. Anglo-German banks were particularly pronounced by 1914, constituting eleven out of the twenty banks engaged in acceptance business. The major houses enjoyed enormous prestige that became the hallmark of London's standing in international finance.

Appearances were to some extent deceptive, however. British merchant banks were not masters of financial alchemy as they have often been portrayed. They were far more dependent on the staple of acceptances than on the more glamorous business of issues. Correspondingly, their fortunes matched the broad flow of world trade, with rapid growth between 1850 and 1870, followed by reduced activity until 1890 when the number of bills of exchange increased sharply to double in volume by 1913. During this last period, British merchant banks, according to a leading authority, lost much of their earlier 'vigour and boldness'.[18] They did not take up opportunities in the field of financing small and medium-sized businesses in the domestic economy. They became increasingly conservative in their traditional business. They were, in other words, not unlike much of British industry: family firms that were experiencing growing competition from 'faster-growing and more capital intensive' German and American rivals, that were more directly involved in industrial finance in Europe and the USA.

The promotion and flotation of loans to launch commercial and industrial operations abroad did not depend on merchant banks alone. Individual financiers such as H. O. O'Hagan and Sir Ernest Cassel made large fortunes in this way.[19] And from the 1880s

18. S. Chapman, *The Rise of Merchant Banking* (1984), p. 179.
19. H. O'Hagen, *Leaves From My Life* (1929, 2 vols); P. Thane, 'Financiers and the British State. The Case of Sir Ernest Cassel', *Business History*, 28 (1988), pp. 80–99.

onwards, the mining riches of Southern Africa offered enormous promotional opportunities and enabled men such as Barnarto, Beit and Rhodes to acquire prodigious wealth.[20] Yet more typical of British international finance than capitalist buccaneers were British multinational banks that had their headquarters in London but operated outside Europe and the USA, particularly in the empire, South America, the Middle and Far East. They were multinational trade banks which financed the movement of commodities around the globe, ranging from West African cocoa to Siamese tin.[21] They fostered their activities by developing retail banking in the regions in which they operated. In these ways they improved the flow and quality of commercial information and lubricated the mechanism of international trade from which Britain was a major beneficiary. But again, like merchant banks, their business performance was characterized by conservatism and a growing aversion to risk. They effectively exploited the advantages which Britain's position in the world economy gave them and, in turn, they contributed to it through their operations. Yet, significantly, they did not make headway in Europe and the USA where well-developed banking institutions already existed, and this serves to emphasize the facilitating as opposed to the promotional nature of their activities. Whether this role reflected the broader contribution of the City to Britain's position in the world economy is a central issue to which we must now turn.

CAPITAL EXPORT AND DOMESTIC ECONOMIC PERFORMANCE

The question that has been much debated is whether too much capital was invested abroad, in the sense that home industry was kept short of funds, and that this was an additional element in slow

---

20. Useful studies are provided by R. V. Kubicek, *Economic Imperialism in Theory and Practice. The Case of South African Gold Mining Finance 1886–1914* (Durham, N. C., 1979); J-J. Van Helten and P. Richardson, 'The Development of the South African Gold-Mining Industry, 1895–1918', *Economic History Review*, 37 (1984), pp. 319–40. For more colourful accounts see P. H. Emden, *Randlords* (1935) and S. Joel, *Ace of Diamonds. The Story of Solomon Barnato Joel* (1958).

21. My information is drawn from the major study by G. Jones, *British Multinational Banking 1830–1990* (Oxford, 1993), of which see especially pp. 83–102.

growth and the sapping of competitiveness of the economy.[22] There is, too, the issue of whether overseas investment further exacerbated these domestic weaknesses by helping to promote competitive foreign industries to an extent that more than outweighed any complementary feedback effects of foreign demand for British goods and services. The answer might be simply that overseas investment was wholly a response to new opportunities; and it is well to bear in mind that in the receiving economies foreign capital was always a small proportion (usually less than 10 per cent) of total domestic capital formation, so that economic development abroad was essentially domestically based.

Attempts have been made to estimate the costs and benefits of overseas investment, based on a neo-classical economic model with a given production function.[23] The basic tenet of this approach is that the market will equalize returns between home and foreign investment and, consequently, any switch in investment at the point of equilibrium will result in a fall in the marginal rate of return to the economy as a whole. However, this analysis is open to criticism on a number of grounds. First, it depends on the quite unrealistic assumptions of perfect competition. Secondly, it is necessarily based on comparative statics and thus assumes that at any point during the period the economy was at or near equilibrium. Thirdly, conditions are held constant to the extent that there can be no dynamic effects from, say, technical change, business reorganization or the quality of entrepreneurship, which could alter the nature of the production function and, therefore, create new investment opportunties. And, finally, the model can only be estimated if it is assumed that the economy was one of full employment – an assumption quite at odds with reality in late-nineteenth-century Britain. In short, even a small measure of realism renders this analysis somewhat irrelevant.

Yet the problem remains. Contemporaries were divided on the issue. Those who focused on imperialism saw overseas investment as either desirable or as an inherent part of the evolution of

22. The case has been put most forcibly by W. P. Kennedy, *Industrial Structure, Capital Markets and the Origins of British Economic Decline* (Cambridge, 1987). This is, however, but part of a large literature. A useful summary of the issues is provided by M. Collins, *Banks and Industrial Finance in Britain 1800–1939* (1991), pp. 52–64. A more comprehensive survey and analysis is given by Pollard, *Britain's Prime and Britain's Decline*, pp. 58–114.

23. See D. N. McCloskey, *Enterprise and Trade in Victorian Britain* (1981), pp. 94–135.

capitalism. Leading bankers and financiers claimed that it brought nothing but benefit to these shores in the form of dividends and demands for goods which in turn created employment. Others, especially during the Edwardian period, were worried that fear of socialism was causing capital to flee the country at considerable cost to the population at large. Yet others, and most notably Hobson, argued that whilst overseas investment was part of the excesses of capitalism, the solution was at hand in terms of the more equal distribution of income and wealth at home. Reforms would benefit the poor and revive the fortunes of industry.[24]

Such differences of view in part reflect differences of analysis, but in part also they reflect differences of interest. This latter aspect has perhaps not been given sufficient weight by economic historians, who implicitly define 'too much' foreign investment in relation to an implied optimal social rate of return. But how is such a return to be defined and measured? Less investment in South American railways and more in slum clearance would clearly have had domestic welfare effects, but the calculation of the balance of losses and gains is dependent on prior value judgements. Victorians and Edwardians got the investments they wanted, given the distribution of political and economic power. In this sense, at least, the outcome was optimal. It is both legitimate and important, nevertheless, to evaluate economic performance according to certain stated measures and, on this basis, to indicate the consequences of the decisions actually made. These consequences can be given fuller meaning when set within a comparative framework, and the clearest way of doing this is to examine the nature of and return on foreign investment against the performance of the economy in general.

Foreign investment is thought by some to have been strongly conditioned by the imperfect nature of market information resulting from an institutional bias in the London financial market which was dominated by internationally orientated merchant banks.[25] The effect was to make it far easier to invest in companies abroad than in enterprises at home. Various attempts have been made to estimate the foregone benefits to the domestic economy, and the answers given depend on the assumptions made about the strength of the bias and the potential rates of return on alternative

24. J. A. Hobson, *Imperialism: A Study* (1968 edition). This book was first published in 1902 and there are some variations in later editions.
25. Kennedy, *Industrial Structure, Capital Markets*.

domestic investments. At one extreme a counter-factual world can be conjured up that presents a picture in which higher domestic investment transforms the pre-First World War economy from one of slow growth into one of bounding expansion matching the best of the international field.

The main counter to these claims has been to present a comparative analysis of the actual rates of return on domestic and foreign securities. Investment for the period 1870 to 1913 has been aggregated into foreign and domestic issues and then broken down into the three main types of equity, preference and debenture capital.[26] It has been calculated that returns on investment abroad were consistently higher than on investment at home. And it is claimed, more strongly, that this difference holds when the data are refined to take account of the assumed differences of risk attached to each type of security. But this apparent refinement immediately raises a major theoretical inconsistency. If risk is discounted and there was perfect market information, why was not more investment switched from domestic to foreign markets until the marginal rates of return were equal? There are, moreover, a number of practical problems with this analysis. For one thing, the sample is biased because it excludes securities of high risk. More seriously, when the sample is broken into much shorter sub-periods and into commercial and industrial sectors, the differences between home and foreign returns do not follow a consistent pattern and thus call into question the results obtained from aggregate data.[27]

The reality was that there was nowhere near perfect information. Contemporary commercial law required only minimal financial disclosure by companies. This meant that prospectuses were of very uneven quality; many were misleading, and quite a number were downright fraudulent. There is, too, accumulating evidence which shows (not surprisingly) that investment decisions were by no means the outcome of prudent and precise calculations of alternative rates of return, with due allowance for risk. For example, Charles Morrison, one of the most prominent financiers in the nineteenth century, headed an investment group with large holdings in Argentinian companies. In making investment decisions, this group was powerfully influenced by the idea that capitalist investment could provide the foundations for the development of liberal political structures in New World republics.

26. Edelstein, *The Export of Capital From Britain.*
27. Pollard, *Britain's Prime and Britain's Decline*, pp. 76–81.

A profit on these investments was anticipated but they were not made according to calculations of maximum rates of return.[28] More generally, risk was not a constant, uniform element in the dynamic process of investment activity. It varied over time according to the form as well as the type of security, between sectors and industries and between firms within those divisions. As well as variations in the denominator of risk, there were variations in how the numerator of return was defined. For example, differences in investment behaviour could arise according to whether decisions were based on the potential of capital gains as opposed to the flow of income over a given period. And in any retrospective evaluation of investment behaviour, the choice of time periods is crucial. What might seem irrational in terms of income over a given period might appear quite different over a longer span in terms of capitalized gains.

In the case of firms making direct investments overseas, their strategies can often only be understood within the context of their total operations. What might appear as a low-yielding (even misguided) investment in a foreign subsidiary might have been the means of thwarting the establishment of foreign producers who would have added to competition in a number of markets, or it could be the mechanism for securing scarce raw materials.[29] In short, investment decisions were the outcome of prudence and incomplete information frequently mixed with elements of prejudice, passion, altruism, hunch or just plain speculative urge. When it comes to the effects of these decisions, there is no neat statistical test which can be applied to determine whether too much British investment found its way abroad at the expense of domestic economic development before the First World War. Nevertheless, there is what appears to be a more firmly based exercise that seeks to measure the actual return on Empire investment before 1914, which accounted for some 40 per cent of total British foreign investment.[30] The performance of British Empire Ltd. is measured on the credit side by the returns on portfolio investment and on the debit side by government expenditure in support of business (including law and order, public works and human capital), defence

28. C. A. Jones, 'Great Capitalists and the Direction of British Overseas Investment in the Late Nineteenth Century: The Case of Argentina', *Business History*, 22 (1980), pp. 152–69.

29. For example, C. E. Harvey, *The Rio Tinto Company. An Economic History of a Leading Mining Concern 1873–1954* (Penzance, 1981), pp. 1–110, 148–66.

30. L. A. Davis and R. A. Huttenback, *Mammon and the Pursuit of Empire. The Political Economy of British Imperialism, 1866–1912* (Cambridge, 1986).

costs, government loans, direct assistance and the operation of the Crown Agents Department. This method avoids the counterfactual world of what might have been but the results have a clear implication in terms of the opportunity cost of Empire investment.

The main conclusions are that British Empire Ltd. was not a money-making enterprise, that the ownership of imperial business was concentrated in the hands of the traditional elite and London merchants, that the location of ownership was disproportionately in the metropolis and that when taxation is brought into the account, the middle classes bore the main cost of the Empire both in absolute and proportionate terms. In the judgment of Davis and Huttenback, British imperialism can be viewed as a mechanism to effect an income transfer from the British middle class to the British upper class with a slight net transfer to the colonies in the process.[31]

These calculations, based on imperial investment during the period 1885–1914, present huge difficulties, however.[32] The data involve problems of definition and interpretation, to which reference has already been made; direct investment is not accounted for at all; and the estimates are short-term, in the sense that they are concerned with current rates of return and not with cumulative returns over time. Furthermore, they make no attempt to measure the longer-term effects of the economic connections which were established. This last is, of course, a more general issue in the debate on overseas investment. It is akin to (and in part related to) the idea of over-commitment of resources to the staple industries in the domestic economy. To what extent, in other words, did Empire investment contribute to inflexibility within the economy which became very costly in the longer run? How these elements would figure in the final balance is a major question and one to which it will be necessary to return (Chapter 5).

There are further conceptual limitations to this kind of statistical analysis. Is it even realistic, for example, to divide defence expenditure into home and imperial? British commercial interests

31. Davis and Huttenback, *Mammon and the Pursuit of Empire*, pp. 248–52.

32. B. W. E. Alford, Review of Davis and Huttenback in *Economic History Review*, 41 (1988), pp. 321–4; A. Offer, 'The British Empire, 1870–1914: A Waste of Money?', *Economic History Review*, 46 (1993), pp. 215–38, makes a case for the Empire in political/strategic terms and also provides a comprehensive survey of the literature on the issue; but see, in particular, A. Hopkins, 'Accounting for the British Empire', *Journal of Imperial and Commonwealth History*, 16 (1988), pp. 234–7 and A. Porter, 'The Balance Sheet of Empire, 1850–1914', *Historical Journal*, 31 (1988), pp. 685–99.

were world-wide and this carried with it the need for Britain to play a major international policing role with or without the Empire. Similarly, the interests of Empire constituted a powerful element in both Britain's domestic and international politics, and the welfare effects that this might have had – impossible though they are to quantify – are a very significant omission from any assessment. These effects might be taken to range from the sense of status imperial rule gave to the British working class (whether as a form of social control or not) to the strategic importance of the Empire in the First World War.[33] And whilst it is possible to define the Empire as a geographical unit of account, there is the question of the extent to which, over space and time, it possessed an economic coherence and unity which makes it sensible to evaluate it in a separate balance sheet. For all the fact that the Union Jack flew over a large area of the world's land mass, the countries which made up the Empire were part of the wider multilateral economic system.

Meaningful calculations of comparative rates of return in home and foreign investment may well be impossible but there may still be sufficient evidence of an 'institutional bias' that channelled funds overseas. The case for the prosecution rests on the fact of the hugely disproportionate amount of foreign and imperial shares traded on the London market in comparison with domestic securities. And within the domestic sector itself, shares in manufacturing industry made up only a small fraction against the large quantities of railway stock and government paper. It is now clear, moreover, that overseas investment was not directly linked to demands for British exports.[34] The defence protests that the charge is a case of mistaken identity. The London Stock Exchange, it is argued, has to be seen as just part of the capital market and concerned with secondary trading. It was, moreover, easily open to new listings – much more so than the New York exchange, for example.[35] Capital issues, themselves, were the business of specialist company promoters and underwriters and, here again, the market was open and receptive to new proposals, whether domestic or foreign. In addition, the domestic capital market included active

33. See for example, A. Offer, *The First World War. An Agrarian Interpretation* (Oxford, 1989) for an argument in terms of the strategic importance of the empire.

34. Davis and Huttenback, *Mammon and the Pursuit of Empire*, pp. 188–91; T. J. Hatton, 'The Demand for British Exports', *Economic History Review*, 43 (1990), pp. 576–94; Pollard, *Britain's Prime and Britain's Decline*, pp. 103–4.

35. R. C. Michie, *The London and New York Stock Exchanges, 1850–1914* (1987).

provincial markets which operated to some extent through formal institutions but largely through well-tried local networks. Provincially based manufacturing firms were thus well served.

Evidence on the detailed working of provincial capital markets is still hard to come by. What exists does indeed tend to confirm the importance of local networks, but equally it raises questions about the scale and scope of these activities in the context of the nature of industrial development in the late nineteenth and early twentieth centuries.[36] Whilst it is true that throughout the period, and since, ploughed-back profits accounted for something like half industrial investment, for new types of industry or for major new developments in existing firms, capital might have been required on a scale which was beyond the resources of the individual firm and the local capital market. Added to which it could be a matter of the need for new forms of company organization that tended to be associated with new and larger sources of finance. Deficiencies in this latter respect became increasingly significant, as our earlier discussion has shown (Chapter 2). In a cause and effect manner, the nature of company organization and the provincial character of the capital market might well have stifled the flow of information on domestic industry to the investing public at large. The performance of British merchant banks, to which attention has been drawn, does tend to support the idea of institutional bias. It is important to note, however, that this decline related to a growing conservatism among these family-dominated financial houses (which matched British industry) and was not the outcome of a conscious anti-industrial attitude. The need for more detailed evidence must be reiterated, but the balance of proof at this stage marginally favours the prosecution.

Finally, the merits of foreign investment have to be balanced against a total volume of investment which, on average, amounted to 13 per cent of national income, a relatively low proportion in comparative international terms. The differences in domestic capital formation cannot be explained as part of the catching up process by industrializing countries. By 1900 income per head in the USA was already higher than that in the UK. More generally, these higher investment ratios were associated with different mechanisms of capital formation, especially in relation to the role

36. P. L. Cottrell, 'The Domestic Commercial Banks and the City of London, 1876–1939', in Y. Cassis (ed.), *Finance and Financiers in European History 1880–1960* (Cambridge, 1992), pp. 39–62.

Table 3.5 Comparative capital formation proportions – late neneteenth to early twentieth century (% (GNP))

	Gross domestic capital formation	Capital exports or imports (–)	Gross national capital formation
UK			
1880–99	8.4	3.9	12.3
1900–14	8.7	5.3	14.0
Germany			
1871–90	18.9	2.1	21.0
1891–1913	23.0	1.1	24.1
Italy			
1881–1900	10.8	0.0	10.8
1901–10	15.9	1.4	17.3
Sweden			
1881–1900	11.2	–1.6	9.6
1901–20	13.1	–0.5	12.6
United States			
1869–88	20.6	–0.9	19.7
1889–1908	21.4	0.5	21.9
Japan			
1887–1906	10.1	–2.1	8.0
1907–26	14.1	–0.6	13.5

Source: Kuznets (1966), 236–8.

of banks and new forms of company organization. With the advantage of hindsight it is clear that, judged by the standards of much higher levels of income, British investment ratios of the pre-First World War period were decidedly on the low side.

Attention has already been drawn to the argument that by the late nineteenth century 'the United Kingdom had ceased ... to be a net lender, and was living on the returns from earlier lendings out of which in macro-economic terms, new loans were financed ...'.[37]

37. Pollard, *Britain's Prime and Britain's Decline*, p. 69.

This left a surplus of 'unrequited foreign payments'. This assessment does not, however, distinguish sufficiently between capital and income. The fact that income from investment was rising as the stock of investment grew, does not make it any the less income which could either be spent or saved and invested. More importantly, it shows that if net receipts from abroad (income) were exceeding lending abroad (capital), whilst overseas investment as a proportion of national income was rising, the dependence of the economy on overseas income was increasing. This was not a matter of living off capital – and certainly not of selling off the family silver – but of depending to an increasing degree on rentier income.

The low level of investment was paralleled by low growth rates and low rates of interest. This last factor might indicate that there was no shortage of domestic capital. But the prevailing rate does not tell us what would have happened to the marginal rate as demand for funds increased. The growth of 'unrequited payments' may be taken to suggest that under such conditions the rate might have risen quite sharply. Moreover, the relationship between these variables is more complex than much of the debate over the level of British overseas investment implies. The problem turns on the assumed theoretical relationship between capital investment and economic growth.

Most of the literature draws on traditional neo-classical economics and thus capital is seen as a factor of production which, in combination with others (mainly labour), produces output and growth. Marxist historians of imperialism follow a related approach in which capital accumulation is seen as the dynamic force. Modern economic theory is less clear cut, and applied economic analysis which seeks to identify the sources of growth casts even further doubt on the earlier assumed relationship. These investigations indicate that if growth is, so to speak, stripped down into its various components, the most important factor (or rather group of factors) is not the rate of growth of capital or of labour but what is left. Originally this third element was termed the residual and was thought to be made up mainly of technical change, but it is now defined as total factor productivity, and it includes, among a number of other things, technical change, improvements in human capital, improvements in labour organization and industrial relations, and government policy. In other words, the most important factors in economic performance in scale, at least, are those which cannot be individually measured. But more than this, and in line with some modern theory, it supports the view that capital investment may be either a dependent variable or that it occurs in step with other factors and is thus not a pre-condition of economic growth.[38]

What all this amounts to is that the concern over the level of British overseas investment during this period, and its possible consequent effects on economic performance, may, indeed, be a case of mistaken identity. The best available statistical analysis of manufacturing output and investment indicates that their levels were predominantly determined by elements in domestic economic activity as opposed to change in exports and foreign investment.[39] Britain did not invest too much capital overseas at the expense of the domestic market. Domestic investment was low because economic performance was poor.

BRITISH IMPERIALISM AND THE INTERNATIONAL ECONOMY

The direct economic importance of the Empire to Britain was, as has been shown, but part of a much wider involvement in the world economy. Yet was British imperialism no less than the manifestation of the power and influence of a narrow and identifiable group of economic, social and political interests which controlled the wider reaches of external and domestic economic policy? Does the history of British imperialism provide the clearest lens through which to focus on the dynamics of the British economy within the world economy between 1880 and 1914?

---

38. Total factor productivity analysis must be treated with great caution. It is based on identities and, therefore, it describes rates of changes in factor inputs in relation to the rate of growth of output; it does not provide an explanation of changes in economic performance because it cannot specify causal relationships between these variables – it simply measures them. It is, in other words, a measure of outcomes. Moreover, the basis on which capital and labour inputs are calculated and combined involves tight (unrealistic) assumptions as to the nature of factor markets and production functions. At best the method can suggest where investigation might focus in order to discover the reasons for a given level of economic performance; and such an approach can be useful when conducted on a comparative basis. The major example of these techniques as applied to the British economy is R. C. O. Matthews, C. H. Feinstein and J. C. Odling-Smee, *British Economic Growth 1856–1973* (Stanford, 1982). This work is far less formidable than it appears since the authors provide a clear exposition of their methods, and it contains a wide range of historical interpretation.

39. Matthews *et al, British Economic Growth*, p. 282.

There was a sense in which contemporaries had a holistic view of the Empire, though it was as an image refracted through a haze of imperial glory. Politically and culturally the imperial idea, as it has been called, helped to define what it meant to be British or, more accurately, English; it contributed to the invention of the national identity.[40] Economically it was increasingly seen as a defence against the competitive onslaught of foreign industrialization. A leading commentator of the day expressed this in terms of economic paternalism, tinged with racism and vague sentiments about international peace. 'The economic organisation of the Empire is needed, not only to introduce a greater measure of free intercourse within its bounds, but to be a bulwark against the evils of cosmopolitan competition. A great Empire, thus built up, need not exercise either a political or an industrial tyranny over its neighbours, but may help to serve as a foundation on which the Peace of the world can rest securely... . In the face of cosmopolitan competition [and the Asian races were particularly singled out] how can English "wages be kept up, unless there be constantly increasing markets found for the employment of labour" .'[41] Such sentiments, which struck a chord with the masses as much as with middle- and upper-class traditionalists, were part of the ideology of the fair trade movement at the turn of the century which, whilst unsuccessful in its immediate aims, sowed seeds which were to grow strongly later on.

Contemporary writers on the political economy of the empire swam either in the currents of British Liberalism or continental European Marxism. Of the former, J. A. Hobson became the best known.[42] He was much affected by the scramble among the great powers to colonize the remaining open territories of Africa and by what he saw as the imperialistic nature of the Boer War. But his analysis was based on a longer historical perspective and driven by concern for the welfare of the mass of the domestic population. For

---

40. J. M. MacKenzie, *Propaganda and Empire. The Manipulation of British Public Opinion, 1880–1960* (Manchester, 1984) and *idem.* (ed.), *Imperialism and Popular Culture* (Manchester, 1986).

41. W. Cunningham, *The Rise and Decline of the Free Trade Movement* (1904), p. 168.

42. In addition to the original study by Hobson, see P. J. Cain, 'J. A. Hobson, Cobdenism and the Radical Theory of Imperialism 1898–1914', *Economic History Review*, 31 (1978), pp. 565–84; *idem.*, 'J. A. Hobson, Financial Capitalism and Imperialism in Late Victorian and Edwardian England', *Journal of Imperial and Commonwealth History*, 13 (1985), pp. 1–27; A. M. Eckstein, 'Is There a "Hobson-Lenin Thesis" on late Nineteenth-Century Colonial Expansion?', *Economic History Review*, 44 (1991), pp. 297–318.

Hobson, imperialism was predominantly the result of the need of industrial economies to find outlets for surplus capital; it was surplus because it could not find profitable outlets in the mature industries at home which were alleged to be experiencing rapidly declining rates of profit. To this extent he failed to see the potential opportunities for investment in new science-based industries. His solution was, nevertheless, the truly liberal one of redistributing income and wealth by means of taxation which, he claimed, would lead to higher standards of living generally through increased consumption and greater social welfare provision, which at the same time would involve the restoration of industrial prosperity. Not surprisingly, Hobson's ideas on political economy have been recognized as forerunners of Keynes's *General Theory* which appeared some thirty years later.

Marxists such as Rosa Luxembourg and Rudolph Hilferding had much in common with Hobson since they, too, diagnosed surplus capital as the driving forces of imperialism. But unlike Hobson, for them this process was but a stage – finance capitalism – in the inevitable march of capitalism towards its eventual nemesis. The course of events was no more than the confirmation of a predetermined theory of history. The most chilling prophesy of impending collapse was made later by Lenin in *Imperialism: the Highest Stage of Capitalism*. Published in 1916, this book purported to lay bare the forces which had led, ultimately and inevitably, to the First World War which he was convinced was capitalism's Armageddon.[43]

Neither of these approaches attracted widespread support at the time, but the historical issues they raised were revived after the Second World War. Aside from the fascination of the subject itself, this interest reflected two broader issues. First, there was the problem for neo-Marxist historians and theoreticians of reconciling the historical record with the predictions of earlier writers of the impending demise of capitalism. They attempted to square theory with fact by redefining imperialism in terms of global relationships between the developed and the developing (or third) world. Nineteenth-century imperialism was thus reduced to a stage in this longer-term process which was defined as the development of underdevelopment. Unequal rates of exchange, trade protection,

43. V. I. Lenin, *Imperialism, the Highest Stage of Capitalism* (Moscow, 1964, *Collected Works* 22). An excellent survey is provided by A. Brewer, *Marxist Theories of Imperialism: A Critical Survey* (2nd edition, 1990).

foreign investment, multinational corporations: these were the devices used by the capitalist classes for maintaining the subjugation of the poor nations.[44] This defence is a characteristic retreat by neo-Marxists into generality. It does not match the history of the white dominions or take account of the major indigenous and pre-colonial elements in the nature and character of what are now independent countries of the Third World.[45] Faced with this challenge, neo-Marxists have responded in terms of the international division of labour and the necessary international conspiracy of economic interests between the ruling classes in rich and poor nations. In this way, even territorial boundaries become an irrelevance. Imperialism loses all meaning.

The second issue that contributed to the reopening of the historical debate on imperialism was Britain's loss of Empire and the effect, perceived or imagined, that this was having on Britain's political and economic position in the world.[46] The first major historiographical revision of the pedigree of imperialism, by Gallagher and Robinson, sought to demonstrate that it was developments in the peripheral or quasi-imperial areas of the nineteenth century that had drawn Britain and the European nations into imperial relationships. Foremost for Britain were strategic considerations, such as the need to establish a presence in Egypt and South Africa in order to protect the route to India. Missionaries, explorers and political adventurers all played a part. Livingstone, Rhodes and Raffles spring readily to mind. The economic connections made with these regions thus became part of the broader framework of Britain's international economic relations under a system of free trade. And because of the interconnections of this system, exponents of this view do not entirely rule out the influence on the periphery of economic interests at the centre. Nevertheless, it is emphasized that the recently acquired territories of the late nineteenth century – and those which fuelled much of

44. A. G. Frank, *Dependent Accumulation and Underdevelopment* (1978); I. Wallerstein, *The Capitalist World-Economy* (1979). And for a critique see Brewer, *Marxist Theories of Imperialism.*

45. See for example A. G. Hopkins, *Two Essays on Underdevelopment* (Geneva, 1979).

46. For an overall view see B. Porter, *The Lion's Share: A Short History of British Imperialism, 1850–1970* (1984 edition). A more specific survey in relation to the City and the sterling area is provided by P. J. Cain and A. G. Hopkins, *British Imperialism: Crisis and Deconstruction 1914–1990* (1993), pp. 265–96. For an analysis that is highly critical of influence of imperial ties in the post-1945 period see S. Newton and D. Porter, *Modernisation Frustrated* (1988).

contemporary debate – received less than 5 per cent of British overseas investment. And those parts of the Empire which were of greatest importance in finance and trade were those which, by that time, were moving rapidly towards effective independence from Britain.[47]

On this reading, British economic interests were a major but by no means the sole element in imperial expansion, though the weight given to economic interests varies considerably among what might be termed the peripheral school of historians. Thus political and religious interests played their part, together with a growing sense of duty born of a feeling of superiority, and a widely shared belief that upper-class Englishmen were destined to civilize large areas of the world in their own image. The fundamental assumption was, of course, that this form of civilization would preserve both the English class system and the inherent and inalienable superiority of the white man. According to some writers, these influences, both economic and non-economic, were so powerful that Britain benefited from an informal imperialism, in parts of South America in particular. Territories were drawn into Britain's orbit and led to serve its interests without the need for formal annexation. The Empire was, therefore, the hub of Britain's wider economic relations in the world economy. By definition, evidence is hard to come by, and such relationships are hotly disputed.

The most recent and detailed revision, by Cain and Hopkins, follows earlier traditions to the extent that the dynamic of imperialism is seen as being generated at the centre[48]: this 'stems not from a stereotype of capitalist advance or from a vague multi-causality, but from a particular pattern of economic development'.[49] This pattern was formed by the powerful and dominant influence of metropolitan financial interests and the weight of the old and ailing staple export industries. The ruling cadre was made up of gentlemanly capitalists who 'were not a small, covert group who hi-jacked economic policy and made it serve their ends. On the contrary, they were acknowledged by contemporaries to be leading participants in the economy as well as ornaments of

47. J. Gallagher and R. E. Robinson, 'The Imperialism of Free Trade', *Economic History Review*, 6 (1953), pp. 1–15. A broad survey of this large literature is given by D. K. Fieldhouse, *Economics and Empire* (1984 edition). This author gives considerable weight to the role of the periphery.

48. Cain and Hopkins, *British Imperialism: Innovation and Expansion* and *idem.*, *British Imperialism. Crisis and Deconstruction*.

49. P. J. Cain and A. G. Hopkins, 'Gentlemanly Capitalism and British Expansion Overseas II: New Imperialism, 1850–1945', *Economic History Review*, 40 (1987), p. 19.

society, and their political prominence was both open and, in general, accepted.'[50] Free trade and the pre-eminence of sterling were the twin pillars which supported the edifice of British imperialism. The influence of gentlemanly capitalism was exerted in order to ensure that this structure was maintained by informal means if possible but by formal imperialism if necessary; and its control extended to cover 'economic policy formation in Britain itself; and it also had a major impact on the outside world through London's role as the chief provider of economic services ... . Suitably modified, the aristocratic ideal survived because it was adapted and supported by the gentlemanly class which arose from the service sector in the nineteenth century and proved to be the most successful and dynamic element in British economic life between 1850 and 1915.'[51] On this reading the Empire is truly the lens through which Britain's position in the world before 1914 should be viewed.

It may be that economic historians have unduly stressed the facts and fortunes (or misfortunes) of manufacturing industry in comparison with the service sector. But to claim so much on account of the services is hardly supported by the available evidence. The performance of service industries is notoriously difficult to measure and, for what they are worth, the figures suggest that whilst services in total (and this goes well beyond the coterie of financial services located in the square mile of the City) might have had a marginally higher level of productivity than manufacturing industry, their rate of productivity growth was slower than that for manufacturing between 1880 and 1914, which was far from buoyant, whilst the productivity performance of the economy as a whole was weakening.[52] This record hardly adds up to one of success and dynamism. Whatever its influence, gentlemanly capitalism was clearly taking things easy.

Given the amorphous nature of the service sector, can the concept of the gentlemanly class be condensed into a real entity? The implication of the description offered is that contemporaries knew a gentlemanly capitalist when they saw one – 'they were acknowledged by contemporaries to be leading participants in the

---

50. Cain and Hopkins, *British Imperialism: Crisis and Deconstruction*, p. 300.

51. Cain and Hopkins, *British Imperialism: Innovation and Expansion*, p. 138 and back cover.

52. C. Lee, 'The Service Industries', in R. Floud and D. McCloskey, (eds.), *The Economic History of Britain since 1700. Vol. 2: 1860–1939*, pp. 138–42 and generally pp. 117–44.

economy as well as ornaments of society'. Leading merchant bankers were prominent among the class but they hardly conformed to this image. A leading authority on this group has shown that whilst there were obvious connections between banking houses these did not amount to tight relationships. And from the 1880s onwards, these family units were breaking down, not least because improved telegraphic communications increased the flow and quality of financial and commercial information, making family networks less necessary. It has to be recognized, also, that some City houses made much of their money out of exclusively foreign transactions and, interrelatedly, the most dynamic elements in this field were to be found among the growing number of foreign bankers operating in London. They did not easily join the club of gentlemanly capitalists. 'Their immediate environment, social circle, church and principal employees often remained foreign, and their loyalties continued to be *international* in scope'.[53] The social glitter surrounding the Rothschilds and their immediate circle has perhaps dazzled historians as well as contemporaries. Merchant banking was not an exclusive preserve of a powerful and dominant group but was relatively open at this time to new entrants with a particular expertise. The looseness of association within these ranks makes it hard, therefore, to accept that the wider ranks of financiers, aristocrats and politicians were part of a cohesive and coherent metropolitan interest.[54]

If, for the moment, the identity of metropolitan gentlemanly capitalists is taken for granted, their relationship to other interest groups is by no means clear. The central contention is that they dominated industrial capitalists, resulting in a kind of North/South divide – and 'where a choice had to be made, gentlemanly interests invariably took precedence [over industry]'.[55] But against this claim, it has been shown that, on the one hand, vigorous industrial and provincial elites and interest groups existed and came together in varying and effective alliances whilst, on the other hand, there was

---

53. Chapman, *The Rise of Merchant Banking*, pp. 65–9, 98.

54. S. Chapman, 'Aristocracy and Meritocracy in Merchant Banking', *British Journal of Sociology*, 37 (1988), pp. 180–93 and J. Harris and P. Thane, 'British and European Bankers in Pre-1914 Europe', in P. Thane, G. Crossick and R. Floud (eds), *The Power of the Past* (Cambridge, 1984), pp. 215–34.

55. Cain and Hopkins, *British Imperialism: Crisis and Deconstruction*, p. 300. A major critique of Cain and Hopkins is M. Daunton, ' "Gentlemanly Capitalism" and British Industry, 1820–1914', *Past and Present*, 122 (1989), pp. 119–58; also see A. Porter, 'The Balance Sheet of Empire, 1850–1914', *Historical Journal*, 31 (1988), pp. 685–99.

cross-over and fragmentation between metropolitan, provincial, financial, industrial and landed groups. Kaleidoscopic variations of this kind are well illustrated in debates on bimetallism in the 1880s and tariff reform at the turn of the century; issues that were directly part of imperial policy but having major implications for Britain in the wider world economy. Which side an individual chose to support was not predetermined by whether he was a financier or an industrialist but by the type and geography of the markets in which he operated. And on the tariff, the working class with its interest in cheap food had a power of its own.

Those who stress the dominance of the City make some allowance for the fact that on occasions financial and industrial interests coincided, especially in relation to the ailing staple export industries. There is, however, little evidence of new sectors of industry being held back by these sectional interests. Technical backwardness, outdated business methods and dislike of state intervention affected all sectors of industry. On the side of the state, the alternative depended not just on political will; it involved the deeper problem of the progress of knowledge and understanding to overcome Britain's growing and peculiar form of economic backwardness. State-promoted advances in technical education and management training, for example, did not conflict with the maintenance of the gold standard and free trade. The need for such reforms was simply not understood.[56] A growing challenge to the 'official mind' arose from the swelling tide of political radicalism and so-called collectivism. But even here the political and practical appeal was in terms of social welfare and working conditions; it was not much concerned with industrial reorganization. It was perhaps appropriate that the most serious jolt to contemporary complacency came from the imperial quarter. The Boer War brought to the surface the poor physical condition of working class recruits to the army. To the public concern that arose was added growing fears of the competitive force of German industry. The official mind began to sense a self-interested connection between the prosperity of the nation and the quality of its human capital.[57]

56. H. F. Gospel, (ed.), *Industrial Training and Technological Innovation: A Comparative and Historical Study* (1991).

57. This concern was registered officially in the *Report of the Interdepartmental Committee on Physical Deterioration*, B. P. P., 1904 Cd. 2175. By no means radical in its proposals it did, nevertheless, mark a significant change in official attitudes.

Doubts as to the historical value of hegemonic concepts such as gentlemanly capitalism do not alter the fact that the Empire and the ideology surrounding it are central to an understanding of Britain's position in the world economy before 1914. At one level, what is revealed is 'the strength of *all* the competing economic interests of land, industry, finance and labour; all of them too strong for the state not to take serious account of their interests'.[58] They moved in and out of alliance with one another; they were not the puppets of gentlemanly capitalists. At a deeper level, there was a wide degree of *common* interest, particularly among the business classes whether in Bradford, Birmingham, Glasgow or London. It was a shared attitude to economic change which amounted to a belief in minimum change. The empire more and more symbolized the belief of finance and industry alike that Britain's place in the world was assured.

58. Thane, 'Financiers and the British State', pp. 94–5.

CHAPTER FOUR

The First World War and the Return to Gold

THE EFFECTS OF WAR

The First World War was the first total war. War had always imposed exceptional demands on the economy and frequently led to financial crisis. But war economy took on an entirely new meaning when the state used its power to impose total command over human and material resources. This was not simply the outcome of a new strength of political will; it was, also, a consequence of economic might. Modern technology had not only created mass production, it also permitted mass war.

The war ended in 1918 when acute shortages of food and materials and desperately low morale at home forced the German leadership to accept that its armies could no longer sustain the struggle.[1] The entry of the USA into the conflict had been the final crushing blow. The allies, led by Wilson, Clemenceau and Lloyd George, proceeded to construct a peace settlement at Versailles which satisfied few and which laid the foundations for future disasters. The settlement clearly had economic effects on Britain but before these are considered it is necessary to examine the direct impact of the war on Britain's position in the world economy.

The declaration of war stimulated a wave of popular nationalism in Britain. But excitement gradually gave way to anxiety, alarm and ultimately despair. The political crisis of 1915–16 brought a new and much-needed sense of urgency to the war effort, though costly mistakes had already been made. At an early stage the government

---

1. An excellent general account is T. Wilson, *The Myriad Faces of War: Britain and the Great War 1914–1918* (Cambridge, 1986). Of particular interest is A. Offer, *The First World War. An Agrarian Interpretation* (Oxford, 1989). The political aspects are carefully analysed by J. Turner, *British Politics and the Great War. Coalition and Conflict 1915–1918* (1992).

had decided to meet the major part of the cost by the traditional means of borrowing. A series of long-term loans was issued. In 1917 these were supplemented by a new short-term financial device, the Treasury Bill, which by 1918 had become by far the most important source of war finance. This policy was very expensive because of the need to pay high rates of interest. And since many of the loans were financed out of credit newly created by the government's market operations, credit inflation was generated which was then sustained at successively higher volumes of borrowing. After 1917 the efficiency of borrowing was substantially improved through a combination of National Savings schemes and much more effective control of short-term borrowing and interest rates. Nevertheless, by 1919, prices were two and a quarter times the 1914 level.[2]

Taxation played a limited role in war finance. Estimates of its contribution vary between 25 per cent and 30 per cent of the total, which was lower even than the proportion raised in this way during the Napoleonic wars. Income tax was successively increased from 1s 3d (6.5p.) to five shillings (25p.) in the pound, and some new direct taxes were imposed, the most important being the Excess Profits Duty. Quite apart, however, from the limited scale of direct taxation, the progressiveness of the system was not significantly increased since exemption limits were lowered. And for all the publicity given to it, the Excess Profits Duty was substantially evaded.[3]

Trade was an early casualty of the war. All kinds of shifts and stratagems were employed to meet the crisis, and these entailed increasing government control. After early difficulties and failures, considerable success was eventually achieved, and vital supplies were adequately protected from German U-boat attacks through the adoption of the convoy system. But in Eastern markets especially, India and Japan lost few opportunities to supplant erstwhile British exporters. The volume of trade necessarily contracted during the war years, particularly on the export side.

2. E. V. Morgan, *Studies in British Financial Policy, 1914–1925* (1952). Some corrective is provided by T. Balderston, 'War Finance and Inflation in Britain and Germany, 1914–1918', *Economic History Review*, 42 (1989), pp. 222–44 who argues that the sophistication of the British money market, in contrast to that in Germany, acted as a stabilizing influence through its ability to finance government debt. In other words, without it the situation would have been much worse.

3. B. W. E. Alford, 'Lost Opportunities: British Business and Businessmen During the First World War', in N. McKendrick and R. B. Outhwaite, *Business Life and Public Policy* (Cambridge, 1986), especially pp. 215–16.

Table 4.1 UK trade by value and volume, 1913–25

| | (£m) | | | (1913 = 100) | | |
| | | Domestic | | | Domestic | |
	Imports	Exports	Re-exports	Imports	Exports	Re-exports
1913	769	525	110	100.0	100.0	100.0
1914	697	431	96	90.0	82.2	93.5
1915	852	385	99	97.5	67.9	96.4
1916	949	506	98	83.2	70.4	78.4
1917	1,064	527	70	69.6	58.9	48.4
1918	1,316	501	31	71.7	40.5	18.2
1919	1,626	799	165	87.0	52.2	80.9
1920	1,933	1,335	223	87.4	69.0	88.6
1921	1,086	703	107	76.1	49.2	77.8
1922	1,003	720	104	87.4	69.0	84.4
1923	1,096	767	119	96.3	77.4	93.1
1924	1,277	801	140	107.8	80.3	102.4
1925	1,321	773	154	111.0	79.6	102.8

Source: Mitchell (1988), 453, 522.

To the turmoil in trade was added the crisis in international finance. In most respects Britain weathered the storm well because of the accumulated strength of its international capital and financial positions. By cutting down substantially on short-term credits and by eating into the large current account surplus as trade worsened, Britain just about managed to balance the books on its own account. There was, however, the additional problem of providing financial assistance to Dominion and European allies. The total commitment on this score was approximately £2,000 million, and this had to be financed mainly by raising loans in the USA and Canada, supplemented by short-term foreign loans raised in London and by enforced sales of some private securities, especially in the USA.

In one way this can be viewed as no more than switching assets from one account to another, and Britain's overseas capital holdings were reduced by, at most, one-quarter during the war. In other respects, however, these movements marked an important change. Since the mid-nineteenth century, the advance in the nation's prosperity had depended in a major way on its ability to generate large and increasing surpluses on international financial transactions. This capacity was lost, at least for the time being. Britain was now raising loans in New York. Was it the beginning of a permanent change? In response, it has to be said that there is no significant evidence that contemporaries saw these arrangements as anything but temporary. Indeed, the operations were seen as proof of Britain's underlying strength and its ability to lead the new world into its responsibilities for helping to redress the balance of the old.

The exchange rate was maintained without much difficulty, since the general upward movement of international prices matched rises in domestic money income. Wage earners in general and those in war industries in particular bid up their rates. Earnings rose proportionately more because of overtime working, especially in munitions production. Correspondingly, the share of wages in national income rose from 52 per cent to 64 per cent between 1913 and 1918.

Whilst there had been major technical developments in armaments and *matériel* since the Boer War, British generals stuck doggedly to time-honoured methods of trench warfare until the sheer weight of losses and casualties forced them to make some concessions to more modern technology. The armed forces recruited a total of 5.7 million men of whom 616,000 were lost and 1.7 million were wounded. The civil labour force dropped from 19.4 million in 1914 to 17 million by 1918, but it did not fall in a direct relationship to enlistment. The industrial workforce fell by only 5 per cent, from 8.4 million to 8.0 million. Approximately one million women entered the labour force. In addition, the number of school leavers was increasing because of long-term demographic effects and this was supplemented by a large number of male workers who continued to work into old age. The needs of particular industries were met by a switch in occupations. The largest shift was that of 400,000 females who left domestic service to join the industrial workforce. Most dramatically, the number of female workers in munitions and allied industries rose from just over 200,000 to almost one million. By 1918 two-thirds of the labour force were working either directly or indirectly for the government.[4] Even so, the deployment of labour for the war effort could have been much more effective. It has been estimated, for example, that as a result of misjudgements by the government and pressures from within the industry, the output of cotton textiles was maintained at

4. J. Lawrence, 'The First World War and its Aftermath', in P. Johnson (ed.), *Twentieth Century Britain* (1994), p. 153.

an unnecessarily high level during the war, which had the effect of tying up 250,000 workers who would otherwise have been available for alternative occupations. In addition, lower output would have released shipping space for vital imports and supplies of coal for other uses.[5]

The government quickly recognized that effective mobilization of the labour force depended on cooperation with trade unions. The status of unions and their leaders was thus enhanced and, for their part, they accepted a fair measure of labour direction and the dilution of skills as a short-term necessity. The appalling ravages of trench warfare might well have created an even more severe shortage of labour but for the marked effects of demographic change. Long-term trends in birth and death rates resulted in a 50 per cent acceleration in the rate of growth of the labour force which, in purely numerical terms, meant that the losses of the war were speedily replaced.[6]

Peacetime demands for *matériel* had been largely met by government ordinance factories and naval dockyards, but even these very large-scale enterprises could not provide the nation's full requirements, and the proportion of supplies purchased from private industry had been steadily increasing. War presented a wholly new order of demand. In a preliminary barrage before a big battle, for example, British artillery would regularly use one and a half million shells which can be compared with an annual output of 0.5 million shells in 1914.[7] Yet despite the fact that at a very early stage of the war the government had taken large powers of requisitioning and control of supplies, it initially persisted in satisfying its ever-increasing needs through the market. This led to shortages, inefficiency and, ultimately, a crisis in shell production in 1915. The outcome was the establishment of the Ministry of Munitions which fundamentally changed the organization of armaments production.

Controls were extended to other parts of the economy. What resulted was a major change in the relationship between government and private enterprise. Yet the manner of the change was such that private enterprise was by no means supplanted. Businessmen were recruited into government to command the new

5. J. Singleton, 'The Cotton Industry and the British War Effort, 1914–1918', *Economic History Review*, 47 (1994), pp. 601–18.

6. R. C. O. Matthews, C. H. Feinstein and J. C. Odling-Smee, *British Economic Growth 1856–1973* (Stanford, 1982), pp. 51–63.

7. W. K. Hancock and M. Gowing, *British War Economy* (1949), p. 6.

agencies that were set up. In many instances – for example in agriculture – policies were directed through local organizations run by those supplying the goods and services. Even when food rationing was introduced towards the end of the war, it was done on a quasi-voluntary basis through the organization of regional groups of retailers.[8]

Business attitudes towards traditional free trade changed. Calls for tariffs were led by iron and steel manufacturers who lobbied the government through their trade associations.[9] Underlying these demands was the belief that foreign, especially German, firms had been increasingly successful in international competition before the war because they had benefited from state support that gave them unfair advantages. The war was seen by businessmen – particularly those in the staple industries – as providing the opportunity and the means of extirpating insidious German competition. The true extent of these demands was not revealed until immediately after the war, however. Furthermore, as anxiety about raw material and shipping shortages receded, so too did support for protection. Even more to the point, many businesses and businessmen did extremely well out of the war and this had the effect of stimulating a heady self-confidence and self-interest that drove out any ideas of closer connections between business and government.

Lever Bros., for example, was the second largest manufacturing company in the UK by 1919, and it dominated the soap, edible oil and fats industry. Initially the war brought problems: 'the loss of several continental businesses, the shortage of capital, labour and raw materials, growth of government interference in industrial affairs ...'. But the clouds soon parted and the first substantial increase in the soap market for many years came as a result of 'the increase in employment and purchasing power as well as the social changes which resulted from these things'.[10] Exports boomed, especially to the USA. Over and above this, the war brought Levers into margarine production because of the impossibility of securing adequate supplies from the Continent. In the short run it required changes in the organization of production, with the establishment

8. An interesting contemporary analysis was made by E. M. H. Lloyd, *Experiments in State Control* (Oxford, 1924).

9. The remaining paragraphs of this section draw heavily on Alford, 'Lost Opportunities: British Business and Businessmen', which contains extensive references.

10. C. Wilson, *The History of Unilever: A Study in Economic Growth and Social Change. Volume 1* (1954), p. 216.

of new factories in Britain; in the longer run the consequences of this were profound since it strengthened the position of the British industry against its Dutch rivals. During the war, an annual loss in the USA of £20,000 was transformed into a profit of £300,000, and capitalization rose from £12 million to £47 million between 1913 and 1920.

Motor vehicles, rubber, pharmaceuticals, artificial fibres, tobacco, biscuits, chemicals, electrical goods, glass, petroleum, iron and steel, shipbuilding, shipping, cotton: all these were industries in which major companies did well out of the war. Buoyant demand fed by rising incomes within insulated markets spelt big profits that rose rapidly in real terms and not simply as part of the froth of wartime inflation. Profitability on this scale became profiteering in the eyes of the public, and the government found it impossible to remain indifferent to blatant excesses. The Excess Profits Duty (1915) was introduced but, as has been noted, whilst this did something to create an impression of public probity, it was not effective. The state of company law meant that those who were determined could relatively easily escape substantial liability, and those less determined or plain honest benefited from the backward state of accounting practices. Moreover, the assessment procedures not only created many loopholes, they ensured that efficient firms did well anyway; and official investigations to catch up on tax evasion, both during and immediately after the war, were somewhat naive in their approach to the task.

Other industries experienced mixed fortunes and the war brought mixed blessings. Coal-mining had for long been the fount of British industry. Output and productivity remained fairly constant during this period, with the extra demand being largely met through a decline in exports. Even so, shortages occurred from time to time, though as has been noted in the case of the cotton industry, coal supplies were far from being efficiently distributed. But, for the coal owners, buoyant demand eased the pressure to push ahead with mechanization and the closure of uneconomic pits. Similarly in the steel industry, domestic supplies were maintained by means of a large diversion of output from the export to the home market. Old locations were kept going beyond their peacetime economic life. Technical improvements occurred in specialist areas linked to munitions but not in the main ones where they were needed.

In the multifarious engineering industry, trade unions agreed to labour dilution, especially through the employment of female workers. These changes to some extent weakened the bargaining position of semi-skilled male workers, though craftsmen, who were in increasingly short supply, were able to extract undertakings from employers which protected their traditional labour practices and traditional production techniques.[11] Similar conditions existed in the shipbuilding industry. Other sectors undoubtedly suffered from the war. Electricity supply lost key men to war service. Coal was in ever-shorter supply and electrical equipment was hard to obtain because suppliers transferred their capacity to more profitable armaments production. Nevertheless, the increasing need for electricity in war production could not be ignored and this led the government to call in an expert to direct the reorganization of electricity generation on a more efficient basis. In turn this resulted in the establishment of the Department of Electrical Power Supply in 1916. Much was subsequently claimed on behalf of this department but investigation has shown that developments during this period were dominated by immediate wartime needs which did not match long-term requirements. A combination of low optimum generating plant, inappropriate locations and a new battery of legislative controls, was a heavy drag on progress towards the establishment of the industry on a basis which could reap the enormous potential demand for cheap electricity.[12]

Rail transport was another sector which lost out. Parts of the system were placed under intense pressure by the need to convey materials to munitions factories and soldiers to ports of embarkation. Equipment and track were run down for want of finance and skilled manpower. Even so, these costs have to be balanced within a broader measure of account. Excesses of competition before 1914 produced an excess of service which can be measured in terms of severe over-capitalization. Half-hearted and *ad hoc* rationalization schemes of the pre-war years were superseded by more direct planning during the war and this led finally to the Railways Act of 1921. But this Act, which failed to meet the

---

11. A. Reid, 'Dilution, Trade Unionism and the State in Britain During the First World War', in S. Tolliday and J. Zeitlin (eds), *Shop Floor Bargaining and the State: Historical and Comparative Perspectives* (Cambridge, 1985), pp. 46–74; *idem.*, 'The Impact of the First World War on British Workers', in R. Wall and J. Winter (eds.), *The Upheaval of War and Welfare in Europe 1914–1918* (Cambridge, 1986), pp. 221–33; J. Zeitlin, 'The Labour Strategies of British Engineering Employees, 1890–1912', in H. F. Gospel and C. R. Littler (eds), *Management Strategies and Industrial Relations* (1983), pp. 25–53.

12. L. Hannah, *Electricity Before Nationalization* (1979), pp. 53–104.

commercial needs of the rail system, was part of the bigger failure to develop a national transport policy which took account of the rise of motor transport. The number of motor vehicles in the UK rose from 108,000 to 0.5 million between 1910 and 1921; and as the experience of the USA indirectly indicated, this was no mere wartime phenomenon. By 1921, there were 10.5 million vehicles in the USA and the number was rising rapidly.

The remaining casualty of war was agriculture, though as with electricity and rail transport, it was a case of aggravated damage within a changing world economy. The industry was directly stimulated by war needs but in a manner which reversed the trend of the previous 40 years. The acreage under arable cultivation was expanded by some 30 per cent. Quite independently, US agriculture had been expanding production, especially of arable crops, as a result of the widespread adoption of tractors which dramatically raised productivity. The dislocation of Continental European agriculture caused international primary product prices to rise sharply to the advantage of British and American farmers. But once the war was over and Continental European production began to recover and add to world supplies, prices began to fall precipitously. The response was a massive change in the structure of land ownership. Large estates were broken up and the English countryside returned to the older pattern of family farming. But this was only the beginning of a long drawn out and painful adjustment to agricultural depression on a world scale.[13]

The financial spoils of war were not distributed evenly, as might be expected. In broad terms, manufacturing industry enjoyed something of a profits bonanza whilst building and construction, internal transport and services lost out. The manner in which these gains were used, however, varied considerably. Steel makers, for example, indulged in what can only be described as an orgy of acquisition and amalgamations. Steel and the other major staples could have applied high monetary profits as a solvent to dead-weight capital liabilities which inflation was already reducing in real terms. Instead, to varying degrees these industries used these funds, during the war and immediate postwar years, to expand capacities within existing technologies for supplying traditional markets and to promote amalgamations with the aim of sustaining monopolistic profits through a system of regulated competition.

13. A. Offer, 'Farm Tenure and Land Values in England, c. 1750–1950', *Economic History Review*, 44 (1991), pp. 1–20.

Little or no attention was paid to the need to use greater concentration of ownership as a means for promoting modern methods of business organization and management. The strength of the belief among businessmen that with the return of peace the world would be their oyster is revealed by the evidence given by a wide range of witnesses from these industries when they appeared, some ruefully, before the Balfour Committee some seven or eight years later.

For firms in a wide range of manufacturing, profligate use of war profits was compounded by the easiest of easy credit from the clearing banks. Some years ago the celebrated economist, Pigou, ascribed to the banks major responsibility for the postwar inflation, and others since have similarly drawn attention to it.[14] The banks were not compelled to lend; they chose to do so. What is more, they were lending short in the form of overdrafts without seemingly realizing that they were providing the cash flow to support long-term commitments, the success of which would determine whether they would ever see their money back. All of this warns against the danger of seeing British businessmen of the period – as many themselves did – as in some way the victims of postwar inflation that was caused by world conditions. Businessmen in industry and finance were, themselves, substantially the guilty parties.

It might be claimed, however, that swelling wartime profits and the defeat of Germany lulled the senses and encouraged the belief that peace would deliver to Britain the level of economic ascendancy it had enjoyed at the end of the nineteenth century. If this was the case, it cannot be counted as a cost of war. It was the direct result of the poor judgement of British businessmen in failing to understand the nature of the economic world in which they had to operate; a failure that had existed from well before the war. Moreover, over the latter years of the war, when many misguided investment decisions were being made, worries began to arise among businessmen about the postwar resurgence of German competition. The crucial point was that German competitive advantages were not seen as arising from superior industrial organization and technical efficiency, but from state subsidies and protection which, it was assumed, had guaranteed German success in the pre-war years.

14. A. C. Pigou, *Aspects of British Economic History 1918–1925* (1947), pp. 169–83.

There is thus ample evidence of the war providing the opportunity for firms in the staple industries to make structural adjustments and thus open the way for development in newer, expanding sectors of industry. These conditions apply to a substantial proportion of the core of manufacturing industry. Whilst the needs of war stimulated invention and innovation including, for example, the development of new alloys and chemical processes, technical change remained narrowly conceived within existing structures of business organization. The most serious error was the manner in which firms in product markets facing permanent decline threw away the financial advantages which the war gave them. This was not simply a loss: it turned an enormous advantage into a crippling handicap.

THE POLITICAL ECONOMY OF PEACE

The Versailles settlement amounted to the triumph of revenge over economic good sense. Germany was to be forced to pay for the war but at the same time her permanent economic weakness was to be ensured by the expropriation of some of her major resources. Some contemporaries saw clearly enough that the extent of Germany's dismemberment would not so much weaken her as create dangerous instability in Central Europe and a feeling of deep national resentment in Germany itself. A brilliant attack on the settlement was launched by Keynes in *The Economic Consequences of the Peace* (1919). Though polemical in tone, the argument was unanswerable: the economic health of Europe depended on an economically sound Germany; to persist in a policy which stripped the country of resources and killed economic incentive was to espouse the economics of the madhouse. The outcome would be economic and political disaster. What was unanswerable was ignored by policy makers and by a popular press crazed with xenophobia.

The solution Keynes offered was a policy of internationalism based on a multilateral system of trade and finance. Postwar British politics, however, were the politics of victory. And the country was certainly not faced with the economics of defeat. There was no pressing need to plan for peace because the years immediately after 1918 were not ones of shortage. In 1919 British imports were 87 per cent of their 1913 level in real terms, and the balance of payments was almost in equilibrium.

Table 4.2 UK balance of payments – current account, selected years 1913–25 (£m.)

	Merchandise exports[x]	Merchandise imports	Visible balance	Invisible balance	Overall current balance
1913	637	719	−82	+317	+235
1918	540	1,170	−630	+415	−275
1919	990	1,460	−470	+425	−45
1920	1,585	1,761	−176	+493	+317
1925	943	1,208	−265	+317	+52
1920–25[xx] (annual average)	1,040	1,196	−156	+330	+174

[x] Includes re-exports
[xx] Excluding Southern Ireland

Source: Feinstein (1972), Table 15.

Nevertheless, in the same year Britain left the gold standard because of inflationary conditions, since the alternative of deflationary action would have been a direct admission by the government that it had abandoned its promises of new social policy. Ministers directly involved in organizing the return to peacetime conditions (such as Auckland Geddes, Director of National Services) expressed considerable fears about the possible reactions of large numbers of demobilized soldiers, if the needs of finance and financiers were put before theirs. There was a whiff of revolution in the air, with isolated mutinous acts in the forces and a surge of radical socialism north of the border.[15] So the boom was let rip. Expansionary investment in various industries was largely misplaced when judged in terms of longer-term needs, but in the immediate period it created the capacity to absorb large numbers of returning workers. Added to this, demands for a shorter working day were widely conceded, resulting in a marked upward movement in unit wage costs, since the reduction in hours was not matched by improved productivity.[16]

15. C. L. Mowat, *Britain Between the Wars 1918–1940* (1955), pp. 1–79. This brilliant book is the outstanding general history of the period.
16. J. A. Dowie, '1919–20 is in Need of Attention', *Economic History Review*, 28 (1975), pp. 429–50.

The politics of victory incorporated the widespread wish to return to normality. In economic terms normality was understood as the system which had existed before the war, with the exception that Germany would no longer pose a threat to British prosperity. Yet there were obvious signs that the world had changed. The most obvious was the international emergence of the USA.[17] It was, after all, that country's entry into the war which had precipitated the collapse of Germany. And the role of the USA at Versailles amounted to a recognition of its economic power as much as it was a consequence of President Wilson's idealism, even though the latter fell victim to the cynical politics of the other allied powers. Less pronounced, but in many respects no less significant, was the emergence of Japan as an industrial nation and the increased sense of economic independence being shown by the Dominion territories. Where change was strongly desired by the allies, vigorously pursued and thought to have been achieved, was in the case of Germany. But this amounted to little more than hope chasing delusion.

Two questions arise. To what extent had the war changed the economic world and Britain's place within it? How clearly did contemporaries understand the economic circumstances in which they now found themselves? In attempting to answer the first question, the obvious starting point is to examine the comparative data on production, trade and finance.

Table 4.3 Relative shares of world manufacturing output selected years 1880–1928 (% share)

	1880	*1900*	*1913*	*1928*
United Kingdom	22.9	18.5	13.6	9.9
France	7.8	6.8	6.1	6.0
Germany	8.5	13.2	14.8	11.6
Italy	2.5	2.5	2.4	2.7
Japan	2.4	2.4	2.7	3.3
United States	14.7	23.6	32.0	39.3

Source : Bairoch (1982), 296, 304.

17. K. Burk, *Britain, America and the Sinews of Power, 1914–1918* (1985).

Table 4.4 Comparative measures of total output, selected years 1890–1929 (UK = 100)

	1890	*1913*	*1929*
United Kingdom	100	100	100
France	66	64	77
Germany	43	59	63
Italy	36	43	51
Japan	28	33	52
Netherlands	10	11	18
USA	166	267	390

Source: Maddison (1991), 198.

The point to highlight in terms of output is the rise in the relative world position of the USA and, to a lesser extent, Germany from the late nineteenth century onwards, and the steady but substantial decline in that of Britain.

Table 4.5 Comparative shares of world exports of manufactured goods, selected years 1899–1929 (%)

	1899	*1913*	*1929*[1]	*1929*[2]
United Kingdom	33.2	30.2	23.0	22.4
Belgium-Lux.	5.5	5.0	5.5	5.4
Canada	0.4	0.6	3.6	3.5
France	14.4	12.1	11.1	10.9
Germany	22.4	26.6	21.0	20.5
India	2.4	2.4	2.4	2.3
Italy	3.6	3.3	3.8	3.7
Japan	1.5	2.3	4.0	3.9
Netherlands	–	–	–	2.5
Switzerland	4.0	3.1	2.8	2.8
Sweden	0.9	1.4	1.8	1.7
USA	11.7	13.0	21.0	20.4
Total	100.0	100.0	100.0	100.0

[1] Excludes Netherlands.
[2] Includes Netherlands.

Source: Maizels (1963), 189.

Table 4.6 Direction of UK trade, selected years 1904–1929 (Annual averages – % shares)

		1904–13	1920–29
Foreign:	Imports	76.0	70.0
	Exports	65.0	57.0
	Exports & re-exports	69.0	61.0
Empire:	Imports	24.0	30.0
	Exports	35.0	43.0
	Exports & re-exports	31.0	39.0

Source : Capie (1983), 19.

Similar features show up in respect of international trade in manufactured goods. Added to which, in the case of Great Britain, there is the continuing and pronounced swing of exports away from foreign and towards Empire markets (see Chapter 2.)

Whilst Britain remained the leader in international finance in 1913, its relative position had already declined from what it had been in the late nineteenth century. This decline accelerated in the years after the war. Net invisible income fell by something between a quarter and a third in real terms between 1913 and the early 1920s; and the ratio between the surplus on invisibles and the deficit on merchandise trade fell from 4:1 to 2:1 over the same period (Table 4.2). Moreover, the latter fall was cushioned by the sharp movement of the terms of trade in favour of Britain. The fall in world primary product prices compensated for the large reduction in the volume of exports (Table 4.1). Another indicator of this change in Britain's external position is provided by the ratio of overseas assets to GDP (Table 4.7).

The loss of overseas investments during the war, the disruption to international finance arising from war debts and reparations, the devaluation of sterling: these were obviously important elements in the decline in invisible income. In addition, earnings from shipping fell disastrously, mainly as a consequence of the contraction of British trade but, also, as a result of growing competition from the technically more advanced merchant ships of other nations. More intriguingly, earnings from financial and other services, centred on

Table 4.7 UK overseas assets and liabilities, selected years 1873–1937[x]
(£billion at current prices)

	Assets	Liabilities	Net assets	Ratio of net assets to GDP
1873	1.1	0.1	1.0	0.8
1913	4.6	0.4	4.2	1.8
1924	6.8	1.6	5.2	1.3
1937	5.3	1.3	4.0	0.9

[x] These figures include estimates of net investment for the intervening
years and adjustments for defaults and alterations in the value of
existing assets and liabilities.

Source : Matthews, Feinstein and Odling-Smee (1982), 128.

the City of London, performed poorly. The effects of the war on
financial confidence, the decline in trade and growing competition
both within and between financial markets (especially between
London and New York), are reasons commonly advanced to explain
this performance. Yet there is evidence to suggest that merchant
banks and other financial institutions (including British
multinational banks overseas) proved slow to adapt to changing
conditions. Lack of entrepreneurial enterprise was no less evident
in City banking parlours than it was in company boardrooms.[18]
And, as will be seen, these characteristics became even more
pronounced in the 1930s.

These comparative measures clearly illustrate Britain's relative
decline in the world economy. They show, moreover, that it was not
something resulting from the war but part of a continuing process
that had begun in the late nineteenth century. The margins on
which Britain operated in international trade and finance by the
mid-1920s were highly vulnerable to the forces of international

18. An excellent study is S. Tolliday, *Business, Banking and Politics. The Case of
British Steel, 1918–39* (Cambridge, Mass., 1987). G. Jones, *British Multinational Banking
1830–1990* (Oxford, 1993), pp. 136–222, is perhaps a little too mild in his assessment
in view of the large amount of evidence he produces. A valuable study of a merchant
bank is R. Roberts, *Shroders. Merchants and Bankers* (1992), but in the absence of
similar studies its typicality cannot be measured.

competition, even when allowance is made for Britain's still strong asset position in the world economy. Dominant economic power now rested with the USA. But it was power without responsibility since, unlike Britain, the dependence of the USA on the international economy was marginal.

The changing pattern of world production and trade was the outcome of the changing process of industrialization that had been well in evidence before the First World War. Technical change had become increasingly capital-intensive and, correspondingly, net value added in manufacture accounted for a growing proportion of the final value of goods produced and inputs of raw materials for correspondingly less. Trade patterns were directly affected. Producers of primary goods were forced to seek ever-higher levels of productivity in order to maintain their real incomes. At the same time the emergence of newly industrialized economies reduced the complementarity in world trade between producers of primary products and manufactured goods, and led to increasing competitiveness between the major economies. These were not once-for-all adjustments. They were the dynamics of a new international economic environment.

The difficulties and challenges of the war economy have already been described. The question is whether these conditions imposed costs on the economy of such a scale as to cause serious damage to its longer-term development. The most sophisticated contemporary estimate of the costs of the war was made by the celebrated statistician, Sir Arthur Bowley. He reckoned that the war had cost Britain the equivalent of four years' capital accumulation at 'normal rates'.[19] More recent estimates have broadly corroborated this figure.[20] And in the most exhaustive analysis of national income data, it is claimed that, 'the absolute fall in GDP across the war, not made good until the 1920s, is one of the most spectacular features of recent British economic history'. Unfortunately the war period is defined as 1913–24 and thus incorporates a substantial postwar period, the nature of which requires separate examination.[21]

Such calculations can exercise a bewitching appeal whilst acting as treacherous guides to historical explanation. For example, it could have been that whilst the war caused the loss of production

19. A. L. Bowley, *Some Economic Consequences of the Great War* (1930), pp. 87–8.

20. W. A. Lewis, 'World Production, Prices and Trade', *The Manchester School*, 20 (1952), p. 127, and I. Svennilson, *Growth and Stagnation in the European Economy* (Geneva, 1954), pp. 18–19, who corroborate Bowley's estimate.

21. Matthews *et al*, *British Economic Growth*, p. 543.

through the run-down of large sectors of industry, subsequently this stimulated their rapid modernization through the need for capital re-equipment and thence led to higher rates of growth than would have been achieved without the disturbance. Much is made of this kind of conjunction, for example, in explaining the high rates of growth in Western European economies and Japan in the post-Second World War period (see Chapter 10). Other circumstances were clearly different between the two periods, but the point is that these kinds of direct losses from war do not necessarily result in a negative growth effect in the longer run. Furthermore, the calculation of 'losses' in aggregate, based on assumed foregone peacetime production and capital accumulation, take no account of the redistributive effects of war, which have already been examined. In sum, the calculation of costs in narrowly defined statistical terms is a hazardous and imprecise exercise. When costs are defined more broadly to include non-quantifiable elements such as business expectations, the outcome becomes indeterminate.

To the question of whether the war had changed the economic world and Britain's place within it, there is similarly no clear-cut answer. But the evidence points strongly to the war having had only a marginal effect. In the case of Britain's leading export industry, cotton textiles, for example, the wartime advantages gained by neutrals in foreign markets is obvious, but the most careful analysis of the industry's development provides an overwhelming case that the war hastened the process of permanent loss of comparative advantage, and that more perceptive businessmen would have recognized this fact and adjusted to it under what were favourable wartime financial conditions.[22] To the contrary, as has been noted, a combination of official incompetence and special pleading by the owners served to sustain the industry in a bloated condition.

The break-up of the old British empire and the redrawing of the map of Europe as a result of the war created new economic uncertainties and difficulties. The Habsburg empire was

---

22. L. Sandberg, *Lancashire in Decline: A Study of Entrepreneurship, Technology and International Trade* (Columbus, Ohio, 1974). It is important to note that whilst Sandberg offers a persuasive case to the effect that businessmen in the industry were not fundamentally responsible for its decline, he fails to acknowledge that they lacked the ability to adjust to the loss of comparative advantage. For a survey of the debate on the performance of the industry see W. Mass and W. A. Lazonick, 'The British Cotton Industry and International Competitive Advantage. The State of the Debates', in M. B. Rose (ed.), *International Competition and Strategic Response in the Textile Industries since 1870* (1990), pp. 9–65.

dismembered, the Ottoman empire suffered its ultimate demise and post-revolutionary Russia withdrew into isolation. The number of independent customs units in continental Europe rose from 20 to 27, and tariffs rose up like palisades. These political changes are well recorded but the relationship between them and the economic conditions of the post-war period is complex. The political divisiveness of the period in part arose from the changed and changing nature of the world economy. The United States had emerged as the leading economic power and its dominance was set to increase. By 1920 the USA accounted for nearly half the world's industrial output. Yet, as has been noted, under normal circumstances there were no strong economic imperatives acting on the USA, leading it to impose a degree of order and stability on the international economy. But in the abnormal conditions of the First World War the USA had been brought into a position of international prominence. This major opportunity to establish a new system of international economic relations was lost amid the wranglings of the European allies which strengthened the ever-present urge in the USA to revert to type. The dislocations and uncertainties affecting trade as a result of the war undoubtedly presented problems to Britain and the other major trading nations, but these difficulties were both secondary to and symptomatic of more fundamental structural shifts in the world economy which had been occurring since before the war. Competitive relationships had substantially replaced complementary ones in international trade and a new system of trade regulation was needed. Until the USA felt this need and was prepared to take the lead in the formation of a new system, the prospects for world trade would be poor. The war simply added variation to this dominant theme.

Keynes understood the nature of the international economy better than any of his contemporaries. Hence his charge against the allies: 'Moved by insane delusion and reckless self-regard, the German people overturned the foundations on which we all lived and built. But the spokesmen of the French and British peoples have run the risk of completing the ruin, which Germany began, by a peace which, if it is carried into effect, must impair yet further, when it might have restored, the delicate, complicated organisation, already shaken and broken by war, through which alone the European peoples can employ themselves and live'.[23] Keynes's remedies of reduced reparations, free trade, the consolidation of

23. J. M. Keynes, *The Economic Consequences of the Peace* (1919), pp. 1–2.

inter-allied debts and an international loan to Germany, were far too strong a medicine for contemporary policy makers. And the sharpness of his international focus probably caused him to overlook real and understandable concern with national economic self-interest, not least in his own country. But the vehemence and hostility which his proposals met from those in power betrayed a basic ignorance which went way beyond self-interest. Keynes, himself, was far from possessing the degree of knowledge and understanding that was required to remedy affairs.

The records of a wide range of businesses and businessmen provide no evidence of shock or despair in face of the economic impact of war. The overall response was a mixture of optimism and complacency.[24] Moreover, the direct involvement of top businessmen in government during the war does not appear to have done anything to persuade them, in general, that Britain's wider economic needs required closer cooperation between government and industry. There were notable exceptions such as Dudley Docker, who argued for postwar protectionism and closer trade relations with the Empire.[25] Such ideas were part of a broader corporatist strategy that was finding favour in some quarters during the latter part of the war. But it never gained widespread support and it certainly did not represent the views of industrialists generally. Nor was it based on a clear and coherent understanding of Britain's underlying industrial problems. The attitude of Sir Alfred Mond, chairman of the chemical firm Brunner Mond, was far more typical:[26]

> ... As Minister and businessman [I am convinced] that it is impossible to carry on the industries of this country from a Government Department .... A curiously paralysing influence seems to come over everybody as soon as they begin to work for the State.

As has been noted, businessmen were aided and abetted in their delusions in the early years of peace by the clearing banks which provided the easiest of easy credit. One of the most vivid accounts

24. Alford, 'Lost Opportunities'.
25. An excellent study is R. P. T. Davenport-Hines, *Dudley Docker, The Life and Times of a Trade Warrior* (Cambridge, 1984), especially pp. 105–32, 187–98.
26. Cited by S. Marriner, 'Sir Alfred Mond's Octopus: A Nationalized House-Building Business', *Business History*, 21 (1979), p. 40. Lloyd George thought that Mond was the best business brain ever to serve the state, *loc. cit.* p. 27.

of this episode is provided by Lord Brand, writing of his own experiences as a director of Lloyds Bank in 1919:[27]

> My impression of Board meetings ... at that time was that we ladled out money; we did it because everybody said they were making and were going to make large profits, and while you had an uneasy feeling yet you thought that while they were making large profits there could be nothing said about ladling out the money.

This reveals both the nature of the relationship between finance and industry and the limited competence of financial entrepreneurship itself.

One potential source of pressure to adopt a new business outlook was organized labour. Through being brought into direct cooperation with the government, the status of unions – especially those representing the skilled and semi-skilled – was substantially enhanced. Labour leaders were seen by the ruling classes as the personification of the essential patriotism and cooperative spirit of the British working class. For its part, organized labour had accepted direction and the dilution of skills as necessities of wartime. But whilst dilution to some degree weakened the position of the semi-skilled, this had been counteracted by an ability of craftsmen to extract undertakings from employers. In so far as the war forced employers to accept that they had to negotiate with organized labour rather then confront it, this had a perverse effect on the potential for change. Central to the needs of business reorganization was technical change involving new labour practices and reduced manning levels. The war conspired to fuse the interests of businessmen and organized labour in their resistance to innovation.[28]

There is some debate over the impact of war on the advance of state welfare and more general social change, and this obviously has economic implications. The balance of opinion is that whilst the war set the basis and direction for future policy, the practical extent of change was limited and did not develop until somewhat later in the interwar period. There is evidence that the war promoted freer social relationships, not so much between classes as between the sexes. This freedom especially applies to women. 'When they were

27. Cited by S. Howson, *Domestic Monetary Management in Britain 1919–38* (Cambridge, 1975), p. 10.
28. Reid, 'The Impact of the First World War on British Workers'.

freed from tight corsets, the popular hour-glass figure gave place to the neatly cylindrical'.[29] And soon the pace and style of social life responded to the new pleasures of the petrol and electric age. But promises of increased social welfare could not be sustained, and the fruits of modern consumer goods industries were restricted to the upper and better-off middle classes. Moreover, the form and nature of mass marketing and mass consumption were conditioned by developments in the USA and in this respect Britain lagged well behind.[30] This is not to deny that the war brought about a measure of change in social, cultural and political life. But because it did little to alter the economic system and outlook with which those changes were interdependent, their impact was correspondingly limited.

There was no intellectual conversion among policy-makers during the war as to how the economy functioned. In part this reflected the unchanging nature of political leadership. 'The older men hung on to the positions of power without being challenged until the thirties; then the challengers were the young men who had not been in the war, between whom and the older generation the gap was unduly wide, with no influential members of the middle-aged in between. Partly this was because of the coupon elections. Shut out then, and rebelling against the tone of the campaign, the wartime generation acquired a distaste for politics which never left it. There was a lost generation in this sense: lost to politics. The men who came back from the war have counted for less, perhaps, in the political life of their country than any generation during the last two or three centuries. An ageing second team remained on the field.'[31] In part, also, the lack of government initiative can be explained by the absence of any plausible alternative theoretical rationalization to that long provided by the classical economists. How else did the international financial system operate if not to the dictates of the gold standard? For all his international vision, Keynes, the most formidable critic of

29. R. Graves and A. Hodge, *The Long Week-End. A Social History of Great Britain 1918–1939* (1961 edition), p. 39. A brilliant evocation of the period, especially of middle and upper-middle class mores.

30. *Idem., The Long Week-End*, Chapters 3, 8 and 9; S. M. Bowden, 'Demand and Supply Constraints in the Interwar UK Car Industry: Did the Manufacturers Get It Right?', *Business History*, 32 (1990), pp. 52–75; *idem.* and P. Turner, 'Some Cross-Section Evidence on the Determinants of the Diffusion of Car Ownership in the Inter-War UK Economy', *Business History*, 35 (1993), pp. 55–69.

31. Mowat, *Britain Between the Wars*, p. 9.

contemporary economic policies, had no coherent alternative political economy to offer. Political inertia, combined with an antediluvian administrative system, whose vested interests deepened with each passing year, were formidable barriers to innovative political economy. Contemporaries thus remained largely oblivious to the changed and changing position of Britain within the world economy.

FINANCIAL POLICY AND THE RETURN TO GOLD

However little understood, the practical demands of the postwar world could not be avoided. The central international economic need was for the restoration of a financial system. This need bore particularly heavily on Britain because of its external economic dependence, which amounted to nearly one-third of national income. By contrast, the USA, now the world's strongest creditor nation, drew less than 5 per cent of its income from international transactions. From the outset, therefore, need and capacity in international finance were basically out of balance.

In the turmoil and dislocation of financial markets immediately after the war, the defence of the pre-war sterling exchange rate was impossible and, as has been noted, Britain went off gold in 1919. The decision was, nevertheless, accompanied by a clear declaration that Britain would return to the gold standard as circumstances permitted.[32] This was a commitment not simply to return to the pre-war system of international finance but to pre-war parity. Viewed from the standpoint of contemporary policy-makers the decision is understandable. There was nothing approaching an obvious alternative. And Britain was still at the centre of a large imperial trading network which needed the restoration of a reliable sterling exchange. The USA was thus uncooperative in the sense that, despite its financial strength, it was not willing (and did not need) to assume international financial leadership; though it has to be borne in mind that the American financial system was far less centralized than that of Britain and the Federal Reserve System was weak as a central bank. The USA was thus cooperative in encouraging Britain to resume its traditional role as international lender in the last resort but the position of the US monetary authorities was ambivalent on this score because, in the early 1920s,

32. Howson, *Domestic Monetary Management.*

they were intent on reducing Britain's international financial influence as part of their opposition to British imperialism.[33]

In one sense these conditions amounted to a case of *force majeur*. The fact was, however, that Britain was not being forced to act against its better judgement. Treasury ministers and officials, the Bank of England and leaders of financial opinion, were in no doubt that Britain should return to the gold standard and to what was believed to be its natural leading international role. This innate sense of superiority was enhanced by a wave of imperial sentiment which, a little later, was registered in the Empire Settlement Act (1923). It involved, also, putting pressure on the financial authorities in the Dominions to become more closely integrated with London and sterling.[34] Along with this, there was limited understanding of the relationship between external policy and its internal effects.

Policy-makers thus took no account of the evolution of the world economy which involved a continuing decline in Britain's relative economic power. Deflation was vigorously pursued. Bank rate was raised, public expenditure was cut, short-term debt was reduced and the budget balanced. The task was difficult because British prices remained out of line with those ruling in the USA, in terms of pre-war relativity. An added problem was the supply-side shock to the economy resulting from substantial increases in wage rates, unmatched by increases in productivity, conceded by employers during the turbulent years of 1919–20.[35] Thereafter the strength of organized labour declined and the government seized its opportunity. It was not until April 1925, however, that the chancellor of the exchequer, Winston Churchill, announced the return to gold. Somewhat paradoxically, financial policy had a high political profile even though government leaders regarded the objectives of that policy to be above party politics. Such was the nature of financial orthodoxy. Moreover, the issue has been the focus of fierce historical debate. The question is whether this debate amounts to much more than a form of historical shadow-boxing. In short, was the British economy crucified on a cross of gold which bore the inscription $4.86 to the £?

33. F. C. Costigliola, *Awkward Dominion: American Political, Economic and Cultural Relations with Europe, 1919–33* (Cornell, 1985); M. J. Hogan, *Informal Entente: The Private Structure of Co-operation in Anglo-American Economic Diplomacy 1918–28* (Columbia, Missouri, 1977).

34. P. J. Cain and A. G. Hopkins, *British Imperialism: Crisis and Deconstruction 1914–90* (1993), pp. 109–45.

35. Dowie, '1919–20 is in Need of Attention'.

A number of economic historians have been in no doubt as to the answer to the question. Putting to one side the issue of the level of understanding that could be expected of contemporaries, and adopting an *ex post* Keynesian view of the world, the argument has been made that deflation and tight money squeezed life out of the economy and created the scourge of long-term unemployment.[36] It is pointed out, furthermore, that what was restored in 1925 was not a gold standard but a gold exchange standard. The level of liquidity needed to finance international transactions meant that the exchange reserves of countries had to be made up of both gold and the major currencies. In the case of smaller countries, reserves were held almost entirely in the form of other currencies. This was no more than a recognition of the fact that the pre-war system had effectively been mainly a sterling standard and that sterling was no longer available in quantities sufficient to finance international requirements. Equally, this development implied the complete abandonment of gold movements as the adjustment mechanism. Exchange rates would need to be managed within a fixed rate system. This was a change from the pre-1914 period, not so much of kind as of major degree. The dangers inherent in such a system in terms of competitive central bank actions were enormous.

On the broader front, stress has been laid on the greater politicization of international finance following the war.[37] Central banks became subject to more direct control by their respective governments because of the latters' need to take account of the domestic, and particularly the employment consequences of external financial conditions. Furthermore, the settlement of war debts and reparations upset the commercial flow of capital, and international capital movements in the early 1920s did not seem to have the same stabilizing effects as in the pre-1914 period. According to one authority, the war created a major imbalance because of the manner in which 'it strengthened the competitive position of American industry and transformed the United States from a net foreign debtor into a creditor nation'.[38] Above all, postwar international politics were so soured that the degree of international economic cooperation necessary for world stability was simply unattainable.

36. S. Pollard (ed.), *The Gold Standard and Employment Policies Between the Wars* (1970), pp. 1–26 for a trenchant statement of his viewpoint.
37. B. J. Eichengreen, *Golden Fetters: the Gold Standard and the Great Depression, 1919–1939* (New York, 1992), pp. 390–9.
38. *Idem.*, p. 392.

This analysis has a strong *a priori* appeal and it has been reinforced by reference to contemporary opinion. Keynes is cited as the major figure who argued that the return to gold damaged Britain's international economic position. However, this was the pre-*General Theory* Keynes and his argument was that the choice of the dollar/sterling parity (at the pre-war rate) was mistaken, not the return itself. Britain should have returned at 10 per cent below the previous rate – but return it should. Keynes claimed that the action taken priced industries out of overseas markets with calamitous consequences for the level of economic activity and employment. To add to self-inflicted injury, the major continental countries, Germany, France and Belgium, returned to the standard at devalued rates on 1914 levels. And to complete the agony, international prices continued to fall, placing even greater stress on Britain's competitive position.

Any attempt to validate Keynes's claims faces the same problem as confronted contemporary policy-makers, namely, the quality of the available statistical data. Contemporaries relied heavily on indices that were based on wholesale prices and these were heavily influenced by international price levels of raw materials and primary products. The net statistical effect was a pronounced narrowing of national price differences and, hence, this gave a distorted view of price differences between traded manufactured goods. To make matters even more complicated, individual countries did not collect and calculate data on a universally consistent basis. But given these problems, it is claimed that British manufactured goods appeared more price-competitive internationally than was, in fact, the case, thus strengthening Keynes's position.

The case against the return to the gold standard is much less strong than it appears, however, and to a significant extent is beside the point. To begin with, in relation to the issue of the direct effects on Britain of the return to gold there are four overriding conditions. First, the relevant exchange rate for making judgements is the effective rate and not the nominal rate. In other words, a general price index, however accurate, may well not match the relative distribution of British trade between different markets and correspondingly different price structures.[39] Such was obviously the case during this period since nearly half of British trade was within

39. The effective rate is the value of a country's currency in terms of a 'basket' of other currencies weighted according to their importance in that country's trade.

the sterling area and, therefore, the choice of the sterling/dollar rate had absolutely no effect on the price-competitiveness of British goods in this theatre. And this condition applied especially to staple industries which were experiencing the major problems. Attempts to estimate the effective rate for 1925 indicate that sterling was overvalued by as much as 20 per cent. The difficulty with these calculations, however, is that they are based on weighting the composite of other currencies (and hence relative price changes since 1913) against the pound sterling according to the shares of their respective countries in international trade. Whilst these estimates provide a measure of the price disadvantage that *might* have been suffered by British exporters in world markets, they do not reflect the *actual* distribution of British trade.[40]

The matter of the effective rate is clearly related to the second condition, which concerns the assumptions that can be made about the price elasticity of demand for British goods. The usual device is to apply retrospective measures, adjusted for specified contemporary conditions. This procedure is unconvincing when set against the evidence.[41] There was a shift downwards in world demand for staples because of changes in technology. The shifts from coal to oil and from natural fibres to synthetics, are major examples of this process. In the British case the shift in demand was further propelled by a shift in comparative advantage in such industries to lower-cost foreign producers. Cotton textiles, which

40. *Cf.* N. H. Dimsdale, 'British Monetary Policy and the Exchange Rate 1920–38', *Oxford Economic Papers*, 33 Supplement (1981), pp. 306–49 and J. Redmond, 'The Sterling Overvaluation in 1925: A Multilateral Approach', *Economic History Review*, 33 (1980), pp. 83–91.

41. D. E. Moggridge, *The Return to Gold 1925* (Cambridge, 1969), pp. 69–79 and *idem.*, *British Monetary Policy 1924–1931: The Norman Conquest of $4.86* (Cambridge, 1972), pp. 245–50, where Moggridge calculates that a 10 per cent devaluation would have improved the balance of payments on current account by £70m. and lowered unemployment by 729,000 by 1928. The assumptions underlying these calculations have been criticized by B. W. E. Alford, *Depression and Recovery? British Economic Growth 1918–1939* (1972), pp. 35–6 who argues that price-elasticity data based on long time series do not reflect the market conditions facing the staple trades in the 1920s. Dimsdale, 'British Monetary Policy', p. 322 uses a lower price-elasticity of demand and estimates that unemployment would have fallen by just 450,000 over four or five years, assuming that wages did not rise in response to increased prices of imports. Similar difficulties apply to L. S. Presnell, '1925: The Burden of Sterling', *Economic History Review*, 31 (1978), pp. 67–88, who suggests that the sterling area might have benefited from a 10 per cent devaluation, but his final judgement is highly conditional. My argument is much in line with that originally put forward by R. S. Sayers, 'The Return to Gold, 1925', in S. Pollard (ed.), *The Gold Standard and Employment Policies Between the Wars* (1970), pp. 85–98.

accounted for 26 per cent of British exports was the prime example. In order to compete with Japanese and Indian producers, Lancashire firms needed far more than an adjustment of the exchange rate could provide, notwithstanding the large share of trade conducted within the sterling area. Even in those industries which remained vital to Britain's economic progress, the remedy to the lack of price competitiveness lay not in the manipulation of the exchange rate but in substantial and long overdue improvements in productivity which would have led to cost/price reductions.

Thirdly, the case for a lower parity tends to rest narrowly on the visible trade sector. Britain's overall current balance was positive in the 1920s, apart from the one year of 1926. A substantial balance of trade deficit was more than covered by invisible earnings, despite less favourable conditions in this sector, to which reference has been made. There is no strong evidence to suggest that demand for invisibles was significantly price-elastic, especially since the largest element of this sector was property income from abroad. The reasonable assumption would be, therefore, that a lower sterling rate would have reduced income from invisibles. More broadly, it is somewhat perverse to argue for a devaluation when the balance of payments was in overall surplus. The authorities had the power to regulate overseas investment during this period but it was used little and intermittently.[42]

Finally, UK exchange rate policy could not operate in isolation. The claims made for a 10 per cent devaluation on pre-war parities involves the large assumption that other countries would not have adjusted their rates accordingly. Yet this is precisely what happened, as has been noted. Moreover, there is clear contemporary evidence to the effect that this would have happened correspondingly if Britain had chosen a lower dollar parity.[43]

The case for the alleged advantages which would have resulted from a 10 per cent lower sterling/dollar exchange is thus not a convincing one. But this still leaves the issue of whether the effects of the deflationary policies which were adopted seriously damaged the capacity of the economy to adjust to changed international conditions. Was industry, as some contemporaries and modern historians have claimed, sacrificed on the altar of finance? The evidence suggests otherwise.

---

42. J. Atkin, 'Official Regulation of British Overseas Investment, 1914–31', *Economic History Review*, 23 (1970), pp. 324–35. See also A. T. K. Grant, *A Study of the Capital Market in Postwar Britain* (1937).

43. Sayers, 'The Return to Gold', pp. 321–4.

The financial authorities were faced with the serious problem of inflation at the end of the war. It was a problem of their own making as a result of resort to borrowing rather than to taxation in order to finance the war. But inflation continued after the war, rising to a peak in 1920. This boom in prices was associated with a shift in the distribution of income in favour of profits which, in turn, fuelled what was little less than an orgy of investment. But as has been shown, this investment went overwhelmingly into old technologies and working practices and much of it into traditional staple industries. It amounted to a major misallocation of resources when judged against the requirements of higher longer-term economic performance. By the same token, these investment decisions were proof positive that the war did little, if anything, to alter outdated business attitudes or the business organizations in which they were nurtured. Indeed, the outcome of the war might well have had the opposite effect of reinforcing commercial complacency. Yet, either way, this surely amounts to a damning indictment of British business and business- men. There is thus every reason to believe that under less deflationary conditions than were subsequently imposed, British industry would have done little to alter its accustomed practices. Correspondingly, it is wide of the mark to represent these events as evidence of the conscious triumph of 'gentlemanly capitalists' over the 'industrial elite'. In so far as these distinct interests can be identified, there is nothing to suggest that one was any less incompetent than the other.

Much has been made of the rights and wrongs of Britain's return to gold. But the importance of the decision should be measured in terms of what it symbolized rather than by indices of industrial output and unemployment. The return and the policies which led up to it had little fundamental economic effect. Part of what lay behind the event was the failure of industry and government to develop a new relationship to meet the changed needs of the world economy. In the broader context, whilst the dislocations resulting from the war were serious, they were so in the sense that they came on top of more fundamental and longer-term problems concerning the structure of world trade and finance. It is fanciful to claim that, however delicately, the gold standard had operated automatically before the war.[44] It has already been shown (Chapter 2) how the system was subject to substantial manipulation and adjustment. And so far as capital flows were concerned, it was not a case of the

44. *Cf.* D. H. Aldcroft, *From Versailles to Wall Street 1919–1929* (1987 edition), p. 46.

abnormal replacing the normal, but one of the degree of randomness in the system increasing as the distribution of global economic power shifted. The lack of political cooperation was a problem but to attach major importance to it is somewhat misplaced. Cooperation without much better understanding of the changing nature of the world economy could not have achieved a great deal. Seen in this light, Britain's failings were not all of its own making.

CHAPTER FIVE

Britain and the World Depression

OFF GOLD AND UNDER PROTECTION

In 1931 Britain left the gold standard and abandoned free trade, thereby renouncing the political economy that had guided previous generations. Whether the renunciation of practice extended to principle is a major question to be considered. But these events, together with the limited economic impact of the First World War, should warn against political and economic interpretations which treat the interwar years as a more or less self-contained period. It was not until the economic crisis of 1929–31 that Britain's secondary role in the world economy was clearly exposed.

The New York Stock Exchange crashed in October 1929, and whilst it was initially the collapse of a speculative domestic boom, it signalled and then interacted with critical conditions in the USA and the wider world economy.[1] The persistent dollar gap of the 1920s, together with the short-term nature of much of US foreign lending (a great deal of it made in connection with German reparations payments), led to a rapid withdrawal of American dollars from international finance that could only have the effect of precipitating severe exchange crises, since the dollar was the main pillar of the gold exchange standard.[2] Exchange crises were superimposed on a fall in international prices, especially of primary products. As primary producers struggled to maintain their incomes by increasing their exports, the fall in prices was transformed into a

1. An excellent analysis is C. P. Kindleberger, *The World in Depression 1929–1939* (1987 edition).
2. M. E. Falkus, 'United States Economic Policy and the "Dollar Gap" of the 1920s', *Economic History Review*, 24 (1971), pp. 599–623. The plain fact was that the USA needed to purchase very little on international markets whereas other countries needed to buy a great deal from the USA. Hence, there was a dollar shortage.

spiral; primary producer incomes continued to fall and this soon had effects on demand for industrial goods.[3]

At first, the British authorities prepared to weather the storm by raising the bank rate. For a while, this seemed to work and the inflow of short-term funds seeking refuge from New York even allowed the bank rate to fall. But then the currents of international instability returned and bore in on Britain and the other European economies with increasing and ultimately devastating force. Production in Britain fell away and unemployment began to rise sharply from its already high level: from 10.4 per cent (1.25 million) of the insured workforce in 1929 to 16.1 per cent (1.98 million) in 1930 and to 21.3 per cent (2.7 million) in 1931. It was to go even higher, to 22 per cent (2.8 million) in 1932. Gold began to trickle out from the Bank of England to support the pound, but this soon turned into a swelling flow. There was little cooperation between the major economies, and France and the USA in particular added to Britain's acute problems by actively adding to their gold reserves.[4]

Economic turmoil stimulated political turmoil and the fact of a Labour government in power served only to increase the sense of instability in the minds of international bankers and financiers. At the time of its election, however, the government had shown itself aware of the need to do something about the by then persistent problem of unemployment and declining trade. In November 1929 it had established the Macmillan Committee 'to enquire into banking, finance and credit, and to make recommendations calculated to enable these agencies to promote the development of trade and commerce and the employment of labour'.[5] The Committee included a galaxy of experts among whom were Keynes and Bevin, but their deliberations were overtaken by the pace of events in international finance when, in May 1931, the Austrian Kredit-Anstalt collapsed. This quickly had serious repercussions on the states of central and eastern Europe. Germany ran into acute problems which were transmitted to London in the form of

---

3. The outstanding analysis is I. Svennilson, *Growth and Stagnation in the European Economy* (Geneva, 1954). It sets the European experience in an international framework.

4. A. Cairncross and B. J. Eichengreen, *Sterling in Decline: The Devaluations of 1931, 1949 and 1967* (Oxford, 1983); S. Howson, *Domestic Monetary Management in Britain, 1919–38* (Cambridge, 1975). More generally see Kindleberger, *The World in Depression*.

5. *Report of the Committee on Finance and Industry*, Cmd. 3987, 1931, p. vi.

demands for funds to balance Germany's external liabilities. London simply did not possess the short-term credits required because of the decline of the volume of its claims on the rest of the world as a direct result of the large contraction in British trade. Hence the outflow of gold which, by early summer, was reaching unsustainable levels. The urgency was not lost on the government, and in March a Committee on National Expenditure (the May Committee) had been established with the clear remit to recommend 'all possible reductions in the National Expenditure on Supply Services'.[6]

It was something of an irony that the publication of the Macmillan Committee's report in July increased the pressures on sterling. The report presented a critical analysis of the operation of the banking and financial system and laid stress on the heavy and unsatisfactory reliance of London on short-term capital. Furthermore, certain of its members felt that the terms of reference they had been given were too narrow and did not allow for a full examination of the interrelationships between finance and industry. Their misgivings were expressed in a series of addenda which, taken together with the main report, conveyed a picture of serious weaknesses in the British economy that required urgent remedial action. For all this, the tone of the Macmillan report was mild compared with the polemical language of the May report which was published on the last day of July. It declaimed against wasteful public expenditure with a zealousness which would have done justice to a sixteenth-century tract against sin. Whether mistaken or maleficent, the report had an obvious effect on international financial confidence in Britain. Thus it was not until the government agreed to significant cuts in public expenditure along the lines recommended by the May report, that the Treasury was able to secure an international loan raised in Paris and New York. This proved too much for the Labour government to accept, and in August of 1931 it split and was replaced by the euphemistically named National Government.

The brave words of politicians in times of crisis are usually less credible than their normal utterances. And so it proved in 1931. The pound sterling was forced off the gold standard on 20 September. Financial fever quickly subsided and the dollar/sterling rate dropped from $4.86 to $3.40. Other countries quickly followed Britain's move and by the spring of 1932 the currency had

6. *Report of the Committee on National Expenditure*, Cmd. 3920, 1931, p. 5.

stabilized. Bank rate was falling rapidly from a high of 6 per cent in 1931 to a low of 2 per cent by June 1932. On the international front, Britain found itself in a world of currency regulation by multifarious means. Some major economies, including the USA, France and Germany, remained on gold – to form the so-called gold bloc – which gave Britain an export price advantage, but only for a short period since tariff protection was soon introduced by these countries.[7] Even so, by chance rather than by judgement, Britain, unlike the USA and major European economies, had extricated itself from the gold standard without suffering the collapse of its banking system.

In order to maintain the stability of the pound at its lower level, the Exchange Equalisation Account was set up in 1932. It was a fund of sterling and foreign exchange to be used to counteract short-term fluctuations in the exchange rate by means of purchases and sales of currency. During the 1930s it was never put under strain since London was a comparatively safe haven in an otherwise turbulent world.[8]

Table 5.1 UK balance of payments – current account, selected years 1925–39 (£M)

	Merchandise* exports	Merchandise imports	Visible balance	Invisible balance	Overall current balance
1925	943	1,208	−265	+317	+52
1932	425	641	−216	+165	−51
1937	614	950	−336	+289	−47
1930–39 (Annual average)	519	779	−260	+209	−51

* Includes re-exports

Source: Feinstein (1972), Table 15.

7. B. J. Eichengreen and J. Sachs, 'Exchange Rates and Economic Recovery in the 1930s', *Journal of Economic History*, 45 (1985), pp. 925–46 for an account of policies pursued by gold bloc countries.
8. S. Howson, *Sterling's Managed Float: The Operations of the Exchange Equalisation Account, 1932–9* (Princeton, N. J., 1980).

If anything, the operations of the Account contrived to hold the pound down below the longer-term market level, though from the evidence it seems unlikely that this had a significant effect on the balance of payments.

Protection was introduced as an emergency measure in 1931, to be followed by a full-blown tariff in February 1932, established under the Import Duties Act. A 10 per cent *ad valorem* duty was imposed on a wide range of goods, the major exceptions being leading foodstuffs and heavily used raw materials. And, for the time being, Empire goods were exempt. In addition, the Import Duties Advisory Committee was established to make recommendations for the extension of tariffs and alterations to rates, particularly in the light of evidence put forward by representatives of industry. This system led to substantial increases in rates and, for example, the duty on steel imports reached 33⅓ per cent. These were, however, nominal rates, whereas the actual impact of tariffs has to be gauged in terms of effective rates that measure the actual cost/price advantage or disadvantage to the domestic producer. Under a tariff regime, the production of a good can be subject to nominal tariffs directly on the value of its outputs and indirectly on the cost of its inputs that are purchased on the world market. The precise degree of protection afforded to an industry by tariffs depends, therefore, on two sets of variables: first, the relative nominal rates on inputs and outputs; secondly, the proportionate relationship between the cost of inputs and the net value added in manufacture. The effective rate is thus the weighted outcome of these variables and it can range from being much higher than the nominal rate to a negative value if the tariff on inputs is disproportionately high to that on output and especially if the cost of inputs forms a large share of the final price. Shipbuilding and the building industry were two industries that suffered negative protection in the 1930s, amounting to 6 per cent in the former and 7 per cent in the latter case. More typically, effective rates were double nominal rates.[9]

Detailed analysis has shown that tariffs had a minimal effect on industrial performance in the 1930s when judged in aggregate terms. Three qualifications must be made, however. First, the data on which these calculations are based are highly aggregated and thus could obscure the impact of tariffs on sectors within industry. Secondly, output was determined by a wide range of variables,

9. A full discussion and explanation of these technicalities is provided by F. Capie, *Depression and Protectionism. Britain Between the Wars* (1983).

Table 5.2 UK trade by volume, 1925–38 (1925 = 100)

	Total imports	*Re-exports*	*Net imports*	*Exports*
1925	100	100	100	100
1926	103	87	104	90
1927	106	91	108	103
1928	103	88	104	105
1929	109	85	111	108
1930	105	81	108	88
1931	108	77	111	68
1932	95	68	97	68
1933	95	64	98	68
1934	99	58	103	73
1935	100	66	103	78
1936	106	66	111	80
1937	113	68	118	87
1938	108	65	112	77

Source: Mitchell (1988), 519.

Table 5.3 World production and trade, 1926–38 (1926–30 = 100)

	Production		*Trade volume*	
	Manufactures	*Primaries*	*Manufactures*	*Primaries*
1926–30	100	100	100	100
1931–33	78	98	72	89
1934–35	94	102	74	93
1936–38	112	110	88	102

Source: Maizels (1963), 80.

whereas measures of the impact of the tariff rest on very crude estimates of correlations between a narrow range of variables. Thirdly, evidence from business history indicates that businessmen, in so far as they took account of tariffs in their investment decisions, were influenced by nominal rates. Quite apart from these considerations, however, modern trade theory shows that under a regime of floating exchange rates, the tendency is for the exchange rate to rise in response to protection, thus neutralizing the effect of a tariff. On the balance of evidence to date, and paying particular attention to the performance of British industry, there seems good reason to attach minor economic importance to tariff policy during this period.[10]

Empire trade was brought into the system following the Ottawa Conference on the summer of 1932. Whatever the reasons for the introduction of protection – which have yet to be considered – the negotiations with the Empire countries were seen by the British as an important means of drawing the Empire closer together into a defensive union within an unfriendly and turbulent world. Protection thus had a deeper meaning than trade policy in political vocabulary. At all events, British negotiators at Ottawa appear to have misjudged the strength of economic self-interest that existed among Empire countries, especially in Australia and Canada, which were keen to develop their own industrial sectors. In the case of Australia, for example, this threatened the multilateral settlement of Britain's accounts with Japan. The preferences granted by Britain to Empire countries were not effectively reciprocated and this laid the basis for continued wrangling throughout the 1930s, as the mists of imperial sentiment dissolved.[11]

Trade with the Empire grew during the 1930s, but this has to be seen in the broader context of an accelerating trend towards trade with the Empire in both imports and exports, beginning at the turn of the century.

In a major study of protectionism various factors – Empire sentiment, capital flows, sterling balances, exploitation, geography, income levels, the First World War – have been tested for their influence on this pattern of trade. All, with the exception of sterling

10. This is an issue that still generates controversy. The view above is broadly in line with F. Capie, 'Effective Protection and Economic Recovery in Britain, 1932–1937', *Economic History Review*, 44 (1991), pp. 339–42. See also G. D. N. Worswick, 'The Sources of Recovery in the UK in the 1930s', *National Economic Review*, 110 (1984), pp. 85–93. The alternative view based on a range of statistical assumptions is argued by M. Kitson and S. Solomou, *Protectionism and Economic Revival: The British Inter-War Economy* (Cambridge, 1990) and M. Kitson, S. Solomou and M. Weale, 'Effective Protection and Economic Recovery in the United Kingdom During the 1930s', *Economic History Review*, 44 (1991), pp. 328–38.

11. Some idea of these attitudes may be gained from I. M. Drummond, *British Economic Policy and the Empire, 1919–39* (1972) and J. B. O'Brien, 'Australia-British Relations During the 1930s', *Historical Studies*, 22 (1987), pp. 569–86.

Table 5.4 Direction of UK trade, 1920–38 (Annual averages – % shares)

		1920–29	*1930–38*
Foreign:	Imports	76.0	64.0
	Exports	65.0	54.0
	Exports & re-exports	69.0	57.0
Empire:	Imports	24.0	36.0
	Exports	35.0	47.0
	Exports & re-exports	31.0	43.0

Source: Capie (1983), 19.

balances, have been found to be of little importance.[12] As for sterling, throughout the period it provided exchange stability, and probably a measure of price stability, in trading relationships. It is likely, moreover, that the importance of these elements increased during the 1930s. The dominant influence, however, was the dependence of the British staple export industries on demand from primary producers, of which the Empire countries formed a significant part.

POLITICAL ECONOMY IN THE DEPRESSION

Devaluation and protectionism marked the end of *laissez-faire*, though the extent to which these actions were matched by firm commitment is far less clear. Yet a critical change was that, whereas in 1925 Britain could be seen as taking the lead in establishing the gold exchange standard, during the years of international crisis from 1929 to 1933 Britain was driven to respond to circumstances beyond its control. At times Britain was reduced to client status in international finance, as when the Bank of England petitioned for loans to bolster the pound sterling. The weakness was there from the start, of course. The gold exchange standard was highly vulnerable to short-term capital movements ('hot money') since exchange rates were backed by reserves, not just of gold, but of claims on major currencies, predominantly dollars and sterling. In

12. Capie, *Depression and Protectionism.*

itself, this was not a problem, provided the availability of these currencies matched the liquidity needs of international transactions. The flaw was that they did not.

British trade was declining both as a proportion of world trade and in absolute terms. Balance of payments surpluses shrank in proportion, with the obvious effect on the availability of sterling. The USA, by contrast, was generating large and increasing surpluses on its trading accounts, because of the heavy world demand for its goods combined with its own near self-sufficiency. These two elements led to a growing dollar gap as countries could not generate through trade the currency needed to purchase goods from the United States. For a while the system was relieved by the provision of short-term finance by the USA, mainly to finance German reparations payments. But these loans were made through the private banking system and within a context in which external transactions accounted for no more than 5 per cent of US gross national product as compared with a dependency of approximately 30 per cent in the case of the UK. In other words, official US commitment to international finance was of a tenuous and unreliable nature, yet the scale of US operations was of enormous importance to the rest of the world. The withdrawal of US funds from Europe from 1928 onwards made this fact painfully obvious.[13] The strong self-interested nature of French financial policy, measured by the determination of the Bank of France to accumulate as large a stock of gold as possible, made matters worse. As for Germany, it posed a perennial problem of financial instability, confirming Keynes's dire predictions of the consequences of the allies demanding massive reparations; and the Reichsbank followed French fashion of changing as large a proportion as possible of its exchange reserves into gold.[14]

13. The relative importance of domestic as opposed to external elements in the German depression is a subject of debate but this has not undermined the importance of the withdrawal of US loans. See M. E. Falkus, 'The German Business Cycle in the 1920s', *Economic History Review*, 28 (1975), pp. 451–65; P. Temin, 'The Beginning of the Depression in Germany', *Economic History Review*, 24 (1971), pp. 240–8; T. Balderston, 'The Beginning of the Depression in Germany, 1927–30. Investment and the Capital Market', *Economic History Review*, 36 (1983), pp. 395–415. For a detailed study of the German economy see H. James, *The German Slump* (Oxford, 1986).

14. A useful summary of events is provided by D. H. Aldcroft, *From Versailles to Wall Street 1919–1929* (1987 edition), pp. 168 *ff.* See also B. Eichengreen, 'The Bank of France and the Sterilization of Gold, 1926–32', *Explorations in Economic History*, 23 (1986), pp. 53–84.

The upshot was that the distribution of world holdings of gold changed markedly. The US stock increased from just over 25 per cent to approximately 40 per cent of the world's total between 1913 and 1929, France held just short of 20 per cent by the latter date, whilst Britain's share was a mere 7 per cent. Contemporaries expressed concern about the adequacy of the world's supply of gold, the production of which fell somewhat over the 1920s. This concern has been echoed by others subsequently. However, this reduction was easily compensated for by the fact that the proportion of gold stocks held by central monetary authorities increased rapidly, at the expense of private holders, to a level of 92 per cent of world stocks as compared with 50 per cent in 1913. The real problem was not the total amount of gold but its distribution and the substantial quantities held in an ultra-precautionary way, in particular by the US and French monetary authorities.

For all the technicalities of the gold exchange standard, the crisis in international finance was the basic one of liquidity. However such a system is organized, it depends on the existence of an institutional arrangement, formal or informal, that will act as lender in the last resort. Before 1913, this role had been performed by Britain through the Bank of England though, as has been shown, it depended increasingly on the support of other central banks. The restoration of 1925 could only have worked over the longer run if the US had succeeded to Britain's earlier role. Self-interest had to be supplanted by a political will which placed international interests, under US leadership, ahead of immediate national concerns. In the circumstances of the time, the reasons why the US did not meet this need are understandable. But, historically, what is of importance is that, whoever was at fault, the 1929–31 crisis arose from a breakdown of international political cooperation and was not simply a malfunctioning of the market requiring a technical solution. At the same time, the achievement of cooperation and the removal of the fetters of the gold standard could not, by themselves, restore prosperity. International economic relations were interlinked with domestic economic conditions that varied widely between the major economies which, in turn, were subject to similarly divergent regimes of political economy. In the case of Britain, release from the gold standard played a part in stimulating an upturn from the depression through permitting lower interest rates and an easy money policy. Whether it promoted economic recovery is quite another matter, as will be considered shortly. Failure to see events in this light can lead to historical misinterpretations which match the myopia of contemporary policy-makers.[15]

The 1931 crisis was a classic case of the ability of markets to clear – at a price. More accurately, it imposed a huge cost on countries as measured by the high levels of unemployment. The authorities in Britain, however, regarded leaving the gold standard as the result of a technical failure in the sense that the natural market forces had not been allowed to operate free of national interest. Thus the governor of the Bank of England, Montagu Norman, could reconcile the fall in the pound sterling to $3.40 in terms of the wilful (and unnatural) undervaluations of other major currencies by foreign monetary authorities when they returned to the gold exchange standard from 1925 onwards.[16] Moreover, the speed with which sterling stabilized at the lower rate was taken as powerful confirmation of the operation of the natural forces of the market. Hence, the broader question arises: what was the nature of Britain's response to the world depression in relation to how it saw its place in the world economy? In order to attempt to answer this question, it is necessary to examine British economic policy at both the international and domestic level in a little more detail.

There has been a great deal of debate on this issue which has been strongly conditioned by two alternative frameworks of analysis.[17] The first approach may be broadly defined as Keynesian.

15. *Cf.* B. Eichengreen, *Golden Fetters: The Gold Standard and the Great Depression, 1919–1939* (New York, 1992) and *idem.*, 'The Origins and Nature of the Great Slump Revisited', *Economic History Review*, 45 (1992), pp. 213–39. Whilst Eichengreen provides a convincing analysis of the operations and failings of the gold standard, his explanation of so-called economic recovery in the 1930s fails to carry conviction because it is too generalized. His emphasis on the effects of US policy is truly counter-factual when measured against the levels of economic development of the other major economies in the 1930s and the historical reality of the differing political economies of the period. In short, domestic politics were the outcome of much more than international economic conditions. A useful collection of brief surveys of individual countries and guide to the literature is W. R. Garside (ed.), *Capitalism in Crisis. International Responses to the Great Depression* (1933). For monetary policy see E. Nevin, *The Mechanism of Cheap Money* (Cardiff, 1955) and S. Howson, 'Cheap Money and Debt Management in Britain, 1932–51', in P. L. Cottrell and D. E. Moggridge (eds), *Money and Power* (1988), pp. 227–89.

16. Norman expressed these views in evidence before the Macmillan Committee and was coldly disdainful of alternative suggestions put to him under cross-examination from Maynard Keynes and Ernest Bevin. For a detailed biography of Norman see H. Clay, *Lord Norman* (1957).

17. A useful survey is provided by A. Booth, 'Britain in the 1930s: A Managed Economy', *Economic History Review*, 40 (1987), pp. 499–522. This provoked some exchanges which perhaps have produced a little more heat than light but, together,

It incorporates powerful elements of hindsight to the point where economic policy in the 1930s is interpreted as leading ultimately (in a teleological sense) to the eventual triumph of Keynesianism in the post-1945 period. Variations on this approach range, on the one hand, from characterizing policies of the 1930s as a series of *ad hoc* but conditioned responses to economic problems to, on the other hand, a process of incipient Keynesianism, especially as it incorporated actions to deal with unemployment through state intervention and through a greater willingness to place domestic economic needs ahead of external considerations.

This approach can be squared with the growth of economic nationalism, particularly when the range of policy is extended to include tariffs and imperial preference. Likewise, regional policy in the form of a Special Areas Act (1934), which attempted to revive declining staple industries and reduce high levels of unemployment, can be represented as a recognition that markets (and more generally the capitalist system) must be managed if industry is to adjust successfully to changed economic circumstances, particularly if these emanate from international competition. In combination with this approach, more or less weight is given to the persistence of orthodox beliefs in balanced budgets, economic liberalism and internationalism. The greater the weight, the greater the emphasis on the *ad hoc* nature of the advance towards the nirvana of Keynesianism.

The second approach operates within the contemporary framework of neo-classical economics. Mainly, it attempts to explain policy in terms of the reaction to circumstances which (at least temporarily) so openly and directly challenged the prevailing view of how the economic world operated. No more clearly was this challenge presented than by the continuing high levels of unemployment which were stubbornly resistant to market adjustment. The focus of this analysis is on those elements which were at the centre of neo-classical economics, namely, profits, rents,

---

these contributions cover the literature. See R. Middleton, 'Britain in the 1930s: A Managed Economy?', *Economic History Review*, 42 (1989), pp. 544–7; G. Peden, 'Britain in the 1930s, A Managed Economy?', *Economic History Review*, 42 (1989), pp. 538–43; A. Booth, 'Britain in the 1930s: A Managed Economy? A Reply to Peden and Middleton', *Economic History Review*, 42 (1989), pp. 89–94. Important studies of the period are R. Middleton, *Towards the Managed Economy: Keynes, the Treasury and the Fiscal Debate of the 1930s* (1985) and D. Winch, *Economics and Policy: A Historical Study* (1969).

wages and, above all, prices. The direct link with the international economy is made through the exchange rate. The official British response to the consequences of the world economic crisis, it is claimed, was one of aiming to restore the market system to full vitality. The method was to raise wholesale prices through the depreciation of the exchange rate. It was hoped that, in turn, this would raise retail prices, and that profits would be increased as a consequence of wages showing a similar measure of rigidity in the upswing as they had done in the downswing during the 1920s and early 1930s. Raising prices was seen by Treasury officials as part of an international need though, in fact, it failed to achieve the necessary international cooperation. The tariff is fitted into the scheme of things as the means for protecting the balance of payments under conditions of a floating exchange rate, though the fallacy in this analysis has already been noted.

In the case of industrial policy, unlike the Keynesian approach, the emphasis is less on the statutory provisions for regional economic development and much more on the facilitative nature of policy. Stress is laid on the support given to rationalization programmes in coal, cotton, shipping and steel, and how it was provided either formally, as in the case of the Coal Mines Act (1930) or, more frequently, indirectly through contacts with industry or by using the clearing banks and the Bank of England as 'proxy rationalizers'. The aim of this industrial diplomacy, as it has been described, was that of raising profits and prices and improving market efficiency, and similar principles guided the deliberations of the Import Duties Advisory Committee. As with the Keynesian approach, the strength of this interpretation varies according to the consistency claimed for policy objectives, but the crucial difference is that it stresses the evolution of contemporary orthodox ideas on their own terms and not in relation to an emerging heterodoxy.

These two approaches are seen by their proponents to be in sharp conflict. Yet this is a false opposition which stems from the common, implicit assumption that policy responses are necessarily coherent. There were diverse views and influences at work. In so far as something called Keynesianism informed economic policy after the Second World War, it is unconvincing to claim that it followed directly from policy decisions in the 1930s. The eclecticism of policy in the 1930s is exemplified by the fact that evidence can be found to support either approach. It is revealing that a great deal of discussion and analysis in the Macmillan Report centred on the need to raise prices, and Keynes was a major contributor to those recommendations. Keynes's opinions on the subject subsequently changed as his analysis of the economy shifted from monetary to real factors. Officials in the Treasury and the Bank of England changed their views much less. Yet the greater consistency of the latter implies nothing directly about the coherence of the theory which underlay their opinions. Indeed, ideas of stimulating price rises hardly sit well with the theory of competitive markets.

Officials might have supported the imposition of tariffs as a device to protect the external balance, given the floating exchange rate. The contemporary theoretical debate in support of the policy was weak, however; and, as has been noted, subsequent analysis has shown that the tariff had minimal economic impact. But the overwhelming evidence is that the tariff was introduced and extended for political reasons.[18] Pressures from commercial interests had built up steadily during the 1920s. During the same period there were political realignments which eventually led to a clear majority in parliament for tariff protection. There was a perceived need to defend British interests in a world in which other countries were not playing according to the rules of the game, and these interests were naturally defined to include the Empire.

Industrial policy in the form of rationalization was a crude mixture of vested interests – mainly those of the clearing banks and dynastic family firms in the staple industries – and notions of efficiency.[19] The outcome was the creation of a number of conglomerate, oligopolistic business organizations whose market operations hardly squared with ideas of free competition; and they certainly did not become models of business efficiency. Industrial policy in the guise of regional policy was a weak affair in which government officials based in London had little understanding of the realities of industrial decline and regional decay. Industrial self-help was the guiding principle. By comparison, the Industrial Transference Scheme, established in 1929 but effectively abandoned in 1931, contained some understanding of the crucial links between regional policy, industrial structure and labour

18. T. Rooth, *British Protectionism and the International Economy: Overseas Commercial Policy in the 1930s* (Cambridge, 1992). See also a detailed analysis in terms of commercial diplomacy in respect of two major industries, steel and cotton, in C. Wurm, *Business, Politics and International Relations. Steel, Cotton and International Cartels in British Politics 1924–1929* (Cambridge, 1993).

19. B. W. E. Alford, 'New Industries For Old? British Industry Between the Wars', in R. Floud and D. McCloskey, *The Economic History of Britain Since 1700. Volume 2: 1860 to the 1970s* (Cambridge, 1981 edition), pp. 309–31.

mobility. But the resources and administrative competence it required were not forthcoming.

The policy response to the international economic crisis was neither a case of *ad hoc* decisions nor of consistency, but one of eclecticism constrained by two basic beliefs. First, it was taken as axiomatic that the primary economic role of the government should be to exercise control over public expenditure, both in the sense that expenditure should be properly accounted for and that it should be kept to a minimum. The minimum was not defined in precise terms but it implied a limited role for the state in economic affairs. How could it be otherwise, with the Treasury in control of economic policy? And the growth in the power of the Treasury was one of the most significant developments in the period. Moreover, limiting public expenditure was believed to be an essential part of maintaining the external balance, though this consideration did not figure prominently in contemporary arguments because, for the most part, the external position was not under pressure. Even so, it was with an eye to external relations that on occasions the Treasury adopted the technique of 'window dressing' in its annual budget accounts.[20] During the 1930s, this belief in financial orthodoxy was not so much challenged as that concessions had to be made around it as a result of the sheer practicalities of dealing with unemployment. But there is no evidence that such concessions were seen as other than temporary, an attitude exemplified by the initial Treasury resistance to increased expenditure on armaments which could not be compensated for by savings elsewhere. It was only when the threat of German militarism was fully recognized that the necessary concessions were made.[21]

Adherence to a cautious financial orthodoxy at home contrasted with a grandiose view of Britain's role in world affairs, which constituted the second basic belief underlying policy.[22] Paradoxically, the failures of 1931, after the initial shock, served to reinforce this delusion. One way this has been represented is as the persistence of a deeply entrenched belief in liberalism and

---

20. A technique whereby deficits could be concealed. For example, between 1932 and 1936 payments to the sinking fund to pay off the national debt were dropped from the annual accounts; see Middleton, *Towards the Managed Economy*, pp. 80–3, 115.

21. G. C. Peden, *British Rearmament and the Treasury, 1932–1939* (Edinburgh, 1979).

22. R. W. D. Boyce, *British Capitalism at the Crossroads, 1919–1932: A Study in Politics, Economics and International Relations* (Cambridge, 1987).

internationalism. But these principles have always incorporated a strong sense of national superiority.[23] The upsurge of economic imperialism after 1931 represented a change only in the sense that it was a redefinition of Britain's world role, more specifically, as the head of an empire. It was a view of Britain's position in the world as through a looking glass.

TRADE AND INDUSTRY

In comparative international terms, the depression in Britain was marked by its mildness. Whereas the main indicators of economic activity in the major economies dropped sharply, the decline in Britain was but a further downturn on an established downward trend.

Table 5.5 UK comparative GDP per head, selected years 1913–37 (1913 = 100)

	1913	1929	1932	1937
UK*	100	105	98	119
France	100	130	109	124
Germany*	100	113	94	163
Italy*	100	115	110	124
Japan	100	146	141	167
USA	100	133	91	121

* Adjustment for boundary changes.

Sources: Feinstein (1972), Table 55; Maddison (1991), 204, 212–15, 220, 232–5.

And British trade had been declining absolutely for some time (Tables 4.1 and 5.2). By contrast, for example, Germany experienced the cataclysm of military defeat and hyperinflation from which it never fully recovered during the 1920s.[24] The shock

---

23. *Cf.* the somewhat simplistic view advanced by R. Skidelsky, 'The Reception of the Keynesian Revolution', in M. Keynes (ed.), *Essays on John Maynard Keynes* (Cambridge, 1975), pp. 89–107.

24. James, *The German Slump.*

of economic collapse in the USA was cataclysmic, too, since it shattered the myth of the land of opportunity and of the continuously self-regulating and expanding economy.[25] It must be borne in mind, however, that contemporaries had very limited statistical measures of relative economic performance. Nevertheless, the rising economic power of other nations, especially that of Germany, had clearly been recognized as a matter of concern in Britain for some time, and the severity of their subsequent economic problems gave rise to an attitude of *Schadenfreude* that provided a kind of vicarious reassurance that, after all, the British economy had proved to be more stable and durable than its major rivals. But even under these conditions Britain's position in world trade continued to slide.

Table 5.6 UK comparative trade shares, 1929 and 1937 (% world total)

| | Exports of manufactures | | Exports of capital goods | |
	1929	1937	1929	1937
United Kingdom	22.4	20.9	17.4	16.4
United States	20.4	19.2	36.1	40.3
Germany	20.5	21.8	19.7	17.9
France	10.9	5.8)		
Japan	3.9	6.9)		
Belgium-Luxembourg	5.4	6.6)		
Canada	3.5	4.8)	26.8	25.4
Netherlands	2.5	3.0)		
Italy	3.7	3.5)		
Others	6.8	7.5)		
Total	100.0	100.0	100.0	100.0

Source: Maizels (1963), 189, 279.

As to the broader picture of economic and social change, some historians claim that during the 1930s there were important developments in state provision of welfare benefits, reflecting the

25. An excellent short account is J. Potter, *The American Economy Between the Wars* (1974). A good basic text is P. Fearon, *War, Prosperity and Depression. The US Economy 1917–45* (Oxford, 1987).

emergence of new principles of social policy which expanded to form the basis of post-Second World War welfare state.[26] Yet to the extent that there were changes, they did not involve significant costs or anything that could be described as radical institutional reform. To the contrary, the stress on the need for economic stability and orthodoxy enormously strengthened the traditional institutions of government, especially the Treasury. And, somewhat ironically, social pressures were eased by the favourable movement in the terms of trade. Despite Britain's poor export performance, the price of imported foodstuffs, in particular, fell dramatically, with a consequent effect on real incomes for the mass of the people. Agricultural depression, which was such a major destabilizing force in many countries, had only a weak effect in Britain because of the contraction in the industry that had occurred much earlier as part of the process of the development of an export economy. By 1930, only 6 per cent of the labour force was employed in agriculture in Britain, compared with 29 per cent in Germany, 36 per cent in France and 22 per cent in the USA.

In this context, any kind of radical, alternative ideology had little appeal. When, later in the 1930s, a challenge to the existing orthodoxy came with the publication of Keynes's *General Theory of Employment, Interest and Money* (1936), it attacked the operation of liberal, market capitalism but not the system itself. The message was that capitalism could be managed. For all its intellectual originality, moreover, Keynes's theory had one major thing in common with policies adopted by other nations: like charity, the solution was seen to lie at home. Accordingly, for Keynes, international economic relations would more or less look after themselves if domestic affairs were handled correctly:

> ... If nations can learn to provide themselves with full employment by
> their domestic policy ... there need be no important economic forces
> calculated to set the interest of one country against that of its
> neighbours. There would still be room for the international division of
> labour and for lending in appropriate conditions ... International trade
> would cease to be what it is, namely, a desperate expedient to maintain
> employment at home by forcing sales on foreign markets and
> restricting purchases which, if successful, will merely shift the problem
> of unemployment to the neighbour which is worsted in the struggle,

26. These issues are examined by R. Lowe, *Adjusting to Democracy. The Role of the Ministry of Labour in British Politics, 1916–1939* (Oxford, 1986).

but a willing and unimpeded exchange of goods and services in conditions of mutual advantage.[27]

The British response to the international crisis is not to be measured just in terms of official policy, however. Individual sectors of the economy were forced to react to the practicalities of changed circumstances. So far as the international financial and services sectors were concerned, the response was largely determined by exchange rate policy and through the influence which City interests exerted on the government. The problems of industry and, in particular, of the major staples, were of a different nature. Their importance in British trade is shown in Table 5.7.

Table 5.7 The major staple industries in UK export trade, selected years 1925–37 (% shares)

	1925	1929	1932	1937
Coal	7.0	7.0	9.0	8.0
Cotton textiles	26.0	19.0	17.0	13.0
Iron and steel	9.0	9.0	8.0	7.0
Total share of domestic exports	42.0	35.0	34.0	29.0

Source : Mitchell (1988), 453, 484.

These industries were particularly affected by import substitution, thus reflecting their basic nature.

The long-term decline of the staple industries, beginning in the late nineteenth century, is an issue which has been hotly debated, most often in terms of entrepreneurial performance (See Chapter 2). By the 1930s, however, conditions had become so acute that various forms of assistance to these industries were being provided

27. J. M. Keynes, *The General Theory of Employment Interest and Money* (1936), pp. 382–3. The literature on Keynes is vast to the extent that it has become an academic industry which has now surely run into rapidly decreasing returns to scale. A convenient short survey which contains an excellent biography is provided by G. C. Peden, *Keynes, the Treasury and British Economic Policy* (1988).

Table 5.8 UK loss of trade through import substitution and foreign competition, 1929–37

	% share of loss due to		
Import substitution		*Foreign competition*	
Industrial markets	36.0	Industrial markets	2.0
Semi-industrial markets	50.0	Semi-industrial markets	12.0
Total	86.0	Total	14.0

The figures are rounded.

Source: Maizels (1963), 228.

by the state and by financial institutions.[28] Firms sought refuge in the formation of combinations which then set about protecting themselves by means of price-fixing, market- and profit-sharing, and trade barriers. Many of these activities were pursued under the banner of rationalization: a vogue word that gave the impression of reform and efficiency, whereas, the reality of what was done in its name was very different. As the work of business historians has shown, business organization and industrial structure were not modernized in line with best practice, as defined in international terms. There were exceptions, of which ICI is the leading example. But even in this case, the introduction of new structures of organization and management was not thoroughgoing enough to overcome the separate (divisional) interests which stemmed directly from the original three companies from which ICI had been formed in 1926. For example, the power of the fertilizer division was such that it was able to commit the company to a huge and

28. A survey and analysis is provided by Alford, 'New Industries For Old?'. See also L. Hannah, *The Rise of the Corporate Economy* (1983), pp. 27–40. There are a number of individual studies but among the best are J. Bamberg, 'The Rationalization of the British Cotton Industry in the Inter-War Years', *Textile History*, 19 (1988), pp. 83–101; J. R. Hume and M. S. Moss, *Beardmore. The History of a Scottish Industrial Giant* (1979); E. Green and M. Moss, *A Business of National Importance. The Royal Mail Shipping Group, 1892–1937* (1982) – though in this case the authors tend to downplay the strength of the evidence they have amassed; M. W. Kirby, 'The Lancashire Cotton Industry in the Inter-War Years. A Study in Organisational Change', *Business History*, 16 (1974), pp. 145–59; P. Payne, *Colvilles and the Scottish Steel Industry* (Oxford, 1979); S. Tolliday, *Businessmen, Banking and Politics: The Case of British Steel, 1918–1939* (Cambridge, Mass., 1987). See also R. H. Campbell, *The Rise and Fall of Scottish Industry* (Edinburgh, 1980).

misplaced investment in this low-technology area that nearly brought the firm to its knees, with the consequence that exciting new developments in plastics were blocked until much later; by which time, the Americans, under the lead of Du Pont, had stolen the march.[29]

Studies in business history show, also, that successful modern organization did not require slavish adoption of what has been defined as US competitive managerial capitalism. Correspondingly, the definition of British business failure in terms of personal capitalism (the family firm) is similarly wide of the mark. Family firms performed successfully in a range of economies, including the USA, and alternative company forms, noticeably different from those in the USA, were well established and developing successfully to match modern needs, as German and Japanese evidence shows. Modernization consisted essentially of methods and practices operating in a variety of business organizations that facilitated adaptability and flexibility, attributes which were as much characteristic of the businessmen running them as they were of the organizations themselves.[30]

Adaptability in industry depended on more than industry itself. Attention has been drawn (Chapter 2) to the relationship between industry and the state. This involved both state intervention and wider provision of support, especially in the fields of education and training. The point to be made, however, is that there was little fundamental change in this relationship to meet changed needs during this period. Evidence of the backward state of affairs in education and training, for example, had been provided in plenty to the Balfour enquiry into industry and trade in the mid-1920s, but it led to little action.[31] There were, of course, some changes with the passage of time, but they did not squarely address the problem of the efficiency and competitiveness of British industry.[32]

One other response to the crisis must be examined, namely that of labour. If anything undermines a neo-classical analysis of the

29. W. J. Reader, *Imperial Chemical Industries. A History. Volume II. The First Quarter Century 1926–1952* (Oxford, 1975), pp. 98–115, 338–64.

30. For a useful survey see R. Church, 'The Family Firm in Industrial Capitalism: International Perspectives on Hypothesis and History', *Business History*, 35 (1993), pp. 17–43.

31. See Committee on Industry and Trade (Balfour Committee), *Factors on Industrial and Commercial Efficiency* (1927), pp. 135–264 and *Minutes of Evidence* Volume I (1930), Volumes II and III (1931).

32. H. F. Gospel (ed.), *Industrial Training and Technological Innovation: A Comparative Historical Study* (1991).

British economy during these years, it is the behaviour of the labour market. By all the rules, high and rising unemployment, deflation and orthodox policies should have led to falling wage rates and widespread reductions in real wages for those remaining in work. It did not happen. Not surprisingly, there have been attempts to rationalize this phenomenon in neo-classical terms, and the most controversial argument, based on aggregate economic data, has been that wage rates and labour immobility were underpinned by social welfare benefits which were 'too high' – the so-called replacement ratio.[33] For all its appeal in some quarters, this hypothesis has not stood up to critical and detailed analysis. The alleged effects of welfare payments are based on an excessively simplistic view of the labour market which, for example, takes no account of the displacement costs of labour mobility. One of the most obvious and heavy of such costs was the much higher levels of rents and house prices in the more prosperous regions of the country compared with the areas of high unemployment, differences which far outweighed any possible marginal reductions in welfare provisions. In addition, the regional nature of the labour market, linked to the geographical concentration of the massively depressed export industries, resulted in a level of structural unemployment which totally swamped any increase in the 'natural rate' caused by alleged generous welfare benefits.[34] But even these criticisms do not take account of the complexity of the labour market. Variations in labour practices, including short and part-time working, and occupations in both depressed and prosperous regions of the country in which casual unemployment was still the norm, meant that underemployment was still an important characteristic of the labour force, as it had been in Edwardian Britain. Significant numbers fell into these categories; they were

33. D. K. Benjamin and L. A. Kochin, 'Searching for An Explanation of Unemployment in Interwar Britain', *Journal of Political Economy*, 85 (1979), pp. 441–78.

34. M. Collins, 'Unemployment in Interwar Britain: Still Searching for an Explanation', *Journal of Political Economy*, 90 (1982), pp. 380–5; R. Cross, 'How Much Voluntary Unemployment in Interwar Britain?', *Journal of Political Economy*, 90 (1982), pp. 380–5; D. Metcalf, S. J. Nickell and N. Floros, 'Still Searching for an Explanation of Unemployment in Interwar Britain', *Journal of Political Economy*, 90 (1982), pp. 386–99; N. H. Dimsdale, S. J. Nickell and N. Horsewood, 'Real Wages and Unemployment in Britain During the 1930s', *Economic Journal*, 99 (1989), pp. 271–92. The analysis in S. R. Dennison, *The Location of Industry and The Depressed Areas* (Oxford, 1939) is still of major relevance.

unable to claim state benefits and thus were not even recorded in unemployment statistics.[35]

There were, however, major rigidities in the labour market as part of the nature of industrial decline. Added to which, trade union organizations simply did not disappear during the depression so that their bargaining strength in resisting wage cuts was removed. Union leaders did not feel inalienable obligation to those workers who simply left the union, whilst most of the workers who could no longer afford union dues because of unemployment showed little inclination to become blacklegs. For their part, employers showed little enthusiasm for breaking down existing working patterns. In coal mining, for example, the interests of coal owners and miners were fused in opposition to pit closures following the Coal Mines Act of 1931. Labour practices and union organization in newer sectors of industry, moreover, followed much along traditional lines, though their full effects did not show up until much later.[36] At all events, conservatism ruled in the boardroom as strongly as it did in the union lodge.

ECONOMIC RECOVERY?

An assessment of the effectiveness of the response of government or of individual sectors of the economy to the world depression must rest, in part, on an analysis of the causes of the crisis, though it is important to recognize that, as in other areas of human experience, the recognition of a cause of a problem does not necessarily point in a directly connected way to its solution. Economic problems, for example, may well require non-economic solutions (see Chapter 9). Moreover, any attempt to analyse the causes of the crisis immediately comes up against the problem that the result is determined by the theoretical assumptions that are made. This kind of problem exemplifies the fact that economic theory is a weak science, because in the real world the number of variable conditions is such that it is impossible to specify one set of assumptions with a high degree of confidence. Economic theory describes a number of possible worlds. There are, it can be suggested, five credible theoretical frameworks of analysis in this

35. N. Whiteside and J. A. Gillespie, 'Deconstructing Unemployment: Developments in Britain in the Interwar Years', *Economic History Review*, 44 (1991), pp. 665–82.
36. See below note 48.

case, and each gives rise to a distinct historical interpretation of the depression. The five can be described in turn as Marxist, monetarist, Keynesian, cyclical and structuralist. These can be applied separately to the international economy and to individual countries. But account has to be taken, also, of the interaction between international and national economic experiences. The main elements of these theories are as follows.

Marxist analysis emphasizes the crisis nature of capitalism. The depression is thus viewed as the inevitable outcome of declining rates of profit and the consequent increasingly monopolistic nature of the mode of production. The difficulty with this theory is that it is self-evident that whilst the depression was universal in its impact, individual economies were far from being at similar stages of capitalist development, as defined in Marxist terms. And if this was the ultimate crisis of capitalism, how is the subsequent recovery of capitalism to be explained? Marxist analysts are nothing if not resourceful, but their defence of doctrine in terms of the rescue of capitalism through a new form of imperialist exploitation (the development of underdevelopment) has failed to persuade non-believers, who explain the conditions that developed in Third World economies somewhat differently.[37]

The monetarist explanation emphasizes the critical need for a balanced relationship between the quantity of money available to finance demand and the capacity of the economy to produce a flow of goods and services. If the balance is allowed to get widely out of kilter, then inflation or deflation and economic crisis inevitably follow. The fundamental problem with monetarism is that of defining and measuring the quantity of money in an individual economy, and this becomes insuperable at the international level. Thus, 'the analysis is limited to a single country, without the mechanism by which financial crisis in one country is propagated to others without commodity prices, asset prices, capital flows or exchange rates'.[38]

37. See for example M. Dobb, *Political Economy and Capitalism* (1937). Underdevelopment theories are considered in Chapter 3.

38. Kindleberger, *The World in Depression*, p. 5. Kindleberger provides a succinct survey of theoretical approaches to the depression. In particular, he provides a convincing criticism of the main proponents of the monetarist explanation, M. Friedman and A. J. Schwartz, *A Monetary History of the United States, 1867–1960* (Princeton, 1963). See for example Kindleberger, *The World in Depression*, pp. 127–30 and *passim*. A more recent survey is provided by Eichengreen, 'The Origins and Nature of the Great Slump', but, to my mind, his conclusions are not convincing and do not supplant Kindleberger. See note 15.

Keynesian analysis at an international level is similarly constrained by the single fact that it is a closed theory (that is, it has no international sector) and because it is concerned only with short-term equilibrium. It requires an enormous and implausible stretch of analysis to claim that the length and depth of the depression at the international level during the 1930s was the result of a convergence of Keynesian-type downswings in economic activity in the wide range of national economies which made up the world economy.[39]

There are various forms of trade cycle theory, but the most comprehensive and theoretically elegant was that developed by Schumpeter in an attempt to explain what he observed contemporaneously.[40] However, whilst economies fluctuate, the available evidence cannot be made to show that they do so in a regular fashion according to fundamental and immutable laws of economic motion. The observed irregularity and unpredictability in economic activity are explained away by some theorists in terms of stochastic shocks, but this is no more nor less than a euphemism for events which are the stuff of historical reality. And, for example, a great deal of empirical investigation during the period following the end of the 'long boom' of 1950–73, based on far more detailed statistical data than are available for the inter-war years, has failed to establish the case for cyclical theory.

There remains the structuralist approach which, at the international level, is based on two hypotheses.[41] The first is that international economic activity depends on the efficient operation of international institutions, especially in international finance, which are the outcome of explicit or implied negotiations between nations. The second is that the process of economic development results in changes in international relationships which at intervals (usually quite long) create conditions that require reforms in the institutions and mechanisms which govern those relationships. In such circumstances, minor adjustments will no longer meet new needs. Thus the structuralist explanation of the depression is that

39. See for example P. Temin, *Did Monetary Forces Cause the Great Depression?* (New York, 1976); *idem.*, *Lessons From the Great Depression* (Cambridge, Mass., 1989).

40. J. A. Schumpeter, *Business Cycles: A Theoretical, Historical and Statistical Analysis of the Capitalist Process* (New York, 1939) is the classic study. See also A. Maddison, *Dynamic Forces in Capitalist Development. A Long-Run Comparative View* (Oxford, 1991), pp. 85–127.

41. Svennilson, *Growth and Stagnation*; Kindleberger, *The World in Depression*.

there was an institutional failure to provide a lender in the last resort to fill the role which Britain, through the Bank of England, had performed before 1914. The unwillingness of the USA to meet this need, and the inability of the major economies to achieve some alternative form of arrangement, caused the financial breakdown with the serious repercussions that have been described. Moreover, this failure was paralleled by a breakdown in trading patterns. Overproduction of food and primary goods was the symptom. Immediate relief was required through an internationally agreed mechanism for dealing with these so-called distress goods. The device would have cut off the downward and widening spiral of prices and incomes. Instead, multifarious forms of beggar-my-neighbour trade restrictions were practised. Yet the problem went deeper. Underlying the collapse in trade was the impact of technical change on manufacturing production, to which reference has already been made, and which resulted in net value added in manufacturing accounting for an increasing proportion of the value of output. This development had income effects that made it increasingly difficult for primary producers to maintain a balance of trade with industrialized economies. At the same time, no new workable and acceptable pattern of comparative advantage emerged in the trade between the major industrialized economies.

Whilst the structuralist analysis provides the most convincing explanation of the international collapse, it cannot stand alone. Questions of comparative advantage and the length as well as the depth of the depression point to the interaction of international and national conditions. At this level, it can be argued, there is a wider range of explanation. And whilst the focus here is on Britain, the wider literature reflects the differences between countries. Indeed, it was differences of economic structure interwoven with different forms of political economy that made international cooperation in the 1930s unattainable. Space does not permit comparative analysis. But, for example, there is considerable evidence to support the view that in the USA the uneven pattern of demand for consumer durables, combined with scarce consumer credit and weak banking practices, were powerful elements in the continuing depression.[42] There are strong indications, moreover, that the economy was Keynesian, in the sense that it would have responded to a vigorous fiscal policy of deficit finance. For the most

---

42. Eichengreen, 'The Origins and Nature of the Great Slump', pp. 214–16.

part, Roosevelt's New Deal was a period of balanced budgets.[43] When the Second World War came, the US economy demonstrated its responsiveness to massive increases in federal expenditure and economic activity expanded enormously.

The situation in Britain was very different. Nascent Keynesian policies appeared in the Liberal Yellow Book (1928)[44] and in the Mosley Memorandum (1929).[45] But they suffered early deaths. There remains the question, however, of whether Lloyd George could have done it: whether Keynesian deficit finance would have restored health and vigour to the economy. It is, of course, a counter-factual question, but one that is open to plausible testing. On conservative assumptions it can be shown that large budget deficits would have had but limited effects on employment levels, and that to restore the economy to anything approaching full employment would have required levels of public expenditure that reached into the realms of fantasy. One plausible estimate suggests that a fiscal stimulus equivalent to 15 per cent of GDP – which would have been enormous – would have been necessary to reduce unemployment to 3 per cent between 1932 and 1935. And the supply-side assumptions built into these calculations, in terms of the flexibility of factor and product markets, are of heroic standards.[46]

A Marxist interpretation of the domestic depression is open to the same kinds of objections as have been applied at the international level. British capitalism did not collapse, and after the Second World War it entered one of its most successful phases, judged against its previous record. Whether it still suffered from some kind of underlying state of crisis remains a question, however,

---

43. Fearon, *War, Prosperity and Depression. War, Prosperity and Depression*, pp. 230–4. It is necessary, also, to take account of state budgets, and this probably added a deflationary effect to the Federal budget.

44. *Britain's Industrial Future. Being the Report of the Liberal Industrial Inquiry* (1928). The committee which produced the report included Lloyd George, Maynard Keynes, B. S. Rowntree, Herbert Samuel and John Simon. It put forward a whole range of proposals and argued for substantial expenditure on public works. For the contrasting narrowness of the Treasury view at that time see P. J. Grigg, *Prejudice and Judgement* (1948). Sir James Grigg, as he was known, was in the Treasury from 1921 to 1930.

45. Mosley's proposals were secret because they were incorporated in a Cabinet document CAB 24/209, CP (25) 211, but the main points leaked out. They centred on increased state expenditure and direction of industry as remedies for unemployment. It is not difficult to see how they marked the beginnings of Mosley's lurch from socialism to fascism.

46. Middleton, *Towards a Managed Economy*, pp. 176–80; Peden, *Keynes, the Treasury and British Economic Policy*, pp. 27–33.

but one which, it will be argued shortly, is best answered in other than Marxist terms. So far as a cyclical explanation is concerned, this does not measure up to the pattern of events either, as will be seen.

The monetarist approach to British economic performance in the 1930s has attracted considerable support as part of an upsurge in the popularity of market, or new classical, economics following the demise of Keynesian economics in the stagflation of the early 1970s. The fact remains, however, that the 1930s was a period of cheap money whilst unemployment remained stubbornly high, aggregate growth rates were low and productivity growth was abysmal. Monetarists have countered these facts by stressing the imperfections in the labour market which can be measured in terms of own-product wages and replacement ratios. In other words, wages in particular industries were higher than was justified in relation to productivity and product prices in those industries; and the high level of social welfare benefits reduced mobility and competition in the labour market. But such claims are unconvincing as the primary cause of the persistence of the depression as against the evidence of persistently high rates of unemployment, which ranged way beyond what those market imperfections could possibly explain. The fallacies of the replacement ratio argument have been discussed above.[47]

More directly, the pattern, degree and persistence of unemployment in Britain strongly reflected the structural, supply-side nature of the depression. Whereas the US economy might be likened to a sound engine turning over well below its full power, the British economy, on the same analogy, was an engine in a very poor state of repair, and any attempt to increase the power would have soon led to overheating and even worse. Analogies can easily be misleading, of course, and to this one it might be objected that the economy did recover from 1934 onwards; and although there were still depressed areas, large parts of the economy showed ample signs of rising prosperity. Leafy suburbs in the Southeast, mock Tudor on the by-pass and the growing ubiquity of the motor car: what were these other than part of the new consumer age? Government policy, it can be claimed, assisted these developments.

47. A useful discussion of these issues from different viewpoints is Bank of England, Panel of Academic Consultants, *The UK Economy in the 1930s* (1984). A clear survey of the most recent literature is provided by T. Hatton, 'Unemployment and the Labour Market in Inter-war Britain', in R. Floud and D. McCloskey, *The Economic History of Britain since 1700. Volume 2: 1860–1939* (1994 edition), pp. 359–85.

Thus fiscal orthodoxy in the form of balanced budgets can be presented as being more than offset by the low interest rates of a cheap money policy made possible by careful monetary management.

If recovery is defined in terms of fluctuations in economic activity, there can be no doubt that there was a recovery up to 1937. From the low point of the depression in 1931–2 GDP grew at a rate just short of 4 per cent per year to 1937. The upswing then faltered before it was rescued by increasing expenditure on defence. If, however, recovery is defined as adjustment in the economy which substantially overcame the problems of low productivity growth and the switch of resources out of industries in which Britain could no longer retain comparative advantage consistent with rising levels of real income, there is no case for claiming that the period was one of economic success, especially when viewed in comparative terms.

Table 5.9 UK economic peformance compared with six other industrial countries, 1873–1937 (GDP per man year – annual average growth %)

	UK	US	Sweden	France	Germany	Italy	Japan
1873–1899	1.2	1.9	1.5	1.3	1.5	0.3	1.1
1899–1913	0.5	1.3	2.1	1.6	1.5	2.5	1.8
1913–1924	0.3	1.7	0.3	0.8	−0.9	−0.1	3.2
1924–1937	1.0	1.4	1.7	1.4	3.0	1.8	2.7

Excess over UK growth rate

	UK	US	Sweden	France	Germany	Italy	Japan
1873–1899	–	0.7	0.3	0.1	0.3	−0.9	−0.1
1899–1913	–	0.8	1.6	1.1	1.0	2.0	1.3
1913–1924	–	1.4	0.0	0.5	−1.2	−0.4	2.9
1924–1937	–	0.4	0.7	0.4	2.0	0.8	1.7

Source: Matthews, Feinstein and Odling-Smee (1982), 31.

The record of domestic investment performance provides further evidence of the limits to economic recovery.

Table 5.10 UK investment as a percentage of gross national product
selected years 1900–38 (Average annual rates, current prices)

	1900–09	1920–29	1930–38
Gross domestic capital formation			
(a) Dwellings	1.5	2.3	3.4
(b) Other	6.9	6.7	6.9
Net investment abroad	4.4	2.1	−0.6
Stock building	0.5	0.9	0.8
Total %	13.3	12.0	10.5

Source : Feinstein (1965), Table 3.21.

Even though the upturn in investment from the low point of the
depression was strong, the record for the 1930s as a whole was
dismal. The rate of increase in newer sectors of industry was
certainly comparatively high in relation to industry generally, but
the actual amounts were relatively small. The five industries
registering an increase in capital formation of more than 100 per
cent between 1920 and 1938 (motor vehicles, rayon and silk,
leather, rubber, paper and hardboard) still only accounted for 17
per cent of investment in manufacturing during the period.

The performance of the more buoyant sectors of the economy –
sometimes defined in terms of new industries – needs to be
interpreted with care, moreover. Investigation has shown that there
were tight limits to market opportunities for new consumer durable
goods, because of the stratified nature of market demand and the
restricted level of real incomes. In the case of motor cars, for
example, there was nothing approaching a mass market in the
1930s, a fact which modifies criticisms that have been made of
motor manufacturers, who persisted in supplying a wide range of
models in comparison with, for example, their counterparts in the
USA. This had corresponding effects on business structure and
organization.[48] All of this points to the fact that structural change in

48. S. Bowden and P. Turner, 'Some Cross-Section Evidence of the Determinants of
the Diffusion of Car Ownership in the Interwar UK Economy', *Business History*, 35
(1993), pp. 55–69. And on the organization of the industry see S. Tolliday,

the British economy was dependant on complex interrelationships between supply and demand and that these, in turn, were influenced by social and political, as well as economic factors, especially in relation to the distribution of income. But to the extent that these combined to reinforce ingrained behaviour and practices, it simply amounted to storing up more trouble for the future.

In sum, two things emerge from this analysis of the depression in the 1930s which were of critical importance to Britain's position in the world economy. First, explanations of domestic economic depression differ according to the nature of the economy concerned. Similarly, differences in political and institutional structures led to widely differing policy responses. The contrasts between Britain, the USA, Germany and Japan, for example, need no elaboration. The central point is that in these circumstances, international economic relations fell an easy victim to fierce national self-interest. This caused a disjunction in the international economy. What was needed to cross the divide was a new set of institutions that could take account of the competitive nature of economic development. The depression is testimony to the fact that markets do not adjust and equilibrate smoothly at full employment, according to the principles of neo-classical economics. Market adjustment is always a rough-and-ready process operating under conditions of imperfect knowledge. At times, the system jams in ways which require some form of centralized intervention even to the point of a complete reform of the system. The depression of the 1930s was an outstanding case of extreme need. In these circumstances Britain could be none other than a major victim because of its heavy dependence on the world economy.

The second thing the analysis reveals is that in order to sustain a major position in the world economy over the longer run, Britain could not simply rely on some form of international solution to its difficulties. Industrial weaknesses had to be overcome. More fundamentally, there was the problem of how dependent on external trade the economy should be. At the lower levels of world

---

'Management and Labour in Britain, 1896–1939', in S. Tolliday and J. Zeitlin (eds), *The Automobile Industry and Its Workers; Between Fordism and Flexibility* (Oxford, 1987), pp. 29 56 and *idem.*, 'The Feature of Mass Production Unionism in the Motor Industry, 1914–1939', in C. Wrigley, *A History of British Industrial Relations, Volume III, 1914–1937* (Brighton, 1987), pp. 298–322. For a comprehensive survey see R. Church, *The Rise and Decline of the British Motor Industry* (1994).

income prevailing in the nineteenth century, there was a large section of British industry – the staples – that thrived on the integration of domestic and foreign markets. Cheap textiles were much the same whether sold in Manchester or Madras. But the changed character of technology, involving more value added in manufacture, combined with higher and rising levels of income, correspondingly changed the markets which advanced economies needed to serve. Here again, there was a problem of discrete adjustment, such that large markets did not yet exist either at home or abroad for the new kinds of consumer and capital goods. The challenge to Britain was no less for all that. How could a medium-sized industrial economy adjust to match changed and changing circumstances?

The historian is blessed (or cursed) with the power of hindsight, though it frequently functions somewhat dimly. It is clear enough from the evidence which we have surveyed, however, that contemporary perception of Britain's economic problems and of its place in the world was very different from the one just defined. From 1933 onwards the government displayed a spirit of optimism, typified by Neville Chamberlain's statements to the nation made in popular appearances on cinema newsreels. The stockade of Empire gave reassurance as a defence against a threatening world, whilst at home traditional policies and institutions were seen as vindicated when set against the turmoil occurring in other major nations. Even Keynes offered a solution to mass unemployment which could be applied within the closed economy. It may well be the case, as some social historians claim, that there were radical developments in social welfare during the period. But the link between enhanced social provision and the need to reform the economy in order to support it, was not made. Social reformers were reacting to the symptoms of economic distress and failing to understand its causes. Those responsible for the economic health of the nation, whether as politicians or as businessmen, were no less deluded.

Viewed over the long run, 1937 and 1938 were more critical years for the British economy than 1931. There was plainly no sensible alternative to the abandonment of the gold standard. Britain was subject to the dictates of international finance. In late 1937, the economy once again began to turn down. The limits of recovery based on new consumer goods and on the building boom had been reached. The maintenance of even the modest growth which had been achieved in the preceding years depended on structural changes, involving difficult choices at various levels of the economy. But before such issues became imperative, conditions were transformed by the need to prepare for war. The return of an old enemy gave a new lease of life to traditional industries, and infused new confidence into traditional attitudes towards Britain's role in the world.

CHAPTER SIX

Britain, Europe and the New Postwar World Economic Order

1945 was a year of celebration for Britain; it also marked the beginning of a critical period in modern British economic history. The 'years of recovery' between 1945 and 1951 shaped the subsequent development of Britain in the world economy in the latter half of the twentieth century. It did not come as a surprise that there was a need for major postwar economic reconstruction at both the domestic and international levels or that it would require enormous effort; indeed, preparation for it had begun in official circles in late 1942.[1] But equally there was a widely shared belief that the success of the people's war should bring reward in terms of a fairer and more just society than had existed before the war. Whilst much had been destroyed, victory had ensured that much had been preserved that was available for 'fairer shares for all'. Seen in this way, the task of reconstruction would have to start from a position that provided the prospect of real gains for the mass of the population. If this was a delusion it was one affecting the better-off sections of society who were fearful of what the landslide Labour victory of 1945 would mean for them.[2]

THE COSTS OF WAR

What was the cost of the war to Britain? What did this cost amount to in its effect on Britain's international economic standing? These

---

1. B. W. E. Alford, R. Lowe and N. Rollings, *Economic Planning 1943–51. A Guide to Documents in the Public Record Office* (1992), pp. 22–5.
2. This attitude is reflected in R. Lewis and A. Maude, *The English Middle Classes* (1953 edition). This book was first published in 1949 and the cover of the Pelican edition in 1953 bore the statement: 'A critical survey of the history, present condition and prospects of the middle classes, from whom come most of the nation's brains, leadership and organizing ability.'

are questions that raise difficult conceptual and practical issues, as has been shown in our discussion of the First World War (Chapter 4). Those costs which are theoretically quantifiable are, nevertheless, often extremely difficult, and sometimes impossible, to measure in practice. Direct costs in the form of the allocation of resources for war purposes are reasonably clear, but the costs of destruction of physical and human capital are far from straightforward because of the difficulty of devising methods of valuation which take account of quality on the one hand and obsolescence on the other. Moreover, the destruction of some capital cannot be counted as a permanent loss since it would have been used to provide for consumption which was foregone anyway during the war. In addition, there is a whole range of indirect costs arising from the diversion of resources and dislocations in economic activity, both at home and abroad.

These costs may be defined as the first-round effects of the war. Much more intractable are the second-round effects, particularly since their impact on the economy may not be wholly negative. The question is whether war is good or bad for the economy in the longer run; and historical evidence suggests that there is no general rule for either victors or vanquished. Thus the widely accepted position is that the Napoleonic wars had only marginal effects on British economic growth during the early stages of industrialization, though the longer-term and non-quantifiable economic effects, in terms of institutional change, are far less clear.[3] By contrast, there is a currently fashionable view that for some major countries the Second World War proved to be a powerful element in what is defined as a process of catch-up and convergence, that was the driving force of their rapid economic growth in the quarter-century after 1945. According to this analysis, the impact of enormous losses of physical and human capital produced a reaction that overcame barriers to growth, many of which were of pre-war origin.[4] It will be necessary to examine whether this claim is borne out by the evidence, but, even so, it is worth adding that the capacity of industrialized economies to respond to extraordinary demands was demonstrated by the war effort. German production of armaments reached a peak in 1944–45, for example.[5] There was, therefore, an

---

3. P. Hudson, *The Industrial Revolution* (1992), pp. 58–61.
4. See below, Chapter 10.
5. M. Harrison, 'Resource Mobilization for World War II: the USA., UK, USSR, and Germany, 1938–1945', *Economic History Review*, 41 (1988), pp. 171–92.

important sense in which the war ended, not because of the total destruction of one side by the other, but because the allies were able to outperform the enemy in the supply of the resources for waging war. For all the belligerents, except the USA, it was an exhausting process because ultimately the huge productive effort that was generated did not translate into economic welfare. But these achievements demonstrated that the potential capacity for economic advance in peacetime was large, a fact that has perhaps not been sufficiently recognized.

There are some broad statistical measures of the direct costs to Britain of the war, which fall into two groups.[6] The first covers the financing of the war. The external cost of supplies and materials amounted to £10,000 million, financed by the sale of foreign assets (mainly in the USA) amounting to £1,000 million, by borrowing £3,500 million, mainly in sterling from poor countries within the Empire, by the receipt of lend-lease aid totalling £5,000 million from the USA and by direct aid from Canada of £500 million. The total was equivalent to two years' gross domestic product, on average, for the war years. Initially the lend-lease arrangements carried the obligation of eventual repayment though, in the event, only the comparatively small sum of $650 million (£162 million). was demanded and that on particularly favourable terms. Within the domestic economy the cost was borne mainly through reduced personal consumption. As a share of national income, personal consumption fell from approximately 80 per cent in 1938 to 57 per cent in 1944. This reduction was achieved by a sharp increase in direct taxation and by various means of enforced saving. In real terms the fall in consumption was less – to approximately 80 per cent of the 1938 level for most of the war – because of the growth of GDP. The pattern of growth was not even, however; GDP peaked in 1943 and then fell away to 1945 to just below its 1940 level, but it was still 16 per cent above the 1938 level. Moreover, during the war

---

6. I have drawn my information from a variety of sources in order to give a broad picture. A particularly useful survey of information is provided by S. Pollard, *The Development of the British Economy 1914–1980* (1983), pp. 192–234. A. K. Cairncross, *Years of Recovery. British Economic Policy 1945–51* (1985), pp. 3–46 provides a convenient overview of the financial aspects. Those seeking more detail will find M. M. Postan, *British War Production* (1952) and R. S. Sayers, *Financial Policy, 1939–1945* (1956) particularly useful. The major account of the war in this respect is W. K. Hancock and M. Gowing, *British War Economy* (1949). I have based more specific calculations on the relevant tables to be found in C. H. Feinstein, *Statistical Tables of National Income, Expenditure and Output of the United Kingdom, 1955–1965* (Cambridge, 1972).

there was, on average, a real fall in capital formation of 50 per cent on the 1938 level, which was already low even by British historical standards. As with personal consumption, however, this figure masks major redistributional effects. There was substantially increased investment in military establishments and armaments production, though this was more than compensated for by a heavy run-down in other forms of fixed capital, among which road and rail transport and domestic housing figured large. Finally, there was implied cost incurred through the contribution made by those women who surrendered their domestic role for wartime employment. These were distinct from female workers who were diverted from peacetime to wartime production. In addition, 400,000 workers gave up retirement and returned to work.

Taken together, these figures provide no more than broad indications of the direct costs of the war. They are both subject to overlap and omission. The fact remains, however, that for the first time in nearly 200 years Britain had become a major international debtor. By 1945 the stock of external debt amounted to £5,000 million, the equivalent to approximately half current gross national income. Even worse, the debt was rising at the rate of £1,200 million a year because of Britain's inability to match expenditures on imports of food and materials and on the maintenance of large overseas military operations with exports of goods and services. The volume of exports stood at 45 per cent of their 1938 level in 1945 and imports at 62 per cent (see Chapter 7). Import prices rose particularly strongly during the war, mainly because of the shortages and problems associated with wartime trade, but also because of a rise in the proportion of finished goods needed for the war effort. The gap was equivalent to 12 per cent of current national income.

The second group of costs covers physical loss and damage. Enemy bombing destroyed half a million houses and seriously damaged 4 million more. Further destruction was sustained by factory and commercial buildings. These losses amounted to a substantial charge against gross capital investment in addition to the unusually heavy rundown in capital stock during the war. At sea, half the nation's merchant marine was sunk and, combined with the sale of overseas assets, this resulted in a significant fall in foreign income.

The severe damage done to Britain's international economic position was plain and at the forefront of the minds of policy-makers. Most critical was the enormous gap that now existed between Britain and the USA though, as Table 6.1 shows, the UK still appeared to be well placed in relation to the other European economies, and Japan seemed to be well and truly vanquished.

Table 6.1 UK comparative international position, selected years 1937–50

(a) GDP per worker (UK = 100)

	1938	*1948*
United Kingdom	100	100
Denmark	86	84
France	64	62
Germany	74	52
Italy	64	57
Japan	49	28
Sweden	74	86
United States	135	172

(b) % share of world exports of manufactures

	1937	*1950*
United Kingdom	20.9	24.6
France	5.8	9.6
Germany[*]	16.5	7.0
Italy	3.5	3.6
Japan	6.9	3.4
Sweden	2.6	2.8
United States	19.2	26.6

* 1950 area of West Germany

Sources: (a) Feinstein (1990b), 286. (b) Maizels (1963), 189.

But did these relative positions amount to Britain gaining some kind of comparative advantage in the pursuit of postwar economic recovery? If so, how effectively was it exploited? If not, what was the reality which lay behind the appearance?

The harsh nature of economic conditions in Britain in the immediate postwar years is well chronicled, though perhaps the emphasis has been too much in the direction of allowing the facts to speak for themselves. Whilst Britain experienced many problems in common with other major economies, it faced others of a more exceptional kind which were to have a decisive bearing on its longer-term position in the world economy. In an attempt to answer the questions posed, in the remainder of this chapter and the following one, it is necessary to begin by examining the interrelationships between immediate needs, economic policy and economic potential.

POSTWAR ECONOMY

A recurrent and heavy charge was placed on Britain through the accumulation of war debts, the full implications of which will be considered later. However, the massive diversion of domestic resources to the war effort amounted to far more, in terms of what was lost to peacetime use, than the accumulated foreign debt. In one sense, of course, this sacrifice produced an enormous welfare benefit to the nation through the defeat of fascism. And the cost can be viewed as past and paid-for. But this still leaves the issue of whether, in meeting war needs, the structure and nature of the economy was affected in ways that had a more lasting impact on Britain's capacity to respond to the economic challenges of the postwar world.

A major contrast between the First and Second World Wars was that in 1945, unlike in 1918, the government did not face a potentially explosive credit boom. Between 1939 and 1945 war finance had been constructed on the basis of increased taxation and careful recourse to borrowing, some of it enforced on the population through a system of deferred savings. The success of these policies was such that the Second World War has been dubbed the 3 per cent war. Even so, the record of the post-1918 period exercised a strong influence on official minds during the war, and by its end there was a widely shared view in government circles that the danger to the peacetime economy was a short period of rapid inflation followed by a prolonged deflation and rising unemployment.[7] The initial price instability, it was thought, would result from pent-up war demand that would be released by

7. A detailed account of these attitudes is to be found in A. Chester, 'Planning, The Labour Governments and British Economic Policy 1945–51', unpublished Ph.D. thesis, University of Bristol, 1983.

the easing of rationing and the freeing of some wartime savings but that this would soon be swamped by postwar dislocation leading to contraction and deflation. In the event, these fears did not materialize, partly as a result of policy and partly because the economy behaved somewhat differently than predicted. Rationing and controls remained firmly in place and these were combined with a policy of cheap money to guard against medium-term deflation and to keep down the cost of commercial borrowing.[8] At the same time, the overwhelming need to produce to meet glaring shortages, together with a still large number of men under arms, removed any threat of heavy unemployment.

The wartime rundown of capital stock was economically debilitating, and it came on top of a particularly weak investment performance in industry in the interwar years, especially in the 1930s. Comparative measures of labour productivity calculated during the war showed that in the 1930s in a wide range of industries British productivity was approximately half the corresponding level in the USA.[9] This gap widened significantly during the war. A major cause of the difference was the use of less capital-intensive methods of production in the UK, resulting in overall higher unit costs of output, even when allowance is made for differentials in labour and capital costs between the two countries. Comparisons with other major economies cannot be made satisfactorily because of the devastating effects of the war. Nevertheless, over the longer term the record had been unfavourable to Britain in core industrial sectors, particularly in comparison with Germany. Yet there is no evidence of a clear recognition in government or in business that the continental challenge would re-emerge at some point after the war.

It was frequently claimed that there was some compensation in the form of investment in plant and buildings during the war which could be converted to peacetime use. There was, indeed, some attempt to take advantage of this windfall by incorporating it into a newly conceived regional policy. But for obvious strategic reasons,

8. Low interest rates were achieved through persuading the public to take up government loan stock but this increasingly had to be supplemented by government support and by 1947 there was no alternative but to allow interest rates to rise. See S. Howson, 'The Origins of Cheaper Money, 1945–47', *Economic History Review*, 40 (1987), pp. 433–52.

9. L. Rostas, *Comparative Productivity in British and American Industry* (Cambridge, 1948) and *idem.*, *Productivity, Prices and Distribution in Selected British Industries* (Cambridge, 1948). This work was carried out under the auspices of the Board of Trade in 1946.

many of these installations were not in areas appropriate to peacetime needs. Another potential bonus from wartime investment was the stimulus it gave to strategic areas of technical change. Important cases in point were the development and expansion of the motor industry and the development of electronics production, both of which offered major commercial opportunities in international markets. The other obvious case was aircraft production, though it is one for which longer-term gain is far from clear cut. Output increased from 2,800 aircraft in 1938 to over 26,000 in 1944, figures which make no allowance for the major advances in the complexity and technical sophistication of the machines.[10] These increases involved investment and the employment of a specialist workforce on such a scale that it enabled the industry to promote its commercial interest in a powerful way regardless of broader economic considerations. The outcome was the continuing growth of an industry in which development costs and the demand for skilled labour were high and rising rapidly and which, in international terms, involved very considerable risk.

The total number in civil employment remained roughly constant over the war, though some allowances has to be made for increased hours of work on the one hand and some dilution in the quality of the labour force on the other. The most noticeable change was the re-deployment of the workforce between peacetime and wartime occupations. Substantial readjustments had been achieved by 1948 but industrialists continued to petition the government to do something to ease the persisting shortage of labour. Moreover, the armed forces still claimed over 800,000 men at this date. During the war, productivity measured in terms of gross domestic product per head grew by 1.3 per cent per annum and the rate increased marginally to 1.5 per cent per annum between 1945 and 1948. These rates were low and did little to reduce the backlog of Britain's comparative productivity performance.

The Labour government was certainly aware of the pressing need to raise productivity in industry. A major comparative international study had been sponsored by the Board of Trade in 1946.[11] Efforts to address the problem ranged from the setting up of industry working parties to the establishment of the Anglo-American Council on Productivity (AACP) in 1948. These activities produced a great

10. Details of munitions production are to be found in Central Statistical Office, *Statistical Digest of the War* (1951), Tables 117–29 and generally 111–41. This is perhaps one of those cases where the facts do speak for themselves.

11. See note 9.

Table 6.2 Changes in employment in Great Britain, 1938–48 ('000s)

	1938	1944	% of 1938	1948	% of 1938
Armed forces and auxiliary services	385	4,967	1,290	846	219
Total in civil employment	17,378	16,967	98	19,064	110
Agriculture and fishing	949	1,048	110	1,123	118
Mining and quarrying	849	813	96	839	99
Metals, engineering, vehicles, shipbuilding	2,590	4,496	174	3,546	137
Chemicals, explosives, paints, oils, etc.	276	515	187	367	133
Textiles	861	635	74	835	97
Clothing, boots, shoes	717	455	63	613	85
Food, drink, tobacco	640	508	79	628	98
Cement, bricks, pottery, glass	271	159	59	263	97
Leather, wood, paper	844	536	64	775	92
Other manufactures	164	129	79	223	136
Building, civil engineering	1,264	623	49	1,375	109
Gas, water, electricity	240	193	80	275	115
Transport and shipping	1,225	1,237	101	1,472	120
Distributive trades	2,882	1,927	67	2,354	81
Commerce, banking, insurance, finance	414	268	65	344	83
National and local government	1,386	2,091	151	2,229	161
Miscellaneous services	1,806	1,334	74	1,813	136
Registered insured unemployed	1,710	54	3	272	16
Total working population	19,473	22,008	113	20,367	105

Source: Alford (1995), 21.

deal of evidence on the causes of low productivity and the AACP, in particular, drew attention to management shortcomings in this country when measured against standard practices in the USA.[12]

12. J. Tomlinson, 'Productivity Policy' in H. Mercer, N. Rollings and J. D. Tomlinson, *Labour Governments and Private Industry. The Experience of 1945–51* (Edinburgh, 1992), pp. 37–54; *idem.*, 'A Missed Opportunity? Labour and the Productivity Problem, 1945–51', in G. Jones and M. Kirby (eds), *Competition and the*

Nevertheless, the focus of concern was on labour productivity and, even more narrowly, on labour efficiency. The result was that the nature of productivity was basically misunderstood. Thus, higher productivity was measured in relation to a given set of techniques, instead of in terms of achieving productivity growth both by the efficient application of inputs of factors of production and, more importantly, through altering their combination in response to the opportunities of technological change. A clearer understanding, of course, would have involved the need to examine management practices and business organization.

The failure to match up to the productivity problem was of crucial importance to Britain's longer-term position in the world economy. The reasons for this failure are part of the complex relationship between the effects of war and persistent weaknesses in economic performance. The immediate postwar need for output was obvious. Shortages were acute throughout the economy and there was the black hole of the deficit in the balance of payments. The official reaction was strongly conditioned by immediate wartime experience. Manpower planning had been the device which had successfully met wartime needs, and whilst it was officially recognized that the same degree of direction could not be exercised in peacetime, the problem of production was defined essentially as one of labour supply. The alternative way of meeting demands, in part at least, was through increased productivity achieved by means of more capital-intensive methods of production, workshop reorganization and the application of modern business and management practices. Capital supply presented a formidable dilemma, however. In total, the production of more capital goods for domestic use could only be met by reductions in the already low levels of consumption. There was a system of capital controls in operation, though detailed investigation has shown that, even within the limits of what was politically possible and economically desirable, this system was not robust enough to overcome the conflicts between short-term needs, long-term planning and commercial self-interest.[13]

State. Government and Business in Twentieth Century Britain (Manchester, 1991), pp. 40–59. My interpretation of the evidence differs from that of Tomlinson who argues that the nature of the problem was understood by the Labour government and what was lacking was the effective execution of a policy to deal with it.

13. For detailed analysis of this system see M. Chick, 'Economic Planning, Management Decision-Making and the Role of Fixed Capital Investment in the Economic Recovery of the UK 1945–55', unpublished Ph. D. thesis, University of London, 1986.

Labour and management practices were even more intractable. The war had done something to remove the obstacles of the past through the need for rapid expansion of output and the development of new products. Organized labour cooperated with employers and government by agreeing to relax traditional labour practices, especially in relation to the employment of less skilled and female workers. But as part of a longer-term process of modernization these changes by no means amounted to net gains. Trade union cooperation brought with it enhanced status and bargaining strength for union leaders, a development personified in the charismatic Minister of Labour, Ernest Bevin, erstwhile leader of the Transport and General Workers' Union. With their experience of the 1930s much in mind, labour leaders were determined to use their new-found influence to restore the defences of their unions. Postwar reform of labour organization and practices thus offered limited possibilities.

Conservatism on the side of labour was reinforced by the increased political influence of businessmen. This was particularly the case with iron and steel, cotton and shipbuilding in which representative industrial bodies, such as the Cotton Board and the Shipbuilding Committee, established to deal with the problems of the 1930s, became the vehicles for directing production to meet the demands of war.[14] The position of traditional management was thus powerfully confirmed and placed in a strong position to defend its interests against any attempts at postwar reform. These conditions were intensified by the heavy dependence on outdated methods of production under conditions of short supply. A somewhat special case was agriculture which played a critical role in maintaining food supplies and in saving dollars in the immediate postwar years. As a consequence it achieved the unique position of becoming the most regulated and protected industry in Britain, and its fortunes were transformed from pre-war depression to postwar affluence at the expense of the British taxpayer.[15]

14. See for example, M. Dupree (ed.), *Lancashire and Whitehall. The Diary of Sir Raymond Streat, Volume 2, 1939–57* (Manchester, 1987); J. Vaizey, *The History of British Steel* (1974); M. Chick, 'Private Industrial Investment', in Mercer *et al.*, *Labour Governments and Private Industry*, pp. 74–90; L. Johnman, 'The Shipbuilding Industry', in *idem.*, pp. 186–211; S. Tolliday, *Business, Banking and Politics. The Case of British Steel, 1918–1939* (Cambridge, Mass., 1987).

15. B. A. Holderness, *British Agriculture Since 1945* (Manchester, 1985); P. Self and H. J. Storing, *The State and the Farmer* (1962).

In important respects, therefore, the situation was one in which Britain suffered from a form of sclerosis as a result of being on the winning side. In making their contribution to victory, traditional attitudes and practices became more resistant to change. In sharp contrast, in the other European countries (whether ally or enemy) and Japan, there was more willing acceptance of the fact that, since they had lost the war, economic reconstruction would require radical changes. Somewhat paradoxically, this acceptance was facilitated by economic structures that, in major ways were more advanced than those which existed in Britain, as they had been before the war.[16]

The looming problem of the external deficit has already been highlighted. The volume of exports had fallen to 45 per cent of its pre-war level, major sources of invisible earnings had been lost and many pre-war markets had been virtually destroyed. Yet the need, over the longer term, was for an increase of at least 50 per cent in exports on pre-war levels. This daunting task was all the more formidable when account is taken of what it meant in financial terms. Sterling had become a soft currency whilst the economy's needs depended crucially on financing imports from the hard currency, dollar area. The situation was further complicated by the manner in which the sterling area had developed.

During the 1930s Britain had actively promoted the sterling area through preferential trade relations, though this policy was in line with the flow of UK trade towards the Empire against a background of depressed international demand.[17] During the war Britain drew on supplies from the Empire on the basis of credit, and in addition

16. The major work on Europe is A. S. Milward, *The Reconstruction of Western Europe 1945–51* (1984). In the case of Germany this work needs to be balanced against A. J. Nichols, *Freedom with Responsibility: The Social Market Economy in Germany* (Oxford, 1994). For Japan see M. Morishima, *Why has Japan 'Succeeded'?* (Cambridge, 1982), though it is probable that he underestimates the impact of the US occupying administration on the Japanese economy in the immediate postwar years. A more detailed but difficult study is W. M. Frewin, *The Japanese Enterprise System: Competitive Strategies and Co-operative Structures* (Oxford, 1992).

17. A great deal of information on and analysis of the sterling area is to be found in L. S. Pressnell, *External Economic Policy Since the War. Volume 1. The Postwar Financial Settlement* (1986); C. R. Schenk, *Britain and the Sterling Area from Devaluation to Convertibility in the 1950s* (1994). S. Strange, *Sterling and British Policy* (Oxford, 1971) is an outstanding study which examines the issue from the standpoint of international relations. J. H. B. Tew, *The Evolution of the International Monetary System 1945–85* (1985) is an excellent broad study.

these countries allowed earnings from dollar countries to accumulate in London as sterling credits. It was in these ways that the sterling balances grew to the large sum of £3,500 million by 1945, and hence the dilemma. If the balances had simply been released they would have drained mainly to the dollar area; but in the process their value would have plummeted because of the consequent fall in the sterling/dollar exchange rate. For most of the countries concerned that would have been a catastrophe, since they were poor. For Britain it would have amounted to a monumental exchange crisis. Thus for Britain, any postwar international financial settlement had to take account of this unique feature of its external finances.

THE INTERNATIONAL ECONOMIC SETTLEMENT

The manner in which these difficulties were met was strongly conditioned by the fundamental change in the role of government that had occurred during the war. The command economy had rapidly superseded the limp economic liberalism of the 1930s. A new elite cadre of 'temporary' civil servants was recruited and armed with new techniques such as national income accounting and manpower planning. Nevertheless, the state apparatus was far from having become totally *dirigiste*. There was, for example, negotiation and cooperation between government, employers and unions. Moreover, it was fully understood by the government that many of the special powers it took in wartime could not and should not be maintained once the war was over. But experience of the exercise of wartime control, combined with the imposition of much higher rates of taxation than governments had ever before contemplated, gave politicians and civil servants a new sense of what might be achievable, even in peacetime. The requirements of postwar reconstruction and expectations raised by the Beveridge report and the white paper on *Employment Policy* ensured that big government was here to stay. In 1937 all forms of public expenditure amounted to 26 per cent of GDP; by 1948 the share was 37 per cent.[18]

In some ways the change in the role of government in external economic affairs was more fundamental than in relation to

18. A short survey and analysis of the major changes is provided by Alford *et al.*, pp. 1–29. See also P. Addison, *The Road to 1945* (1977).

domestic matters. Despite the introduction of protection in 1932 and the strengthening of imperial bonds, the British approach to international finance before the war was based on the principles of market competition. The isolationism of the USA, combined with the stability of sterling after the devaluation of 1931, sustained traditional British belief in its version of economic liberalism in a world that was increasingly driven by rabid political and economic nationalism. The war forced both Britain and the USA to accept that in the future international political stability, and the economic prosperity needed to underpin it, would require a negotiated international economic settlement. What this would involve was by no means clearly understood and was to be the subject of detailed and difficult discussions between the USA and Britain.[19]

The outcome of these events contains a significant element of paradox. The problem of international trade and finance was defined in terms of the conditions which had been experienced in the 1930s. The solution was formulated in the circumstances of the allied victory. In that process the USA had moved from a position of isolation to one of economic dominance. Whilst accepting that this economic power carried the responsibility on the part of the new world to redress the balance of the old, the USA was still imbued with a strong belief in economic liberalism, however much this stood in contradiction to the monopolistic structure of its own domestic economy. Thus the USA accepted that it would play the leading role in constructing a new world order involving the establishment of international regulatory mechanisms, and that it would have to bear a cost in the process. But it was equally determined that these arrangements would be completed within a specified and relatively short period, and that their subsequent operation would preserve the maximum market freedom for individual economies, such that the USA would not have to carry any special responsibilities.

The British approach was no less idiosyncratic. Whatever the case on the domestic front, there is little doubt that there was wide political consensus on Britain's postwar international role. The influences which led to this position were somewhat diverse, however. The mainstream was formed from the political coalition

---

19. The best accounts are R. N. Gardner, *Sterling-Dollar Diplomacy* (1969 edition); W. R. Louis, *Imperialism at Bay 1941–1945: The United States and the Decolonisation of the British Empire* (1977); Pressnell, *External Economic Policy Since the War*; Strange, *Sterling and British Policy*.

which had run the war and regarded victory as confirming Britain's world status. The leadership of the Labour party (soon to become the government) no more questioned the need to maintain a large military presence overseas after the war than did their Conservative opponents.[20] The extremes of the political spectrum did not dissent from this view, though for very different reasons. As politics shaded to the right the belief was held, with matching intensity of emotion and prejudice, that the war had vindicated Britain's imperial role. Had not Churchill, himself, invoked the cause of Empire in the nation's finest hour! As politics shaded to the left the degrees of emotion and prejudice of the right were paralleled by opposition to the USA. For the left, imperialism *qua* colonialism was anathema; but Britain as the leader of a commonwealth of (non-American) nations was a role which exercised a strong moral appeal.[21]

The British view of the world was not shared by the Americans. To the contrary, they were deeply suspicious of Britain's imperial intentions and, anyway, they wanted Britain to form an integrated group of Western European nations which, as prosperity returned, would act as a bulwark against the threat and designs of communism from the East. For its part, Britain was determined to keep Western Europe at arm's length for a mixture of reasons. The fact of having stood alone against Germany in 1940 naturally created a strong sense of having stood against Europe and correspondingly reinforced the traditional attitude of being apart from it. Added to which, it became increasingly clear in negotiations from 1944 onwards, that the commitment of the Americans to an international economic settlement was essentially a limited and self-interested one. Why, then, should Britain surrender what it considered to be its longer-term interests to those of the USA? These are understandable attitudes but they had little to do with the careful weighing of the nation's economic interests. The failure to give serious consideration to Britain's relationship to Europe was to prove extremely costly in the longer run.

20. For Attlee's views on this need see PRO, CAB 21/2216, CM (47)9, 17 Jan 1947. For Ernest Bevin's strong commitment in this area see A. Bullock, *Ernest Bevin, Foreign Secretary 1945–51* (1983), pp. 233–4, 239–41, 244, 322–3, 330, 354, 522–4, 581–2. See also D. K. Fieldhouse, 'The Labour Governments and the Empire–Commonwealth, 1945–51', in R. Ovendale (ed.), *The Foreign Policy of the British Labour Governments, 1945–51* (Leicester, 1984), pp. 83–120.

21. The politics of this period is attracting increasing attention. See Alford *et al*, *Economic Planning 1943–1951*, pp. 1–29; P. Hennessey, *Never Again: Britain 1945–51* (1992); K. O. Morgan, *Labour in Power 1945–51* (Oxford, 1984).

The *Realpolitik* of the postwar settlement was that it was a settlement primarily in American interests, albeit modified by negotiations between Britain and the USA which stretched back to the very early stages of the war. In 1941 the Atlantic Charter formalized the mutual friendship between Britain and America. Following on from this declaration was the Mutual Aid Agreement through which lend-lease supplies were made available. The USA was still a neutral country and the issue for it in domestic political terms was what recompense the UK should make for the aid provided. This became known as 'The Consideration' and the specific clause of the Mutual Aid Agreement was Article VII, which was eventually agreed in late 1942 after lengthy and often acrimonious discussion. The outcome was, in the words of the historian of the events, a combination of acquiescence and misunderstanding. American suspicion of Britain as Perfidious Albion had certainly not been lifted. Article VII simply stored up trouble for the future.[22]

Talks between the British and Americans continued through 1943 and what they revealed was that American political cooperation with Britain and the allies was not to be matched with extensive economic support during the period of reconstruction. The eventual settlement amounted to a series of agreements: Bretton Woods; the American loan to Britain; the establishment of the General Agreement on Tariffs and Trade. The first of these was the result of the United Nations conference at Bretton Woods (New Hampshire) in 1944. Agreement was reached – to be ratified by individual governments – on the establishment of a new international financial mechanism. Britain and the USA dominated the discussions. Keynes was the intellectual driving force but he certainly did not have things all his own way. The Americans were wary of Keynes's smooth logic and subtle proposals and were hard-headed in their response. They knew well enough that he who pays the piper calls the tune.

The aims of the Bretton Woods conference were twofold: to secure stable exchange rates and to ensure the supply of long-term international capital. The first was met by the establishment of an International Monetary Fund which was to provide a mechanism for multilateral financial settlement. The fund was a currency reserve accumulated through the contributions of its member states. Quotas were set for countries according to their size and resources.

22. Pressnell, *External Economic Policy Since the War*, pp. 28–65.

Each contribution could be paid in a country's own currency subject to a minimum in gold 'equivalent to 25 per cent of its quota or to 10 per cent of its net official holding of gold and dollars, whichever was the less'.[23] A member could borrow 25 per cent of its holding in any one year up to a maximum of four consecutive years. Exchange rates were fixed at those pertaining on July 1944, but each member was allowed one initial adjustment of up to 10 per cent. Thereafter rates were allowed to vary by only plus or minus one per cent. In sum, it was a system for meeting balance of payments deficits without resort to competitive devaluation. Borrowing from the IMF would provide the breathing space for domestic adjustment aimed at bringing the balance of payments back into equilibrium. By its nature, however, the system made no provision for the possibility of individual countries experiencing persistent surpluses or deficits. There was, in other words, no built-in mechanism for adjusting the structure of exchange rates in relation to major shifts in relative economic performance.

The need for international capital mobility was to be served by a new International Bank for Reconstruction and Development. It did not begin operations until 1947 and was heavily dependent on US funds, which proved to be by no means liberally available. So far as Britain and the other major economies were concerned, the Bank's operations were of little direct significance since private international lending soon became far more important.

Once the war had ended the confirmation of the Bretton Woods agreement became urgent. This brought Britain hard up against its fundamental dollar shortage. There was no immediate crisis because there was still a large flow of dollars from the USA into international finance through agencies and obligations arising from the war. But this supply was for a limited period, and Britain had virtually no dollar reserves and no obvious prospect of earning sufficient currency to pay for more than a tithe of what it needed from the USA. In addition to this, in August 1945, lend-lease was stopped. Whatever hopes the Labour government might have had as to the willingness of the USA to make a large grant-in-aid to the UK, they were misplaced in the context of US attitudes to the postwar settlement. In reality there were two alternatives: an intensification of austerity in Britain or the raising of a loan from the USA. Despite a lack of enthusiasm and some fierce opposition

23. W. Ashworth, *A Short History of the International Economy since 1850* (1987 edition), p. 272.

at home, a mission under Keynes was despatched to Washington to secure the latter.

The twists and turns, the plots and sub-plots of the negotiations have been chronicled in detail elsewhere.[24] The basic issues are clear, however. On the British side it was a matter, first, of how much could and should be borrowed, given the best terms available. Secondly, it was considered essential that the terms of the loan were consistent with the broader pattern of Britain's international economic interests, especially in relation to the sterling area. On the American side, there was the imperative that such a loan should be defensible in domestic politics, and this required a combination of commercial terms and broader undertakings that would amount to substantial progress towards the goal of free trade and multilateral financial settlements. In the latter respect, the US negotiators were particularly concerned to weaken, or preferably to remove altogether, what they judged to be the discriminatory and anti-American nature of the sterling area with its ring fence of imperial preference.

Detailed research has shown that in arriving at an agreement there was confusion and prejudice on both sides.[25] In the case of Britain, in particular, ministers at home were not well advised, since all the leading experts on international trade and finance were with the delegation in Washington. Agreement was finally reached in December 1945, though it was not approved by Congress until July 1946. It was not well received in the United Kingdom and was pushed through parliament with difficulty and with grudging acceptance that there was no viable alternative. Keynes had expected a loan of $5,000 million but had to settle for $3,750 million, to which was added $650 million as a final payment for lend-lease. In relation to current UK dollar earnings this was a large amount, but the terms were quite generous at a nominal rate of 2 per cent per annum or 1.6 per cent over the 50-year period of the loan. As it turned out, the burden of the loan became negligible by the 1950s. In addition, the Canadian government provided a loan of $1,275 million on the same terms, so that the total of $5,000 million was achieved. Together, these loans covered the United Kingdom's prospective dollar gap, but this dealt with only part of the problem.

24. Pressnell, *External Economic Policy Since the War*.
25. American attitudes are well brought out in A. Van Dormael, *Bretton Woods: Birth of a Monetary System* (1978).

If the commercial terms were satisfactory the further conditions attached to the loan were certainly not. Contrary to the general understanding of Bretton Woods, that a period of something like five years would be necessary for a satisfactory transition to peacetime conditions, the agreement radically shortened the period to one year from the taking up of the loan. In mid-1947, sterling was to become freely convertible against the dollar. In addition, there was a less tightly specified requirement that Britain would make every effort to reduce the sterling balances as a move towards full multilateral financial settlements. In this respect, the Washington negotiations were far from successful from the British viewpoint; but was this mainly the result of American prejudice and short-sightedness backed by the ability to pay?

The evidence leaves no doubt that the Americans did not comprehend the enormous disparity which existed between their own and the European economies (Table 6.1). Furthermore, all the intellectual force Keynes could bring to bear could not break down the hard-headed and somewhat prejudiced determination of the Americans to establish a largely free-trade world in which British imperialism would be safely corralled. But the matter went deeper. Unlike the experiences of Britain and the Western European nations, in the USA the war had not brought about a fundamental questioning of its political economy. The fact that war expenditures had acted as a kind of Keynesian deficit finance in banishing unemployment and restoring prosperity was, in effect, interpreted as demonstrating the capacity of traditional American capitalism to recover from cyclical depression. The economic policies of the New Deal began to fade as shadows of the past – they had never been particularly successful anyway – and the return to postwar domestic economic policy increasingly confirmed the belief in economic liberalism. This was an attitude of mind which simply did not understand the essential requirements for European economic recovery.[26]

Whatever the failings of American policy, when judged in terms of international needs, these were by no means the sole cause of the increasing predicament in which Britain found itself and which, within a year of receiving the American loan, had erupted into an economic crisis. In 1945–6 it was reasonable for Britain to take the position that the dissolution of the sterling area was a difficult and

26. For a perceptive study see J. K. Galbraith, *American Capitalism: The Concept of Countervailing Power* (Boston, Mass., 1952).

costly business. Any straightforward repayment of sterling balances – even staged over a few years – would have placed intolerable strains on Britain's external position, since there would have been a flight from sterling to the dollar which would have crashed in mid-air as the sterling/dollar exchange rate collapsed. The implications for British and erstwhile sterling countries' trade would have been correspondingly disastrous. But for all the force of this argument in 1946, it is not strong enough, by extension, to counter the charge that the cardinal error on the British part had been made much earlier during the events leading up to the Bretton Woods agreement.

Throughout the negotiations, from 1941 onwards, British policy remained committed to maintaining the country's status as a world power, complete with large armed forces, an international currency and the girdle of empire. Keynes's schemes for international finance modified the extremes of this policy, but they were not basically inconsistent with it. The government and leading financial interests wished to maintain a major role for sterling, and Keynes was a Treasury man after all.[27] This is not to deny that there was an enormous problem in sustaining the sterling area. The point at issue is the official approach to it. In this respect, the alternative was to have taken the Americans at their word and to have surrendered the position of sterling in return for direct financial assistance in settling the sterling balances. As it was, this possibility was resisted by the British; and whilst there was some feeling of moral obligation to the holders of sterling balances lest some part of their assets would be written off, this concern was obviously not decisive. It has to be recognized, of course, that for Britain to have adopted this alternative approach would have almost certainly carried with it the corollary of having to submit to American pressure to become more closely tied to continental Europe, both politically and economically. Whether this is judged the major missed opportunity

---

27. It is impossible to be anything other than selective in references to Keynes because he has become the subject of a vast literary industry, in part, no doubt, a consequence of the need economists feel for a hero figure in a profession that has somewhat fallen from grace. Ways into the literature are provided by D. E. Moggridge, *Maynard Keynes: An Economist's Biography* (1992); A. Booth, *British Economic Policy 1931–49: Was There a Keynesian Revolution?* (1989); G. C. Peden, *Keynes, the Treasury and British Economic Policy* (1988). And for the ultimate aficionado there is R. Skidelsky, *John Maynard Keynes: A Biography. Vol. 1. Hopes Betrayed, 1883–1920* (1983) and *idem., John Maynard Keynes: A Biography. Vol. 2. The Economist as Saviour, 1920–1937* (1992) which chronicle the subject's life in great detail.

of the second half of the twentieth century for Britain will be considered later in the light of subsequent events.

The alternative was a real one but as a policy it was unrealistic given the dominant political and economic perceptions of British interests. So, Britain negotiated itself into the responsibility for operating a second-line international reserve currency, albeit after being allowed a period for postwar adjustment. The terms of the 1946 loan turned what was already an enormous task into an impossible one. And by placing Britain in a client position to the USA, these same terms amounted, paradoxically, to sealing the postwar economic settlement as, first and foremost, one that served American interests. Paradoxically so, because initially it was not seen in this light by either side.[28]

EXTERNAL ACCOUNT

Almost immediately following the receipt of the loan, the restoration of Britain's international finances did not go according to plan.[29] In July 1947 sterling was duly made convertible. The result was a disastrous drain on reserves and within a month convertibility had to be suspended. Little more than two years later (18 September 1949) following continuing intense pressure on the balance of payments, the pound sterling was devalued from $4.02 to $2.80. It is important to note, however, that since most other countries matched this devaluation against the dollar, the trade-weighted value of sterling fell not by 30 per cent but by 9 per cent. Moreover, throughout this critical period appearances were somewhat different from the underlying reality, in a manner which was of central importance to Britain's position in the world economy.[30]

The problem presented itself in the form of the scale of the deficit on the current account of the balance of payments. As Table 6.3 shows, a deficit had been anticipated, though not of the size that the current estimates revealed.

---

28. For a succinct analysis of the American loan see Cairncross, *Years of Recovery* (1985), pp. 88–120. For the European side of the story see Milward, *The Reconstruction of Western Europe*.

29. The outstanding account of postwar economic policy is J. C. R. Dow, *The Management of the British Economy 1945–60* (Cambridge, 1964). It offers a clear and balanced analysis but is abstemious in its interpretation and judgments.

30. A. Cairncross and B. Eichengreen, *Sterling in Decline. The Devaluations of 1931, 1949 and 1967* (Oxford, 1983); Cairncross, *Years of Recovery*, pp. 165–211.

Table 6.3 UK balance of payments forecasts, 1945–52 (£m.)

	Current account as forecast at beginning of year	First published estimate of current account	Latest estimate of current account	Drain on reserves as forecast at beginning of year	Actual drain on reserves
1946	−750	−450	−230	−750*	−225
1947	−220	−675	−381	−500*	−1,024
1948	−270*	−120	+26	−450*	−406
1949	−30*	−70	−1	−400*	−348
1950	+50	+229	+307	−280***	+308
1951	−100	−521	−369		−407
1952	–	+291**	+163		−175

*   Twice half-year forecasts.
**   Includes defence aid of £121m.
*** 1950–51

Source : Cairncross (1985), 84.

The external situation worsened considerably between 1946 and 1947, and this was exacerbated by a domestic crisis and the intervention of the Almighty. Coal stocks, on which the economy was utterly dependent, had sunk to a level below that at which distribution and use could operate efficiently.[31] The shortfall was mainly a consequence of low output over the last two years of the war, though it was made worse by poor planning in the Ministry of Fuel and Power. The Almighty then inflicted on the nation the harshest winter on record for many years. The coal industry simply could not produce enough to meet the nation's needs. The fuel crisis reduced Britain's export capacity by maybe as much as £200 million, and this shortfall was combined with a sharp adverse movement in the terms of trade, disproportionately so in relation to dollar goods. In addition, it made Britain's still large external defence commitments all the more costly. The loss of gold and dollar reserves accelerated and the American loan was exhausted by mid-1947. The loss of reserves turned into a massive drain with the introduction of convertibility and its suspension thus became unavoidable.

31. The authoritative account is W. Ashworth (with the assistance of M. Pegg), *The History of the British Coal Industry. Volume 5. 1946–1982: The Nationalized Industry* (1986), pp. 130 *ff.*

The postwar settlement was rapidly giving rise to the horror of a siege economy. Events on the international front were developing even more dramatically. Relations between East and West reached crisis point in April 1947 with the breakdown of the Moscow conference. In Churchill's phrase, 'an iron curtain rang down across Europe and the cold war set in with a vengeance'. The economic recovery and strength of Western Europe thence became a matter of strategic importance to the USA as the major part of its resistance to the spread of communist totalitarianism. The practical means of meeting the threat were the substantial increase in US military forces in Europe and the introduction of the Marshall Aid programme (European Recovery Programme – ERP) inaugurated in June 1947 with the first payments being made in April 1948.

The amounts distributed in Marshall Aid to the main beneficiaries are shown in Table 6.4.

Table 6.4 Total net European Recovery Programme aid after the utilization of drawing rights as a percentage of 1949 gross national product

	A	B
France	9.9	11.5
Italy	8.8	9.6
Netherlands	16.1	23.1
United Kingdom*	5.2	7.5
West Germany**	4.7	5.9

*   GDP
**   1950

A = pre-September 1949 exchange rates.
B = post-September 1949 exchange rates.

The period for the calculation of aid is from 1 July 1948 to 30 June 1951. 'Defence support' aid for the period 1 July 1951 to 30 December 1951 is added.

Source: Milward (1984), 97.

As a proportion of the gross domestic product of the UK, the amounts received might appear marginal when averaged over the period, and this has led a leading authority to argue that the economic significance of the programme was not crucial and was of very limited effect in postwar economic recovery.[32] This assessment has been challenged on the grounds that the impact of the aid was much greater than the figures in the tables suggest because it was concentrated on the balance of payments and in this way it substantially enhanced the capacity of the nation to import. Rough calculations indicate that the income effects of the aid allowed gross national product in 1949 to be something between 10 per cent and 20 per cent higher than it would otherwise have been. Although only a rule of thumb, this calculation takes no account of the multilateral and multiplier effects of these additional dollars on international trade generally.[33] It will be argued shortly, moreover, that the importance of Marshall Aid for the UK was even greater when the true nature of the balance of payments problem is understood.

The immediate official response to the payments crisis was the inauguration of an 'export drive' sponsored by the Board of Trade under the near-messianic leadership of Stafford Cripps, the minister responsible. The gains in exports were impressive.

Table 6.5 UK visible trade by volume, 1947–51 (1947 = 100)

	Imports					Exports	
	Food, drink, tobacco	Basic materials	Fuel	Manus.	Total	Manus.	Total
1947	100	100	100	100	100	100	100
1948	100	102	125	106	104	123	127
1949	108	111	125	119	112	138	140
1950	104	117	138	113	112	156	162
1951	115	122	183	144	125	160	164

Source: Mitchell (1988), 523.

32. Milward, *The Reconstruction of Western Europe*, pp. 90–125.
33. J. Foreman-Peck, 'Trade and the Balance of Payments', in N. F. R. Crafts and N. W. C. Woodward (eds), *The British Economy since 1945* (Oxford, 1991), pp. 172–3. The counter view is also taken by Cairncross, *Years of Recovery* and C. P. Kindleberger, *Marshall Plan Days* (1987), pp. 245–65.

On the face of it these were supreme achievements, yet more recent research has shown that, for all the publicity surrounding them, they owed little to the efforts of the Board of Trade. Far more significant was the general growth in world trade (facilitated by Marshall Aid). In essence, a number of countries, whose industries had been more severely disrupted than their counterparts in the UK (especially in the late stages of the war) were desperately short of basic capital goods. These were good markets for Britain and thus new capital goods were being exported which were, themselves, produced in plants that had been seriously run down during the war and which were becoming increasingly obsolescent. By the same token, these countries could not offer much competition in the supply of a whole range of consumer goods, at least in the short run.[34]

It may seem unduly harsh to criticize the export achievement but, whether avoidable or not, it was purchased at a high longer-term cost, as will be seen. Yet even in the short run, whilst exports to the dollar area rose threefold between 1947 and 1951, as a share of total exports the increase (from 11.5 per cent to 14.5 per cent) was marginal. In 1948 exports to the hard currency countries (which, in order of importance were South Africa, Canada, the USA, Argentina, Belgium, Switzerland) amounted to only 25 per cent of the total. The remaining 75 per cent relied very heavily on soft currency markets hungry for basic manufactured goods. Textiles alone accounted for nearly one-quarter of this trade. The dilemma faced by Britain was that any switch from soft to hard currency areas would cause the former to seek exports from the latter thus causing a drain on the sterling area dollar pool, which was accumulated from the dollar trade of the sterling area countries.

The historical irony is that the external performance of the economy was much more successful than contemporaries appreciated. Subsequent recalculation of the statistics has revealed that the deficit on current account was substantially less than that shown by the figures available at the time (see Table 6.3). The main source of the discrepancy was the under-recording of invisible trade. What is particularly striking is the swing from substantial deficit to modest surplus in 1948 and the achievement of virtual balance in 1949. Yet the pound sterling was devalued in 1949. Behind this historical irony lies the key to understanding the true

34. A. Maizels, *Industrial Growth and World Trade* (Cambridge, 1963), pp. 200–1.

nature of Britain's external problem.

The general point to be made is that balance of payments figures (whether original or corrected) are end of year figures and, therefore, they do not indicate the extent of fluctuations within the year. Such fluctuations might be self-correcting or, as is more likely if they are large, they might be countered by strong policy prescriptions. 1949 was certainly a year of fluctuations. There were sharp movements in the economy resulting from the self-reinforcing effects of a mild depression in the USA, short-term stock-piling adjustments in the UK which resulted in high imports, speculative expectations of devaluation and short-term measures to safeguard very slender reserves. There was, however, a deeper problem of which these fluctuations were the stormy surface.

By a careful analysis of the data, Cairncross has shown conclusively that the basic problem, which contemporaries did not understand, was 'that the balance of payments on current account and the change in gold and dollar reserves would bear little relationship to one another'.[35] The mechanics of the problem are shown in Table 6.6. The current account deficits which totalled £692 million were far less than the loss of reserves of £2,401 million. So far as direct UK settlements with the dollar area were concerned, these were met by gold and dollars received through the US/Canadian loan and Marshall Aid; in addition there were some small amounts from other sources. In order to explain the loss of reserves, therefore, it is necessary to examine closely transactions with the sterling area. When this is done, it immediately becomes clear that the explanation of the heavy loss of reserves was not a reduction in sterling balances through withdrawals financed by gold and dollars. The *net* reduction on this account between 1945 and 1952 amounted to the comparatively small amount of £70 million as against a total of £3,500 million. Equally clear is that Britain's surplus with the sterling area on current account was, in effect, eaten into by investments to the tune of £892 million; operations in which exchange control did not apply and thus the amounts were used to acquire dollar supplies which could only be financed by the rundown of reserves. Most went to Commonwealth countries plus a certain amount to oil companies in the Middle East and elsewhere. The remainder of the loss (£817 million) went in loans and repayments and to settle accounts with hard currency areas directly.

35. Cairncross, *Years of Recovery*, p. 79.

Table 6.6 The dollar drain, 1945–52 (£m.)

Net gold and dollar deficit	–2,401
Sectoral balance of payments	
Balance on current account with the dollar area	–2,181
Balance on current account with the sterling area	+1,642
Balance on current account with other countries	–153
Balance on UK current account (apparent net loss of dollars)	–692
Transactions with the sterling area	
Net investment in the sterling area	1,158
Less addition to sterling balances	220
Less grants from sterling area governments	46
Net capital transfer	892
(represents drain on reserves)	
Net UK purchases of gold	619
(including South African gold loan)	
Net transfers to other areas on behalf of the rest of the sterling area	127
Other transfers	5
Current account surplus	1,642

Source: Cairncross (1985), 118.

Put another way, the current account balance masks the dollar shortage, and the problem was not so much one of exports but of capital transfer and the undervalued dollar rate of exchange. In relation to our earlier discussion, this analysis reveals that Marshall Aid was important, whichever way it is regarded. With aid, the payments problem was significantly eased; without it the issue of devaluation would have been forced earlier. What is far from clear, because it must remain a matter of speculation, is what would have been the effect of an earlier devaluation with or without capital controls. Obviously, the most powerful variable would have been whether the USA would have provided a large flow of compensating aid. It can only be observed that the actual record of loan negotiations makes this seem unlikely, at least without a much more radical change in British policy towards the sterling area. What does appear certain is that under the terms of Bretton Woods the dollar was undervalued, particularly so against sterling. Once again, however, the consequences of a more realistic dollar exchange in the conditions of 1945–48 are by no means obvious.

Britain's international payments position was part of the complex process of postwar economic adjustment and recovery to which further attention is given in Chapter 7. For the moment, however, it can be noted that by 1949 the time was right for a structural adjustment of the dollar exchange in relation to sterling and other major currencies. By that time the UK had sufficient productive capacity to take advantage of the added price-competitiveness in dollar markets that devaluation would provide, whilst still needing to rely heavily on imports from those areas. Even at this juncture the potential advantage was not understood: devaluation was made too late, after a period of dithering, and it was not effectively exploited. Cripps, the chancellor of the exchequer, regarded devaluation 'as an act of foreign policy quite as much as of economic policy';[36] and the final decision was formulated by three junior ministers outside the cabinet.[37]

The existing parity had for some time been working against exports to the dollar area. It required a clear act of policy, however, to set conditions in which exporters would find it relatively unattractive to sell additional output into soft currency markets. During 1948 sterling was increasingly trading unofficially at below the set rate. What was happening, in particular, was the movement of dollars from the dollar pool and from UK reserves into countries within the sterling area which were then buying dollar goods at prices which represented a discount on sterling. This form of transaction (known as currency shunting) created a state of affairs in which Britain was suffering the worst of two worlds: losing dollars through the sterling area and unable to earn more dollars directly from the USA. Reference has already been made to ministerial and official dithering during the year prior to devaluation. In fact, the issue of the appropriate rate for sterling went back to the war period and discussion became more active from 1945 onwards with differences of opinion emerging within the Treasury and in the Bank of England, all of which contributed to the eventual

36. Cairncross and Eichengreen, *Sterling in Decline*, p. 141.
37. The three junior ministers were Hugh Gaitskell, Douglas Jay and Harold Wilson.

overwhelming indecisiveness of ministers. Cripps did not remove his opposition to devaluation until the last moment, and for most of the time he was supported by Attlee and Bevin. Alone among senior cabinet ministers in 1948, Morrison became convinced of the need to devalue.[38]

The most important thing which emerges from the evidence is that throughout the period under review the government had no coherent international economic policy. Some commentators have, in effect, explained this failure away by arguing that the government was unavoidably driven hither and thither by powerful forces of international instability. Our analysis accepts this defence only as a plea in mitigation. The need for short-term adjustments was not independent of the lack of a coherent policy over the longer run. International economic policy during these years suffered from ideological muddle, theoretical confusion, official machination and effective lobbying from industry and the unions.[39] Perhaps it is ever so. At all events, more detailed examination of the full effects of these elements is given in the following chapter, but certain points stand out clearly in this context. The Labour government was never seriously willing to consider the implications of its ideological commitment to and the potential practical consequences of economic planning in the domestic economy for its external policy. But economic planning at home could not be made effective without close and continuing regulation and control of external trade and finance. Yet successive international economic commitments entered into by Britain worked entirely in the opposite direction. It was not just a matter of economics, however. Bevin pursued a foreign policy that was based on the principles of the minimum of Western European involvement and the firm maintenance of the Anglo-American relationship. Senior officials were constantly reminding Bevin that the Americans were deeply suspicious of state planning, but he hardly needed it since his concern to secure Britain's place as the major European power in concert with the USA was paramount in his policy. To this extent, matters of economic policy came second.

38. By this time Herbert Morrison had lost considerable influence in the government. Apart from anything else he was exhausted through having piloted the enormous nationalization programme through parliament. See B. Donoughue and G. W. Jones, *Herbert Morrison: Portrait of a Politician* (1973), p. 354 *passim*.

39. These various elements are surveyed in Alford *et al.*, *Economic Planning*, pp. 1–21. This view is also informed by the author's current research into the official records of this period.

So far as theoretical economics was concerned, Keynes was the economic colossus of the period, and his ideas continued to gain influence after his death in 1946. Yet these served only to add confusion to indecision. Keynes had played a dominant role in formulating the basic principles on which the system of multilateral postwar international finance was based. But in the case of domestic economic policy Keynesian prescriptions were still those encapsulated in his *General Theory*, which was defined in terms of a closed economy. Economists probably exercised a stronger influence on policy during these years (especially through the Economic Section of the Cabinet Office) than at any time since, but it is difficult to avoid the conclusion that their role was one of accommodation. They shied away from radical proposals on planning, avoided the difficult but central issue of wages and incomes policy, generally eschewed microeconomic policy and concentrated on how best to apply methods of macroeconomic management in order to avoid inflation and to sustain high levels of employment. Economists in government can, perhaps, be expected to aspire to little more.[40]

Ideological differences and the client role of economic theory were skilfully exploited in time-honoured ways by the mandarins of Whitehall, especially by those in the Treasury. This ministry had lost power during the war when the chief administrative tasks were directed towards the mobilization of men and materials. But it regarded this period as an interregnum. By skilful manipulation on the part of senior officials, progress towards the restoration gathered pace after 1945, though it suffered a setback when the Treasury failed to predict the 1947 convertibility crisis. Nevertheless, subsequent political changes, combined with the importance of international financial negotiations through the Organisation for European Economic Co-operation (the agency for Marshall Aid), served to advance the Treasury's cause. Triumph was complete when, in late 1947, Stafford Cripps, the most powerful economics minister, moved from the Board of Trade, via the short-lived Ministry of Economic Affairs, to the Treasury as chancellor of the exchequer. Despite Cripps's erstwhile strong commitment to economic planning, he now adopted the position that planning

40. See for example A. Cairncross and N. Watts, *The Economic Section 1939–1961* (1989); *idem.* (eds.), *The Robert Hall Diaries, 1947–1953* (1989); F. Cairncross (ed.), *Changing Perceptions of Economic Policy* (1981), pp. 259–66, comments by James Meade; Chester, 'Planning, The Labour Governments and British Economic Policy 1945–51'; R. Jones, *Wages and Employment Policy* (1987).

largely amounted to budgetary control. To what extent he was persuaded to this view by Treasury officials it is impossible to say, but the permanent secretary to the Treasury, Sir Edward Bridges, in alliance with the cabinet secretary Sir Norman Brook, was working assiduously to restore Britain's international role in cooperation with the USA and to resist attempts to develop economic planning in the broad sense, since it would have substantially weakened Treasury power. At least there was coherence to administrative self-interest.[41]

The aims of industry and organized labour can be briefly stated (see Chapter 7). Customary markets, outdated business organizations and traditional labour practices were elements powerfully resistant to change. During the export drive, complacency over the prospects of international competition was easily clothed in the rhetoric of 'Made in Britain'.

TRADE REGULATION AND THE EUROPEAN PAYMENTS UNION

The regulation of trade was an integral part of the postwar settlement. Britain's trade performance is examined in detail later (see Chapter 7) but the main institutional arrangements within which it operated were the General Agreement on Tariffs and Trade (GATT) which came into force in 1947, and a range of import controls. GATT was a residual survival from a much grander scheme promoted by the Americans and given some support by Keynes. The original idea was to establish a system of universal free trade under the auspices of a new international organization to be known as the International Trade Organisation. It was a policy fully in line with the USA's mission to create a new liberal world order and its narrow suspicion of the British Empire with its protective mechanism of preferential tariffs. For Britain and the Continental European nations, free trade in the conditions of 1946 and 1947 was an impossibility.

The GATT system, which in essence has remained until this day, was based on concurrent bilateral trade negotiations aimed at lowering tariffs. When a round of negotiations was completed, the common elements would be cancelled out in order to achieve the

---

41. Alford *et al.*, *Economic Planning*.

maximum multilateral reduction in duties. At Geneva in 1947, 123 such bilateral arrangements were made, which allowed an overall reduction in tariffs.

The parlous state of the postwar economy made import controls essential. Without them the exchange rate would have been put under intolerable pressure and the inevitable devaluation would have been of such proportions as to set in motion rampant inflation. Moreover, the controls discriminated against the dollar area. Immediately after the war, 96 per cent of imports were controlled, but by 1951, the proportion was down to one half, mainly as a result of a large-scale scrapping of regulations in 1948. At no time, however, did these controls form part of a strategy of economic development. They were operated as regulators to limit the damage of the pressures of shortages and short-term fluctuations in the balance of payments (see Chapter 7).

The remaining institutional arrangement of this period was the European Payments Union (EPU) established in 1950.[42] Once again, the Americans viewed the process which led to its formation as one aimed at closer economic integration of Western Europe (including Britain) and the rapid introduction of convertibility. This approach was not shared by the Europeans, though there were very significant differences in their motivations. Britain was resistant because it was felt that it would weaken the position of the sterling area and draw Britain further into a continental European orbit. France was guarded in its approach because if was formulating a political and economic policy based on a Franco–German alliance from which Britain would be largely excluded. Belgium was strongly opposed to the arrangement because it believed that its strong balance of payments would be undermined. Altogether, the bargaining position of the Europeans was much stronger than it had been five years earlier at Bretton Woods and the Americans were forced to make major concessions. Their desire to promote a system of payments settlement as a move towards complete convertibility led them to commit substantial financial support to the project. Hedged with in with various provisos, the main nations agreed to the formation of the EPU and, reluctantly and belatedly, the Belgians acceded.

42. An excellent account is provided by A. S. Milward (with the assistance of G. Brennan and F. Romero), *The European Rescue of the Nation-State* (1992), pp. 345 *ff.* See also H. van der Wee, *Prosperity and Upheaval. The World Economy 1945–1980* (1986), pp. 444–7.

The EPU system involved each member country depositing a quota sum fixed at 15 per cent of its visible and invisible trade with all other members. The amount was to be made up of its own currency and of credits not amounting to more than 60 per cent of the total. If a country incurred a payments deficit within the Union, it was allowed to finance it by drawing off the accumulated funds; but depending on the size of the deficit there was a sliding scale for its settlement which increasingly weighted the share that had to be financed by the purchase of the required currency with gold or dollars. There was an automatic overdraft equivalent to 20 per cent of the quota and from 20 per cent to 60 per cent the sliding scale operated. The essential point was that the system provided both a breathing space and a tightening discipline within which a member country could make adjustments to correct its imbalance. Despite its difficult birth, the EPU proved to be enormously successful during the 1950s, though for somewhat different reasons than were originally envisaged (see Chapter 7).

THE REVIVAL OF 'GENTLEMENLY CAPITALISM'?

What has been represented in our analysis as a failure in Britain to develop a coherent international economic policy which took measured account of the nation's economic potential, might, instead, be regarded as a consequence of an overriding yet clearly focused set of values that reflected the exercise of real power in Britain. A number of references have been made to the deep determination among politicians to sustain a world role for Britain, albeit in tandem with the USA; an aim that was shared by financial, and particularly City, interests through the medium of the sterling area. Imperial ties and wider military undertakings easily took precedence over the economic welfare of the nation at large.

The most elaborate analysis of this kind is that by Cain and Hopkins which has already been examined in some detail in relation to the pre-1914 period. According to this analysis, the 'Gentlemanly Capitalism' that directed 'the expansion of the Empire before 1914' matured into a political economy which proved remarkably resilient, first in sustaining the Empire and Commonwealth connection and then, most recently, in securing 'a new role, though an uncertain one, in a new financial order functioning on a scale far greater than that encompassed by nation states or empires'.[43] That an amalgam of economic interests and political and social networks played an important role during the critical years of postwar reconstruction, is supported by the preceding analysis. But it hardly conformed to the precepts of gentlemanly capitalism any more than it did in the late nineteenth century. Thus whilst the Foreign Office needed little encouragement to support City interests, it could not have wished for a firmer champion of Britannia than Ernest Bevin. In Bevin's own words, Britain was 'not just another European country'. But, by no stretch of the imagination, was Bevin a member of the ranks of gentlemanly capitalists nor a toady to them. There was, in short, a variety of interests at work which led to confusion and indecisiveness when it came to economic policy formation. It will be argued in the next chapter that, together, these interests were effective, not in promoting change, but in resisting it. This is but another way of saying that Britain was not dominated by gentlemanly capitalism: it was afflicted with weak capitalism.

43. P. J. Cain and A. G. Hopkins, *British Imperialism. Crisis and Deconstruction 1914–1990*. The book carries this claim on its cover.

CHAPTER SEVEN

Comparative Performance and Competitiveness, 1945–61

MEASURES OF COMPARATIVE DECLINE

The arithmetic of Britain's relative economic decline between 1950 and 1961 is well recorded. In some respects it was a dramatic fall from grace, though it should be judged as much by the superior performances of international competitors as by that of Britain itself. Moreover, Britain's performance was a distinct improvement on its past record. And as well as the risk that such statistical exercises may give rise to a growing sense of tedium, there is the fact that numbers tell only part of the story. Britain continued to aspire to a major role in the international economy and in world affairs more generally. Economic perception and policy were thus clearly at odds with economic capacity and performance.[1]

Economic policy and performance intersect through complex relationships such that economic prescriptions frequently lead to unintended and unexpected outcomes. In broader terms, however, British economic policy during this period traced what might be described as a curvilinear path. It began with a firm commitment to economic planning, but this was soon abandoned in favour of a mixture of economic regulation and state direction, with decreasing emphasis on the latter. By the early 1950s, economic policy was being reformulated into the doctrine of the 'mixed economy'. To its ideologues it was an advanced form of political economy which embodied the best of both socialism and capitalism. More mundanely, it meant policy consistent with the coexistence of public and private sectors and, as such, it was flexible enough to be

---

1. A general survey of this period is contained in B. W. E. Alford, *British Economic Performance 1945–1975* (Cambridge, 1995).

acceptable to the Conservative administrations of the 1950s.[2] By the end of the 1950s, however, the comparative shortcomings of British economic performance began to give rise to official concern, especially since the success of the major European economies and Japan seemed to owe a great deal to government intervention.

In 1961 a Conservative government, no less, established the National Economic Development Council (NEDC). Economic planning, in the sense in which it was understood immediately after the war, is far too strong a description of this new approach, and the term was used in an extremely vague way by the chancellor of the exchequer when he introduced the proposal. The Cabinet, moreover, were by no means happy with the idea, whilst the trade unions were deeply suspicious of it. Even so, this was a change of course away from a completely free private enterprise market economy, but precisely where policy was heading was far from clear.[3]

The main indicators of comparative performance are shown in Table 7.1. Three things are immediately obvious: growth in Britain was significantly slower than in the other major economies, with the major exception of the USA; Britain still retained a significant lead in terms of comparative levels of output and income per head, again with the major exception of the USA; the most dramatic changes were in international trade shares. These comparisons, however, have to be placed in context in the sense that in the late 1950s the data available on comparative economic performance were far less comprehensive than the historical statistics now available. Indeed, the manufacture of economic statistics, incorporating new techniques of measurement, was part of the new culture of economic growth and the quest for affluence. 'Growthmanship' was just beginning to emerge as a new form of international rivalry. The world in which Britain now found itself was very different from that of the early postwar years.

2. The classic statement is A. Crosland, *The Future of Socialism* (1956). See also S. Brittan, *Steering the Economy* (1971 edition); A. Shonfield, *British Economic Policy Since the War* (1959).

3. J. C. R. Dow, *The Management of the British Economy 1945–60* (Cambridge, 1965), p. 398, note 1; F. T. Blackaby, *British Economic Policy 1960–74* (Cambridge, 1978), pp. 22–3.

Table 7.1 UK comparative economic performance, 1950–60

	GDP growth per year % 1950–60	GDP per person hour % per year 1950–60	GDP per head UK = 100 1950	1960	Share of world exports of manfuactures % 1950	1960
United Kingdom	2.9	2.3	100	100	25.5	16.5
France	4.6	4.6	73	82	9.9	9.6
Germany	8.0	6.9	59	90	7.3	19.3
Italy	6.0	5.7	50	84 }*		} 5.1
Benelux	–	–	–	–		}*
Canada	4.6	3.1	108	102 }	26.6 }	21.0
Sweden	3.2	3.4	94	95 }		}
Switzerland	4.6	3.0	116	125 }		
Belgium	3.0	3.1	75	74	–	–
Netherlands	4.6	4.2	83	90	–	–
Japan	8.8	5.7	28	45	3.4	6.9
United States	3.3	2.5	152	139	27.3	21.6

* Bracketing for comparability.

Sources: Brown and Sheriff (1979), 241; Maddison (1991), 198–9, 236–9, 274–5.

THE LABOUR GOVERNMENT AND ECONOMIC PLANNING

The platform on which Labour came to power in 1945 included the pledge: '[We shall] plan from the ground up, giving an appropriate place to constructive enterprise and private endeavour in the national plan'.[4] Polemics aside, those framing the party's programme were focusing on the fundamental problem of the British economy: the need for major changes in industrial structure. It was generally recognized that the staple industries, in particular, had failed in the 1930s, even though the seriousness with which this was viewed varied because of the intensely regional nature of the

4. This section is based on B. W. E. Alford, R. Lowe and N. Rollings, *Economic Planning 1943–1951* (1992), pp. 1–29.

depression and its associated high levels of unemployment. The depressed areas seemed less of a problem in Whitehall than in Glasgow or Liverpool, for example. Moreover, by the late 1930s it was clear that the Fates had at least spared Britain some of the horrors that accompanied economic crisis elsewhere in the world. At all events, the war strongly reinforced the demand for a new beginning with the return of peace, though there was far from consensus on how economic recovery and prosperity should be achieved, and such cross-party agreement as did exist at the end of the war soon evaporated in the heat of party politics.

Political attitudes to postwar reconstruction were reflected in the debates over nationalization, though divisions in this respect were not as sharp as is sometimes suggested. The major instances of nationalization, in scale and complexity, were those dealing with coal and transport. These industries had fallen to such a low point that there was no serious alternative to reorganizing them under state direction and control. The other cases of nationalization were more or less accepted as unavoidable, with the exception of the iron and steel industry which was the last in the programme. In this case, there was fierce opposition from the Conservatives, who succeeded in delaying the final act until 1951, just before the Labour government lost office. The final revenge was exacted by the Conservative government when it denationalized the industry in 1953.[5]

The opposition to the nationalization of iron and steel was the outcome of a number of things. Firms within the industry could claim to have a good independent future, unlike the benighted colliery companies, for example. Furthermore, the industry had developed its own national organization in the 1930s, and although this was revamped as the Iron and Steel Board in 1946, it remained a powerful defender of the interests of private enterprise. More broadly, the issue became a convenient focus for the growing differences that existed between government and opposition over how the British economy should be run in peacetime. And by the time of the debate on iron and steel the Labour government itself had modified its principles and shifted its policy objectives from those it had averred in its 1945 election manifesto.

On the face of it, those principles had been incorporated into

5. Road transport was denationalized in the same year. For details see W. Ashworth, *The State in Business, 1945 to the Mid-1980s* (1991), p. 27.

the nationalization programme.[6] As a leading commentator has observed: 'The strength of the "general welfare" approach was evident in the statutes. The avoidance of contradiction [with commercial need] was sought mainly by expressing the public interest in requirements broad enough to be compatible with a range [but by no means unlimited range] of business practices, and by including commercial and financial objectives but referring to them explicitly only in minimal terms ... "Profit" was a dirty word to the nationalisers ... [Accordingly the undertakings] were all told to pursue the efficient and economical development of their industries'.[7] In this sense, therefore, nationalization was part of the Labour government's broader commitment to planning since it gave formal recognition to long-held aspirations and it certainly demonstrated a high degree of political will. But in many ways the new organizations which were constructed reflected the administrative preoccupations of civil servants rather than immediate and longer-term commercial needs. An enormous amount of parliamentary time was used to complete the programme, and the primary issues were those concerning owner-ship and procedures for compensation rather than those dealing with the coordination of economic control of the so-called commanding heights of the economy. To what extent the nationalization programme was pursued too far, too quickly, at the cost of effective economic planning is an extremely interesting question but one that must wait upon further research.

Between 1945 and 1947, the government established some rudimentary machinery for planning. The *Economic Survey* was invented. It was designed to provide an analysis of the current state of the economy and set out targets for the coming year.[8] A Ministry of Economic Affairs under Stafford Cripps was established in 1947

6. An excellent survey is *idem*. The official history, which contains an enormous amount of detail, is D. N. Chester, *The Nationalisation of British Industry 1945–51* (1975). There are good histories of individual nationalized industries: W. Ashworth (with M. Pegg), *The History of the British Coal Industry, Volume 5, 1946–1982. The Nationalized Industry* (Oxford, 1986); T. Gourvish, *British Railways. A Business History* (Cambridge, 1986); L. Hannah, *Engineers, Managers and Politicians: The First Fifteen Years of Nationalised Electricity Supply in Britain* (1982).
7. Ashworth, *The State in Business*, pp. 45–6.
8. The *Survey* was based on the system of national income accounting that had been invented by two economists, James Meade and Richard Stone, in 1941. See J. E. Meade and R. Stone, 'The Construction of Tables of National Income, Expenditure, Savings and Investment', *Economic Journal*, 51 (1941), pp. 216–33. See also A. Booth and A. W. Coates, 'Some Wartime Observations on the Role of the Economist in Government', *Oxford Economic Papers*, 32 (1980), pp. 177–99.

to oversee economic planning, and although it was short-lived because Cripps became chancellor of the exchequer later in the same year and carried his planning responsibilities with him, other changes were made at that time. A Central Economic Planning Staff was set up; an Economic Information Unit was given the task of coordinating publicity on planning and ensuring that ministers were more effectively briefed on planning matters; an Economic Planning Board was appointed with the object of involving management and unions in policy formulation; ministerial responsibility was clarified with overall responsibility being concentrated in Cripps's hands; and, finally, the Cabinet committee structure was reformed in order to streamline planning decisions.

These changes amounted to little more than sound and fury since they were not matched by any kind of clear formulation of the principles on which economic planning should be based and the techniques through which it should be implemented. The theoretical pedigree was mixed and uncertain and there was certainly no blueprint available. There was, too, an apparent conflict between planning and Britain's international economic relations. Strictly conceived, economic planning assumed a closed economic system or, at least, one in which external relations were tightly regulated. These requirements, however, are easily overstated. Planning was not a case of all or nothing, it was a matter of degree within a process of learning by doing. The issue was the extent to which the state should direct the reconstruction of the postwar economy rather than seeking to promote a return to the traditional operation of the market. The fact that the Labour government's commitment to planning was based on ideology rather than on closely formulated theoretical principles, was of much less importance to the outcome than whether ministers possessed the necessary political will to change things.

The nationalization programme epitomized the Labour government's success in achieving the worst of both worlds. Ideological demands were met but not in a manner that amounted to a planned response to industrial needs. Accordingly, the state was now in business in a big way but found itself in an uncertain and increasingly difficult relationship with private enterprise which, from 1948 onwards, the government was vigorously promoting through the rapid and general abolition of economic controls.[9]

9. This was the so-called 'bonfire' of controls, a phrase used by Harold Wilson when he made the changes in November 1948.

This outcome, it will be argued, had serious and long-lasting consequences for Britain's comparative performance in the world economy. The immediate question is whether this resulted from a failure of political will or a conscious and independently determined set of policy decisions.

As a defence against the charge that the Labour government all too easily abandoned its commitment to planning, there is undoubtedly some force in the claim that the demands on ministers and civil servants were enormous and exhausting and that, together with the shocks of international crises, both were stretched to the limit. Yet much of this pressure was of their own making. Among ministers there was a conflict of priorities. At the very top, the prime minister, Attlee, and the foreign secretary, Bevin, were determined to sustain a position for Britain as a leading world power, a policy which involved heavy military commitments and close attention to the international interests of the USA. How foreign policy objectives matched domestic economic needs and capacities was never seriously considered. By 1948 there was, in addition, growing support in the government for more orthodox methods of economic regulation and, in combination with foreign policy objectives which had the aim of promoting wider internationalism as a defence against greater European integration, this led to the vigorous abolition of controls. There is evidence, too, of a conflict of economic ideas in the latter stages of the Labour government. As late as 1951, by which time the government had done much to restore the market economy, a leading minister, Gaitskell, was preparing a comprehensive planning bill.[10]

Ministerial abandonment of economic planning was aided, abetted and even promoted by senior civil servants, particularly by those in the Treasury and the Cabinet Office. During the war, the Treasury had lost much of its influence in government because of the primary concentration on supplies, manpower and materials, which were the responsibility of other ministries. With the return of peace, senior Treasury officials were set on restoring the dominance of their ministry over economic affairs in particular and over the administration of government in general. At first, therefore, they were cautious in their approach to peacetime economic planning

10. For a detailed discussion of this bill see N. Rollings, ' "The Reichstag Method of Governing?" The Attlee Governments and Permanent Economic Controls', in H. Mercer, N. Rollings and J. Tomlinson, *Labour Governments and Private Industry. The Experience of 1945–51* (Edinburgh, 1992), pp. 15–36.

and at the very most gave lip-service to it. But at every opportunity these same officials resisted any moves towards effective economic planning, since these would have directly increased the influence of the supply and trade ministries in the formulation and direction of economic policy. Foreign exchange crises and the translation of Cripps from the Ministry of Economic Affairs to the Exchequer in 1947, marked the road to the Treasury's triumph. For all its good intentions, the Central Economic Planning Staff was neutralized within the Treasury. Even the leading economists in the Economic Section of the Cabinet Office, who had advocated a planning approach to economic policy through some form of investment planning, began to shift their ground when confronted with real-world problems. Maybe because economists have a natural predilection for clear-cut and short-term solutions or at times understand the art of the possible, the Economic Section began to urge the need for a more rapid return to free markets and the operation of the price mechanism.[11]

Opposition to planning came from outside government, directly from employers and indirectly from trade unions. With the former, the most effective resistance was mounted through those industrial organizations that had been established to promote industrial reorganization in the 1930s and then had been strengthened during the war as agencies of wartime production. Iron and steel, shipping and cotton were the main ones. More generally, groups of employers and their umbrella organization, the Federation of British Industry, resolutely opposed government control of industry beyond the acts of nationalization. Private enterprise became the clarion call, despite the dismal record of British business in the years before the war. In part, this was an understandable reaction to the pettifogging nature of some postwar controls. In larger part these attitudes were the problem when it came to the task of modernizing British business.

Trade union attitudes to economic planning were paradoxical in their formulation but in practice they were no less conservative than those of the employers. On the one hand, as an integral part of the Labour party, trade unions supported demands for economic planning and were fully in support of the nationalization programme. On the other hand, whilst unions had submitted to a high degree of manpower direction during the war, they had never surrendered their independent status and were totally committed to

11. A. Cairncross and N. Watts, *The Economic Section 1939–1961* (1989).

the restoration of free collective bargaining in peacetime. If economic planning involved any kind of direction of labour, the unions wanted none of it. In their subsequent dealings with government, therefore, union leaders tended to subscribe to the rhetoric of planning whilst steadfastly resisting its practical implementation.

Any programme of economic planning had to establish itself against the growing popularity of what has become known as Keynesianism.[12] As a result of Keynes's central role in economic affairs during and immediately after the war, his economic prescriptions had acquired a near unimpeachable pedigree. Moreover, Keynes had never directly challenged free market capitalism; his claim was that it required a degree of central management. The rhetoric of Keynesianism was easily adaptable to the theme that such management was best operated through the mechanisms of Treasury control. And, as has already been observed, Keynes was a Treasury man after all. Planning, by contrast, was easily presented by its opponents as the antithesis of capitalism, even though in principle there was a powerful case to be made for it in terms of the postwar economic reconstruction of what would remain predominantly a free enterprise economy. Whether, in practical terms, this amounted to a lost opportunity is doubtful in view of the narrow competence of the civil service and the cumbersome nature of the administrative system. Diverse political aims on the part of ministers, orthodox administrative self-interest, the possible lack of expertise, industrial opposition, lack of political appeal: these combined to sap the political will of the government to promote economic planning, whilst Keynesianism easily became the opiate of postwar political economy.

There has been considerable debate over the extent to which, during the war, a political consensus developed between the Conservative and Labour parties that formed the basis of postwar centrist politics.[13] But this is something of a case of mistaken identity. In the field of economic policy, the objectives of the

---

12. The debate over whether and, if so, when, there was a Keynesian revolution in economic policy is now in danger of matching the disputations of medieval casuistry on the proverbial angels on the head of a pin. Those who wish to pursue the issue should begin with A. Booth, *British Economic Policy 1931–49: Was There a Keynesian Revolution?* (Hemel Hempstead, 1989).

13. P. Addison, *The Road to 1945* (1977); K. O. Morgan, *Labour in Power 1945–1951* (1984).

Labour party were in major respects fundamentally different from those of the Conservatives. It was not so much a case of opposing views in response to new needs, but rather one of Labour being committed to a new approach, whereas the Conservatives had not developed their ideas much beyond the position they had held in 1930s. Evidence of this dichotomy is contained in the records of wartime discussions within government on postwar reconstruction. The sharpness of these differences was exposed in postwar debates on nationalization and economic policy generally. Yet, as we have seen, by 1948 economic planning was receding into the background whilst traditional approaches to government handling of the economy were coming rapidly to the fore, albeit within the framework of a much larger government sector than had previously existed. Furthermore, this approach was strongly conditioned by a consensual view on Britain's international, political and economic role. In addition, the Conservatives came to accept a commitment to full employment and relatively high state welfare. But the crucial point is that a measure of shared commitment to broad aims did not amount to a consensus on what needed to be done: it was a kind of consensus by default, through the government's failure to achieve its own stated objectives.

LABOUR SUPPLY

Labour supply was a problem of which the government throughout the period was acutely aware. The war had caused a massive distortion of labour deployment in comparison with peacetime conditions. Substantial readjustments had been achieved by 1948, though the armed forces were still at twice their 1938 level and considerable concern was being expressed about labour shortages in key industries. There was some recognition of the need to raise productivity levels, not least because of an officially sponsored study of comparative levels of productivity in British and American industry.[14] And as part of the Marshall Aid programme, the Anglo-American Council on Productivity was established with the objective of enabling British industry to learn from its American counterparts, mainly through visits to the USA. Official initiatives achieved very little, however. The gains in productivity that were

14. L. Rostas, *Comparative Productivity in British and American Industry* (Cambridge, 1948).

made between 1945 and 1951 resulted mainly from postwar recovery. British firms faced a sellers' market that allowed them to achieve improving returns and good profits without the need for significant changes in existing practices.

Complacency among management was complemented by the determination of organized labour to profit from its wartime cooperation with government, by gaining official recognition under the banner of free collective bargaining. Success in this campaign could only result in the restoration of traditional labour practices. Labour shortages simply added to the compliance of management and the bargaining strength of labour.[15] And whenever conditions eased firms hung on to workers for fear that labour shortages would return. This response developed in the 1950s into the chronic condition of labour hoarding. Matters might have improved if there had been better understanding of the nature of productivity gains, though that, in itself, was part of the problem. As has been seen (Chapter 6), in official discussions on the subject, the terms productivity and efficiency were used interchangeably, the stress being on the latter, and the approach was strongly influenced by wartime methods of manpower planning, with the emphasis on improving the flow and distribution of the labour force. There was no firm grasp of the fact that the quantity of labour needed for a given activity was a function of labour productivity. In turn, of course, productivity depended not only on the choice of technique, but also on the availability of associated factors of production, most importantly of capital. Whether there were constraints in this respect will be considered shortly, but the critical point is that during the period an attitude and approach to labour productivity was formed that was truly counterproductive.[16]

15. H. Phelps Brown, *The Origins of Trade Union Power* (1986 edition), pp. 147–87; *idem.*, 'A Non-Monetarist View of the Pay Explosion', *Three Banks Review*, 105 (1975), pp. 3–24, for a perceptive analysis of changing trade union attitudes in the postwar period. For comparisons see R. P. Dore, *British Factory–Japanese Factory: The Origins of National Diversity in Industrial Relations* (1973).

16. The difficulty is to distinguish the extent to which, on the one hand, overmanning was the consequence of the perceived need to retain a sufficient labour force to meet boom demand under conditions of generally full employment and, on the other hand, the extent to which it resulted from some combination of union bargaining strength and poor-quality management. The evidence from nationalized industries is indicative of the complexity of the problem. See Ashworth, *The State in Business*, p. 168. See also, J. Foreman-Peck and R. Milward, *Public and Private Ownership of British Industry 1820–1990* (Oxford, 1994), pp. 300–18.

One area in which change was strongly needed was education and training. Technical education had been a matter of debate for many years. But as subsequent research has shown, Britain lagged behind best practice in Western Europe and the United States.[17] Educational reform was high on the postwar political agenda and the much-vaunted 1944 Education Act commanded considerable cross-party support, albeit strongly influenced by exceptionally powerful vested interests in education, with the result that the outcome was a masterpiece of compromise and restraint. But even among the radical proponents of educational change the dominant theme was equality of educational opportunity rather than major reconstruction of the system which provided it. The Act went some way to meeting this demand through widening access to and expansion of grammar school education. The main achievement was that some working-class children were given the opportunity to receive the benefits of the fairly traditional liberal education that had previously been largely restricted to the middle and upper classes. As for technical education, whilst it figured in the provisions of the Act, little was achieved. Thus, the so-called tri-partite system degenerated into a bi-partite one of grammar and secondary modern schools – a system of segregation into academic and basic education based on a highly unsatisfactory examination test of eligibility at the age of eleven. Whatever the claims made during the discussions and consultations that led up to the 1944 Act, in the event little serious consideration was given to designing educational provision in relation to commercial and economic need, or to individual need for that matter. To the extent that such requirements were taken into account, the belief appears to have been in line with tradition, that an English liberal education provided the ideal training for management and that technical education was best left to the established apprenticeship system. For the majority of the labour force a basic education to the age of fifteen was considered adequate to meet Britain's needs in the world economy of the second half of the twentieth century. An opportunity to expand the provision of technical education came again in the mid-1950s with a growing awareness that Britain was

17. D. H. Aldcroft, *Education, Training and Economic Performance 1944–1990* (Manchester, 1992); M. Sanderson, *Educational Opportunity and Social Change in England* (1987); *idem.*, 'Social Equity and Industrial Need: A Dilemma of English Education since 1945' in T. R. Gourvish and A. O'Day (eds), *Britain Since 1945* (1991), pp. 159–82; *idem.*, *The Missing Stratum, The Technical School in England* (1994).

finding it hard to keep up with the international rate of technical change. Dramatic evidence of the power of modern technology came with the launch of the first Soviet space satellite in 1957. A flurry of official activity ensued and some advances were made. But much remained on the drawing board whilst Britain continued to slide down the international league. By the early 1960s it is doubtful whether more than 20 per cent of the workforce had vocational qualifications.

Closely allied to the quantity and quality of the labour was the issue of the location of industry.[18] The problem had been identified in the 1930s in the form of the depressed areas and some associated, though not particularly effective, legislation. Just after the beginning of the war, in 1940, the Royal Commission on the Distribution of Industrial Population (Barlow), which had been set up in 1937, issued its report. In many ways it was a landmark because it examined industrial location within a framework of economic and strategic objectives, though because of its timing little action flowed directly from it. In essence, these problems persisted into the postwar period. To some degree the national-ization programme was seen as addressing important parts of the problem in so far as it dealt with the old industries such as coal and steel. More generally, under the Distribution of Industry Act, 1945, combined with the imposition of investment controls and the introduction of industrial development certificates in 1947, the government pursued a vigorous regional policy. By the beginning of 1948, however, opinion in official circles was rapidly moving to the position that the regional problem had been largely overcome and that this was reflected in the sharp decline of expenditure under the terms of the 1945 Act. Subsequent economic development revealed clearly that this was a mirage but it was not until the end of the 1950s that things were seen a little more clearly.

Regional variations in unemployment during this period are clearly discernible but overall absolute levels were low because of buoyant demand conditions. In the late 1940s the strong sellers' market enjoyed by British industry gave a powerful fillip to those staple industries closely associated with erstwhile depressed areas, conditions that served either to arrest their terminal decline, as in the case of cotton, or to underwrite outdated practices that were

18. A. J. Brown, *The Framework of Regional Economics in the United Kingdom* (Cambridge, 1972); G. McCrone, *Regional Policy in Britain* (1969); D. W. Parsons, *The Political Economy of British Regional Policy* (1986).

costly in terms of productivity growth, as in the case of iron and steel. Central government approached regional problems in terms of the relief of unemployment. This approach was influenced, no doubt, by the experience of worker transfer policies between the wars which had demonstrated that the number who could be persuaded to move was small and that such movements could make matters worse because the most mobile were also the most valuable, and moving them reduced further the economic viability of a region. The subsequent policy of taking jobs to the workers fared little better, however, because it was uncoordinated and opportunistic.

Table 7.2 Regional unemployment rates as a percentage of the United Kingdom rate, selected years, 1929–73

Region	1929	1937	1951	1964	1973
London	50	52	{ 69	{ 59	56**
South East & East Anglia	52	65			70***
South West	77	70	92	88	89
West Midlands	{ 86	{ 61	31	53	81
East Midlands			{ 54	{ 65	78
Yorkshire & Humberside	132	99			107
North West	126	125	92	123	133
North	–*	169	169	194	174
Wales	187	210	207	153	130
Scotland	115	151	192	212	170
Northern Ireland	131	214	469	389	237

*   Included in the two previous categories.
**   South East and London
*** East Anglia

Source: Matthews, Feinstein and Odling-Smee (1982), 83.

The alternative was to develop a structured policy of national industrial development which placed the needs of and potential for regional employment in the context of the development of the economy as a whole. In this, as in a lengthening catalogue of economic matters, Britain stood in sharp contrast to Western

Europe and Japan.[19] In this field of policy, perhaps more than in any other at this time, much difficulty was being stored up for the future.

COMPARATIVE BUSINESS STRUCTURE AND ORGANIZATION

The detailed examination of British industrial performance owes much to the work of business historians. This has involved both the study of individual firms and comparative studies of business organization and management, especially in relation to US corporate structures and business methods. By the 1940s the multi-divisional company form, complete with a system of managerial hierarchy, was common in American big business, and it has been extolled by some economic historians as a triumph of modern capitalism.[20] These corporate giants are seen as combining the greatest degree of efficiency with a diversified range of activities that made a major contribution to producing the highest level of income per head in the world. In Britain, however, the multi-divisional company was the rare exception and the few firms that came nearest to the form were pale reflections of their American counterparts.[21] In Continental Europe and Japan, the picture was one of sharper contrasts since large-scale business organizations had been long-standing features of those countries' industrialization, though alongside the gargantuan cartels of Germany and zaibatsus

19. Among the various analyses along these lines the most stimulating is A. S. Milward, *The European Rescue of the Nation-State* (1992), pp. 329 *ff*. See also S. Newton and D. Porter, *Modernization Frustrated. The Politics of Industrial Decline in Britain Since 1900* (1988); S. Pollard, *The Wasting of the British Economy: British Economic Policy 1945 to the Present* (1982) for approaches that are somewhat different from my analysis. A survey and critique of the 'decline' literature is M. W. Kirby, 'International Rigidities And Economic Decline. Reflections on the British Experience', *Economic History Review*, 45 (1992), pp. 637–60.

20. The multidivisional (MD) form is a structure in which a number of managerially independent divisions (each usually based on a main product) operate independently subject to overall strategic control from the head office which distributes resources between them. The forerunner of this form of large company organization was the centralized, functionally departmentalized company in which managerial functions (selling, technical, finance, etc.) operated across the whole company. It is clear that the MD form allowed expansion through diversification. For the origins and application of these terms the seminal work remains A. D. Chandler Jnr., *Strategy and Structure, Chapters in the History of Industrial Enterprise* (Cambridge, Mass., 1962).

21. D. F. Channon, *The Strategy and Structure of British Enterprise* (1973).

of Japan, small and medium-sized firms flourished to the extent that British manufacturing industry still held the position it had attained between the wars as the most concentrated among the advanced economies.[22]

Industrial concentration did not equate to modern business organization, however. Hence the charge has been made that Britain suffered the shortcomings of personal capitalism, so-termed because of the allegedly still strong and debilitating influence of unreconstructed family firms. By contrast, it is claimed that the USA enjoyed the bounties of competitive managerial capitalism, whilst the major European economies and Japan benefited from co-operative managerial capitalism, the latter being a form of business organization intermediate between that of the USA and of Britain but distinctly superior to the latter.[23] The neatness of this comparative analysis lends it much superficial appeal and it has certainly exercised a strong influence on explanations of comparative economic performance. On closer examination, however, it proves far less satisfactory as an explanation, since it is highly over-generalized and, more seriously, it mistakes form for substance.[24]

To begin with, the pattern of business organization was variable across all the major economies. Family firms, for example, existed on a significant scale in France, Germany and the USA and, more importantly, their alleged unique feature of internal managerial succession, can be shown to operate in an alternative form in large companies in America and Japan.[25] Because of dispersal of owner-

22. G. P. Dyas and H. T. Thanheiser, *The Emerging European Enterprise: Strategy and Structure in French and German Industry* (1976); W. M. Frewin, *The Japanese Enterprise System: Competitive Strategies and Co-operative Structures* (Oxford, 1992). On concentration see L. Hannah and J. A. Kay, *Concentration in Modern Industry* (1977). Also of interest is S. Aaronovitch and M. C. Sawyer, *Big Business: Theoretical and Empirical Aspects of Concentration and Mergers in the UK* (1975).
23. For the most detailed statement of this argument see A. D. Chandler Jnr., *Scale and Scope: The Dynamics of Industrial Capitalism* (Cambridge, Mass., 1990).
24. For critiques of this approach see B. W. E. Alford, 'Chandlerism, The New Orthodoxy of US and European Corporate Development', forthcoming in *The Journal of European Economic History*, 24 (1995); L. Hannah, 'Scale and Scope: Towards a European Visible Hand?', *Business History*, 33 (1991), pp. 297–309; B. Supple, 'Scale and Scope: Alfred Chandler and the Dynamics of Industrial Capitalism', *Economic History Review*, 44 (1991) pp. 500–14. For further criticism see Chapter 8, pp. 267–8.
25. The evidence is well surveyed in R. Church, 'The Family Firm in Industrial Capitalism: International Perspectives on Hypotheses and History', *Business History*, 35 (1993), pp. 17–43. An excellent example based on Dutch evidence which runs directly counter to Chandler's generalizations is K. T. Sluyterman and H. J. M. Winkleman, 'The Dutch Family Firm Confronted with Chandler's Dynamics of Industrial Capitalism, 1890–1940', *Business History*, 35 (1993), pp. 152–83.

ship through shareholdings, the management hierarchies in many large corporations took on the nature of family dynasties. Furthermore, the impact of multidivisional corporate structures in the USA on economic performance is problematical. The growth of the US economy in the post-Second World War period has not been particularly impressive, though this fact has to be balanced against the much higher levels of performance achieved by the US over many years in comparison with the other major economies. Two important conclusions can be drawn from the evidence of business history, however. First, business performance was not so much a matter of structure and organization as of practice. Secondly, business success or failure was as dependent on conditions external to firms as on their internal operations.

Modern business training and the associated need to keep abreast of technical change in all its aspects from methods of production to techniques of marketing and financial control, were the keys to high business performance. What the UK experience during this period shows is that shortcomings on these fronts were common across widely differing business structures, and this was the vital difference between Britain and its major competitors. To explain why it was so is far more difficult – to the point of being impossible until much more evidence is available. One obvious question is to what extent did the level of provision of business training in Britain reflect a lack of demand from business itself, as much as a failure on the part of the state? It is certainly the case that there is no strong evidence from either quarter of a real concern about management training until the late 1950s, even though there had been some moves towards the professionalization of management with the establishment of the British Institute of Management in 1947. Business schools were, however, still a thing of the future.

There has been much debate on the social esteem attached in Britain to a career in business, and more especially in manu-facturing industry. Unfavourable comparisons have frequently been made with Germany and much emphasis has been given to the different systems of education in the two countries. German education, it is alleged, gave more attention to scientific, technical and commercial subjects than was the case in Britain and thus helped to create a culture that was more favourable to business and industry. As has been noted, however (Chapter 2), differences at this level have been exaggerated, since there are many common elements in the content of education in the two countries. Likewise, attempts to substantiate the claim of an anti-business culture in Britain by drawing on contemporary literature and social comment have been shown to be highly selective in their use of evidence. Money-making and the ethics of capitalism have always been convenient Aunt Sallies, not least for the pecuniary interests of those who write about them. And no-one has yet demonstrated a high inverse correlation between the desire for money and social status.

The pattern which emerges from a wide range of evidence, however, is that from whatever area of business activity individuals drew their incomes they found it necessary, in order to achieve and sustain high social status, to engage in those activities in ways that conformed to the norms of the English class system. Thus it was possible to pursue a career in the top professions and still match those requirements since professional status was, itself, the means of maintaining class difference. A career in banking and finance at the highest levels was a socially insulated activity. By contrast, in industry such division could only be achieved by means of a club-like boardroom which segregated top management from the factory floor, and this division was highly conducive to amateurism at the top. The histories of individual firms are replete with examples of such gentlemen amateurs, who lacked expertise in finance, marketing, technology and labour organization, all of which involved direct and continuous involvement with the shop floor. As it was, these matters were left to other ranks who continued, as had their predecessors, to rely heavily on the rule of thumb and customary practice.[26]

The structure of British business was ostensibly brought under tighter control by means of the Monopolies Act of 1948. The guiding principle of this legislation was that of the protection of the public interest against monopoly power. The agency charged with its implementation was the Monopolies and Restrictive Practices Commission. In reality, the Commission had little direct influence on industrial structure, since the public interest proved to be, not surprisingly, a very flexible concept. Monopolistic organization had become a necessary element of modern economic development,

26. As indicated, the literature has been surveyed in Chapter 2 and, moreover, there is need for more detailed investigation of the post-Second World War period. An excellent example is D. C. Coleman, *Courtaulds. An Economic and Social History. Volume 3. Crisis and Change 1940–1965* (Oxford, 1980). See also A. Pettigrew, *The Awakening Giant: Continuity and Change in ICI* (Oxford, 1985). Somewhat similar weaknesses occurred in nationalized industries, see for example, Gourvish, *British Railways 1948–73*, pp. 31–67 and *passim*.

mainly for technological, financial and marketing reasons. The real issue was how to match this need with high levels of efficiency and business performance which, in turn, would be the basis of securing the broader public interest. In the longer run, the most effective arbiter would be international competition, but during the period under consideration British industry was not exposed to its full force because, in common with foreign industry, it was still benefiting from the economic recovery after the war.

Between 1950 and 1960 there was a sharp increase in concentration in manufacturing industry.[27] In 1948 the 100 largest firms accounted for 20 per cent of manufacturing net output; by 1963 this share had grown to 38 per cent. Mergers played a dominant part in this process, with a particularly sharp rise in their number in the late 1950s. Between 1959 and the mid-1960s the value of merger activity averaged between 20 per cent and 25 per cent of total investment expenditure in manufacturing. The nature of this process, however, was more important than the increase in concentration as such. At the time, mergers were commonly justified to the public in terms of production and marketing advantages which would result from larger-scale operations. The techniques of creating them were stock market manipulations, which frequently enabled their promoters to reap substantial capital gains (which, unlike profits and dividends, were untaxed) on undervalued assets. Such undervaluation was, itself, often a sign of sleepy management. For example, one of the most publicized takeover bids of the 1950s was for the brewing firm of Watney, and it was only at a late stage in the battle that its owners realized that the bidder was not interested in the core business but in the large number of sites valued in the balance sheet at the absurdly low levels of historic cost.[28]

The increased stockmarket exposure of British firms during this period might be taken, together with increased competition

27. Hannah and Kay, *Concentration in Modern Industry*. The manner in which concentration is measured involves both conceptual problems as to how concentration is defined and methodological problems in terms of statistical techniques and the data used. Hannah and Kay's measurements, which are the ones preferred here, differ sharply in both respects from P. E. Hart and R. Clarke, *Concentration in British Industry 1935–75* (Cambridge, 1980). The issues are brought out sharply in P. E. Hart, 'On Bias and Concentration', *Journal of Industrial Economics*, 27 (1979), pp. 211–26, but to my mind the argument does not meet the original criticisms made by Hannah and Kay.

28. For the story see T. R. Gourvish and R. G. Wilson, *The British Brewing Industry 1830–1980* (Cambridge, 1994), pp. 449, 451, 459–65.

resulting from the activities of the Restrictive Practices Court (1956) and the general reduction in international trade protection, as a spur to much-needed change in business methods. The outcome was very mixed, however. Research has shown that, whatever the rewards secured by their promoters, the claims made by them in support of takeovers and mergers were not subsequently justified by improved performance and an associated development of modern business practices.[29] Advances were made but in many cases mergers were promoted as a means of defending monopolistic power. In yet others, firms became the hapless victims of marauding asset-strippers, who exploited the open nature of British financial markets and the permissiveness of company law. These conditions placed increasing pressure on managements to make decisions consistent with maintaining the market value of their companies as reflected in share prices, lest they became prey to takeover predators; tactics that worked against medium and longer-term investment strategies and marked the beginnings of what has subsequently become known as 'short-termism'. These conditions were in sharp contrast to the business environment, including company law, ruling in France, Germany and Japan, in particular. In those countries, large-scale and long-term were far more synonymous and integral to the nature of business structure and organization. Equally, these differences constitute a major illustration of the critical importance of conditions external to the firm in explaining business organization and performance.

One other feature of industrial structure must be commented on, namely, the problems of the old industries, in particular coal, shipbuilding and textiles. After a period of remission that has already been described, in the 1950s the longer-term problems affecting these industries returned with a vengeance. Coal was partially protected under the carapace of nationalization but shipbuilding and cotton textiles, especially, felt the full force of international comparative disadvantage. As cotton typified the

---

29. K. Cowling, *Managing Capitalism* (1982); *idem.*, P. Stoneman, P. Cubbin, J. Cable, G. Hall, S. Dernberger and P. Dutton, *Mergers and Economic Performance* (Cambridge, 1980); G. Meeks, *Disappointing Marriage: A Study of The Gains From Merger* (1977); *idem.* and J. G. Meeks, 'Profitability Measures as Indicators of Post-Merger Efficiency', *Journal of Industrial Economics*, 29 (1981), pp. 335–43. The efficacy of legislative control had not been a significant factor since the war. See H. Mercer, 'The Monopolies and Restrictive Practices Commission From 1949–1956: A Study in Regulatory Failure', in G. Jones and M. W. Kirby (eds), *Competitiveness and The State: Government and Business in Twentieth Century Britain* (Manchester, 1991), pp. 78–99.

industrial revolution of the late eighteenth and early nineteenth centuries, so it came to represent much that was at the heart of industrial weakness in post-1945 Britain. Throughout the 1950s it hung on by whatever defensive stratagems came to hand, except that diversification and the redeployment of much of its 200,000 workforce never entered those calculations. 'The survival of the cotton industry was only in the interests of particular groups: elderly workers, owners of small family firms, and trade union leaders who were threatened by a loss of power and prestige as their unions declined. It was not in the interests of the country at large.'[30] The government resisted appeals for protection but, it has been argued, did not go far enough in its neglect of the industry and thus indirectly prolonged its drag on the economy.

The international position of the shipbuilding industry began to slip away quite rapidly from the early 1950s onwards. In comparison with France, Sweden and especially Japan, its production methods were excessively labour-intensive. From 1955 onwards the international challenge was clear, yet it was a further ten years before radical changes were made, by which time it was too late. As with cotton, management through its incompetence and labour through its intransigence ensured that the final outcome could not be in doubt.[31]

In 1960 coal, shipbuilding and cotton accounted for 13 per cent of the labour force employed in mining and manufacturing. If iron and steel are added, the share was 17 per cent. Yet overmanning was not just an infection in old industries. The needs of war stimulated the growth of new branches of industry and these brought with them new peacetime opportunities. But opportunity and good business judgement did not necessarily accompany one another. They certainly did not do so when it came to what was in many ways the most successful wartime industry, aircraft production. During the war, the Air Ministry and the Air Chiefs of Staff developed a powerful pressure group for the building up in peacetime of a large civil and military aircraft industry.[32] These

30. J. Singleton, *Lancashire on the Scrapheap* (Oxford, 1991), p. 140 and generally for a very good analysis of the industry. Special pleading by the industry is indirectly revealed in M. Dupree, *Lancashire and Whitehall: The Diary of Sir Raymond Streat, 1931–57. Volume Two – 1939–57* (Manchester, 1987). This diary is also of more general interest in relation to government/industry relations during this period.

31. A graphic survey is provided by P. Pagnamenta and R. Overy, *All Our Working Lives* (1984), pp. 124–49.

32. M. M. Postan, *British War Production* (1952), p. 435.

demands fell on ready ears since they matched the aspirations of great power status that were cherished in official circles. Government and industry held a shared belief that defence needs and a bid to become a world leader in the development of production of civil aircraft could be easily and profitably combined. Yet the appetite of the industry for skilled manpower and resources was wildly out of proportion to the capacity of the economy. By 1962, for example, aircraft accounted for 35.4 per cent of research and development expenditure in Britain as compared with 27.7 per cent in France and nothing in Germany and Japan. By contrast, the corresponding figures for instruments, electricity, machinery and chemicals in the four countries were 35.6 per cent, 42.5 per cent, 66.7 per cent and 56.3 per cent. Overcommitment and comparative disadvantage continued to go hand in hand.[33]

TRADE PERFORMANCE

A country's ability to pay its way in the world is recorded in its balance of payments, but these accounts have to be interpreted carefully. Some countries are much more trade dependent than others due to the nature of their resources and the pattern of their comparative advantages, within the system of international trade and its regulation. But except over the very short run or in exceptional circumstances of overseas aid, both the commercial and basic balance of the country will tend to zero or, in other words, to balance. The former is defined as imports and exports of goods and services and the latter as including, in addition to the former, the balance of all government receipts and payments (including transfers), net property income from abroad and long-term capital investment.

33. C. F. Freeman, 'Technical Innovation and British Trade Performance', in F. T. Blackaby (ed.), *De-industrialisation* (1979), p. 67. See also *idem., The Economics of Industrial Innovation* (1982). It is important to note that expenditure on research and development is not, by itself, a direct indicator of economic performance. The problem is much more one of quality and distribution and there is far less information available on this score. An aspect of this problem is addressed by D. E. H. Edgerton and S. M. Horrocks, 'British Industrial Research and Development Before 1945', *Economic History Review*, 47 (1994), pp. 213–38. This presents a favourable picture of the *level* of British R and D within a comparative international framework. But, as the authors admit, this is only one aspect of technical change and their analysis relies almost wholly on quantitative data. See also R. P. Smith, 'Defence Procurement and Industrial Structure in the UK', *International Journal of Industrial Organization*, 8 (1990), pp. 185–205.

Table 7.3 UK balance of payments, 1946–65. Main items as a percentage of GDP

	(1) Manufactures	(2) Primary products	(3) Non-government services	(4) Commercial balance = (1)+(2)+(3)	(5) Government services and grants	(6) Interest profits dividends	(7) Long-term investment	(8) Residual balance = (5)+(6)+(7)	(9) Basic balance = (4)+(8)
1946–50	+8.6	−11.4	+0.2	−2.6	+0.4	+1.8	+0.1	+2.3	−0.3
1951–55	+8.8	−12.4	+0.8	−2.8	−0.4	+1.5	−1.2	−0.1	−2.9
1956–60	+8.0	−9.1	+0.5	−0.6	−0.6	+1.1	−0.8	−0.3	−0.9
1961–65	+6.4	−7.1	+0.6	−0.1	−1.1	+1.2	−0.5	−0.4	−0.5

Source: Rowthorn and Wells (1987), 98.

Table 7.4 Comparative UK balance of trade in manufactures and non-manufactured goods and services as a percentage of GDP, 1952–61

	1952		1953		1954		1955		1956		1957		1958		1959		1960		1961	
	M	NM	M	NM	M	NM	M	NM	M	NM	M	NM	M	NM	M	NM	M	NM	M	NM
United Kingdom	+9.1	-10.8	+9.0	-10.5	+8.4	-10.1	+7.8	-10.8	+8.1	-9.9	+8.4	-9.6	+8.1	-7.6	+7.5	-7.7	+6.5	-7.8	+6.6	-6.6
Belgium	n.a.	n.a.	+8.6	-9.1	+8.2	-9.0	+9.7	-7.6	+10.2	-8.4	+9.3	-8.1	+9.0	-5.8	+8.9	-6.9	+8.9	-7.3	+7.1	-7.1
France	+3.9	-4.9	+3.8	-4.1	+3.9	-3.7	+3.9	-3.3	+2.8	-4.8	+3.0	-5.2	+3.5	-4.2	+4.9	-3.0	+4.7	-3.0	+4.0	-2.6
Italy	+1.5	-3.8	+1.0	-2.4	+1.0	-1.4	+1.5	-7.1	+1.7	-2.0	+2.1	-1.9	+2.6	-0.6	+2.8	-0.5	+1.9	-1.7	+2.7	-1.1
Netherlands	+0.6	+4.2	-0.4	+3.4	-1.8	+1.4	-2.9	+2.5	-5.1	-0.1	-5.2	+3.9	-1.4	+2.4	-1.2	+3.5	-2.8	+4.7	-4.6	+4.5
Sweden	-0.6	+0.2	-1.2	+1.7	-1.6	+0.9	-1.6	+0.3	-1.1	+0.2	-1.1	+0.3	-0.7	-0.1	-0.2	0.0	-1.0	+0.2	+0.2	+0.1
USA	+1.8	-0.6	+2.0	-0.8	+1.8	-0.7	+1.5	-0.7	+1.7	-0.4	+1.8	-0.3	+1.5	-0.6	+1.0	-0.6	+1.2	-0.3	+1.2	-0.2
West Germany	+7.5	-6.8	+7.6	-5.6	+8.1	-6.2	+8.0	-6.3	+9.1	-6.7	+9.9	-7.2	+9.0	-6.2	+8.5	-6.4	+8.4	-6.7	+8.4	-6.6

M = manufactures

NM = non-manufactured goods and services

Source: Rowthorn and Wells (1987), 64–7 with minor corrections

It is essential, therefore, that an economy's balance of payments is viewed in relation to the level of performance and output of the economy as a whole.

In broad terms, by 1951 Britain had achieved a substantial recovery in manufactured exports since the war, and the surplus on this trade was equivalent to 11 per cent of GDP, three times more than the 1939 level. Yet this achievement was based on shifting sands. During the following decade the balance of payments showed growing elements of weakness. In common with the economy generally, there was an improvement on pre-war performance – though that had been weak anyway – whereas, in comparative terms Britain was substantially failing to hold its own, even when due allowance is made for the later economic recovery of Western Europe and Japan.

During the 1950s the volume of world trade was increasing at an average rate of 6.5 per cent per year as compared with 7 per cent for Western Europe and 2 per cent for Britain.[34] Tables 7.3 and 7.4 provide an analysis of Britain's trade performance within the context of a heavy dependency on external transactions, equivalent to an average of 30 per cent of GDP. From a high point of 11 per cent of GDP in 1951, the balance of trade in manufactured exports had fallen to 6.6 per cent in 1961 against a relatively slow growth in GDP in international terms. During the same period world exports of manufactured goods grew by 75 per cent as compared with 12 per cent for Britain. The main reason, by far, for this difference was loss of market share. So far as the early 1950s are concerned, some reduction can be discounted as the consequence of the return to full peacetime international competition. But this explanation does not apply to the end of the period. By that time what had been a slippage in Britain's comparative export performance was turning into a serious loss of position.

Exports of manufactures were only part, albeit the major part, of trade. But as the figures show, the total commercial balance worsened between 1951 and 1955 before improving dramatically by the end of the period. This improvement was not, however, the result of an enhanced performance in invisible trade. Both in

34. I have drawn on A. Boltho (ed.), *The European Economy. Growth and Crisis* (Oxford, 1982) which contains much useful comparative information on Britain and Europe. My main source of data is the outstanding study by R. E. Rowthorn and J. R. Wells, *De-Industrialization and Foreign Trade* (Cambridge, 1987) and the excellent earlier analysis by A. Maizels, *Industrial Growth and World Trade* (Cambridge, 1963).

absolute terms and as a percentage of GDP this balance, although positive, was less strong in the latter part of the period. The most active element was the sharp reduction in the negative balance on non-manufactured goods. This reduction applied especially to food and basic raw materials and was a direct result of the sharp, favourable movement in the terms of trade for those commodities, following the end of the Korean war. It has been estimated that between 1951 and 1953 the gain to Britain from falling primary product prices alone was equivalent to 4 per cent of GDP, a gain that almost matches the return from North Sea oil in the mid-1980s.

The commodity composition of British exports more or less matched the changing pattern of world trade, and to that extent performance was satisfactory. A more sharply defined comparison with the six countries of the European Economic Community (EEC) put Britain at a slight advantage in this respect. The pattern of imports is unsurprising except that the share of manufactured goods was rising, though not to a level which amounted to an unduly high degree of import penetration. The difficulty with such analyses, however, is that they are made on the basis of unavoidably broad categories of goods, and this is especially significant in the case of exports of manufactures. Therefore, unless Britain was set on either a path of dramatic export decline or exceptional growth, its commodity pattern of trade is likely to appear to be much in line with that for other major traders. Yet if it were possible to analyse

Table 7.5 Commodity composition of UK visible trade, 1948–61 (annual averages: % share exports/imports)

	Exports	Imports				
	Manufactured goods	Food, drink, tobacco	Fuels, lubricants etc.	Other crude materials inc. oils, fats, etc.	Manufactured goods	Total
1948–9	87.6	59.9	5.0	22.3	12.8	100
1950–55	85.3	37.3	8.4	33.3	21.0	100
1956–61	86.2	35.8	11.0	24.9	28.3	100

Source: Mitchell (1988), 459.

the commodity composition of exports in much more differentiated terms it could well show quite marked differences. Whilst this hypothesis cannot be tested directly in this context, other variables that are estimated in this type of analysis point to the artificiality of commodity comparisons taken on their own.

The main results are shown in Table 7.6. What stands out is the loss through market share or, in other words, the lack of competitiveness.

Table 7.6 UK comparative changes in exports of manufactures attributable to different factors, 1937–59 (% change)

	United Kingdom	France	Germany	Japan	USA
1937–50					
Change attributable to:					
Growth of world market	+24.8	+25.2	+24.7	+24.9	+24.5
Area/commodity pattern	−2.2	−7.0	+4.9	−22.8	+22.3
Market share	+39.2	+96.5	−73.8	−59.3	+18.1
Actual change	+61.8	+114.8	−44.1	−56.6	+65.0
1950–55					
Change attributable to:					
Growth of world market	+38.5	+38.5	+38.7	+37.8	+38.5
Area/commodity pattern	−6.4	−2.0	+9.9	−17.1	+4.2
Market share	−29.6	−11.7	+141.4	+92.7	−19.3
Actual change	+2.6	+24.7	+190.1	+113.4	+23.3
1955–59					
Change attributable to:					
Growth of world market	+26.3	+26.3	+26.3	+26.3	+26.3
Area/commodity pattern	−4.9	+2.9	+8.2	−4.6	−9.4
Market share	−12.6	+7.1	+24.6	+46.9	−16.3
Actual change	+8.8	+36.4	+59.0	+68.0	+0.6

Columns may not sum and world row varies because of rounding.

Source: Maizels (1963), 200–1.

Table 7.7 UK visible trade by area, selected years 1938–65 (% shares imports/exports)

	Imports from:					Exports to:				
	1938	1948	1951	1958	1965	1938	1948	1951	1958	1965
EEC	18.5	13.2	17.9	20.1	23.6	23.7	17.9	17.4	19.6	26.4
Other W. Europe	8.6	8.1	10.1	10.1	12.5	9.0	12.7	11.7	10.5	15.3
USA	12.8	8.8	9.7	9.3	11.7	5.4	4.3	5.7	8.7	10.6
Japan	1.0	0.3	0.4	0.9	1.4	0.4	0.0	0.4	0.6	1.1
White Dominions	23.1	25.3	19.0	20.1	18.6	22.9	23.7	27.5	22.2	18.0
OPEC	3.4	6.9	9.1	12.1	9.7	4.0	7.3	5.3	7.9	5.5
New industrialized countries	1.9	2.5	4.1	2.3	2.4	3.5	4.6	5.9	3.5	3.6
Centrally planned economies	6.5	2.9	2.9	3.2	4.3	7.5	2.4	2.0	3.2	2.9
Other LDCs	24.2	32.1	26.8	21.7	15.8	23.5	27.1	24.1	23.7	16.5

Columns do not sum because of rounding.

Source: Rowthorn and Wells (1987), 176, 185.

Competitiveness is made up of a number of elements of which marketing, selling, price, quality, delivery times and aftersales service are the main ones. But conditions can arise in which differences in these characteristics between what is *nominally* the same product exported by different countries become so wide, that it is more realistic to regard them as defining a different product. In these terms, the potentially large and indistinguishable overlap between the effects of changes in market share and commodity composition in trade performance is obvious.

Similar considerations apply to the direction of trade. Britain served quite widely dispersed markets in comparison with, for example, the EEC countries. The White Dominions noticeably still accounted for 20 per cent of exports of manufactures in 1961, even though this was substantially down on the 31 per cent recorded in 1951. The area effect on British trade was neutral, as has been indicated (Table 7.6) – it was evenly balanced in relation to the distribution of size and rates of growth in national markets. By the same token, however, Britain was not gaining from concentrating more of its trade in the fast-growing markets, particularly in the EEC where growth was substantially above world levels. Put another way, the UK was doing no better than the average for the world. To what extent commodity composition, more finely defined, conditioned the growth of trade and thus adds to the problem of defining causes, remains an intriguing question. The source of imports is unsurprising but, even so, the trend away from the White Dominions and towards the EEC is clear.

It is interesting, nevertheless, that the pattern is widely dispersed in comparison with the more rapidly growing economies of the EEC. Here the pattern was one of concentrated intra-regional trade, with the Federal Republic of Germany acting as both fulcrum and the major link with the wider world (Table 7.8).

The direction of trade involved more than simply matters of geography. A given set of markets involved a commercial and financial nexus. In the British case, this included preferential tariff arrangements with Commonwealth and Empire countries that traders could set against tariffs and trade regulations operating in other markets. And whilst the trade pattern was not static, if the requirement for the more rapid growth of British trade was a substantial and accelerated switch to new markets, this was not something that was easily achieved as part of a smooth process of adjustment. To the extent that it involved international trade bargaining, Britain was in a weaker position at the beginning of the

Table 7.8 European exports to West Germany as a percentage of all exports by value, selected years 1950–58

	1950	*1955*	*1958*
Austria	14.3	25.1	25.1
Belgium-Lux	6.8	11.7	11.6
Denmark	17.4	17.0	20.1
France	7.8	10.5	10.5
Italy	5.9	12.6	14.3
Netherlands	20.9	17.1	19.0
Norway	11.3	11.2	14.1
Portugal	3.6	7.8	7.7
Sweden	12.4	13.2	14.2
Switzerland	9.3	13.4	16.3
United Kingdom	2.0	2.6	3.8

Source: Milward (1992), 138.

1960s than it had been a decade earlier, a measure of which was a decline in its share of world exports of manufactures from 25 per cent to 13 per cent. More fundamentally, it was at this point that the weaknesses in the structure and performance of British industry bore most directly and damagingly on Britain's position in the world economy. The tightening competitive condition of visible trade was not eased by trade in services, which remained roughly in balance and at a volume approximately equivalent to one-third of visible exports. The net balance on invisible trade was mainly attributable to the favourable net return on property income.

The indeterminate nature of the relationship between trade and growth has been examined in an earlier context (Chapter 2). Despite an enormous amount of theoretical work by economists on mechanisms of economic growth in the post-Second World War period, the issue remains unresolved. Even so, a vast amount of circumstantial evidence, especially in relation to the EEC, points strongly to a high rate of growth of trade as a necessary condition of sustained high rates of economic growth. By the same token, well-documented weaknesses on the supply side of the British economy point to its growing inability to exploit those favourable conditions. In general terms, the full impact of these comparative shortcomings was not borne in on the economy because of the improvement in the terms of trade of no less than 30 per cent between 1951 and 1961. As has been noted, this gain resulted overwhelmingly from the big falls in the prices of food and raw materials. The more intriguing question concerns the effect of the direct restrictions on trade that continued from the war.

Trade regulation took the form of tariffs and import controls or quotas. The weakness of *ad valorem* tariffs as instruments of protection has already been considered (Chapter 5) and, in any event, a general process of all round reduction in tariffs followed from the GATT agreement of 1947. Import controls are quite a different matter since they do raise hard issues about trade protection, though these issues are very difficult to resolve. Table 7.9 shows that the proportion of trade subject to quotas fell steadily between the late 1940s and the mid-1950s and then strongly to the point of virtual abolition of quotas by the end of the decade. The exception was a rise between 1951 and 1952 as result of measures taken to meet the sterling crisis of that time. Whilst the overall reduction was in line with OEEC policy, it was strongly influenced, as has been noted, by the foreign policy aim of the government to promote freer international economic relations as a means of countering pressures on Britain, especially from the USA, to become a leading participant in closer European economic integration. Anything that seemed to create freer trade had a bewitching effect on US officialdom.

It has been estimated that import controls produced a saving of £310 million between 1946 and 1949 as compared with actual imports of £1,940 million. In 1952 the corresponding figures were approximately £250 million as against £3,000 million.[35] These estimates are subject to considerable margins of error because of the range of assumptions involved. If anything, these figures could be on the low side. At all events, these savings were clearly significant and they bear directly on the issue of industrial competitiveness. It has already been observed (Chapter 6) that the retention of import controls would have been essential for a high degree of economic planning. More realistically, they could have been a crucial part of microeconomic policy that aimed to raise

35. These estimates were made by M. F. G. Scott, *A Study of United Kingdom Imports* (Cambridge, 1963) and W. M. Corden, 'The Control of Imports: A Case Study in the United Kingdom Import Restrictions of 1951–2', *The Manchester School*, 26 (1958), pp. 181–221.

Table 7.9 UK import controls, 1946–58 (% subject to control)

	1946	1947	1948	1949	1950	1951	1952	1953	1954	1955	1956	1957	1958
Government direct imports	64	58	57	54	46	38	37	24	13	6	6	2	–
Restricted private imports	32	33	34	37	27	16	28	24	21	16	10	7	10
Total controlled imports	96	91	91	91	73	54	65	48	34	22	16	9	10

Source: Dow (1965), 174.

industrial productivity through closer cooperation between government and industry. Did the government's determination to abolish these controls amount, therefore, to a major missed opportunity?

There is no clear answer to this question. Circumstantial evidence suggests that whatever the failings on the part of government, they were well matched by the attitudes of the majority of industrialists who simply wanted to see an end to government interference in their affairs and who were buoyed up by a false optimism, engendered by easy export markets, as to their longer-term ability to compete in international trade. If quotas had been abolished more rapidly, British industry would have been brought up against a problem of import penetration a decade earlier than was actually the case. As it was, British industry enjoyed more protection in the 1950s than it fully realized. Moreover, the effect of trade controls did not end here. They had important consequences for financial policy to which we must now turn.

INTERNATIONAL FINANCIAL POLICY

International financial policy was at the heart of Britain's political economy in the 1950s. The issues were not clear cut because there were important differences of view between the two leading players, the Treasury and the Bank of England; though these differences were never allowed to undermine their common concern to define the limits within which politicians should be allowed freedom of action in these matters, and in economic matters generally. This mixture of motives and interests, not surprisingly, resulted in vacillation and lack of direction in policy. Uncertainty was increased by the limitations of technical and theoretical knowledge in general and by the narrow competence of Treasury and Bank of England officials in particular.

The position of sterling in international finance had to be resolved after what amounted to a period of transition between 1945 and 1949. Nominally, the Bretton Woods system was still in operation. But, as has been examined in detail in Chapter 6, sterling had been devalued in 1949 and, a year earlier, the International Monetary Fund had been superseded by Marshall Aid administered by the Organisation for European Economic Recovery. At the same time the US State Department became even more enthusiastic than it had been in 1945 for a high degree of political and economic integration in Europe, which included Britain. The US Treasury did not share the enthusiasm, though on this issue it was in the subordinate position. These attitudes made little difference, however, since US foreign policy aims were effectively thwarted when Britain joined the European Payments Union in 1950 under conditions which made it quite explicit that this institution would not become the vehicle for the launching of an integrated currency system.[36]

Sterling policy now focused on the long-standing problem of convertibility. The issue was complicated by two contemporary developments. First, in the summer of 1950, the government decided to embark on a major rearmament programme. In immediate terms this was a response to the increased communist threat of which the Korean War was seen as a dire warning of potentially worse things to come. And the speed of the programme imposed quite severe pressures on the balance of payments and precipitated a payments crisis in 1951–2. More fundamentally, rearmament marked the acceptance in principle (by a Labour government) of Britain's continued, and in some ways enhanced, role as a world power. Secondly, relations with the USA became increasingly strained. On the one hand the USA was annoyed by Britain's arm's length policy towards Europe, whilst on the other hand the USA proved unwilling to meet more than a small share of the cost of British rearmament, which was not what Britain had expected and to some extent had been led to believe. These conditions gave added impetus to the determined aim of the Bank of England to re-establish sterling as a major international currency and to restore London as a financial and commercial centre second only to New York and, in some respects, equal to it.[37]

The Bank's chosen instrument was a plan which was given the codename ROBOT.[38] It incorporated a floating rate for sterling, convertibility of what was defined as 'overseas sterling' (i.e. that held outside the sterling area) and the funding (in effect, blocking) of 80 per cent of sterling balances. It was anticipated that whilst

---

36. Milward, *The European Rescue of the Nation-State*, pp. 347–95; R. Triffin, *Europe and the Money Muddle. From Bilateralism to Near-Convertibility, 1947–1956* (New Haven, Conn. 1957).

37. A survey of these events is given by S. J. Procter, 'Floating Convertibility: The Emergence of the Robot Plan, 1951–52', *Contemporary Record*, 7 (1993), pp. 24–43.

38. Cairncross, *Years of Recovery*, pp. 234–71; C. Schenk, *Britain and the Sterling Area from Devaluation to Convertibility in the 1950s* (1994); Dow, *The Management of the British Economy 1945–60*, pp. 86–90.

sterling would float down it would soon stabilize at a level not much below the fixed rate and that, for the future, exchange reserves would not come under severe pressure when the balance of payments worsened, as adjustment would be achieved through the exchange rate. The scheme was invented in the context of considerable debate over exchange rate policy in 1951 and 1952 and it led to bitter discussions within official circles. In fact, Treasury estimates of the impact of the crisis on Britain's dollar reserves were wildly out. Instead of falling by between $600 million and $1,250 million by the end of the 1952, they increased to $1,850 million. As Cairncross has shown, there was a somewhat inexcusable lack of understanding in official circles of what was happening to the balance of payments. The rise in dollar imports in the second half of 1951 was known to be on government account in respect of the rearmament programme, and a corresponding falling back in 1952 should have been predicted. ROBOT was effectively dead by the end of February 1952 but it was not finally dropped until much later in the year.

The Bank was not easily put off, however, and some of its leading officials, with Treasury support, pressed on with what became known as the collective approach. In the new scheme, the aim of flexible exchange rates was replaced with that of floating rates within agreed limits, though obviously much wider than the adjustment limits under Bretton Woods. But the really critical assumptions of the collective approach were that sterling area countries would continue in support of British international financial interests and, much more improbably, that the USA would underwrite this extension of exchange rate flexibility to the tune of hundreds of millions of dollars. In all the toings and froings of these financial negotiations, Britain came up against the US attitude, personified by Foster Dulles, the secretary of state, that a high degree of European integration was a fundamental need, morally as well as politically, to the extent that Dulles was ever aware of such a distinction. Recent research has exposed the naiveté of British official thinking at the time in believing that US attitudes could be otherwise. Commonwealth governments were hardly less forthcoming in their support than the USA. As for the collective approach, it was overtaken by events. Britain's balance of payments improved by 1955 to the extent that sterling became *de facto* convertible, but within a fixed exchange rate system. In 1958 convertibility became official and the European Payments Union was replaced by the European Monetary Agreement.

ROBOT, at least in its essentials of floating rates of exchange, has continued to have its defenders.[39] The claim is that the rejection of the plan in favour of fixed exchange rates imposed a policy of stop-go on the economy because of the need to defend the par value of sterling with only slim reserves of currency and gold. The result was that periodic interest rate increases choked off demand and sapped the forces of economic growth (especially the level of investment). Britain's international competitiveness was thus severely damaged. There are a number of reasons, however, why this claim fails to carry conviction.[40]

First, it is now clear that Britain was no more subject to stop-go policies than a number of other major economies that grew rapidly, indeed rather less so.[41] Secondly, there is overwhelming evidence that investment is determined much more by profit expectations over the medium term than by short-term movements in interest rates. During this period market expectations had the powerful assurance of the government's commitment to a policy of full employment. Thirdly, the advocates of floating rates take no account of the effect their introduction would have had on the European Payments Union and on existing restrictions (agreed with the USA) on dollar imports into Western Europe. The EPU would either have foundered or would have to have been reorganized into a tighter discriminatory grouping. Thus Britain would have faced high barriers and financial complications in its trade with Western Europe and/or intensified competition in remaining markets,

---

39. See for example Brittan, *Steering the Economy*, p. 200. See also R. A. Butler, *The Art of the Possible* (1971), pp. 158–9 who argued that a floating rate would have avoided a number of subsequent difficulties in the economy. His approach to the issue when he was chancellor of the exchequer was certainly not an example of clear thinking – see S. J. Procter, 'Towards Convertibility: The Sterling Policy of the Conservative Governments, 1951–1958', unpublished University of Bristol Ph.D. thesis, 1990.

40. The attacks on the role of sterling have been particularly fierce. For an overall view see Alford, *British Economic Performance*, pp. 74–88. For the attack, see A. C. L. Day, *The Future of Sterling* (Oxford, 1954); F. Hirsch, *The Pound Sterling: A Polemic* (1965); Pollard, *The Wasting of the British Economy*, p. 88; A. Shonfield, *British Economic Policy Since the War* (1959 edition), p. 108; Strange, *Sterling and British Policy*, pp. 318 *ff*. Day was a major witness before the Radcliffe enquiry into the operation of the monetary system – see note 47.

41. M. Artis, 'Fiscal Policy for Stabilization' in W. Beckerman (ed.), *The Labour Government's Economic Record 1964–70* (1972), pp. 262–89; R. C. O. Matthews, 'Why Has Britain Had Full Employment Since the War?', *Economic Journal*, 78 (1968), pp. 195–204; A. Whiting, 'An International Comparison of the Instability of Economic Growth', *Three Banks Review*, 109 (1976), pp. 26–46.

especially from the Federal German Republic in the dollar area. Plausible estimates indicate that these changes would have amounted to a substantial net loss in exports.[42] Fourthly, given conditions of full employment and comparatively slow productivity growth, floating exchange rates as a mechanism for balance of payments adjustment adds up to a recipe for inflation above international levels, which would have been a disaster for British competitiveness. Fifthly, in the light of the distinct improvement in the current account surplus during the 1950s (with the exception of 1955) there are, as Cairncross states, 'no strong grounds for supposing that [Britain] would have done better with a lower rate of exchange'.[43]

So why did the Bank, aided and abetted by the Treasury, persist in its endeavours? As has been suggested above, insufficient understanding of the true position played an important part. But in much larger part the reason was the overriding concern of the Bank 'to strengthen the value and acceptability of sterling both internally and internationally'.[44] In its view what was at stake was the international interests of the City of London – and it went without question that what was good for the City could be nothing other than good for the country at large. The Bank was of the opinion that convertibility and a floating exchange rate were not means for dealing with balance of payments deficits; instead it considered that equilibrium should be achieved quite independently by means of deflation. By contrast, the Treasury, whilst supporting ROBOT and the role of the Bank, saw convertibility with flexible rates as important elements in maintaining balance of payments equilibrium, as well as having international implications. Nevertheless, in so far as the chancellor of the exchequer, R. A. Butler, understood the technicalities and the economic reality, he was fully committed to the objective of acquiring for Britain a position of international financial prestige. When powerful political opposition to ROBOT intervened, Butler's support became characteristically elusive and finally dissolved as if it had never existed.

Once again, it is important to draw attention to the effect of import controls. The extent to which these contributed to the trade balance has been indicated. If they had been completely abolished

---

42. Milward, *The European Rescue of the Nation-State*, pp. 356–8.

43. Cairncross, *Years of Recovery*, p. 268.

44. The Governor of the Bank to the chancellor of the exchequer, 13 February 1952, PRO T236/3240, cited by S. J. Procter, 'Floating Convertibility'.

or substantially reduced by the early 1950s, it is hard to see how the consequences for exchange stability could have been other than extremely serious. Under a system of floating rates, the trade balance would have been disastrous. Whilst import controls were increased as a defensive measure during the 1951–2 crisis, Cairncross states: 'The government appeared in 1952 to have lost faith in its power to control the balance of payments through import restrictions'.[45] A major thrust of both Treasury and Bank policy was the abolition of these controls. There could hardly be clearer testimony to misunderstanding married to preconception on both their parts.

What is equally striking is the total misjudgement of the US position shown by the Bank and to a slightly lesser extent by the Treasury. For the British authorities to have believed that the US would finance British pretensions amounted to high orders of delusion and arrogance. Even more remarkable was the Bank's dogged persistence in pursuit of these objectives after the Suez crisis in late 1956. The Anglo-French invasion of the Suez canal immediately led to a flight from sterling. In the event the consequences proved to be short-lived, but at the time Britain desperately needed international financial assistance which could only be provided by the USA. The sequence of events could not have made clearer the reality of Britain's world status. The money from the USA was forthcoming only on condition that Britain did as she was told and withdrew from Egypt. Britain could do no other than obey, yet it was compliance in a manner akin to a profligate eighteenth-century aristocrat agreeing to a mortgage on his estates with his banker: a temporary financial setback, perhaps a little loss of face, but not something that could fundamentally alter the birthright of the ruling class. The delusion of grandeur became clouded but it was not dispelled.

Britain's misjudgement of the international position was not restricted to the so-called special relationship with the USA. According to the leading authority on European reconstruction, 'The gulf between British views of a reconstructed world order and those of other OEEC members by summer 1954 were so wide, that they were talking about different worlds'.[46] Germany, in particular, had made it quite clear that it did not want the deutschmark to

---

45. Cairncross, *Years of Recovery*, p. 268.
46. Milward, *The European Rescue of the Nation-State*, p. 385. See also D. Reynolds, *Britannia Overruled. British Policy and World Power in The Twentieth Century* (1991).

become an international reserve currency. For their part British officials and political leaders did not believe that France, Germany, Italy and the Benelux countries could form an effective economic union on their own. Yet this is precisely what happened. The Treaties of Rome were signed in 1957 and the European Economic Community was inaugurated in January 1958. Britain was left with promoting a European Free Trade Area which it had first announced in 1956. This plan (and effectively British membership of the EEC) was rejected by the French in late 1958 and Britain was left to establish the European Free Trade Association in late 1959, which came into operation in July 1960. It was little more than a loose arrangement of countries peripheral to the EEC, which pursued joint trade liberalization a little ahead of the international rate of progress. Britain's isolation from decision-making in the most dynamic area of the world economy was virtually complete.

In 1957, the year before convertibility was formally adopted, sterling had been under severe pressure. To the crisis surrounding Suez was added general international instability following the devaluation of the franc and growing alarm at home at what were seen as inflationary wage claims. There was a sharp rise in the number of labour disputes, in particular as a result of unofficial strikes and stoppages of work. At the peak in 1957, the number of working days lost was four times the annual average level for the previous years since 1950. Mining, transport and engineering (especially motor manufacture) were the industries most affected. Full employment underpinned the bargaining strength of workers. More fundamentally, these disputes reflected weakness in management and industrial organization.

What at the time were considered to be severe deflationary measures were imposed. But when the chancellor of the exchequer, Thorneycroft, proposed a further turning of the screw he failed to get the backing of Cabinet and was forced to resign. More favourable international conditions in 1958, in particular a marked improvement in the terms of trade and reduced pressure from the overseas sterling area, produced a dramatic turnaround in the balance of payments. The crisis, however, had given rise to considerable questioning of the working of the monetary system and the role of the Bank of England. Moreover, the behaviour of City financial institutions during the crisis could in no way be described as being imbued with patriotism and the primacy of the national interest. Normal commercial instincts operated. Funds were moved out of sterling with alacrity and impunity, and with a keen eye for the maximum return; there were even charges of a bank rate leak. The upshot was the establishment of the *Committee on the Working of the Monetary System* (Radcliffe Committee).

The report of the Radcliffe Committee came in August 1959.[47] On the face of it, the main recommendations were a setback for the orthodox approach to economic policy. First, in various ways and on the basis of detailed evidence, it challenged the effectiveness of monetary policy, arguing in particular that investment decisions were determined by profit expectations and not by interest rate movements. Secondly, it confronted the role of the Bank of England in policy-making by stating that it was important to make 'more explicit the understanding that monetary policy must fall within the orbit of general economic policy and that the Government must bear the ultimate responsibility' and that the policies of the Bank should be 'from first to last in harmony with those avowed and defended by Ministers of the Crown responsible to Parliament'.[48] Taken together, these propositions could have provided the basis for a shift in economic policy that would have redefined more realistically Britain's international economic aspirations. Yet the Committee's effectiveness in this direction was enormously reduced by its failure to propose any reform of policy-making bodies. Thus any loss of influence by the Bank was more than balanced by confirmation of the central role of the Treasury. So far as international economic policy was concerned, it was a case of Tweedledum and Tweedledee.

STATUS QUO

Sterling was the emblem of Britain's world status in the 1950s. To its adherents, it represented not simply successful economic recovery from a victorious but immensely costly war, but restoration to a position of economic leadership which had been surrendered in 1931. The argument over whether the return to convertibility should be at a floating or fixed rate of exchange was far more than a technical issue: to its proponents a floating rate was the ultimate

---

47. *Committee on the Working of the Monetary System* Cmnd. 827. *Minutes of Evidence* (1960). *Principal Memoranda of Evidence,* 3 Vols. (1960). A mine of information on a range of topics including the attitudes of City financial institutions, the role of the Bank of England and the nature of financial policy formation. It revealed that businessmen's investment decisions were little affected by short-term interest rates.

48. Dow, *The Management of the British Economy 1945–60,* pp. 108–9.

mark of status and confirmation of the Bank of England as an arbiter of both domestic and international finances. Economic sense prevailed, at least to the extent that fixed rates of exchange under the hegemony of the dollar remained the order of the day. But the question remains as to whether even this concession sacrificed Britain's economic progress on the cross of an overvalued rate for sterling. It is a question that will be examined in more detail later (Chapter 8). For the present it is argued that whatever the direct effects on economic performance of sterling exchange rate policy, indirectly it revealed why the issue of international competitiveness was not satisfactorily addressed.

During the 1950s there was an informal and partly unconscious alliance between government and business that reaffirmed the essentials of their pre-war relationship and, more immediately, was a reaction against attempts at economic planning in the postwar period. On the side of business the relaxation and abolition of restrictive wartime and postwar economic controls was blindly equated to the necessary removal of government intervention in the economy. Early, albeit transitory, advantages in export markets and the recovery of domestic demand fed the belief in the virtue of a return to economic liberalism and so-called free markets, despite the rapid expansion of big business and monopolistic practices. There is, in addition, significant evidence of large British companies adopting investment strategies based on a false sense of internationalism.[49] The net result was a resumption of direct overseas investment against a background of low official reserves and low domestic investment ratios by international standards. The productivity record of British industry did not justify this kind of optimism but, as has been noted, it was underwritten by the government's commitment to sustain high demand and full employment. On the side of government, the Treasury had secured a firm grip on economic policy by the early 1950s.[50] Treasury officials adopted the rhetoric of Keynesian economics even though there is dispute over whether they applied its prescriptions. Keynesianism was used to validate macroeconomic management

49. A classic example is provided by Courtaulds in the person of its chairman between 1946 and 1962, Sir John C. Hanbury-Williams. He pursued a policy of securing an international status for the company regardless of profit: Coleman, *Courtaulds. An Economic and Social History*, pp. 25–6, 89–92. More generally, it was not a matter of the quantities of capital involved in aggregate (see Chapter 8) but the attitude of mind behind such decisions.

50. S. Brittan, *The Treasury Under the Tories 1951–1964* (1964), pp. 19–125.

through the levers of fiscal and monetary regulation. The Treasury saw its central task as that of maintaining the balance between full employment at home and the status and value of sterling abroad. What neither business sought nor the Treasury wished to allow was the development of any form of microeconomic policy in which government and business (and maybe organized labour) would combine in planning a strategy aimed at strengthening Britain's international competitiveness. Economic conservatism and administrative vested interests were easily allied.

CHAPTER EIGHT

Britain and the Climax of the Long Boom

THE FOUNDATIONS OF THE BOOM

The economic performance of the Western economies between 1950 and 1973 is now firmly inscribed in the annals as the period of the long boom. After two decades of exceptional economic growth by historical standards, eventually, in 1971, strong signs that all was far from well in the international economy began to appear, when the United States was forced to devalue the once-mighty dollar. Britain, itself, experienced severe economic problems in the following year, arising out of bitter labour disputes. But the *coup de grâce* to international economic stability was delivered in late 1973 when the major oil-producing countries formed a cartel, the Organisation of Petrol Exporting Countries (OPEC), with the result that oil prices were quadrupled almost overnight. Since cheap oil had literally fuelled the long boom, the world economy was plunged into its biggest crisis since the years immediately after the Second World War. Despite Britain's creditable economic performance during the long boom, especially in comparison with its past record, its persistent underlying economic weaknesses were severely exposed in a series of balance of payments crises until, in December 1976, the government was driven to seek international financial support in a manner which, in certain important respects, brought Britain's position in the world economy back full circle to that which it had experienced in the convertibility crisis of 1947.

After a quarter of a century of economic growth Britain was still living beyond its means. Popular demands for levels of consumption that were well up to the highest world standards, combined with the costs of pretension as a world power, were not matched by productive effort. It is far from clear that the latter was necessarily a consequence of the former, as some commentators have sought to argue, given the levels of consumption sustained by other advanced economies. But on all the usual measures of output, British performance maintained its consistency in being markedly inferior to that of the other major economies.

Table 8.1 UK comparative economic performance, 1950–73

	GDP growth per year %	GDP per person hour % per year	GDP per head UK = 100	
			1950	*1973*
United Kingdom	3.0	3.2	100	100
Australia	4.7	2.7	105	103
Austria	5.4	5.9	50	86
Belgium	4.1	4.4	75	94
Canada	5.2	2.9	108	118
Denmark	4.0	4.1	92	105
Finland	4.9	5.2	62	90
France	5.1	5.0	73	103
Germany	6.0	6.0	59	100
Italy	5.5	5.5	50	85
Japan	9.7	7.6	28	92
Netherlands	4.8	4.3	83	102
Norway	4.0	4.3	80	93
Sweden	3.8	4.4	94	112
Switzerland	4.5	3.3	116	131
USA	3.7	2.4	152	140

Source: Maddison (1991), 198–9, 216–19, 274–5.

The long boom created a culture of economic growth, though its precise nature varied according to national circumstances. In Britain and the Western European economies, in particular, the pursuit of economic growth went hand in hand with policies of extensive state welfare. In the USA and Japan this relationship was far more tenuous. But universally the belief took hold that economic growth was a continuing process; expressing it in terms of compound interest transformed this belief into a definition of fact. Economists rushed to give it analytical form through newly fashionable growth theory, though it is somewhat ironical that the most active centres of such theorizing were to be found in Britain and the USA, the two slowest growing of the major economies.

When viewed in historical perspective the long boom is exposed as the exception rather than the rule of twentieth-century economic development. It was sustained by a number of elements specific to the period.[1] First, postwar reconstruction programmes, including US aid schemes, gave a big initial impetus to economic recovery. These involved, either directly or indirectly, a number of radical institutional changes which were conducive to rapid economic growth, though as will be seen Britain lagged well behind France, Germany and Japan in this regard. Secondly, during the 1930s and the war years an accumulation of technical advance was built up by the USA that resulted in a technological gap between that country and the other major industrial nations.[2] The rewards to be gained from the exploitation of this gap by means of technical diffusion, were enormous by the end of the war. These conditions created a tremendous impetus to trade in manufactured goods between the advanced economies, though the extent to which an individual country would gain from this trade would depend on the strength of its comparative advantage; in other words it would depend on competitiveness. Older products ranging from steel to motor cars could be manufactured by new processes, whilst totally new goods in such fields as electronics and artificial fibres were in the vanguard of modern methods of mass production. Technology transfer on this scale generated and was sustained by large flows of commercial capital from the USA, often through the agency of rapidly expanding multinational companies. These transfers also brought with them new forms of organization and management techniques. Even so, the capacity to generate high levels of domestic investment was overwhelmingly important as a necessary condition for exploiting new technological opportunities.

Thirdly, the war had stimulated demands for higher levels and new forms of peacetime public expenditure. It had been in Britain, after all, a people's war fought for a better world that would not only be rid of fascism but also secure from the scourge of unemployment. The New Jerusalem, as it is sometimes called, took on different forms in different countries, but in Western Europe, in particular, it led to widespread provision of social welfare. Public finances were further swelled by defence expenditures when the

---

1. C. J. Allsopp, 'The Management of the World Economy', in W. Beckerman (ed.), *Slow Growth in Britain. Causes and Consequences* (1979), pp. 140–65.

2. OECD, *Gaps in Technology: Analytical Report* (Paris, 1970). J. H. Dunning, *American Investment in British Manufacturing Industry* (1958).

postwar world proved to be much less secure than had been hoped. Quite apart from specific needs and demands, war finance had accustomed both government and public to higher levels of public expenditure. Between 1937 and 1951, public expenditure rose from 26 per cent to 37.5 per cent of GDP. It remained at about this level until the mid-1960s when it again increased to reach 42.9 per cent by 1973. Public expenditure on this scale maintained a high basic level of demand in the economy.[3]

Fourthly, up to the late 1960s the political economy of western countries was suffused with high expectations of growth that acted as a constant stimulus to investment. The ideological framework within which these expectations were formed varied – indicative planning in France, the Social Market Economy in Germany, neo-corporatism in Japan, Keynesian demand management in Britain – but all subscribed to the belief that high levels of economic activity and employment could and would be maintained. At the lowest common factor, it was the political economy. of maximization of return.[4]

Fifthly, there was a conjunction of elements of structural change, centring on the supply and distribution of labour. During the war the labour market had experienced massive disturbance which broke up the pattern of employment of the 1930s and tended to make for greater labour mobility after the war. In addition, France, Germany and Italy, though not Britain, had large reserves of labour in low productivity agriculture. The nature and effects of these elements is disputed, however. Whilst rapid economic growth was accompanied by the rapid growth and redistribution of the labour force, it is by no means clear that these were causative conditions. For one thing, there is much evidence to suggest that, given

3. R. Middleton, 'The Size and Scope of the Public Sector', in S. J. D. Green and R. G. Whiting (eds), *The Boundaries of the State in Modern Britain* (Cambridge, 1995), forthcoming. For an excellent account of the development of welfare policies see R. Lowe, *The Welfare State in Britain Since 1945* (1993). It is important to note that transfer payments, particularly in respect of social welfare, formed a major part of public expenditure in Western European countries and Britain. Even so, in so far as this involved the transfer of income from the better-off to the poorer sections of the community, such payments would tend to raise the level of demand.

4. A contemporary analysis is A. Shonfield, *Modern Capitalism: The Changing Balance of Public and Private Power* (1965). This interpretation has come in for some revisionism in recent years (see below note 17) but the fact remains that, whatever the reality and effectiveness of government intervention during this period, the expectation was that demand would be managed to maintain at near-full employment. A contemporary analysis that fully reflects this attitude is A. Maddison, *Economic Growth in the West* (1964).

demand, labour supply expands relatively easily as, for example, part-time, female and foreign workers are drawn into the labour force. For another thing, the supply is not only a function of the number of people available for work but, also, of their level of productivity. Thus in the case of Britain there was no *a priori* reason why low reserves of agricultural labour should not have been compensated for by higher levels of labour productivity in other sectors. What seems critical in this respect, therefore, was not the supply of labour but its capacity to adapt to the requirements of structural change; though it must be added, that the latter is by no means independent of the former.[5]

Finally, whilst the individual economies experienced fluctuations in activity around a strong upward growth trend, these fluctuations did not occur in a predictable pattern of the kind that generations of trade cycle theorists have vainly endeavoured to discover. Likewise, this degree of variance runs strongly counter to those theories that purport to explain postwar economic growth in universal terms. The random, or as economists term it, stochastic, nature of these fluctuations resulted in a lack of synchronization between economies. In this way the international economy benefited from an in-built economic stabilizer which kept overall fluctuations within safe limits. By the same token, circumstances could change and produce just such a synchronization which could cause extremely serious international economic dislocation. The expectation was, however, that such a conjunction was no more likely than a permanent eclipse. The predominant view of the world economy was that a crisis of the kind that had occurred in 1931 was truly a thing of the past, mainly because it was believed that advances in economic knowledge had provided the necessary remedies.[6]

The nature of these autonomous elements in economic growth changed during the course of the period. Reconstruction programmes had spent their force by the early 1950s. Likewise, the

5. The seminal theoretical position was defined by W. A. Lewis, 'Economic Development with Unlimited Supplies of Labour', *The Manchester School,* 22 (1954), pp. 139–91. A specific analysis of the postwar period is to be found in J. Cornwall, *Modern Capitalism, Its Growth and Transformation* (1977), pp 67–96; C. P. Kindleberger, *Europe's Postwar Growth. The Role of the Labour Supply* (Cambridge, Mass., 1967). A useful survey of the main issues is provided by H. Van Der Wee, *Prosperity and Upheaval. The World Economy 1945–1980* (1986), pp. 174–99.

6. The theory of economic growth became the dominant interest in economics. In economic history this confident approach was reflected in the enthusiasm for W. W. Rostow, *The Stages of Economic Growth* (Cambridge, 1960).

Table 8.2 UK balance of payments, 1961–75. Main items as a percentage of GDP

	(1) Manufactures	(2) Primary products	(3) Non-government services	(4) Commercial balance = (1)+(2)+(3)	(5) Government services and grants	(6) Interest, profits, dividends	(7) Long-term investment	(8) Residual balance = (5)+(6)+(7)	(9) Basic balance = (4)+(8)
1961–65	+6.4	−7.1	+0.6	−0.1	−1.1	+1.2	−0.5	−0.4	−0.5
1966–70	+4.9	−5.7	+1.0	+0.2	−0.9	+1.0	−0.4	−0.3	−0.1
1971–75	+3.5	−6.2	+1.4	−1.3	−0.7	+1.2	−0.3	+0.2	−1.1

Source: Rowthorn and Wells (1987), 98

impact of public expenditure growth had levelled by the early 1970s. The technological gap, technical diffusion and the associated flows in investment and trade, operated throughout the period, but the spectacular growth of Continental Western European economies and, more latterly, of the Japanese economy, steadily reduced the technical leadership of the USA to a position of *primus inter pares* by the early 1970s. The gain in productivity to the European economies in Japan from this technology transfer mechanism was correspondingly reduced.

The weakening of these autonomous elements did not, in itself, mean that the boom was nearing its end. In contrast to the years immediately after the war, the world economy was now based on a number of strong nations operating through systems and organizations of mutual self-interest. And domestic conditions and individual government policies played a part which is yet to be examined. What brought an end to the international feast was the fourfold increase in oil prices in 1973. That act achieved the one thing that had not occurred in the world economy in a quarter of a century: a shock wave that hit all economies at the same time at their most vulnerable point. Simultaneously, there was a crisis of belief in self-sustaining economic growth and in the nostrums associated with it.

TRADE GROWTH

Notwithstanding an improvement in productivity during the late 1960s, British economic performance remained at a fairly constant level throughout the long boom. It was a record that kept Britain firmly at the bottom of the international league (Table 8.1). The trading position remained correspondingly insecure, though the nature of it underwent significant changes (Table 8.2).

Four features stand out from the overall picture. First, the manufacturing balance fell substantially between 1960 and the early 1970s, though it remained positive. Secondly, and relatedly, there was a sharp rise in the degree of import penetration of manufactured goods. Thirdly, the negative balance on primary products continued to fall. And, fourthly, the balance on non-government services recovered to a level above the high point of the early 1950s. These movements must be seen in relation to the rapid growth in world trade based predominantly in trade in manufactured goods between the advanced economies. This feature

Table 8.3 Industrial import penetration of UK domestic market, 1961–75 (imports as % domestic sales)

	Total imports	Remaining imports
1961	11	10
1962	11	9
1963	11	10
1964	14	12
1965	13	11
1966	14	12
1967	15	12
1968	17	15
1969	18	14
1970	18	15
1971	18	15
1972	21	18
1973	25	22
1974	31	28
1975	28	25

Remaining imports = Less import content of exports

Source: Bacon and Eltis (1976), 217–31.

was in marked contrast to the pre-war period and confounded theoretical predictions made in the 1940s based on the idea that as trade rose non-tradable goods and services would form an increasing proportion of domestic consumption. In particular, such theories completely missed the point that comparative advantage existed in the production of manufactured goods and that a very wide range of services is tradable.[7]

The increase in import penetration, in particular, provided a focus for a major debate on deindustrialization in Britain, as measured by the decline in the industrial workforce. The argument has frequently generated more heat than light and it should stand as warning against the facile use of statistics. If Britain had managed to close only half the gap in productivity between itself and its

7. The literature on this debate is surveyed in B. W. E. Alford, *British Economic Performance, 1945–75* (Cambridge, 1995), pp. 34–51. In addition see the outstanding analysis by R. E. Rowthorn and J. R. Wells, *De-Industrialization and Foreign Trade* (Cambridge, 1987). As in the previous chapter I have relied heavily on their work for data on trade.

major competitors, the gain in output would have been many times the loss reckoned to have resulted from the decline in the industrial labour force. Whether such an improvement would have altered the balance of trade in manufactures is, again, not a straightforward matter. The outcome depends on whether Britain was gaining from comparative advantage in other sectors of trade such that it could afford to spend more on those manufactured imports in which it did not enjoy a comparative advantage. With higher productivity in manufacturing industry, this balance of advantage would have been *proportionately similar but at higher levels* of both industrial production and income.

A big contribution to trade gain came from the improvement in the balance of primary products. From the mid-1960s this resulted mainly from a reduction in import volume, even though GDP was rising, and only marginally from a fall in import prices. Some part of the lower import volume reflected the greater efficiency of material use, the continued development of substitutes (as in artificial fibres) and advances in technology which meant that raw materials accounted for a declining proportion of the final value of goods produced. But in much larger part the fall was a direct result of reductions in imported foodstuffs. In comparison with 1958 the biggest gains in self-sufficiency were in cereals (from 46 per cent to 68 per cent), butter (6 per cent to 23 per cent), cheese (41 per cent to 58 per cent) and other milk products (76 per cent to 120 per cent). These gains were hardly the result of unfettered comparative advantage, however. Whilst agriculture achieved major improvements in productivity with only 3 per cent of the total workforce, these were purchased at an enormous cost through protection from cheaper foreign imports and huge domestic subsidies. One estimate puts the total cost of subsidies at £63 billion between 1946 and the early 1980s, and this calculation includes no allowance for environmental damage and public concern for animal welfare.[8]

The increases in non-government service income have frequently been highlighted in their contribution to the balance of payments. The City of London and its defenders have been particularly vocal in this regard. It is, moreover, the case that this sector was far less affected by import penetration than was manufacturing and the fall in its share of the world total, from 25 per cent to 15 per cent between 1955 and 1975, was creditable in view of the enormous

8. R. Body, *Farming in the Clouds* (1984), p. 37, cited by Rowthorn and Wells, *De-industrialization and Foreign Trade*, pp. 105, 399.

growth in the world economy during that period. Between 1966 and 1976 net overseas earnings grew by just over fivefold compared with just over a doubling for manufacturing industries. Within this overall increase, insurance grew by a factor of 11.7, construction overseas by 11.4, banking by 7.7, brokerage by 7.3 and commodity trading by 5.8. Productivity in services is notoriously difficult to estimate, however; indeed, no satisfactory figures are available. The broad issue can be illustrated by comparing insurance, banking and allied services with manufacturing. In very crude terms, the former returned a gross GDP per person of £6,530 in 1976 as against £4,140 for the latter. But these comparisons have to be placed in the context of services maintaining a respectable share of international business, of comparatively low productivity growth in manufacturing industry and comparatively low productivity growth for the economy as a whole. All of which combined, points to the UK gaining from the comparative advantage in a relatively low productivity sector. International services shared a common characteristic with services generally, namely, that they employed a high proportion of female labour concentrated in the lower occupational grades and rewarded at wage rates significantly below their male counterparts. This pattern of employment is probably an important reason why gross profits in services were substantially higher than in manufacturing. In the mid-1960s the ratio was 1.6, and by the mid-1970s this had widened to a remarkable 7.5.[9]

What these underlying movements in the balance of payments reflect is relatively low productivity growth in international terms, but with a superior economic performance the balance between sectors of the economy would probably have remained much the same. A larger surplus on manufacturing trade could have financed a strengthening of reserves and allowed more direct finance of overseas investment than was actually adopted, as will be discussed later. Alternatively or in part, there could have been an increase in import penetration of manufactures as a consequence of the improved balances on the export of services and the import of primary goods. Whether the increase in penetration was exceptional, in the sense of undermining industrial capacity, is the really difficult question (see Chapter 9). The enormous cost of supporting agriculture can be counted as a misallocation of

9. Calculations made by Alford, *British Economic Growth, 1945–75*, p. 57. There are enormous difficulties of definition. Broadly defined manufacturing or service industries may subsume both kinds of activity. For example, is an accountant working in the chemical industry part of the services sector?

resources that might otherwise have been applied to industrial development. At all events, in this regard at least the UK was in line with all the advanced countries. The EEC financed the stupendously costly Common Agricultural Policy, whilst the governments of the USA, Japan and Sweden, for example, acceded to the demands of powerful agricultural lobbies. The truth may be that Britain was the least able to afford this largesse.[10]

The fragile nature of the UK balance of payments has been elaborated into a theory which hypothesizes that British economic growth was constrained by the growth of demand for its exports. In order to maintain external balance the rate of growth of income could not exceed the ratio between the rate of growth of demand for British exports and the income elasticity of demand for foreign imports. If true, this relationship limited UK growth to just under 3 per cent as compared with approximately 5 per cent for France, 6 per cent for Germany and 13 per cent for Japan. The problem with this analysis, however, is that it is based on measures of outcomes. Thus, if the calculations are adjusted to compensate for Britain's loss of world share of exports (that is for competitiveness) it does not appear to have been at a disadvantage. In other words, the constraint was not foreign demand for British goods but supply-side deficiencies at home. The balance of payments simply registered this fact.[11]

Changes in the direction of trade were an obvious sign of Britain's changing position in the world economy. In important respects, what occurred during the 1960s marked the end of an era that stretched back to the beginning of the century. Trade with the EEC nearly doubled between 1958 and 1974 while trade with the White Dominions was halved. There was, moreover, a sharp fall in trade with late-developing countries, a major cause being the general break-up of the Empire and its associated trading arrangements of imperial preference and the extension of these to

10. One rough indication of this pattern is given by figures for the level of output per person employed in agriculture as a percentage of the average for the economy for as late as 1987: France 68%, Germany 42%, Japan 34%, Netherlands 97%, UK 86%, USA 92% – A. Maddison, *Dynamic Forces in Capitalist Development* (Oxford, 1991), p. 151. For a more detailed discussion see A. S. Milward, *The European Rescue of the Nation-State* (1992), pp. 225–317.

11. The strongest argument was originally advanced by A. P. Thirlwall, 'The Balance of Payments Constraint as an Explanation of International Growth Rate Differences', *Banco del Lavora Quarterly Review*, 128 (1979), pp. 44–53. For a useful critique see N. F. R. Crafts, 'Economic Growth', in N. F. R. Crafts and N. W. C. Woodward, *The British Economy since 1945* (Oxford, 1991), p. 266.

third markets. In the process, the Commonwealth lost its economic *raison d'être* and Britain was driven inexorably into the network of trade between the advanced economies. Between 1958 and 1973 the proportion of British visible exports going to the EEC, the rest of Western Europe, the USA and Japan rose from 39 per cent to 53 per cent. The comparable figures for imports of primaries show a rise from 35 per cent to 44 per cent and for manufactured goods the increase was from 66 per cent to 78 per cent.

These shifts in the direction of trade are given even more point when placed against an analysis of changes in the volume of UK exports. This shows that Britain lost out heavily on volume share of world trade in the period up to 1967, overwhelmingly as a consequence of loss of competitiveness. The loss through area was small and the effect of commodity composition was neutral. The net result was that while world trade grew by nearly 46 per cent between 1963 and 1967 the corresponding growth for the UK was 11 per cent. From then until the early 1970s the loss of market share continued but at a much slower rate, though world trade was still growing one-third faster than that of the UK. Attention has already been drawn to the limitations of this kind of disaggregated analysis but, taking the losses together, the pattern suggests strongly that there was a substantial, once-for-all, effect from the switch of British trade into European markets but that the attrition of Britain's competitive position continued, albeit at a reduced rate.

THE ROLE OF THE STATE

Maximizing the rate of economic growth became the central aim of political economy during the long boom. Theoretical, political and popular discourse became suffused with an ever-increasing flow of economic statistics. Perhaps most striking was the manner in which economic growth came to be viewed as the outcome of an evolutionary process. Thus the advanced economies were seen as having reached a stage at which growth was at least sustainable and most probably self-sustaining. Despite the methodological tensions which existed between them, in this field of explanation historians and economists seemed to have achieved a significant measure of analytical reconciliation. Historians, it appeared, could explain the process of economic evolution whilst economists dealt with the functioning of the fully developed system. These forms of analysis were recognized as being far from totally consistent with one another, but what was purveyed was a powerful sense that the advanced economies had achieved a state of economic grace. The most popular historical account, *The Stages of Economic Growth* (1960) by W. W. Rostow, was of American origin but it relied heavily on a schematic description of British economic development from the eighteenth century onwards, around which the other advanced economies were fitted into the picture. Its widespread appeal owed much to the fact that it presented economic development, which led to economic growth, as a repeatable process, and in this form it provided a ready historical pedigree for contemporary theories of economic growth. Alternative historical analyses were developed that were much more sensitive to the variety of historical evidence and correspondingly less grandiose in their claims; the most important of these was A. Gerschenkron, *Economic Backwardness in Historical Perspective* (1962) to which reference has already been made (Chapter 1). Gerschenkron was, however, silent on the question of whether a country that had achieved the breakthrough into industrialization, by devising substitutes that had overcome the handicaps of time, could subsequently fall back into a state of *comparative* economic backwardness. Even so, the whole thrust of the historical analysis which Gerschenkron's ideas stimulated was that the means of over-coming economic backwardness, in themselves, sustained the process of growth. Thus, differences and disputes between historians arose over the nature of the means rather than the outcomes.

The language of historical analysis and economic theory coloured and shaped more popular debate on economic performance, and both were interwoven into what became known as international growthmanship. Appropriately, league tables of economic performance began to proliferate. A new branch of economic statistics was invented which set out to measure the sources of economic growth and, hence, to explain why growth rates differed between nations. This analysis, based on the neo-classical theory of the production function, apportioned the sources of growth between inputs of labour, capital and other factors, or the residual as it was termed.[12] These calculations

---

12. The major pioneering work is E. E. Denison, *Why Growth Rates Differ. Postwar Experience in Nine Western Countries* (Washington, 1967). A broad critique of these techniques is provided by Van Der Wee, *Prosperity and Upheaval*, pp. 138–74. The British equivalent is R. C. O. Matthews, C. H. Feinstein and J. C. Odling-Smee, *British Economic Growth 1856–1973* (Stanford, Calif., 1982). See p. 97 n. 38.

depended on extremely tight assumptions – including perfectly competitive factor and product markets, constant returns to scale and fixed relationships between sectors of the economy during the period measured – that were wide open to the charge that they did not reflect the real world. As has been discussed above, the causal relationships between these variables is indeterminate. They may vary such that, for example, during given periods the rate of growth of capital and/or labour may be the consequence of the overall rate of growth. Viewed from this perspective, the form of the exercise and the pattern of results it yielded were revealing in a way that, perhaps ironically, was perplexing for economists and reassuring for economic historians. What emerged was that the most important factor accounting for both the level and variability of economic growth was not, as had been commonly thought, the combination of labour supply and capital investment, but the residual: that bundle of conditions that could only be measured by elimination but which included such elements as technical change, management techniques, labour practices, education and training, and government policy; in short, the very stuff of economic performance.

In the early stages of the boom, rapid economic growth in Western European economies and Japan had not led to serious questioning of Britain's comparative performance. Those economies were seen as experiencing a natural acceleration from very low postwar levels, whilst Britain was achieving rates of growth that represented a significant advance on its pre-war record. But as evidence and possible explanations of the persistence of these deficiencies accumulated, attitudes in Britain began to show signs of change. The formation of the National Economic Development Council in 1961 signalled this concern. As has been noted, there was considerable opposition to this new approach, especially from within the ranks of the Conservative party. Nonetheless, contrasts drawn with foreign competitors, especially in relation to the planning role of the state, were compelling.[13] This concern was shared in a number of quarters. In 1961 a major report on public expenditure was published (Plowden) that strongly urged the case for a more planned approach based on rolling five-year accounting

---

13. A little later these theories were effectively expressed in the influential book, Shonfield, *Modern Capitalism.*

periods.[14] Further support for a new approach to economic policy came from the Federation of British Industry. Here the emphasis was not directly on planning as such but on the need for a more cooperative approach to economic strategy based on medium-term assessments of economic prospects.[15] Finally, Harold Macmillan, the prime minister, had an active interest in a more interventionist industrial and economic policy. He had never cast off the principles of government management of the economy which he had first set out in the 1930s.[16]

The nature of state involvement in Western economies did not follow a common pattern, however. Indicative planning in France could be contrasted with the powerfully corporate nature of the Japanese Ministry of International Trade and Industry (MITI) which actively protected, subsidized and promoted key sectors of the Japanese economy. Much less overtly than in either of these countries, in Germany government at both the federal and state (*Landes*) level indirectly fostered industrial growth under the banner of the Social Market Economy.[17] But what was common to these countries in contrast to Britain was the central management of the economy in accordance with industrial and commercial objectives conceived, not simply within domestic dimensions but within the broader framework of the world economy. With obvious

14. *The Control of Public Expenditure*, 1961, Cmnd. 1432. This contains much important information but it does not make for easy reading. A critical analysis of Plowden in the context of the Treasury-dominated civil service is R. Lowe, 'Milestone or Millstone? The 1959–61 Plowden Committee and Its Impact on British Welfare Policy', forthcoming. I am grateful to the author for this paper.

15. P. Meadows, 'Planning', in F. T. Blackaby *et al*, *British Economic Policy 1960–74* (Cambridge, 1978), pp. 402–8.

16. H. Macmillan, *Reconstruction: A Plea for a National Policy* (1933) and *idem.*, *The Middle Way* (1938).

17. The difference in extent and effectiveness of government/industry relations between Britain on the one hand and Western Europe and Japan on the other, is subject to debate. See Shonfield, *Modern Capitalism*; J.-J. Carré, P. Dubois and E. Malinvaud, *French Economic Growth* (Stanford, Calif., 1975); S. Estrom and P. Holmes, *French Planning in Theory and Practice* (1983); A. J. Nichols, *Freedom With Responsiblity: The Social Market Economy in Germany* (Oxford, 1994); J. Zysman, *Governments, Markets and Growth: Financial Systems and the Politics of Industrial Change* (Ithaca, NY, 1983). For an interesting case study of the Japanese MITI set within the broader literature see P. A. O'Brien, 'Industry Structure as a Competitive Advantage: The History of Japan's Postwar Steel Industry', *Business History*, 34 (1992), pp. 128–59. Differences of view are brought out in M. Chick (ed.), *Governments, Industries and Markets: Aspects of Government-Industry Relations in the UK, Japan, West Germany and the USA since 1945* (Aldershot, 1990). For some revisionism in the case of Italy see V. Zamagni, *The Economic History of Italy, 1860–1990* (Oxford, 1993), pp. 321–78.

variations, microeconomic direction and manipulation were accorded central importance. Yet it was not simply a matter of cause leading to effect. These policies were the outcome of complex relationships involving management practices, labour organizations, education and training and, more deeply, social and cultural norms. The practical attempts at economic planning in Britain reveal this all too clearly. For this reason it is an open and disputed question as to just how effective government/industry relations were in promoting economic growth in the Western European countries and Japan. Evidence of incompetence and inefficiency can be found, but the circumstantial case in terms of the contrast with Britain remains a strong one. And even if Britain's major competitors gained much less from state involvement than it appears, it does not follow that Britain was that much less in need of it.

The objectives of NEDC were couched in the characteristic prose of civil service mandarins and, therefore, offered the greatest flexibility of interpretation:

a) To examine the economic performance of the nation with particular concern for plans for the future in both private and public sectors of industry.
b) To consider together what are the obstacles to quicker growth, what can be done to improve efficiency, and whether the best use is being made of our resources.
c) To seek agreement upon ways of improving economic performance, competitive power and efficiency, in other words, to increase the rate of sound growth.[18]

The organization was divided into two sections – one concerned with general economic issues, the other with particular sectors of industries. Quite soon, the Council's deliberations became focused on the implications of achieving a 4 per cent annual growth rate. It would seem that this rate was fixed upon as one that was a realistic target in relation to current performance and respectable in comparative international terms. However, for an economy which had been growing at just under 3 per cent a year this was a very tall order. The enormous implications this had in terms of productivity growth were obviously not fully appreciated. There is more than a

18. Meadows, 'Planning', citing Lord Bridges, *The Treasury* (1964), p. 219. Bridges was a Treasury mandarin *par excellence* and as Permanent Secretary to the Treasury from 1945 to 1956 he exercised a powerful influence of economic policy.

suspicion, however, that an unrealistic target was not challenged by senior Treasury officials since it served their interests in discrediting a planning approach to economic policy.[19]

By the end of 1963 the record of economic performance made it clear that the 4 per cent target was not being achieved. There was no downward revision, however, because in 1964 a Labour government came to power committed to a policy of modernization to be achieved by an altogether more professional approach to government in general and economic policy in particular, than had hitherto been the case. Central to this policy was the production of a national plan, and to oversee its formulation and subsequent implementation a new ministry, the Department of Economic Affairs was established in 1964. As had been promised, a 4 per cent growth rate was the keystone of the five-year National Plan announced on 1 February 1965. From the outset, however, the Plan and the Ministry of Economic Affairs ran into severe difficulties and by 1966 both were effectively dead, though the Ministry continued in a comatose state until it was finally laid to rest in 1969.[20]

Part of the failure could no doubt be attributed to political ineptitude. More fundamentally, the central assumption of a 4 per cent growth rate was unrealistic and thus made nonsense of the range of projections contained in the Plan. The Plan and, more importantly, the Ministry thus became easy prey to the Treasury which was set on their destruction. The reasons for the Treasury's opposition will be considered shortly. More immediately, the Plan was overtaken by the establishment, in 1966, of the Industrial Reorganisation Corporation (IRC) with specific charge to promote industrial reorganization with the aim of improving Britain's international competitiveness. It was an independent organization financed by the government to the tune of £150 million and it drew its membership from leading businessmen.

It is beyond the scope of this book to examine the activities of the IRC in detail.[21] Between 1966 and 1970, the latter being the year in which it was wound up, it was involved in nearly 100 projects. The most notable were the promotion of a merger in the

19. R. Opie, 'Economic Planning and Growth' in W. Beckerman (ed.), *The Labour Government's Economic Record, 1964–70* (1972), pp. 157–77.

20. P. Hare, *Planning the British Economy* (1985).

21. On the motor car industry see R. Church, *The Rise and Decline of the British Motor Industry* (1994), pp. 84–124 and Milward, *The European Rescue of the Nation-State*, pp. 408–24. And on the electrical industry merger see R. Jones and O. Marriott, *Anatomy of a Merger: the History of GEC, AEI and English Electric* (1970).

motor industry in 1966–7 to form British Leyland and backing the absorption of Associated Electrical Industries by the General Electric Company in 1968. The attitude of the government at the time was firmly expressed by Anthony Crosland who, as president of the Board of Trade, was the minister directly involved in the latter.

> The government takes the view that the rationalisation which the proposed merger would facilitate would increase the efficiency and productivity of the electrical engineering industries, and in particular the effectiveness of the export effort of the companies whose overseas sales are of the greatest importance to the Balance of Payments.[22]

The Leyland merger proved to be a milestone on the road to the final collapse of the British motor industry. As for GEC, its subsequent development fell well short of expectations. And the case of British Leyland, in particular, illustrates that the IRC was a characteristically British invention in its lack of sufficient professional expertise when it came to the detailed implementation of policy decisions.

For all its initial busying the IRC did not satisfy its political masters and in 1968 the Industrial Expansion Act was passed which gave the government greater freedom of action to intervene in industry and to finance company restructuring than was allowed to the IRC. Aluminium and computers were the two cases of government intervention under this Act. In each the aim was to promote companies which could effectively meet the rigours of international competition. The Act was not used again, mainly because of a more active policy by the IRC which had been given new management. Moreover, actions under both these provisions became part of a larger involvement in industry, that resulted either from broader aspects of policy or from unanticipated developments.[23]

The aircraft industry took the jackpot in the former category. On the civil aircraft side government collaboration was secured by commercial firms on the basis that help with development costs was necessary if the industry was to sustain a credible international position. The overall case was accepted as unanswerable when the

---

22. Jones and Marriott, p. 1.

23. A valuable survey of the policies pursued is given by P. Mottersead, 'Industrial Policy', in Blackaby *et al*, *British Economic Policy 1960–74*, pp. 418–83. See also C. F. Pratten, *Economies of Scale in Manufacturing Industry* (Cambridge, 1971).

development costs of military aircraft were thrown into the scales. Concorde was the most spectacular case in the civil field. Its total development costs rose from between £200 million and £225 million in 1962 to £760 million in 1974 in constant 1970 prices. Of this amount, the government generously provided £460 million. Despite the predicted and subsequent commercial failure of Concorde, the government could at least claim it had played a major part in creating the fastest white elephant in modern times. When direct support to military products is added, total government financial contribution to the aircraft industry between 1960 and 1974 amounted to just under £760 million in 1970 prices.

Shipbuilding and the textile industries were cases in which difficulties arose mainly as a consequence of obsolete technologies, outdated business structures and concentrated geographical location. Here, again, substantial sums of public money were injected. The shipbuilding industry received £150 million between 1965 and 1974 in 1970 prices. £34 million was provided for the textile industry between 1960 and 1967. The sum total of all government expenditure on industrial intervention between 1960 and 1974 was just over £1 billion in 1970 prices. Moreover, this amount does not include the benefits companies enjoyed as a consequence of the highly favourable tax regime under which they operated. This aspect is considered in Chapter 10.

As Crosland stated, the driving principle of government intervention in industry was that it would promote greater productivity and competitiveness. But it was a principle based on the belief that 'big' is beautiful. The assumption was that large-scale organizations naturally achieve economies of scale and that in comparative international terms Britain was at a disadvantage in major sectors of industry. The approach was a mixture of half-truth and mistaken analysis. There was confusion between the unit of ownership, which was the company, and the unit of production, which was the plant. Government intervention was concentrated almost entirely at the former level presumably in the belief that one would somehow follow from the other, while being seemingly unaware that British industry was already among the most highly concentrated in the world.

Below the level of ownership the issue becomes much more complex. Economies of scale do exist but in multidimensional form. If production alone is being measured, then in many industries maximum economies are achieved at low levels of output and in modest-sized plants when compared with the size of the industry as a whole.[24] In addition to production economies of scale, however, there are potential economies of scale in finance, marketing and research and development. The central management task is their optimization since they frequently occur at different levels of activity. Big may be beautiful but the nature, structure and organization of the bigness is critical. This is a problem which will have to be considered in more detail a little later, though it was not one which exercised official minds at the time.

Assessments made in the 1970s of government involvement in industry in the 1960s generally returned an open verdict. Certainly no immediate substantial gains were obvious. With the advantage of longer hindsight it is clear that this policy did not halt the decline in Britain's international industrial competitiveness. To what extent it contributed to continuing decline is an unanswerable question. There is evidence that government pressure and the compensation of large subsidies caused some firms to pursue strategies that did not, in their independent judgement, make long-term commercial sense.[25] In some cases, such as the shipbuilding industry, plain electoral advantage appears to have been high on the list of government priorities. And, whatever the objectives, there was an opportunity cost to the £1 billion expended. Yet even on this count the sum was not enormous in relation to national income. But this still leaves the question of why the intervention took the form it did, and why government–industry relations were less effective in Britain than would appear to have been the case in the economies of Western Europe and Japan.

In part, the answer follows from the fact, namely, that there was a lack of competence at all levels. Business could hardly provide the knowledge when it was itself the problem. To this extent the IRC was an organization effectively based on the principle of the blind leading the blind. There is no evidence that the government made serious efforts to investigate foreign practices as it had attempted to do in 1947 under the Anglo-American Council on Productivity. Formal analysis had little to offer as the academic fashion in Britain was still firmly in the groove of macroeconomic theory. To the lack

24. For a survey of the theoretical literature see D. A. Hay and D. J. Morris, *Industrial Economics and Organization* (Oxford, 1991), pp. 27–57, 226, 228–9, 420, 470.

25. An interesting case is Courtaulds and its involvement in the cotton and artificial fibres industries, see A. Knight, *Private Enterprise and Government Intervention* (1974).

of knowledge was added the pliant nature of intent. The signal fact is that the policy of interventionism was not reinforced by radical reform of the machinery of government and of relations between government and industry. The short and sorry history of the Department of Economic Affairs encapsulates the whole issue.[26]

The determination with which senior officials had sunk the Ministry of Economic Affairs in 1947 was matched by their successor mandarins twenty years later in their destruction of the Department of Economic Affairs. Had the Department survived and succeeded in its aims it would have caused a significant diminution in the power of the Treasury. In mounting this challenge to the vested interests of the Treasury, the Department was largely on its own. Overwhelmingly, economic policy was still conceived within the confines of the Keynesian macroeconomic framework. The IRC and actions associated with it were not coordinated into any kind of industrial strategy. The 'white heat of the technological revolution', that had been the clarion call of the Labour Party's 1964 election campaign, evaporated into rhetoric.

The nationalized industries formed a sector in which it might be anticipated that industrial policy would have taken on a more strategic approach. This proved not to be the case. A leading example of what happened is provided by energy policy. 'What was supposed to be a long-term policy was characteristically changed with every short-term shock and for this reason there was never a long-term energy policy, only the pretence of one.'[27] Other attempts were made, but it has been convincingly argued that whenever government attempted a coordinated strategy of nationalized industries the results were more often adverse than beneficial.[28] At the same time political pressures on these industries increased because ministers and civil servants attempted to use them as instruments of short-term macroeconomic management, most often in the pursuit of some counter-inflationary goal. Price controls and adjustments to investment programmes were the levers most frequently applied. In this sector of the economy, the need for major reform of the machinery of economic policy-making was most clearly demonstrated. But the strength of this criticism must

26. P. Hennessy, *Whitehall* (1989), pp. 169–208.

27. W. Ashworth, *The State in Business. 1945 to the Mid 1980s* (1991), p. 176 and *idem., The History of the British Coal Industry, Vol. 5, 1946–1982. The Nationalized Industry* (Oxford, 1986), pp. 50–60, 642–3, 659–62 and, in particular, pp. 54–5 for a critique of M. V. Posner, *Fuel Policy: A Study in Applied Economics* (1973).

28. Ashworth, *The State in Business*, p. 177.

be judged against the productivity record of nationalized industries. Between 1951 and 1985, total factor productivity for the group as a whole grew at 2.2 per cent a year as compared with 1.6 per cent for manufacturing, though the record for the 1970s was poor in contrast to a sharp upturn in the early 1980s *before* privatization took hold. Even coal and transport achieved productivity growth slightly above manufacturing, whilst the new technology industries such as gas, telecommunications and electricity were ahead of manufacturing by a significant margin.[29] Perhaps this record provides less of a defence for the nationalized industries than an added indictment of manufacturing. In other words, from the failures and weaknesses of industrial policy it cannot be deduced that government intervention was unnecessary and that the operation of the 'market' offered the only true means ot the generation of British industry. It might equally be the case that the government needed to do things differently and better than it had done.[30]

BUSINESS, LABOUR AND INSTITUTIONAL CHANGE

Business organization and management continued to be major sources of weakness in the economy. The activities of the IRC, for example, revealed a wide range of problems even if they failed to solve them. Overmanning, poor cost control, low levels of investment, weak marketing strategies, low rates of innovation: these were prominent among the charges made against management. Such failings were not universal and there were companies that could stand comparison with the best in the world. But the evidence of business history reveals that some problems, especially in the field of management training and labour relations, were endemic in nature. These shortcomings were exposed as losses of market share abroad and increasing import penetration at home. Poor design, late delivery and weak aftersales service were all too common characteristics of British goods.[31] Striking testimony to the

29. J. Foreman-Peck and R. Milward, *Public and Private Ownership of British Industry 1820–1990* (Oxford, 1994), pp. 306–14. An excellent survey is provided by L. Hannah, 'The Economic Consequences of the State Ownership of Industry, 1945–1990' in R. Floud and D. McCloskey, *The Economic History of Britain. Volume 3: 1939–1992* (Cambridge, 1994), pp. 168–94.

30. *Cf.* the implied argument in N. F. R. Crafts, *Can De-Industrialisation Seriously Damage Your Wealth?* (1993), pp. 68–73.

31. For example, D. K. Stout, *International Price Competitiveness, Non-Price Factors in Industrial Trade* (1976).

weaknesses of British management practices has been provided by studies of subsidiaries of US firms operating manufacturing plants in the UK, equipped and planned to the same specifications as domestic plants in the USA. These show that the levels of productivity attained were higher in these plants than in corresponding plants in British firms, but still significantly lower than the levels achieved in the USA.[32]

These studies might also appear to confirm the claim made by the leading American business historian, Chandler, that until the very recent period the American business corporation, based on the multidivisional form of organization, was the most advanced business structure which set the international standard. This form of big business is presented as the central dynamic element in the success of what is defined as American competitive managerial capitalism.[33] On this scale of virtue, British companies are easily discredited. But such comparisons are not convincing. As has been noted (Chapter 7), what is ignored is that the growth performance of the US economy since 1945 has been only marginally better than that of the UK, though the absolute level remained higher. American big business is, by definition, based on monopolistic power and practices and it is thus naive to assert, in effect, that private and social rates of return are equally achieved. Robber barons are well established among the fauna of American capitalism. There are difficulties, too, with the narrowness of this analysis, since it concentrates on what is termed the internal history of firms; in other words, it artificially divorces company organization and performance from the economic context within which it operates. One consequence of this abstraction is the failure to consider the relationship between what is a limited number of firms of a particular type in one sector, manufacturing, to other types of firm and other sectors of the US economy. There is, too, ample evidence that quite different forms of company structure proved to be immensely successful in Continental Western European economies and Japan. German Atkeingesellschaft (AG) were joint

32. C. F. Pratten, *Labour Productivity Differentials Within International Companies* (Cambridge, 1976).

33. A. D. Chandler, Jnr., *Scale and Scope: The Dynamics of Industrial Capitalism* (Cambridge, Mass., 1990). These and other criticisms are developed in B. W. E. Alford, 'Chandlerism, the New Orthodoxy of US and European Corporate Development', *The Journal of European Economic History*, 23 (1994), pp. 631–43.

stock companies operating within a system of corporate law which made them very different animals from big firms in the USA. Zaibatsus such as Mitsui and Mitsubishi were conglomerate structures unique to the Japanese economy. Alongside these different forms there continued to be others such as family-controlled firms, large and small, and comparatively small-scale public companies, that had much in common in whichever country they operated. In short, the classification of firms according to forms of ownership and formal structure does not provide a direct measure either of individual business performance or of the economy. Performance is a matter of activity within organizations and structures and has to be measured by carefully defined criteria such as rates of return on capital and output per worker. When such measures are applied they indicate that there is no predetermined relationship between structure and performance.

Detailed evidence on individual British firms during this period is as yet limited, but what is available tends to confirm the persistence of the same kinds of weaknesses in business organization and management as those that are well documented for the earlier part of the twentieth century. Lack of professionalism and technical expertise in senior management, outdated working practices and the pursuit of large-scale operation and international company status for their own sake are all too prevalent. Further confirmation of these shortcomings is provided by more general studies of the merger wave of the 1960s, to which reference has already been made (Chapter 7).[34] Similarly, studies of modern business strategy provide many illustrations of these processes, whilst revealing that there are no generic strategies for success; neither is success totally random.[35] Put another way, the higher the quality of human capital in a business organization the more likely it is that success will be achieved. But this, in turn, raises the issue of education and training to which we return below.

A substantial amount of evidence on economic performance has been produced by comparative international studies at industry and sector level. The focus has been on productivity, plant performance

---

34. See note 29, Chapter 7.
35. An excellent study which combines theoretical insight and a firm historical and empirical grasp is J. Kay, *Foundations of Corporate Success: How Business Strategies Add Value* (Oxford, 1993). See also A. Pettigrew, *The Awakening Giant: Continuity and Change in ICI* (Oxford, 1985).

and technical innovation.[36] The picture is a depressing one as it reveals Britain's comparative failure during the post-Second World War period. One major study of productivity, for example, shows major British industries lagging behind their counterparts in Germany and the USA by between 30 per cent and 170 per cent in 1975.[37] In the main, these exercises provide statistical measures of performance and thus concentrate on identifying and describing symptoms rather than on exposing the causes of the problem. In so far as there are attempts to explain these outcomes, it is striking that economists are forced to the conclusion that differences in performance are not mainly explained by superior plant but, once again, by less easily quantifiable and unquantifiable elements of managerial and labour practices. And in the particular respect of research and development the critical factor was not the level of expenditure but its composition. It is important to recognize, moreover, that R and D in defence absorbs substantial amounts of scarce scientific manpower which has limiting effects on networks of technical diffusion, and, in any case, the employment of scientists in industry was notoriously low in Britain.

In 1968 the Brookings Institute of the USA published a wide-ranging study under the title *Britain's Economic Prospects*.[38] It was a kind of economic health scan and the prognosis it came up with was not particularly encouraging. The report, which attracted considerable publicity, indicated clearly the gap between current performance and what was needed to match the par rate for OEEC countries. In some respects it offered pointers to what was required, especially in terms of investment, labour relations and research and development. But it, too, was more concerned with the symptoms of the disease than with offering a cure. The continuous failure of Britain to break out of low growth and low productivity into the sunny uplands of high growth and high productivity led a number of economists to employ language more appropriate to Old Testament prophets than to disciples of economic science. They spoke of vicious and virtuous circles of economic performance. The

36. S. J. Prais, *Productivity and Industrial Structure: A Statistical Study of Manufacturing Industry in Britain, Germany and the US* (Cambridge, 1976); M. Panic (ed.), *The UK and West German Manufacturing Industry 1954–72: A Comparison of Structure and Performance* (1976); Pratten, *Economies of Scale; idem., A Comparison of the Performance of Swedish and UK Companies* (Cambridge, 1976); K. Pavitt (ed.), *Technical Innovation and British Economic Performance* (1980).

37. Prais, *Productivity and Industrial Structure.*

38. R. E. Caves (ed.), *Britain's Economic Prospects* (Washington, DC, 1968).

elaborate formularies of econometrics were used to refine identities and correlates between logically separable elements of economic growth. But all this intellectual effort did not produce the key for turning vice into virtue.[39]

Labour markets and industrial relations are probably better understood than other elements in economic performance in the light of historical evidence though, ironically, they were the least fashionable areas of economic analysis at the time. The increasing frequency and sharpness of industrial disputes was a strong feature of the second half of the 1960s. In international comparisons of days lost through labour disputes the UK does not appear as particularly strike-prone. But such data are misleading. In the USA, for example, a large number of days could be lost in an industry at one time while new pay deals were being negotiated, yet the short-term loss was more than compensated for by medium- and long-term productivity gains. In Britain, by contrast, strikes were often unofficial, of short duration and concerned with job demarcation and manning levels.[40] The effects on output quality, delivery dates and labour costs led to a corrosive loss of markets both at home and abroad. The causes were, in many cases, weak management – which simply pushes the need for an explanation back a stage – and, more directly, a change in union attitudes in the mid-1960s, which a distinguished commentator has described as 'the hinge'.[41]

Union leaders' willingness to accept wage constraint as a *quid pro quo* for the maintenance of full employment was replaced by a determination to secure regular increases in wages as a due reward for contributing to economic growth. Growing awareness of rising real wages in Western Europe provided added stimulus. And underpinning this change was a greater 'militancy and *dynamisme de*

39. N. Kaldor, *Causes of the Slow Rate of Growth in the United Kingdom* (Cambridge, 1966); *idem.*, 'Economic Growth and the Verdoorn Law', *Economic Journal*, 85 (1975), pp. 891–6. But see S. Gomulka, 'Increasing Efficiency Versus Low Rate of Technical Change', in W. Beckerman (ed.), *Slow Growth in Britain. Causes and Consequences* (1979), pp. 166–93 and R. E. Rowthorn, 'What Remains of Kaldor's Law?', *Economic Journal*, 85 (1975), pp. 10–19.

40. D. C. Smith, 'Trade Union Growth and Industrial Disputes', in R. E. Caves and L. Krause (eds), *Britain's Economic Performance* (Washington, DC, 1980), pp. 81–134. Valuable surveys of the labour market in all its aspects will be found in successive editions of Prest and Coppock's *A Manual of Applied Economics* which was first published in 1966. See for example, D. Metcalf and R. Richardson, 'Labour', in M. J. Artis (ed.), *Prest and Coppock's – The UK Economy* (1986 edition), pp. 266–332.

41. E. H. Phelps Brown, *The Origins of Trade Union Power* (1986 edition), pp. 159–65.

la base' among the growing number of rank and file members who had not suffered the searing experience of unemployment in the 1930s.[42] The term 'hinge' is, therefore, well chosen since this swing did not cause a break with the past. It occurred within the existing framework of union organization complete with its long-established protective armoury of negotiating procedures and work practices. The contrasts with the different traditions of organized labour in Western Europe, Japan and the USA are clear. In the first two, the postwar settlement had, in addition, involved major changes in union organization and practices.[43]

Whilst a number of important reasons for comparatively poor labour productivity can thus be identified, it is all too clear that the manner in which they might have been remedied does not follow directly. Labour relations and practices cannot be separated from management organization and performance. Moreover, the broad conclusion to be drawn from studies by applied economists and from the work of business historians is that management and labour were powerfully influenced in their behaviour by social and cultural mores. The difficulties involved in defining these conditions and in relating them to business behaviour has been examined in relation to an earlier period. And whilst attitudes have changed during the intervening years, most rapidly as a consequence of social reforms after 1945, recent studies have shown that old patterns of recruitment which preserved the position of traditionally educated amateurs at the head of big business, remained remarkably resilient for some time after the war.[44] Lack of professionalism in the boardroom may be one reason why some large companies became easy prey to outside financiers with professional training in accountancy but with little concern for longer-term industrial development. Whether a different school and social background, which began to occur in the 1970s, signified a more professional cadre of top management is not certain, since the availability of high-level business training was still limited by international standards. This pattern was repeated down the scale.

42. *Idem.*, 'A Non-Monetarist View of the Pay Explosion', *Three Banks Review*, 105 (1975), p. 5.

43. Phelps Brown, *The Origins of Trade Union Power*, pp. 198–228; Van Der Wee, *Prosperity and Upheaval*, pp. 241–51, 323–88 and *passim.*

44. See J. Authers, 'Old Boy Network Loses Hold on Top Boardroom Jobs', *Financial Times*, 10 November 1993, p. 2, reporting on a lecture by L. Hannah at the London School of Economics.

Table 8.4 Vocational qualifications of the labour force in Britain (1974–78) and West Germany (1978) (% of labour force in each group)

	University or equivalent	Intermediate	None
Manufacturing			
Britain	3.3	28.7	68.0
Germany	3.5	60.8	37.7
Non-manufacturing			
Britain	6.5	30.7	62.8
Germany	8.9	59.4	31.6
All activities			
Britain	5.5	30.0	64.4
Germany	7.1	59.9	33.0

Source: Prais (1981), 48.

To the extent that quality of human capital is an important element in economic performance, Britain was clearly placing itself at a comparative disadvantage.

The point can be made that at a general level industry gets the managers and workers it deserves. The basic lack of training was, in other words, largely a consequence of lack of demand for it from business itself. It is true that there is no strong evidence of such demand during the 1960s, though this hardly proves the case. Except for those ideologues who believe in an Alice-in-Wonderland world where virtually all goods and services can be supplied satisfactorily through 'the market', education must be provided as a basic public good; though this obviously does not rule out privately financed education for a privileged minority. In the provision of technical and commercial education there are major external economies to be gained by firms if training is provided through central agencies. The Labour government in the 1960s recognized this need and, early in its programme, stressed the need for greater provision in the area of technical education as a central requirement for improved economic performance, though much of the planning in this field was already underway as a consequence of a fundamental reappraisal of policy by the Conservatives from 1961 onwards. To this end, various steps were taken, including the establishment of Colleges of Advanced Technology that were supposed to achieve parity of esteem with universities. But these and other measures were of limited success as the subsequent transformation of these institutions into more traditional universities signified.

Much more research is necessary before anything approaching a firm understanding of these non-quantifiable elements can be achieved. There is, nevertheless, sufficient comparative evidence available to remove any doubt as to the central importance of social and cultural conditions. For example, in the large literature on Japan's postwar economic success, the most convincing explanations place emphasis on the nature of Japanese society and culture. It is true that Japan gained advantages from the postwar settlement, including a number of economic and labour reforms imposed on it by the US administration but, at the same time, those changes that cut into the hard grain of Japanese traditions were effectively resisted and eventually overturned. Thus, the USA instituted a programme for breaking up the zaibatsus, which had acquired an unsavoury reputation during the period of fascist rule. After some early success the programme was abandoned because of the need to accelerate Japanese economic recovery in face of the advance of communism in the Far East. The zaibatsus survived, albeit in modified forms. Furthermore, Japan outstandingly exemplifies the point made earlier (Chapter 1) that tradition, *per se*, does not necessarily act as a drag on economic performance.[45]

The cultural foundations of American capitalism have likewise attracted much attention, though they cannot be considered in detail here. Among the more important elements, however, are the nature of the frontier in myth and reality and the multifarious and multilayered influences of what was predominantly an immigrant culture. The individual's quest for economic betterment and the absence of a traditional ruling class thus powerfully conditioned American materialism. By the same token, it has been argued that, over time, those traditional values have weakened in ways that help to explain America's muted economic performance in the post-1945 period. More generally, historical comparisons of this kind illustrate the point that there was not a unique cultural and social recipe for economic success but that social and cultural choices had a powerful influence on economic outcomes. How explicit or conscious these choices were is one of the fascinations of economic and social history.

45. M. Morishima, *Why Has Japan 'Succeeded'?* (Cambridge, 1982).

At a more abstract level there have been various attempts to explain the economic rise and decline of nations as part of a process of institutional change. One of the most influential of such analyses has placed great stress on the power and operation of organized groups in British society.[46] That these groups have chosen to behave in what is literally a counter-productive fashion is claimed to be due to the lack of sufficient common, interconnected interests between them which has been fostered by a long period of political stability – or, to use the jargon, these interest groups are not sufficiently encompassing. Furthermore, the fact of Britain being on the winning side in the Second World War enabled most of these institutions to survive more or less intact, whereas by contrast, in the vanquished nations many traditional institutions were destroyed or were forced to make radical changes that rendered them in tune with the needs of modern economic development. Another theory of this kind places emphasis on the greater capacity of Western European countries, Scandinavia and Japan, in comparison with Great Britain and the United States, to solve the distributional problem in society. This problem arises from the costs imposed in the production of economic growth and the rewards which it delivers. The inherent danger is that costs and benefits, if left unregulated, will be shared unequally and the resulting tensions and disruption will undermine the process of growth. Labour disputes are cited as the most obvious manifestations of these difficulties.[47]

Whilst such theories leave much room for argument and indicate the need for much further investigation, the focus of their concern is compelling. Moreover, they give added point to the view that it is naive to presume that economic outcomes can be explained in purely economic terms, and plainly foolish to think that mechanistic economic theory holds the key to the explanation. These are very difficult issues to which there is no quick-fix statistical answer. And in the British case a paradox remains. The competitive deficiencies of the British as producers had been clearly exposed by the 1960s. But as consumers they saw no need to modify their demands. The high and increasing level of import penetration of manufactured consumer goods was a measure of this dichotomy.

46. M. Olson, *The Rise and Decline of Nations* (New Haven, Conn., 1983).
47. Zysman, *Governments, Markets and Growth*.

POLICY AND PERFORMANCE

Economic policy dominated political debate during the period. A party's success at the polls depended heavily on being able to convince the electorate that it, alone, could ensure higher and increasing standards of living. What was on offer came gift-wrapped in manifestos of varying economic design. These combinations of economic statistics and ideology nevertheless had a common theme: if the correct form of technical economic management was adopted then economic problems could be largely, if not completely, solved. The Labour party's success in the 1964 election owed much to the appeal of its claim that, when it came to economic management it offered a professional competence in contrast to the amateurism that had preceded it.

A comprehensive discussion of economic policy is not appropriate to the theme of this book. Accordingly, our main concern is with the manner in which and the success with which economic policy met the international challenge to Britain's competitiveness and economic standing. In one sense the verdict is unequivocal. Between 1960 and 1973 GDP per head grew at the rate of 2.6 per cent in Britain as compared with an average for OECD countries of 3.7 per cent. On this criterion economic policy was a failure. But this is to judge performance rather narrowly and in a way that perhaps gives undue credence to the electoral posturing of politicians. More carefully formulated, the issue becomes one of whether comparatively poor performance can be explained in terms of policy formulation and implementation or whether, because of its very nature, economic policy can never deliver what its practitioners claim for it. In order to address this issue, economic policy can be measured against three yardsticks: actual performance in relation to the objectives that policy sets itself; the impact of the unintended effects of policy decisions; and the relationship between economic theory and economic prescription.

On the first count the verdict has already been given. Even so, it is necessary to refine it. On the grounds that there was widespread agreement by the 1960s that Britain was suffering from structural economic weaknesses that required medium- to long-term solutions, strong criticisms can be made of the implementation of policy. In their pronouncements, the Labour governments of 1964 and 1966 committed themselves to an industrial policy that moved away from the tactics of short-term demand management to the strategy of reversing industrial decline. The collapse of the Department of Economic Affairs signifies not just the overambitious and rhetorical nature of the National Plan, but also the government's inability to achieve appropriate institutional reform. Some commentators have blamed the government for what they term the one-idea-at-a-time syndrome.[48] In response, however, it might be argued that the idea of industrial regeneration at least had the virtue of being a big one. It is neither possible nor appropriate to cover all areas of policy in this context, and in the important area of industrial policy specific problems have already been examined. But the really critical fact is that domestic policy was overridden by external financial policy. Why was this so?

The Labour government came to power in 1964 at the height of yet another sterling crisis. Subsequent and more accurate calculation of the current deficit of that year has revealed that it was by no means as large as was thought at the time – £372 million as compared with £800 million.[49] Nevertheless, contemporary perception was what mattered. An import surcharge was imposed and the pressure eased. Later in the year the crisis returned and when the prime minister, Wilson, threatened to devalue sterling by allowing the pound to float, the governor of the Bank of England quickly prevailed on his City confrères, and through them on certain international bankers, to raise $3 billion to stave off the pressure on sterling. Further arrangements of credit from other central banks were called for and a drawing of $1 billion was made on the IMF. According to a leading authority on these events, the impression of indecisiveness created by the government, especially in relation to deflation, caused nervousness to persist in the international exchange markets.[50] Reserves continued to drain out and the exchange crisis returned in mid-1965. Once again, the UK was forced to make a large drawing ($1.4 billion) from the IMF. In securing international financial support, especially from the USA, the government was required to seek what international bankers would accept as a more effective incomes policy. Loose agreements to this end were made with the Trades Union Congress.

Sterling's difficulties receded until mid-1966. Following a strike by seamen and with worsening reserve figures and a widening trade

48. Blackaby, *British Economic Policy 1960–74*, p. 7.

49. *Economic Trends. Annual Supplement* (1994), p. 120.

50. An incisive commentary on these events is provided by A. Cairncross, *The British Economy Since 1945* (1992), pp. 134–225.

gap, sterling again came under intense pressure. Harsh budgetary measures were brought forward and this led to disagreement among ministers over whether devaluation should be adopted. The deflationists in the Cabinet carried the day, and together with a swing into surplus in the balance of payments, which financed a substantial repayment of international debt, the pressure on sterling again eased. But it was a temporary remission. Labour problems and difficult international trading conditions (partly as a consequence of the Six Day Arab–Israeli War in June) were topped by a growing deficit on the trade account. The British government remained Micawber-like, hoping that something would turn up to rescue sterling. In November, the inevitable came with the announcement of the devaluation of sterling to $2.40. Delay, alone, placed an immediate price tag on devaluation of £356 million, to cover the Bank of England's losses on forward buying of sterling in an effort to maintain the old rate.

There have been numerous studies of the overall effects of the devaluation. Estimates of the benefit to the balance of payments vary between £400 million and £1,000 million over three years with the consensus being around the middle of the range.[51] The really difficult part is the calculation of the indirect and longer-term effects on cost and price structures. Taking all these movements into account, the most convincing analysis indicates that there was very little gain from the devaluation because real productivity and competitiveness did not improve significantly at the same time.[52] Pressure on wages increased and incomes policy became discredited. By the early 1970s wages and prices were increasing at rates that were beginning to move ahead of those for other industrial economies. The slow improvement in the balance of payments caused pressure on sterling to persist, despite a letter of intent that the government had sent to the IMF in November 1967. In line with the undertakings it contained, big cuts in expenditure were made in 1968 and these involved an accelerated withdrawal from defence commitments east of Suez. But a further, supplicant, letter of intent was still necessary in May 1969 since the balance of payments did not begin to pick up until the second quarter of that year.

51. A. Cairncross and B. Eichengreen, *Sterling in Decline: The Devaluations of 1931, 1949 and 1967* (Oxford, 1983), pp. 197 *ff.*

52. National Institute, 'Effects of the 1967 Devaluation', *Economic Journal,* 82 (1972), pp. 442–64.

Overseas investment and military expenditure have generated a great deal of controversy as to their effects on British economic performance. Both have frequently been presented as draining life-blood from the economy. On the investment side, there was a persistent and at times substantial deficit on the long-term account. Under fixed exchange rates this negative flow might have had a serious effect on currency reserves but the circle was squared by financing the deficit through foreign borrowing by UK companies. The upshot was that between the mid-1960s and the early 1970s the long-term capital account contributed a small net balance to exchange reserves. As a result it was reckoned that exchange controls had little restrictive effect on direct investment and, as will be seen, within limits companies could evade them. Portfolio investment, however, was probably quite severely curtailed by these regulations, if the surge in this type of capital export after 1979, when the controls were lifted, is anything to go by.[53]

The failure of the government to restrict overseas investment is, however, still seen by some commentators as a fundamental shortcoming of external financial policy. But such criticism is simplistic. There are a number of reasons for thinking that a complete block on foreign investment would not have resulted in higher domestic investment ratios. As has been noted, much foreign investment was financed overseas anyway. International investment decisions by companies cannot sensibly be viewed in isolation from their domestic investment strategies; and in so far as there were shortcomings in this regard, they were likely to have operated across the board. More positively, there are numerous examples of foreign investment serving strategic interests. In some cases it was linked, directly or indirectly, to the finance of exports. In others, investment in distribution and servicing networks overseas was essential for circumventing various kinds of protective barriers. The export of particular skills in mining and construction was financed to good effect abroad since they yielded substantial returns to the domestic economy.[54] In short, the distinction between domestic and foreign investment is somewhat artificial in economic terms. Investment decisions existed as part of a complex of interrelationships and were part of the multilateral system of

53. J. H. B. Tew, 'Policies Aimed At Improving the Balance of Payments', in Blackaby, *British Economic Policy 1960–74*, pp. 317–42; A. K. Cairncross, *Control of Long-Term International Capital Movements* (Washington, DC, 1973).

54. Rowthorn and Wells, *De-Industrialization and Foreign Trade*, pp. 127 and 400 note 22.

capital flows. These flows often acted as vectors of technical change, particularly through the medium of multinational companies. A policy of investment autarky could well have been very costly in terms of forgone economic growth.

An evaluation of the overall effects of overseas investment is, nevertheless, difficult, not least because of the indirect and non-quantifiable elements within it. The only major attempt to date was made in the 1960s.[55] It proved impossible, however, to construct more than very approximate estimates of the size of overseas investment and even the valuation of known assets was highly problematical. Added to which, despite exchange controls and rules of disclosure, it was relatively easy for international companies to conceal the transmission of funds by means of such devices as internal pricing, the effects of which would be included under current transactions in the trade balance and would not show up under capital transactions in the balance of payments.[56] For what it is worth, the overall assessment was that there was a small marginal gain in export performance arising from overseas investment. When non-quantifiable factors are taken into consideration, together with what is known about individual companies, it is hard to avoid the conclusion that government policy in this area was not the critical issue in economic performance; what mattered was the quality of the investment decisions themselves.

Policy on defence expenditure is a far more contentious issue than overseas investment. Although there was a marked contraction in the global spread of defence commitments, the total did not decline because of continuing major commitments in Europe. Nevertheless, by the end of the 1960s approximately 90 per cent of European expenditure was offset by purchases of defence equipment by Germany and the USA. The issue then becomes much trickier. It can be argued that, despite the offset purchases, these expenditures locked Britain into defence industries – in particular the aircraft industry – which had a debilitating effect on the economy in the manner discussed earlier. Furthermore, in sustaining the illusion of a world power, the UK committed a large absolute amount of expenditure, both direct and indirect, to

55. W. B. Reddaway *et al*, *The Effects of UK Direct Investment Overseas: Interim Report* (Cambridge, 1968).
56. Internal pricing is the system whereby a foreign branch or subsidiary charges the controlling British firm an inflated price for commodities, goods or services and in this way capital finance is indirectly transferred abroad as revenue.

defence. The direct portion alone accounted for 4.8 per cent of GDP in 1970 and in the 1960s it had reached over 6 per cent. In the same year the corresponding figure for France was 4.2 per cent, for Germany 3.3 per cent, for Italy 2.7 per cent and for Japan 0.6 per cent.[57]

In assessing economic policy between 1960 and 1971 against our first yardstick, it is possible to draw parallels with the years between 1945 and 1951. In both periods, it would seem, a Labour government set out with the aim of establishing a system of economic planning but quite soon these efforts were abandoned in face of a series of unanticipated international financial crises. The parallel can be drawn deeper if the failure to press on with a modified version of original plans is ascribed to a lack of sufficient political will on the part of ministers, when faced with Treasury officials determined to defend the existing framework of policy-making that was so effectively under their control. There is, indeed, much evidence to support the view that in the intervening twenty years the fundamentals of economic policy-making had not significantly changed. The Brookings Report pointed out that the role of the UK as banker to the overseas sterling area and to the world financial community in general was carried out with a very inadequate underpinning of foreign exchange reserves.[58]

These strictures amount to the charge that the need to give primacy to international financial policy over domestic economic policy during the 1960s was both consequence and proof of the failure to overcome long-standing economic problems. So far as direct responsibility is concerned, the Treasury was the major barrier to change, whatever the ultimate contribution economic policy can make to economic performance. And it is one of the ironies of British economic history since 1945 that these financial crises, for which the Treasury ultimately bore heavy responsibility were, also, the means through which the Treasury maintained its grip on the conduct of economic policy. Moreover, top civil servants in the Treasury and other departments were not only concerned with policy formulation, they were increasingly responsible for its execution. In a wide range of activities, they were effectively making major business decisions involving the allocation of large resources.

57. I am grateful to my colleague Dr R. Middleton for these figures. See his forthcoming *Government and the Market: The Growth of the Public Sector, Economic Management and British Economic Performance, c. 1890–1979* (Aldershot, 1996).

58. R. N. Cooper, 'The Balance of Payments', in Caves, *Britain's Economic Prospects*, pp. 180–8.

The plain fact is that civil servants at this level were quite untrained for these tasks and the Treasury, which was responsible for training and recruitment, made no serious efforts to remedy matters. Industrial policy during the 1960s is littered with the costly consequences of these shortcomings.[59] The persistence of this attitude of mind in the Treasury is exemplified in the manner in which it resisted major proposals for reform made by the Fulton Report in 1968.[60]

The weaknesses of economic policy cannot be laid wholly at the door of the civil servants, however. The commitment to sterling and Britain's world role was much in evidence among Labour ministers. Whether this was through genuine belief or perceptions of political expedience is not clear. Thus the prime minister, Wilson, declared in the mid-1960s that Britain's frontiers were 'on the Himalayas'. On this and other policy issues, Wilson subsequently demonstrated that his avowed principles were highly flexible in application but this, in itself, hardly made for effective and consistent policy. Nowhere was this weakness better exemplified than in the dithering and delay over devaluation in 1967.

Finally in respect of evaluating policy on its own terms, both in industrial and incomes policy what was achieved fell short of what was promised. However intractable to policy these problems were, there are grounds for arguing that they were seen not only as secondary to, but in large measure separate from, external economic policy. Again, this partly reflects the influence of the Treasury. Yet in so far as policy could meet the increasing challenge to Britain's position in the world economy, it depended on the coordination of domestic and international economic policy. Productivity and competitiveness were at the heart of Britain's international economic problems and these could not be solved by exchange rate manipulations. Exchange rate crises were consequences not causes.

Correspondingly, it is mistaken to see the defence of sterling as the outcome of the powerful influence of the 'City'. It was only when the influence of the 'City' was added to the widespread desire

59. Hennessy, *Whitehall*; A. Ham, *Treasury Rules* (1981); S. Pollard, *The Wasting of the British Economy* (1982). A defence of the Treasury is offered by J. Tomlinson, *Public Policy and the Economy Since 1900* (Oxford, 1990), pp. 249–51, 289–90, 322–5. I find this defence unconvincing since it is focused on certain specific policies and thereby misses the much wider ramifications of Treasury power and attitudes.

60. D. Healey, *The Time of My Life* (1989), especially pp. 13–14, 372 *ff.* where he extols the quality of Treasury officials and the value of a classical education.

among British political leaders to remain at the top table in world affairs, to the belief in official circles that domestic economic stability depended on maintaining the existing sterling exchange rate, to the client status of Britain in relation to the USA in international finance, and to the determination of the Treasury to remain in control of economic policy and of the wider administration of government and to the conservatism of British business and industry, that a diversity of interests coalesced into a uniformity and concentration of aims. Sterling policy in relation to the economic performance of Britain was, in other words, a matter of massively misplaced effort.

The nature of unintended effects of economic policy is the second yardstick to be applied. The most important of such effects was paradoxical in nature. The devaluation of 1967 and the cuts in defence expenditure which led to Britain's withdrawal from east of Suez, were acts which, far from saving the day, effectively undermined sterling's claim as a top currency and marked the end of world power aspirations. The so-called Basle Group Arrangements of 1968, which provided international support to Britain in dealing with reductions in sterling area balances, signalled the new reality. A large dollar credit to Britain was provided by twelve central banks and the Bank of International Settlements to cover large withdrawals of sterling balances. In addition, guarantees were given which underwrote the dollar value of the remaining official reserve sterling holdings of countries. Later events will show, however, that delusion retained a powerful hold on the official mind.[61]

The lack of coordination in government economic policy has already been mentioned. Beyond specific shortcomings and improvements which were practicable lies the much bigger issue of the sheer scale of government activity. Decisions taken in one area of government could easily have quite unexpected and maybe contradictory effects in another. An example is the manner in which taxation policy facilitated types of company merger and takeover which ran counter to industrial policy and the regulation of monopoly. The government was also a large purchaser of goods and services and thus, for example, political decisions on foreign policy and defence could have unintended effects on industrial structure, the use of scarce resources and industrial productivity.

61. A stimulating analysis on this theme is T. W. Hutchinson, *Economics and Economic Policy in Britain 1946–1966* (1968).

Big government became a feature of all modern economies after the war and to that extent the problems associated with this development were common. Accordingly, much more comparative work needs to be done before any attempt can be made to draw conclusions as to whether Britain fared better or worse than other countries in this regard. What is reasonably clear is that the unavoidable complexity of modern government, quite apart from the competence of those running it, produced a systemic inconsistency in large areas of policy-making. Whatever claims governments might make, the outcome of policies should normally be judged within wide tolerances. The fact of unintended effects of policy not only emphasizes the need to distinguish between the exercise of political power and the extent to which its effects can be controlled but, also, it raises the intriguing but as yet unanswerable question of whether this limitation was of more importance in Britain than in many other countries, because the need for directed change was all the greater.

Finally, there is the yardstick which measures the effectiveness between economic theory and economic prescription. The obvious point is that economic policies, in particular those dealing with macroeconomic management, are based on either explicit or implicit models of how the economy works. The problem is that there are a number of alternative models which differ according to the assumptions on which they are based. These assumptions are heavily influenced by value judgements, abstract theoretical relationships, differing views of individual behaviour and assertions about the ways in which industries and sectors of the economy respond to economic stimuli. And whilst models based on unrealistic assumptions may (occasionally) give good predictions, they can offer little or no guide to real world prescription which is the essence of economic policy.

Economic models can only incorporate factors that are quantifiable and thus, for example, they cannot take account of the effects of institutional change which may well be a central element of policy. Even with quantifiable factors there is the sheer complexity of the interrelationships in the economy to which reference has already been made. A well-known statistical test of demand management policy conducted the 1960s revealed that the outcome was contrary to what the government believed it was doing in a central area of policy.[62] A similar limitation arises from the fact

62. R. C. O. Matthews, 'Why Has Britain Had Full Employment Since the War?', *Economic Journal*, 78 (1968), pp. 555–69.

that statements based on past relationships may be of little use in predicting future outcomes, as attempts to predict the future rate of inflation exemplify only too well. Likewise, the demonstration of a relationship may cause a modification of the actions that determine it and thus result in policy creating an overreaction. Permeating and further weakening these fault lines is the poor quality of economic statistics. Accurate and up-to-date recording of data present enormous problems; trade statistics provide one of the most notorious examples. And having collected the data, statisticians still face enormous difficulties in terms of processing and application.

The conclusion that emerges from the application of our three yardsticks is that the impact of economic policies on economic outcomes is not just a matter of the inherent technical weaknesses of economics as an applied science, it is more fundamentally a matter of the nature of political economy. To put it in rudimentary terms, whilst economic analysis may help policy-makers to define and measure a problem it does not follow that the problem thus identified has economic causes or that it is susceptible to an economic solution. This may be to state the obvious, but our historical review of this period reveals that it was not something well understood at the time. Governments persistently presented issues of economic performance as matters of technical economic management. This approach was heavily influenced by political expediency and departmental vested interests. Exchange rates, fiscal regulators and monetary instruments were projected as powerful and effective levers of economic management. Together they made up a mechanism of economic management that was politically highly serviceable. Politicians, as has frequently been observed, are creatures of the short run and this mechanism was ideally suited to short-run manipulation of the economy; it simplified the economic management regardless of the complexity of the problems. And the continued operation of this mechanism was made to depend on the continuing commitment to sterling and the preservation of the existing structure of economic management.

A particularly good example of these relationships in the 1960s was incomes policy. It was, without doubt, an area of critical importance to Britain's international competitiveness and growth performance. Various methods of regulating wages were tried, including manipulations of the tax system. They failed because, *au fond*, the issue was one of distributive justice, of ideas of fairness, that involved relationships between groups of workers and social classes and institutional arrangements in the field of labour relations. In this and in other areas of economic life, such as education and training Britain was obviously less successful than other major economies as measured by performance and by its falling relative position in the world economy.[63]

It is important to emphasize that this analysis does not amount to support for the kind of demands for less government that began to figure more prominently in political and economic debate in the 1970s (see Chapter 10). To the contrary, it points to the need for more effective government within the bounds of practical possibilities, especially when these are defined in comparative international terms. There was a persistent failure in Britain, though lack of political will and administrative opposition, to reform the machinery of government in line with the needs of modern political economy.

It was in this condition that Britain was exposed to the full force of the oil price-rise shock and the collapse of the long boom. The immediate consequences were serious as Britain was thrown into the whirl of financial crises that was outlined at the beginning of this chapter. The economy was brought to a point which in some ways comparable to the crisis of 1947. Yet Britain, after all, had enjoyed over 20 years of rising prosperity, at a rate significantly above anything in contemporary living memory. Unemployment seemed to have become a thing of the past. For all their seriousness, were the crisis events of the early 1970s no more than the outcome of a process of international economic adjustment faced by all the major economies, albeit with more difficulty in Britain than elsewhere? Or did they mark the beginning of a more fundamental challenge to the nation's ability to remain in the premier division in the world economy? These are the questions to which we must now turn.

---

63. For a masterly analysis see E. H. Phelps Brown, *The Inequality of Pay* (Oxford, 1977).

CHAPTER NINE

International Crisis, the EEC and the North Sea El Dorado

THE END OF BRETTON WOODS

'There is no longer any need for the United States to compete with one hand tied behind her back.' With these words, on 15 August 1971, President Richard Nixon justified the devaluation of the once unassailable dollar. Signs of the impending upheaval first appeared when the German and Dutch currencies had been allowed to float in the late spring of 1971. Once the decision on the dollar had been taken, all the other major currencies were forced to follow suit and, after an initial hesitation, the pound sterling was allowed to float in 1972, though it was described officially as a temporary measure. The dollar rate settled at a level which amounted to an effective devaluation of 12.5 per cent against the major currencies. These events marked the end of an era in international finance and in the world economy.[1] Because of this fact, the nature of these developments must be examined in a little more detail before we turn to analyse their impact on Britain.

The fundamental reason for this realignment of world currencies was the relative decline in the economic power of the United States. America's share of world exports of manufactures fell from 27 per cent in 1950 to 18 per cent by 1973, though the dollar remained the primary reserve currency in international finance. In 1950 the US economy was one-third larger than the combined economies of Belgium, Denmark, France, Germany, Italy, the Netherlands, the UK and Japan. By 1960 this group of countries had achieved a position of equivalence to the USA and by the early 1970s it was

---

1. The standard work is J. H. B. Tew, *The Evolution of the International Monetary System 1945–85* (1985 edition). See also R. Solomon, *The International Monetary System, 1945–1976. An Insider's View* (New York, 1977).

ahead by some 10 per cent and the gap was widening. In terms of income per head, the USA retained the lead. But even on this measure, for example, whereas the difference between Germany and the USA was two and a half times in 1950, by 1973 it had narrowed to 40 per cent.

Somewhat ironically, the pressure on America's position was intensified by the enlargement of its international military commitments, especially in Vietnam during the 1960s. The financing of these operations caused huge quantities of dollars to flood onto international currency markets and substantial amounts of these funds became the basis of the secondary banking and credit system known as the Euro-dollar market. The expansion of this market exerted tremendous leverage on the dollar which the central monetary authorities in the USA could not directly control and thus they found it increasingly difficult to maintain the international value of the currency. These difficulties were directly reflected in the US balance of payments. First, large outflows of capital, whether for commercial or military purposes, were not being balanced by surpluses on current accounts. Secondly, there was a consequent loss of gold which undermined confidence in the dollar. Thirdly, incipient deficits on the balance of payments were being financed by short-term dollar holdings by foreigners that were interest rate sensitive. The counterpart of this position was the growth in the foreign exchange surpluses of the two most successful economies, Germany and Japan. In particular, in the late 1960s, US banks were borrowing on the Euro-dollar market as a way round the domestic credit squeeze that was backed by tight regulations relating to bank deposits. Somewhat ironically, therefore, foreign borrowing of this kind had the effect of recycling foreign dollar holdings and thus easing the pressure on the US balance of payments. In the early 1970s, this process was reversed as US banks repaid their loans. The Euro-dollar market then became a major source of instability for the dollar, as it provided funds for speculative attacks on the dollar exchange rate. This pressure was intensified by the currency operations of US importers seeking to reduce their exposure to a possible fall in the dollar rate.[2]

2. Traders bought foreign currencies forward in case the dollar fell and this increased the supply of dollars on international markets, thus exerting a downward pressure on the dollar exchange rate. I am grateful to Professor Tew for a copy of his unpublished paper 'The Bretton Woods Regime – February 1961 to March 1973', which explains a number of technicalities of international finance during this period.

The central flaw in the Bretton Woods system, as argued earlier in Chapter 6, was the absence of a mechanism for the structural adjustment of exchange rates within the fixed rate regime. In turn this reflected the inherent conflict between international exchange stability and the internal policies which individual countries wished to pursue, especially in relation to the level of employment. For a quarter of a century this tension had not brought the house tumbling down because the dollar was able to withstand the strain. The Germans and the Japanese, in particular, benefited from their minimal international financial respons- ibilities, whilst Britain sublimated the pain of sterling crises in a state of delusion over its world role. More than anything, these conditions resulted from the fact that the Bretton Woods settlement had not been an international agreement constructed on the basis of clearly thought out principles and freely negotiated arrangements. It was essentially a system imposed by the Americans in their own interests, and when it no longer served those interests it was unilaterally abrogated. The reality to be set against Britain's delusion is that Britain had become a client of the USA and could not have broken free from its obligations, however onerous they became, until the USA either explicitly or implicitly permitted it to do so.[3]

Various devices were invented during the 1960s to cope with the deficiencies of the International Monetary Fund. In 1961 leading central banks agreed to cooperate in providing temporary credits (the so-called SWAP arrangement). In the following year the system known as General Agreements To Borrow was set up, whereby standby funds were made available to the IMF by countries in substantial surplus on their balance of payments. In 1967 the continuing and growing strain on the dollar was recognized when Special Drawing Rights were introduced. Each SDR, equivalent to one dollar, was based on a basket of mainly strong currencies, and SDRs rather than dollars came to be regarded as the measure of a country's currency reserves. And as has been shown in relation to British financial crises, other international loan arrangements were made as occasion demanded. In short, the dollar could no longer

3. S. Strange, *Sterling and British Policy* (Oxford, 1971). In the event, the conclusion of this excellent study has proved decidedly optimistic. For a view highly critical of the USA's intentions see A. S. Milward, *The Reconstruction of Western Europe 1945–51* (1984), pp. 56–125. In my view Milward gives insufficient weight to the influence of the USA on the subsequent development of international finance. For a critique of Milward's views on Marshall Aid see C. P. Kindleberger, *Marshall Plan Days* (1987), pp. 245–65.

match the requirements of international liquidity; at the same time, confidence in its underlying value was being eroded, because the increased flow of dollars into international financial markets reflected the growing deficit on the US balance of payments. The declining credibility of the gold-convertibility of the dollar is clear from Table 9.1.

Table 9.1 Total international reserves at the end of selected years, 1949–72 ($ billion)

	1949	1958	1969	1972
Gold reserves*				
US	25	21	12	10
Other countries	8	17	27	29
Total ($ billion)	33	38	39	39
Totals as % of year's world imports	55	38	15	10
Non-metallic reserves				
US liabilities	3	10	16	62
Other	10	10	24	59
Total ($ billion)	13	20	40	121
Totals as % of year's world imports	22	20	16	31

* Gold is valued at its official price of $35 an ounce 1949–69, and at $38 an ounce in 1972.

Source: Tew (1994).

The various devices and stratagems promoted by the IMF were *ad hoc* in nature and arose from the fundamental inability of the Bretton Woods system to meet the requirements of international finance as world trade expanded.[4]

Inflation was both a symptom and an added cause of these problems. During the 1960s the international economy had been

4. J. Williamson, *The Failure of World Monetary Reform, 1971–1974* (Sunbury-on-Thames, 1977).

suffused with a rate of inflation of 3.5 per cent, which was high by historical standards and added significantly to the pressures on international liquidity. The increase in world prices began to accelerate in the late 1960s. Moreover, exchange rate adjustments were made all the more difficult by the widening divergence of price increases between countries. The first attempt to provide some stability to financial markets under the new conditions was made under the lead of the USA which promoted the Smithsonian agreement in December 1971. Under its terms, sterling and a number of other currencies were pegged at new rates to the dollar, though degrees of fluctuation were allowed within limits which became known as 'the tunnel'. A variant of this system was adopted in early 1972 by the members of the European Economic Community and known as the SNAKE. As the name implies, this arrangement allowed for considerable variations in the exchange rates of these countries in international markets whilst they remained collectively linked to one another.

These arrangements did not hold and, as has been noted, in June 1972, Britain allowed the pound to float. A further period of uncertainty followed until March 1973 when an agreement was made between the major economies (the Paris Agreement) which sanctioned floating rates. For all its solemnity, this declaration was little more than formality catching up with reality. What had already come into being was a regime of floating but nationally managed exchange rates. The front marker was still the dollar but the other strong currencies – in particular the German mark and the Japanese yen – assumed much greater importance. At the same time, individual countries endeavoured to manipulate their exchange rates to secure maximum advantage in relation to their trading positions and domestic economic objectives. These operations soon earned the system the epithet of a 'dirty float'. To these uncertainties was added the dramatic shock of the quadrupling of oil prices almost overnight in late 1973. The twin forces of inflation and financial instability were thus unleashed.

The effects of the oil price rise, large though they were, came on top of an already weakening performance in world production and trade as the long boom came to an end. Costs of production in the West rose sharply because industrial technology had relied heavily on inputs of cheap oil, and the second-round effects of the oil price rise pushed up the cost of producing raw materials, especially in the extractive industries and agriculture. These increases in costs resulted in large balance of payments deficits which, in turn, were financed by the recycled flows of dollars. This process operated as follows. Oil was priced in dollars on the international market and the huge revenues flowing to major oil producers, particularly in the Middle East, were far in excess of what could be absorbed by economic development in those countries, and the surplus thus had to be recycled as credits and investments in the big Western economies. Almost at a stroke, therefore, the erstwhile excess of dollars was mopped up and the dollar exchange rate hardened across the board. The upshot was that in a world economy suffering the most severe downturn since 1945, the USA was experiencing an improvement in its balance of payments and a strong exchange position.

The temporary nature of these conditions was not understood by contemporaries and thus there was no challenge to the way in which the Americans set about adjusting the post-Bretton Woods system of international finance. Discussions on new arrangements occurred between 1973 and 1976. The leading participants were the USA, Japan, Western Germany, Britain and France, meeting under the umbrella of the IMF. The critical agreement was reached in Kingston, Jamaica in January 1976 and subsequently ratified by the IMF later in the year. In effect, this agreement confirmed what had been the *de facto* situation since 1973, even though it did not formally come into operation until April 1978. *De facto* meant a dollar-dominated system of floating exchange rates in which the level of the dollar would be determined primarily by the needs of US domestic economic policy. To secure their grip on the system, the Americans insisted on limiting the quantity of Special Drawing Rights and the use of gold in international settlements. The latter they were able to achieve by means of sales (or threats of sales) of gold from their still substantial holdings. In addition, SDRs were heavily weighted in favour of the dollar. The consequences of these arrangements for Britain will be considered shortly, but before doing so it is necessary to reflect on what they meant for the operation of the world economy.[5]

During the 1970s many commentators drew parallels with the international crisis of the early 1930s. Superficially, at least, the parallels were obvious. International currencies were thrown into turmoil and international trade was destabilized by massive price movements in primary product markets. The outcome, however,

---

5. M. G. de Vries, *The IMF 1966–71: The System Under Stress* (Washington, 1976); and more generally R. C. Amacher, G. Harbeler and T. D. Willett (eds), *Challenges to a Liberal International Economic Order* (Washington, 1979).

was by no means as severe or ultimately as catastrophic in the 1970s as it had been in the 1930s. Unlike the 1930s, the later crisis did not arise from an unprecedented need to establish the means for international cooperation. On this occasion, the interdependent interests of the group as a whole were threatened. To this extent there already existed a degree of understanding that the reform of international finance and the maintenance of economic growth depended on a degree of cooperative effort among the major economies, especially in face of the unified demands of the oil-producing countries. But over and above these conditions was the fact that since 1945 a political, as well as an economic, framework bound the western economies together in a way that was totally different from the 1930s. In particular, the USA had assumed responsibility as the leader of the western world and, somewhat ironically, as it turned out, its fall from grace in 1971 was quickly followed by a comparative strengthening in its international position directly as a consequence of the oil price rise.

One other major difference between the 1930s and the 1970s was the nature and effects of price changes in primary product markets. In the former case, big price falls resulted in substantial reductions in the income of primary producers with consequent reductions in their demands for manufactured and semi-factured goods. There were then second-round effects on employment and industry in the major economies. The solution involved a shift in international trading patterns towards a concentration on the demands of the industrialized economies. By contrast the problem in the 1970s was a sharp rise in production costs within a highly industrialized world accustomed to rapid technical change. Whilst massive oil price rises were bound to cause serious economic disruption and dislocation to trading patterns, the capacity for adjustment was much greater than in the 1930s because a supply-side problem could be met by innovation and technical change. Furthermore, the crisis was not the outcome of unregulated market forces but of the manipulation of prices by a cartel that could well prove difficult to hold together. None of this, however, is to deny that the crisis was serious and marked an end to the halcyon years of high growth.

Whilst the 1970s did not parallel the 1930s in international finance, it would be mistaken to view the outcome as proof of a deep spirit of international cooperation. For one thing, the financial crisis exposed the highly contingent nature of the postwar financial settlement. The IMF had survived by means of *ad hoc* adjustments under highly favourable conditions of international economic growth. The moment it was really put to the test it was revealed for what it was: a creature of US economic interests that secondarily served international needs. The big difference between the 1970s and the period of the long boom was that the USA could no longer allow its external transactions to take care of themselves: the dollar exchange rate became an increasingly weighty element in US internal price levels and, therefore, in domestic policy decisions that had major international repercussions. This was bad news for exchange rate stability.[6] The dollar strengthened until the late 1970s; it then rose quite sharply, at which point the American authorities agreed to manage the rate more tightly. This undertaking proved to be short-lived, however. For the Western economies, this self-interested neglect by the USA had two serious consequences. First, it contributed to international price instability through its effects on the terms of trade and the value of exchange reserves, which under the Kingston agreement were predominantly denominated in dollars. Secondly, as we have seen, the Euro-currency market, which was based on dollar deposits, became increasingly unstable. It was not subject to effective central control and the banking institutions that constituted it became enmeshed in highly speculative lending based on the classically unsound principle of borrowing short and lending long. The scale of these operations and the now enormous speed of international communication presented a growing threat to the stability of the western financial system.

The upshot of the turmoil of the early 1970s was an international financial system still dominated by the USA but without the elements of stability and favourable trading conditions that had previously underpinned it. Nevertheless, so far as Britain's economic interests were concerned, it might be argued that the Bretton Woods regime had not served it particularly well and the reduction in Britain's international responsibilities which the new regime involved might well amount to a *deus ex machina*. Under the 1968 Basle agreement (see Chapter 8) the withdrawal of sterling balances had involved a substantial cost to Britain because of compensation payments that had to be made between 1972 and 1974 to cover the fall in the sterling rate against the dollar.

6. S. Strange, *'Interpretation of a Decade'*, in L. Tsoukalis (ed.), *The Political Economy of International Money* (1985), pp. 1–43; *idem., Casino Capitalism* (Oxford 1986); J. Williamson, *The Exchange Rate System* (Washington, DC, 1985).

Thereafter, sterling movements were still an added source of exchange rate instability once the pound came under pressure. Britain nevertheless remained extremely reluctant to surrender the functions of sterling as a reserve currency. Lack of the necessary reserves and increasing pressure from the EEC gradually forced the authorities to concede.

STERLING, THE COMMONWEALTH AND THE EEC

The events in the international economy in the early 1970s exposed the fundamental weaknesses in the British economy in dramatic form. There was an eruption of severe labour disputes which culminated in a strike by the miners in 1972 and the introduction of a three-day week by the government. Poor industrial relations were a running sore throughout the 1970s. The dispute with the miners brought down the Conservative government in 1974 and five years later, following a series of disputes that became known as 'the winter of discontent', a Labour government was defeated at the polls. Successive governments grappled with the problem of industrial relations at a national level. Conservatives aimed to curb the power of the unions by means of its Industrial Relations Act (1971) which was repealed by the Labour government in 1974 and replaced by a Faustian agreement known as the 'social contract', in which government proved to be well and truly cast in the principal role. Wages policies became a regular feature of government activity, but whilst the various schemes might be given high marks for ingenuity they failed convincingly in terms of effectiveness.[7] Yet for all the disruption caused by poor industrial relations and for all its central importance in party political debate, from an historical standpoint these events can be seen as the symptoms of a far more serious underlying malady.

Prices had been rising sharply since the late 1960s but in the early 1970s they accelerated alarmingly to reach a peak rate of 27 per cent per annum in 1975. The striking fact was that the UK rate of inflation was significantly above that for industrial economies generally. The UK average rate of increase for 1973–79 was 16.0 per cent per year as compared with just under 9.0 per cent for OECD

7. G. Bain (ed.), *Industrial Relations in Britain* (Oxford, 1983); W. Brown (ed.), *The Changing Contours of British Industrial Relations. A Survey of Manufacturing Industry* (Oxford, 1981); W. J. McCarthy (ed.), *Trade Unions* (1985 edition); E. H. Phelps Brown, *The Origins of Trade Union Power* (Oxford, 1986 edition), pp. 151–97.

countries generally. In this connection the adoption of a floating exchange rate in 1972 was particularly significant. Initially, the downward movement of the rate gave a stimulus to inflation through increased prices for imported goods and services, and this was reinforced by a concurrent easing of monetary policy. In 1971, the Bank of England removed limits on bank credit and altered the regulations governing clearing banks as part of a policy to promote competition in the credit market. Whereas between 1963 and 1972 'bank lending had grown at a little over 12 per cent per annum, in 1972 it increased by 37 per cent and in 1973 by 43 per cent. Whatever the contribution of changes in the stock of money to inflation in other years, their contribution in 1972 and 1973 is beyond dispute'.[8]

In addition to these short-run influences, the operation of a floating exchange rate allowed British prices to rise faster than the world rate of inflation. A depreciating exchange acted as a kind of automatic transmission that maintained external price competitiveness and insulated domestic inflation, at least for the time being. For how long depended on the second round inflationary effects of higher import prices and the point at which domestic inflation and currency depreciation went out of control. But well before this extreme was reached in Britain it was still possible that the government might find it politically expedient, in the absence of the discipline of a fixed exchange rate system, to allow prices to continue to rise out of line with international prices. This was certainly the pattern that emerged and whether this mattered in terms of competitiveness, if it was not fully compensated for by exchange depreciation, depended on the complexities of relative elasticities of demand for British exports. On the record to date, there was no obvious reason why Britain could afford such latitude. Moreover, the prices of goods and the exchange rate were the outcome of demand and supply relationships, and how these were determined contains the key to the explanation of Britain's performance in the turbulent conditions of the 1970s.

The first step, therefore, is to examine the record of external performance as recorded in the balance of payments. The 1970s are impressive mainly in a negative sense and it must be borne in mind that these end of year figures can mask the full extent of the pressures on the external account, since corrective measures were

8. A. K. Cairncross, *The British Economy Since 1945* (Oxford, 1992), pp. 190–1. OECD, *Historical Statistics* (Paris, 1990), Table 8. 1.

frequently taken during the course of the year. The big reduction in the current account surplus in 1972 proved to be just the beginning of a severe worsening in the account that eventually led to a massive deficit in 1974. Matters eased a bit in 1975 and 1976 but the picture was still bleak. A sharp turn around into useful surplus occurred in the latter half of 1977 which brought the year just into surplus, and a strong balance was finally achieved in 1978. Success was short-lived, however, and the external account ended the decade in the red.[9]

Financing the deficit was achieved by a combination of means. Positive long-term capital flows resulting substantially from the inflow of investment for developing North Sea oil met just over half the deficit. To this gain was added short-term capital flows generated by the recycling of foreigners' oil revenue and currency borrowing from foreigners, largely by the public sector industries. These devices did not, however, avoid recourse to crisis borrowing from international bodies and the IMF in 1976. In that year, acute pressure built up on the pound to a degree not fully reflected by the annual out-turn of the balance of payments. Domestic labour disputes proliferated, and together with the obvious weaknesses in the British economy, this caused foreign holders of sterling to draw down heavily on their sterling balances. The British chancellor, Healey, was eventually driven to seek a $3.6 billion loan from the IMF as international bankers were no longer willing to provide independent support. The loan was granted under certain conditions that were inscribed in a Letter of Intent which the British government duly sent to the IMF.[10]

The bankers at the IMF basically required large cuts in public expenditure. These demands were based on characteristic orthodoxy rather than on a clear understanding of the ills besetting the British economy. And, characteristically, the Treasury had seriously overestimated the extent of the crisis. Unemployment was rising and public expenditure as a proportion of GDP was by no means out of line with other major economies. In 1975, for example, public expenditure as a percentage of GDP amounted to

9. *Economic Trends, Annual Supplement* (1994), Table 1.17. Balance of payments, quarterly data.

10. K. Burk and A. Cairncross, *'Goodbye, Great Britain': The 1976 IMF Crisis* (1992) for an excellent account in both political and economic terms. An insider view of the crisis is D. Healey, *The Time of My Life* (1989), pp. 426–37. What this account reveals of Healey's attitudes to public finance and the role of the Treasury should provide a corrective to those who see the Labour government as a victim of Treasury orthodoxy and 'City' financial interests.

46 per cent in the UK as compared with 49 per cent in West Germany and 44 per cent in France.[11] Countries that were out of line were typified by Japan (27 per cent), Switzerland (29 per cent) and the USA (36 per cent). In broad terms, these differences are explained in terms of the level of transfer payments, though there were also significant differences in defence expenditure. The more significant difference was the rate of inflation, and here Britain was well ahead of the field with the exception of Italy.[12] Yet cuts in public expenditure would have needed to be massive before they would have curbed inflation, since they would have operated only indirectly and to a significant degree they would have been self-defeating since, contrary to received wisdom, there was not a continuous trade-off between inflation and the rate of unemployment; this fact was recognized by the invention of the term 'stagflation' to describe the condition that developed in the 1970s. Low productivity and wage demands by the large majority who remained in employment combined to push up unit wage costs and hence prices.[13] To break this vicious circle with the bludgeon of huge public expenditure cuts carried the enormous risk of severe economic dislocation that could only serve to weaken further international confidence.

In the event, resistance within the cabinet and compromise on the part of the bankers led to a reduction in the original demand for cuts of £5 billion to £2.5 billion spread over two years. The loan was essential, even though it covered only a third of what was required and was not available until 1977, by which time the balance of payments was already turning. The critical fact, of course, was its effect on international financial confidence. And the cuts in public expenditure might be seen, also, as important for what they symbolized about the resolve to maintain the value of the currency rather than for what they directly delivered to that end. They were made, moreover, in an atmosphere charged with ideas amounting to ideology that the level of public expenditure was a key element in current economic difficulties.

The tone was set by a white paper, *The Attack on Inflation*, published in the summer of 1975.[14] The policy that was stipulated

11. R. Middleton, 'The Size and Scope of the Public Sector', in S. J. D. Green and R. G. Whiting (eds), *The Boundaries of the State in Modern Britain* (Cambridge, 1995), forthcoming.

12. OECD, *Historical Statistics*, Table 6. 5.

13. J. E. Meade, *Stagflation. Vol. 1. Wage Fixing* (1982).

14. *The Attack on Inflation*, Cmnd. 6151, 1975.

was wrapped in the Social Contract and bore the claim that it served the interests of housewives, pensioners and the unemployed. But it was based on principles which contained much more than an echo of Treasury financial orthodoxy of half a century earlier. More to the point, the leading ministers responsible for economic policy, in particular the chancellor of the exchequer, Healey, appear to have had little difficulty in identifying with it.[15] At a more abstract level a number of economists identified budget deficits as a major source of current economic problems. In particular, the alleged excesses of public finance became part of the increasingly noisy refrain to 'be heard from monetarists.[16] Probably of more immediate influence were those who claimed that weaknesses in the economy, especially in the manufacturing sector, which led to a lack of international competitiveness and external deficits, resulted from 'Too Few Producers'; in other words, public sector employment, which was heavily concentrated on non-marketable output as defined, crowded out the manufacturing sector that produced the goods which were essential for a sound economy and a healthy trading performance. The validity of this analysis will be considered critically later (see Chapter 10), but for the moment the important point is that the claim of 'Too Few Producers' was ideally tailored to the political rhetoric of cuts in public expenditure.[17]

Britain's external financial problems were exceptional among the major economies, but this did not mean that there was a complete lack of shared concern about the structure of international finance. To the contrary, within the European Economic Community there were growing worries about the role of the dollar and the possibility of the German mark being attached more closely to the dollar in opposition to other major currencies. These concerns crystallized into a proposal in late 1977 for a European Monetary System. After various negotiations within the Community what emerged was a mechanism based on a new currency unit, the ECU, an arrangement for the mutual adjustment of exchange rates and a European Monetary Fund. The overall aim was to strengthen the financial system of the Community within the international

15. Healey, *The Time of My Life*, pp. 392–401.

16. An excellent account of this swing in opinion, together with effective criticism, is given by Burk and Cairncross, *'Goodbye, Great Britain'*, pp. 197–208 and more generally pp. 179–214. For a contemporary dose of common sense see J. Hicks, 'What is Wrong With Monetarism', *Lloyds Bank Review*, 18 (1975), pp. 1–13.

17. R. W. Bacon and W. A. Eltis, *Britain's Economic Problem: Too Few Producers* (1976).

economy and to hold out the possibility of much closer economic and political integration within the EEC over the longer run. Difficulties between France and Germany delayed the introduction of the system until the spring of 1979 and, even then, it had very limited immediate impact. But of particular significance in this context was that Britain refused to join the system.[18]

This refusal is perhaps all the more remarkable when seen within the context of Britain's position within the world economy. Thirty years after the 1947 financial crisis, Britain still remained a client state within the sphere of international finance. And, in comparison with the earlier period, America was attempting to steer international financial relations with far less regard for international financial stability and without much concern with the so-called special relationship with Britain. Yet when due allowance is made for the fact that through the IMF the USA was helping to bail Britain out of its immediate difficulties, the depth of official belief in Britain in a continuing special relationship with the USA is remarkable. It may be that this commitment has to be explained in terms of perceived (or misperceived) foreign policy interests. At all events, Britain was still far from defining its external economic interests first and foremost as a member of the European Economic Community.

Applications by Britain to join the EEC had been made in 1961 and 1967 and both were vetoed by De Gaulle. On the first occasion the breakdown came after two years of negotiations, but on the second it occurred almost immediately since the devaluation of sterling in the same year was easily represented as an attempt to reduce the balance of payments cost to Britain of entering the EEC. Intransigence on the part of the French has to be balanced, however, against Britain's strong perception of its world role, based on Commonwealth ties and a belief that it enjoyed a special relationship with the USA. And in practical terms, Commonwealth economic interests were a major problem in relation to the still large, high cost agricultural sectors in France, Germany and Italy. The Common Agricultural Policy (CAP) was a keystone of the EEC, after all.[19]

18. A useful survey is provided by H. Van Der Wee, *Prosperity and Upheaval. The World Economy 1945–1980* (1986), pp. 498–512.
19. A. S. Milward, *The European Rescue of the Nation-State* (1992), pp. 224–317, for a stimulating analysis of the 'Europeanization of agricultural protection'. It may be questioned, however, whether the author somewhat downplays the importance of the Common Agricultural Policy in the light of the evidence he supplies.

The second application had been allowed to lie on the table and, following the resignation of De Gaulle and further difficult negotiations, Britain finally entered the EEC on 1 January 1973. Another important element in this outcome was probably the election of a new government in 1970 under Heath, who was recognized in Europe as being fully committed to Britain's entry into the EEC. The terms of the agreement gave only limited concessions to Commonwealth countries in respect of their preferential trading arrangements with the UK, though a period for adjustment was allowed. For its part, Britain agreed to move towards a common external tariff by 1977, but this requirement had effectively been eased by GATT negotiations in the 1960s; substantial tariff reductions were made in the Dillon Round in 1962 and the Kennedy Round between 1963 and 1967. Britain agreed, also, to contribute 19 per cent of the Community budget by 1977. Other major financial matters – including exchange rates, monetary policy and debt-management – remained under independent control. After much public heart-searching a referendum on the terms was held in 1975. It returned a 2:1 majority in favour of Britain's membership of the EEC. It is difficult to know what this signified, however, since by 1975 membership was widely accepted as largely a matter of *fait accompli*.

At the time of entry and since there has been a great deal of debate on the economic consequences of Britain's membership of the Community. The question is unanswerable in anything like precise terms because of the range of assumptions involved in attempts to calculate costs and benefits. The diversion of British trade was much less than had been commonly predicted, since the swing to EEC markets had occurred substantially before entry, as our earlier analysis has shown.[20] The Common Agricultural Policy was clearly not to Britain's advantage because, for all the subsidy already enjoyed by British agriculture, it was still significantly more cost-effective than continental producers. The upshot was that the CAP was by far the biggest element accounting for Britain's net contribution to the EEC budget. In turn, agriculture accounted for 75 per cent of total EEC expenditure. It has been estimated for 1978, for example, that EEC agricultural policy cost the British consumer an amount equivalent to just under 1 per cent of GNP.[21]

20. See Chapters 7 and 8.
21. F. Giavazzi, 'The Impact of EEC Membership', in R. Dornbusch and R. Layard (eds.), *The Performance of the British Economy* (Oxford, 1987), p. 100.

This was double the average for the other member countries. The loss in comparative international terms was somewhat less than had been feared, however, because European agricultural prices subsequently rose less fast than world prices.

Calculations of gains and losses are, in important respects, beside the point, notwithstanding the high degree of error to which they are subject. The basic issue is the competitiveness of the UK economy. If this could be increased, then the market opportunities within the EEC were substantial. Indeed, if Britain's entry resulted in an economic loss this was a measure of competitive failure rather than some kind of penalty. It is perhaps ironic, therefore, that many of those who argued strongly for Britain's membership did so on the basis that wider market opportunities would stimulate the necessary competitive response. At all events, the market was still subject to both direct and indirect barriers between the member states. Harmonization of regulations would obviously involve a protracted process of negotiation. Different forms and levels of taxation and state procurement of goods and services were two areas in which major differences operated. The level of sales tax could, for example, operate as an indirect and maybe disguised form of tariff. And whilst no formal restrictions applied to labour mobility and entitlement to social security throughout the EEC, there were effective barriers here, too. Indirectly, these involved such things as access to socially provided housing and language problems and, directly, there was the complicated matter of the equivalence of technical and professional qualifications. During the 1980s, mobility within the labour market was gradually increased as some of these barriers were removed.[22]

One of the more serious aspects of Britain's membership of the EEC, and not one which excited major concern at the time of entry, is the impact on regional economic development. Regional economic disparities which had become such an acute feature of the British economy in the 1930s had by no means been eliminated by the 1970s.[23] At the latter date the same areas as in the interwar years experienced significantly higher levels of unemployment and lower levels of income than the economy at large. The EEC recognized the regional problem but the funds available for tackling it amounted to no more than 4 per cent of its budget

22. K. J. Twitchett (ed.), *European Cooperation Today* (1986).
23. The issue is surveyed by H. W. Armstrong, 'Community Regional Policy: A Survey and Critique', *Regional Studies*, 12 (1978), pp. 511–28. See also *idem.*, and J. Taylor, *Regional Economics and Policy* (Oxford, 1985).

expenditure, though it might be claimed that some part of the large cost of the CAP was a form of regional policy. Moreover, the whole thrust of economic growth within the EEC was generated from a central industrial axis made up from France, Germany, the Benelux countries and northern Italy.[24] In other words, the problem of the economic periphery was a point of particular vulnerability for Britain. The evidence is that it has remained so throughout the 1980s.

As has been indicated, the financial aspects of the EEC were much less developed than those of trade, yet they continued to be by far the most critical. So far as Britain was concerned, arrangements during the 1980s did not proceed much beyond credit arrangements between central banks based on the European Currency Unit (ECU). In October 1991, however, Britain joined the Exchange Rate Mechanism, which was but part of a much more fundamental move towards European Monetary Union. This development proved short-lived and just under a year later, Britain was forced to leave the ERM. The fundamental financial issues thus remain unresolved.

The book-keeping approach to Britain's membership of the EEC is extremely narrow in conception in relation to Britain's place in the world economy.[25] International economic development in the 1970s and 1980s was increasingly subject to the somewhat conflicting forces of neo-mercantilism and economic globalization. The former was represented by the economic power blocks of the USA, Japan and the EEC and the latter by huge multinational companies and the rapidly increasing scale of international financial and capital movements. In these circumstances there could be no certainty that the steady liberalization of world trade that had occurred since the Second World War was necessarily a permanent feature. For Britain to continue to regard itself as a major economic power in these circumstances was unreal. Membership of the EEC offered the benefits of collaboration and, potentially, a measure of protection from these powerful international economic forces, though it did not by the same token guarantee Britain's prosperity.

The political element was probably the central issue in the referendum of 1975 which confirmed Britain's membership of the

24. This point is brought out strongly by Milward, *The European Rescue of the Nation-State*, pp. 119–223.

25. See, for example, D. Reynolds, *Britannia Overruled. British Policy and World Power in the Twentieth Century* (1991), pp. 238–92.

Table 9.2 UK visible trade by area, selected years 1965–68 (%)

	Imports						Exports					
	1965	1973	1974	1979	1980	1983	1965	1973	1974	1979	1980	1983
EEC	23.6	33.0	33.4	43.1	40.8	45.9	26.4	32.6	33.4	41.8	42.0	43.4
Other Western Europe	12.5	17.0	14.8	16.7	15.8	16.2	15.3	18.2	17.4	16.4	16.4	13.1
USA	11.7	10.2	9.7	10.2	11.7	11.0	10.6	12.1	10.7	9.5	9.4	14.1
Japan	1.4	2.8	2.5	3.1	3.3	5.2	1.1	2.2	1.9	1.4	1.2	1.3
White Dominions	18.6	11.0	8.7	5.5	5.9	5.1	18.0	10.8	11.3	6.2	5.7	5.3
OPEC	9.7	9.4	16.4	7.0	8.4	4.3	5.5	6.4	7.3	8.9	10.0	10.1
New ind. countries	2.4	3.9	3.2	4.0	4.7	4.8	3.6	3.9	4.2	3.7	3.4	3.3
Centrally planned econs.	4.3	3.7	3.2	3.2	2.8	2.4	2.9	3.3	3.0	2.8	2.7	1.9
Other less developed countries	15.8	9.0	8.2	7.3	7.1	5.2	16.5	10.6	10.7	9.5	9.2	7.5

Figures do not sum because of rounding

Source: Rowthorn and Wells (1987), 176, 185.

Community. And this was reflected in the fact that in subsequent negotiations the Treasury and the Foreign Office took over the main responsibility from the Board of Trade. To the extent that these changes amounted to a major shift in political attitudes towards a more realistic view of Britain's position in the world, this could well have had significant economic effects of the kind that would lead to policies more appropriately designed to deal with some of Britain's economic weaknesses. The subsequent development of economic policy makes it abundantly clear, however, that the depth of political consensus accompanying Britain's entry into Europe was shallow. This became pronounced when Mrs Thatcher, who had replaced Edward Heath as leader of the Conservative party, became prime minister in 1979. Great power status then became the order of the day. Delusions, like old habits, die hard.

TRADE

The main changes in the pattern and composition of UK trade between 1973 and 1983 are shown in Tables 9.2 and 9.3. A number of features stand out, of which the most prominent is the increase in trade with the EEC. In broad terms this increase was matched by a change in trade with OPEC countries and the clear switch away from the high income areas of the Commonwealth and from Third World economies.

These geographical shifts were associated with changes in commodity patterns. Here again, the main features are clear. Trade in manufactures became more intra-EEC, with the balance shifting in favour of Britain's European partners. The overall balance did not swing to the same extent because of the increase in UK primary exports going to Europe. North Sea oil was of particular importance and by the end of the period the EEC absorbed just short of two-thirds of Britain's fuel exports. The trend in the balance of trade in food, also, moved in Britain's favour between 1972 and 1983.

It has been argued convincingly that the decline in the manufacturing balance was not attributable to the 'loss of Empire'.[26] Whilst it is true that trade regulations within the EEC favoured intra-European trade, it remains the case that Britain achieved increases in surpluses with primary producing areas,

26. R. E. Rowthorn and J. R. Wells, *De-Industrialization and Foreign Trade* (Cambridge, 1987), pp. 194–5 and *passim*.

Table 9.3 UK balance of trade in primary products and manufactures by area in 1983 (% of GDP)

	Primary products	Manufactures	Total
All countries	+0.3	−0.7	−0.4
Manufacturing exporters	+1.8	−3.8	−1.9
EEC	+1.5	−2.2	−0.7
Other Western Europe	−0.3	−0.4	−0.7
USA	+0.7	−0.2	+0.5
Japan	0.0	−0.8	−0.8
New ind. countries	−0.2	−0.2	−0.3
Primary producers	−1.6	+3.1	⎯1.5
OPEC	−0.4	+1.5	+1.1
White Dominions	−0.5	+0.5	0.0
Other less developed countries	−0.5	+0.9	+0.4
Centrally planned economies	−0.2	+0.1	−0.1

Source: Rowthorn and Wells (1987), 198.

mainly as a result of reduced fuel and, to a lesser extent, food imports on the one hand, and an increase in exports of manufactured goods on the other. The resulting surpluses would have been somewhat higher if the UK had been able to maintain Commonwealth preferences. But these surpluses would have been used largely to purchase increased quantities of manufactures from the major industrial economies, even though some proportion might have gone in increased military expenditure, overseas aid, foreign investment and services. What the 'loss of Empire' and the decline in the proportion of Third World trade did produce, however, was an increased triangularity in British trade by the early 1980s. Nevertheless, it is important to note that this analysis says nothing about the *level* of British trade. To put it another way, the triangular settlement of surpluses and deficits was a balancing mechanism; the competitiveness of British exports was quite another matter, that will be considered a little later.

The extent of the reduction in UK energy consumption after 1973 is especially interesting. By 1983, consumption was one-sixth lower than ten years earlier, but even this measure fails to capture the full impact of the change when related to contemporary predictions and the energy policy based upon them in the early 1970s. If consumption of energy had continued to grow at its trend rate, consumption in the early 1980s would have been 45 per cent higher than the actual amount. This implied reduction was equivalent to 75 per cent of the output of North Sea oil in 1983.[27] By far the two most important causes of this reduction were energy saving and economic stagnation. Precise estimates of their relative importance would be extremely difficult, if not impossible, to make but rough calculations suggest that just over half the reduction was the result of poor economic performance whilst innovation accounted for the bulk of the remainder.

Trade in invisibles during the period improved in performance both in comparison with other sectors and on its own past record. But within the total there were considerable changes in the relative contributions of constituent elements. The biggest loss was in sea transport which halved in volume between 1973 and 1983 so that a small positive balance of earnings was turned into a substantial net loss. The other significant turnaround occurred in foreign travel which moved into a substantial deficit in the early 1980s in comparison with a healthy positive balance in the 1970s. Financial services maintained a healthy surplus and construction work overseas assumed increasing importance; the latter, it has been pointed out, returned more than either the banks or insurance companies of the City of London, whose role has been frequently singled out for special comment. As with visible trade, however, comparative performances tell us nothing about overall performance in relation to productivity, competitiveness and comparative advantage, to which we must now turn.

THE NEW EL DORADO?

The new and dramatic change in Britain's trade during this period was the advent and then the full flow of North Sea oil production. The impact of this development was intensified by a second round of oil price rises in 1979 and 1980. As has been shown, Britain's balance of trade in fuels was correspondingly transformed into a healthy surplus, which allowed the Bank of England, among others, to claim that North Sea oil cancelled out the effects of the oil price rise on Britain and still added a bonus to the balance of payments.

27. *Idem.*, pp. 116–24.

For all this, in a most careful analysis of the impact of oil on the economy, Rowthorn and Wells have shown that the combined effect of a reduction in imports of food and materials, amounting to a reduction equivalent to 11.5 per cent of GDP between 1950 and 1983, far outweighed the corresponding reduction of 2.4 per cent due to oil.[28] Their measures need to be qualified, however, since over the half the reduction in food and raw materials occurred prior to 1970, so that the added effect of oil in the following decade was clearly of substantial proportions.

The major debate over the impact of oil on the economy is focused on its macro and structural effects on employment. The former relates to the level of employment and the latter to changes in the distribution of labour between sectors at a given level of employment. Contemporary estimates of the macro effect varied widely, from an addition to unemployment of up to 2 million to a 1.7 million reduction in unemployment. This enormous range of estimates results from different counter-factual assumptions made about government policy. For example, the figure of a 1.7 million reduction in unemployment with oil is based on the assumption that without oil the government would have been forced to pursue more deflationary policies than was in fact the case.[29] But there are more fundamental problems with such econometric exercises. Since there is no agreed theory of how the economy works, economists are free to construct possible worlds according to their tastes. The problem of disentangling the multifarious relationships of cause and effect are thus solved by prior definition. Even the data that are used to operate chosen models are themselves subject to significant margins of error. The hypothetical, itself, thus becomes uncertain.

It is not possible, therefore, to provide anything approaching a precise estimate of the macroemployment effects of North Sea oil. The best estimate is that it had a marginal effect on the sharp rise in unemployment from 1979 onwards. There are, in other words, more plausible causes of that rise and, as will be argued later, this view is borne out by the persistent nature of unemployment in the 1980s. It is nevertheless important to distinguish between the impact of North Sea oil and the shock effects of the international oil price rise of 1973, which occurred before North Sea oil came on stream. Britain was no more protected from the effects of this shock

28. *Idem.*, pp. 249–75, 406–7.
29. F. J. Atkinson, S. J. Brocke and S. G. F. Hall, 'The Economic Effects of North Sea Oil', *National Institute Economic Review*, 104 (1983), pp. 38–44; F. J. Atkinson and S. G. Hall, *Oil and the British Economy* (1983).

on inflation and employment than the other industrialized economies.

The structural effects on the economy of North Sea oil production raise more complex and in many ways more important issues than its effect on the level of employment. Those who claim that oil production had major structural effects argue along the following lines. The growth in production is seen as attracting resources away from the manufacturing sector and, at the same time, causing an appreciation in the exchange rate which reduced foreign demand for exports and caused employment in manufacturing to fall. An extension of this analysis claims that since productivity in oil production is higher than in manufacturing, the structural shift will involve an additional net loss of employment. Closer examination of the production and trading pattern suggests, however, that the structural impact of oil on the economy was, as with its macro effects, of marginal significance. There are three main reasons why this was so.

First, prior to the discovery and exploitation of North Sea oil, the combined effect of the decline in domestic coal production and employment, increasing imports of oil and natural gas, and ultimately the sharp rise in the price of oil, was to exert strong pressure for increased output of manufactured goods. To this extent, the domestic production of oil worked to redress the balance. Secondly, it has been noted that over half the improvement in the fuel balance during this period can be attributed to poor growth in the economy, with correspondingly large effects on structural employment. Thirdly, the surplus on trade in non-manufactures was a prior development dominated by the big net improvement in trade in food and raw materials plus the consistent surplus on invisibles. In the words of Rowthorn and Wells: 'Thus, the 1973 price rise induced *re*-industrialisation (or at least should have done), whereas North Sea oil induced *de*-industrialisation ... leaving the overall structure much the same'.[30]

The story does not end here, however. Leaving aside the slow growth of the economy, the large improvement in non-manufactured trade does reflect critical structural changes that were of major importance for Britain's position in the world economy. From the mid-1960s the improvement in this balance ceased to be mainly the consequence of improvements in the terms of trade and instead resulted from structural changes in production. Advances in technology produced new goods in which new materials were a proportionately smaller part of the final value of output, or made

30. Rowthorn and Wells, *De-Industrialization and Foreign Trade*, p. 277.

Table 9.4 Comparative balances of trade in manufactures, 1973–82 (% of GDP)

	1973	1974	1975	1976	1977	1978	1979	1980	1981	1982
UK	+2.0	+2.4	+3.5	+3.9	+4.1	+3.0	+1.4	+2.5	+1.9	+0.9
Belgium	+8.3	+9.7	+7.1	+6.4	+5.3	+4.7	+4.7	+5.0	+6.1	+5.7
France	+1.5	+1.8	+3.1	+1.9	+2.6	+2.2	+2.5	+1.5	+2.0	+0.8
Italy	+3.9	+4.9	+4.9	+7.2	+8.6	+9.0	+8.0	+5.5	+7.5	+7.4
Japan	+6.0	+8.6	+8.6	+9.4	+9.5	+8.0	+7.5	+9.4	+10.4	+10.4
Sweden	+4.1	+3.4	+2.8	+3.0	+3.2	+5.0	+4.5	+3.8	+5.4	+5.2
West Germany	+8.8	+11.5	+9.6	+9.8	+9.4	+8.7	+8.2	+8.1	+9.5	+10.5
USA	0.0	+0.6	+1.3	+0.7	+0.2	-0.5	0.0	+0.6	+0.5	-0.2
Australia	-4.7	-7.1	-5.7	-5.9	-6.5	-6.9	-6.7	-6.1	-7.6	-9.2
Netherlands	-0.8	+0.6	-0.5	0.0	-1.6	-2.2	-1.6	-0.9	+1.0	-0.5
Norway	-5.9	-5.4	-7.2	-10.2	-11.1	-4.3	-5.5	-6.2	-6.8	-8.0

Source: Rowthorn and Wells (1987), 60–7.

for more efficient use of existing materials, or led to the adoption of more cost-effective substitutes. In other cases, the decline of existing industries led to a direct reduction in raw material imports. There are numerous examples of these developments. The production of electronic goods, incorporating solid state technology and cheap materials, grew rapidly; organic materials such as cotton, wool, jute, rubber and wood were replaced by synthetics based on oil and gas; the decline in iron and steel production and shipbuilding reduced demand for basic materials. In addition, there was substitute domestic production for imports as in the case of wood pulp. But by far the biggest substitution effect of this kind was the increased production of foodstuffs leading to a high degree of self-sufficiency. The question of whether this represented the efficient use of resources in agriculture, when judged in terms of the enormous opportunity costs of subsidies and support payments, has already been raised.

The change in Britain's international trading position was not part of a pattern common to major industrialized economies. The variation shows up most clearly when balances of trade in manufactures are compared. It has been argued that unlike Britain, economies such as Germany and Japan had to match the sharp rise in the price of oil by vigorously exploiting their comparative advantages in the production and export of manufactures. Obversely, Britain's improving balance on non-manufactures is seen as being compensated for by an increase in imports of manufactured goods, especially from the EEC.

This analysis is, of course, about proportionate changes and tells us nothing directly about the level of output within which the changes occurred. But before this issue is considered, it needs to be questioned whether the sectoral adjustment is quite as automatic as has been described. Given that, over the longer run, a country's balance of payments will tend to equilibrium (or to zero) it does not follow that the adjustment should be wholly the outcome of compensating movements between trade in manufactures and non-manufactures. As has already been observed, other elements in the balance of payments must be taken into account. These are specifically foreign exchange reserves, overseas investment, foreign aid and overseas defence costs. Thus whilst sterling became, in a sense, a petro-currency this did not give rise to problems of exchange rate appreciation because there was a recognized underlying lack of robustness to the balance of payments. An alternative to a deterioration in the manufacturing balance (which added to import penetration) could have been higher levels of foreign exchange reserves and overseas investment, though this obviously would have implications for the level of domestic consumption. Internationally, an increased surplus on trade in non-manufactures did not automatically exclude higher levels of output and export of certain manufactures achieving comparative advantage in international markets based on improved efficiency of production. The net result could be that manufacturing would still experience a fall in its share of output and employment, imports of manufactures would still rise, but the level of domestic manufacturing output and employment would be higher than was in fact achieved. And in this context the spare capacity in the economy as reflected in growing levels of unemployment at that time, must be firmly borne in mind.

In the context of the actual performance of the economy, however, the importance of oil revenues should not be underestimated. They were highly significant at the margin of the balance of payments. Estimates of the future flow of production varied but the crucial point was that the contribution of oil revenues to the balance of payments was directly dependent on price fixing by a cartel, OPEC. What is revealing, moreover, is how wildly optimistic were many of the estimates of the revenue return from North Sea oil made by economic experts. It did not require exceptional foresight or statistical skill, but simply a little sense of history to be aware that this kind of international price-fixing was extremely difficult to sustain for any length of time. Thus the changing but essentially insecure structure of British trade was a critical element in Britain's longer-term position in the world economy.

CHAPTER TEN

Britain in the World Economy: Falling Behind and Catching Up?

THE ADVENT OF THATCHERISM

By the mid-1960s Britain's consistently poor showing in the international economic league seemed to give the lie to the claim that it was mainly a reflection of postwar economic recovery in Western Europe and Japan. Vigorous debate in political and economic circles produced a variety of diagnoses and a number of suggested cures for the so-called British disease, though some of the proposed treatments had all the sophistication of blood-letting as a cure for fever. And in all the noise, there was no serious questioning of whether the British economy was simply performing to the best of its innate capacity and resources. After all, its record had improved significantly on pre-war levels. But following the crises of the early 1970s, concern about relative performance deepened into a growing conviction that Britain might have entered into a state of more permanent economic decline. Questioning and uncertainty of this kind was fruitful ground for the brand of conviction politics that became known as Thatcherism that took hold in the 1980s. It offered simple solutions to complex economic problems.[1] And as if to confirm the efficacy of these nostrums, the economic health of the nation appeared to improve. Furthermore, this change seemed to corroborate a theoretical challenge to the idea of Britain's economic decline. According to this theory, economic growth among the advanced economies during the twentieth century, and especially since the Second

---

1. H. Young, *One of Us* (1991 edition); A. Gamble, *The Free Economy and the Strong State: The Politics of Thatcherism* (1988). The credo of Mrs Thatcher's economic policy comes through in A. A. Walters, *Britain's Economic Renaissance* (Oxford, 1986) and in K. Joseph, *Reversing the Trend* (1975).

World War, has been a process of catch-up and convergence. Having lost world economic leadership to the USA, Britain was then overtaken by other economies, though the differences were less than in the past because modern economic development depends on a high degree of convergence between the advanced nations. By the 1970s Britain was at the point from which it could benefit from the advantages of being a follower. The catch-up began in the 1980s but, it is claimed, the best is yet to come. Suez marked the beginning of Britain's fall in the world economy. Did the Falklands War symbolize its resurgence?[2]

· The events of this period are too recent to allow the historian to tread with reasonable confidence. Policies that were the outcome of this new form of economic radicalism will perhaps prove to be less radical in their effects than the claims originally made for them would suggest. The controversial area of privatization is a major case in point. Early indications are that far from producing a much wider degree of share ownership, privatization has resulted in more efficient monopolies complete with their own, modern, form of robber barons. Moreover, the long-term consequences of the twists and turns of the Thatcher government's monetary and exchange rate policies will be extremely difficult to disentangle. For these sorts of reasons, this study will conclude by examining the catch-up and convergence thesis within a broad focus on the outcome of what have become known as the Thatcher years, before offering a final assessment of Britain's changing position in the world economy during the past century.

The main statistical indicators of Britain's economic performance are set out in Tables 10.1–10.4.

---

2. The progenitor of the idea of catch-up and convergence is M. Abramovitz, 'Rapid Growth Potential and Its Realization. The Expansion of Capitalism in the Post-War period' in E. Malinvaud (ed.), *Economic Growth and Resources, Proceedings of the Fifth World Congress of the International Economic Association, Volume 1* (1979), pp. 1–51; *idem.*, 'Catching Up, Forging Ahead and Falling Behind', *Journal of Economic History*, 46 (1986), pp. 385–406. See also C. Feinstein, 'Benefits of Backwardness and Costs of Continuity', in A. Graham and A. Seldon, *Government and Economics in the Post-War World: Economic Policies and Comparative Performance 1945–85* (1990), pp. 284–93.

Table 10.1 UK comparative economic performance 1973–88 (% per year)

	GDP		GDP per person employed		Manufacturing output		Manufacturing output per person employed	
	1973–79	1979–88	1973–79	1979–88	1973–79	1979–88	1973–79	1979–88
UK	1.5	2.2	1.3	2.0	-0.7	0.6	0.6	4.0
Canada	4.2	3.2	1.3	1.3	2.5	2.4	1.3	2.3
France	2.8	1.9	2.5	2.0	2.7	0.0	3.7	2.2
Germany	2.3	1.7	2.9	n.a.	1.7	0.6	3.1	n.a.
Italy	3.7	2.4	2.8	1.9	5.5	2.5	5.3	4.0
Japan	3.6	4.1	2.9	3.0	3.6	6.8	5.0	5.8
USA	2.4	2.8	0.0	1.1	1.9	n.a.	0.9	n.a.
Total OECD	2.7	3.8	1.6	1.6	2.3	2.8	2.6	3.3

Sources: OECD *Historical Statistics* (1990), 48, 50–2; *Economic Trends* (1994), 170, 173.

Table 10.2 Comparative unemployment rates 1950–87 (% total labour force)

	1965–73	1974–81	1982–85	1986–89
UK	3.1	5.7	11.7	9.3
France	2.2	5.1	9.1	10.1
Germany	0.8	3.3	7.1	6.1
Italy	5.4	6.8	9.1	8.3
Japan	1.2	2.0	2.6	2.6
USA	4.8	6.8	8.4	5.9

Source: Maddison (1991), 262–5.

Table 10.3 Comparative structure of employment in industry and manufacturing 1973, 1974 and 1987 (% total labour force)

	Industry*		Manufacturing	
	1973	1987	1974	1987
UK	41.7	29.8	34.6	23.6
France	38.5	30.1	28.3	21.6
Germany	46.6	39.7	36.1	32.1
Italy	38.1	31.7	27.0	22.5
Japan	37.2	33.8	27.2	24.1
USA	32.3	26.6	24.2	18.6

* Industry includes mining, manufacturing, electricity, gas and water supply, and construction.

Sources: Maddison (1991), 248–9; OECD, *Historical Statistics* (1990), 41.

Table 10.4 Ratio of balance of payments on current account to GDP, 1980–89 (%)

	Visible trade balance	Services and transfers	Income from abroad	Current balance
1980	+0.6	+0.7	−0.1	+1.2
1981	+1.3	+0.9	+0.5	+2.7
1982	+0.6	+0.5	+0.5	+1.6
1983	−0.5	+0.7	+0.9	+1.1
1984	−1.6	+0.8	+1.3	+0.5
1985	−0.9	+0.9	+0.6	+0.6
1986	−2.5	+1.1	+1.2	−0.2
1987	−2.7	+0.7	+0.9	−1.1
1988	−4.5	+0.1	+0.9	−3.5
1989	−4.8	−0.2	+0.7	−4.3

Source: *Economic Trends, Annual Supplement* (1994), 12, 120.

At one level these figures present a straightforward picture. Within an international framework of a general downward shift in rates of change following the oil crisis, Britain shows up comparatively more favourably than in the previous periods, in terms of the growth of GDP and the rate of productivity gain; just how much more depends on the choice of base years and sub-periods. In productivity, which is widely regarded as the key area in Britain's earlier poor performance, the 1980s appear particularly noteworthy in respect of manufacturing in industry. But this improvement has to be seen largely as a relative one. Britain did better than previously in relation to most countries but the margin of gain did little to compensate for the margin of shortfall in previous periods.

When attention is switched to levels of employment, the distribution of the labour force, import penetration and the balance of payments, the picture becomes more complex. The unemployment rate was significantly above the international average for most of the period, though there was a sharp convergent rise in other major economies towards the end. The decline in the proportion of the work force in industry was a common experience but more pronounced in Britain. The proportions in manufacturing follow a similar pattern to give an overall position, at least, in which Britain is not markedly out of line. More importantly, however, it will be argued that account should be taken of the decline in the absolute number employed in manufacturing industry in Britain in comparison with economies of comparable size. On the external account, the earlier gloom does not appear to have been relieved: import penetration continued to rise to reach 36 per cent by 1985 and the balance of payments moved into a rapidly widening deficit in the late 1980s.

How are these differences to be interpreted?

The changing structure of the economy during the period as a whole has given rise to a long and often sharp debate over whether and to what extent Britain has been suffering from a terminal process of deindustrialization.[3] In broad terms, attempts to provide economic explanations of the fall in industrial employment reduce to three main types. On the positive side there is, first, the mature economy approach. Britain is thus presented as having achieved a level of development at which nothing was more natural than increases in income being spent disproportionately on services as compared with manufactured goods. Most commonly this is attributed to a change in tastes, but recent analysis argues that the shift in expenditure results from the long-run tendency of labour productivity to rise faster in industry than in services. There is thus a corresponding fall in the proportion of the labour force employed in industry. Put another way, if expenditure is measured in constant prices, the proportions spent on goods and services remain fairly fixed. Thus what was occurring was not de-industrialization but more efficient industrial production. The second type of explanation centres on comparative advantage. In Britain's case this process is seen as involving the shift in employment from manufacturing to oil in the manner that was critically examined in the previous chapter. It is important to stress, however, that from neither of these explanations does it follow that a proportionate decline in employment in industry should be accompanied by an absolute decline, if the economy is not at full employment.

3. The literature is huge but most relevant are R. Bacon and W. Eltis, *Britain's Economic Problem: Too Few Producers* (1976 and 1978 editions); W. Beckerman (ed.), *Slow Growth in Britain. Causes and Consequences* (1979); F. Blackaby (ed.), *De-industrialization* (1978); J. Eatwell, *Whatever Happened to Britain?* (1982); R. E. Rowthorn and J. R. Wells, *De-Industrialization and Foreign Trade* (Cambridge, 1987). A useful, brief summary of the latest theoretical forays into this field is provided by N. F. R. Crafts, *Can Industrialization Seriously Damage Your Wealth?* (1993); however, the author's own interpretation in relation to comparative levels of income is open to challenge. See note 14 below.

The third line of analysis is on the negative side and marches under the banner of 'Too Few Producers'. The core proposition is that during the 1970s expenditure on 'non-marketable' services crowded out expenditure on 'marketable output'. The latter was produced mainly by manufacturing, mining, construction and agriculture; and, it is claimed, these sectors generated the wealth on which the former depended for their existence. The major reason for the shift is alleged to be the too rapid rise in public expenditure, especially on so-called non-productive welfare services. Thus starved of resources, manufacturing industry suffered decline.

The first two types of analysis are at least consistent with the direction of changes that occurred in the distribution of the labour force, but they clearly do not provide anything like an explanation of the extent of the decline in industrial employment when this is set against the rapid rise in unemployment. The charge of 'Too Few Producers' founders even more dramatically on this fact. And regardless of high unemployment, this third line of argument is conceptually flawed in the distinction it draws between marketable and non-marketable output, mistaken in its assertions as to the level of public expenditure and logically inconsistent in its analysis of the demand for and supply of marketable output. How else, for example, can human capital be formed without expenditure on education? Public expenditure as a share of output was not excessively high in comparative international terms. Even at high levels of total employment, the potential for increased output from manufacturing industry was still large. If British industry had matched French or German levels of productivity growth between the late 1950s and the mid-1970s, the output of manufacturing industry would have been 70 per cent higher than was in fact the case.[4] And as to demand, the inexorable growth of import penetration proves that British industry did not face 'Too Few Consumers'.

The concept of deindustrialization can still have meaning, however. At fuller employment and high levels of productivity there might well have been a proportionate decline but certainly an absolute increase in industrial output. Moreover, these elements are cross-linked as both causes and effects. The consequences for the level of industrial employment are indeterminate, however, because

4. An excellent analysis along these lines is S. Gomulka, 'Increasing Efficiency Versus Low Rates of Technical Change', in Beckerman, *Slow Growth in Britain*, pp. 166–93.

of the large potential for growth in output per worker. Deindustrialization is thus more accurately defined as the loss of potential output and income rather than in terms of changing patterns and levels of industrial employment.

If the focus of analysis is concentrated on the shorter period of the 1980s, the growth of aggregate output and productivity shows a distinct improvement on the 1970s, though the exact extent varies according to the choice of base year. Nevertheless, this improvement amounted to no more than a return to the levels of the 1960s, which in themselves were undistinguished by postwar standards. The acceleration in productivity growth in manufacturing was the result of the shake-out of less efficient plants and changes in manning systems. The former was to some extent reinforced by the removal of government support from so-called lame-duck industries, whilst the latter to some degree resulted from the removal of restrictive labour practices, in turn the consequence of weaker unions, trade union reform and more effective management.[5] But these gains have to be balanced against a 30 per cent reduction in the manufacturing labour force and rising levels of unemployment. Furthermore, productivity growth in services, especially in retailing and distribution, depended increasingly and thus hazardously on booming imports of consumer goods. And an important element in sustaining steady growth in GDP was the revenue from North Sea oil, at least until the late 1980s. Added to which, oil revenues tended to push up the exchange rate with corresponding income effects which reflected favourably, if relatively temporarily, in international comparisons of British economic performance.

The extent to which Britain's comparative international economic performance and position altered during this period is, on this evidence, unclear. Positive gains in certain directions have to be set against losses in others. Nevertheless, the nature of these developments stimulated a new and optimistic interpretation of the economic growth of advanced economies to which attention was drawn at the beginning of this chapter. According to the theory of 'catch-up and convergence', the pace of economic growth over the past century was set by leader economies (by Britain and then by

---

5. See for example, J. Muellbauer, 'Productivity and Competitiveness in British Manufacturing', *Oxford Review of Economic Policy*, 2 (1986), pp. i–xxv; N. Oulton, 'Plant Closures and the "Productivity Miracle" in Manufacturing', *National Institute Economic Review*, 121 (1987), pp. 53–9.

the USA) which established a lead that became a challenge to the 'followers'. Then as countries achieved full industrialization, levels of performance tended to converge and the process of economic growth became a tighter but intra-variable one of catching up and falling behind. It is a very broadly specified model, the dynamics of which depend critically on the technological gap between leaders and followers and on stochastic shocks which stimulate economic adrenaline for the effort of catch-up. Thus, from the end of the Second World War to the early 1970s, the USA is declared the leader, with Britain holding second place. The specific and critical agents in the process were the wide technological gap that opened up between the USA and the other advanced economies during the Second World War, and the shock effects of the war itself; further stimulus was provided by the oil price rises of the 1970s. Under these circumstances, it has been argued, Britain could not have grown more rapidly than it did.[6] At this point, however, Britain began to fall behind. Thus in the 1980s new hope for Britain appeared; whereas the fast-growing economies of the postwar years had been benefiting as followers, the position had now been reversed. With the possible realization of the need for change on the one hand and the possibility of growing complacency among the erstwhile paragons of postwar economic achievement on the other, the opportunities for Britain are held to be greater than at any time during the past century. The improvements in productivity performance in the 1980s are seen as the green shoots of this new spring of opportunity.

For a country to qualify as a 'follower', it must possess 'social capability' which is defined 'as a certain minimum level of economic activity, of education and culture, of social cohesion, and of political and administrative stability'.[7] If, for the moment, the question-begging and imprecise nature of this concept is put to one side, the extent to which 'in-built attitudes and ossified institutions [are] seen to be barriers to progress, [that] gave way to new and more effective arrangements' during these years, needs to be examined.[8] Whilst space does not permit this to be done in great detail, a number of points stand out.

6. C. Feinstein, 'Success and Failure: British Economic Growth Since 1948', in R. Floud and D. McCloskey, *The Economic History of Britain Since 1700. Volume 3: 1939–1992* (Cambridge, 1994), pp. 115–22.

7. Feinstein, 'Benefits of Backwardness', p. 288

8. *Loc. cit.*, p. 291.

The crises of the early 1970s presented a challenge to what had become the orthodox political economy of the postwar period. The parallels with the early 1930s have already been commented on and, it must be added, like the earlier period, the full seriousness of events in the 1970s resulted from the conjunction of short-term conditions and the eventual breakdown in the fundamental basis of the international economy. Unlike the 1930s, the effect on political economy was not to reinforce traditional orthodoxy, at least not directly. Keynesianism was driven into retreat because what Keynes had predicted could never happen had occurred: rising unemployment was accompanied by rising inflation. After the initial shock to their beliefs, Keynesian economists endeavoured to rationalize events in terms of the new concept of 'stagflation'. But for all their ingenuity, these economists offered only a description and little or nothing by way of prescription.

A challenge was mounted by the Left of the Labour party in the form of a new economic policy but, not surprisingly, the proposals it embodied were not sufficiently encompassing of different interest groups.[9] They contained strong elements of nationalism and neo-mercantilism: they were hostile to the European Community and in favour of tariff protection and the increased state ownership and control of industry. The rejection of these policies by the Labour government was clear indication that whilst the political economy of Keynesianism no longer filled the bill, whatever replaced it would have to fit within the existing framework of economic institutions. More specifically, the Labour governments of the 1970s showed little inclination to challenge the power of the Treasury and the Bank of England. As in the case of the critical years of the 1940s, the defence has been entered that during this period, governments were driven along by the sheer force of international events. As has been noted, however, the scale of economic problems was exaggerated by inaccurate analysis, supplied mainly by the Treasury. But whether better quality economic information and advice would have encouraged alternative policies must remain an open question. What we do know is that the eventual impetus to the shift in political economy came not from the political left but from the right.

9. See for example A. N. W. (Tony) Benn, *Against The Tide: Diaries 1973–1976* (1989) and D. Healey, *The Time of My Life* (1989) for views from left and right. And for an approach sympathetic to Labour and arguing for so-called responsible Keynesianism see M. Stewart, *The Jekyll and Hyde Years: Politics and Economic Policy Since 1964* (1977). For a more radical approach see S. Holland, *The Socialist Challenge* (1975).

Monetarism and market economics became the new credo.[10] It challenged the tenets of the postwar social welfare state and Keynesianism. The message was clear and spelt out in simple propositions: government cannot deliver the goods; unemployment cannot be regulated by demand management policies; the natural rate of unemployment is determined by labour market policies. Consequently, the aim must be to remove obstacles such as 'excessive welfare benefits' which inhibit the efficiency of the labour market operating through real wage adjustment to changing economic conditions; the supply of money must be regulated to match the productive capacity of the economy and thus maintain stable prices; deficit finance is not a real policy option. Trade unions, much of public sector employment and fixed exchange rates were declared anathemas: organized labour means wage monopoly power; state employment is inefficient because it is not subject to the test of the market; fixed exchange rates shield unions from the inflationary consequences of their congenital urge to make wage demands.[11]

The theoretical weaknesses of these teachings and, in particular, the highly abstract nature of the concept of the market, cannot be considered in detail here, though the real world failure of the economic policies that this set of beliefs ultimately engendered will be examined a little later. The important historical point is that monetarism and its associated ideas were taken up by the new Conservative government under Thatcher with zeal and conviction, thus providing further support for Keynes's aphorism: '... the ideas of economists and political philosophers, both when they are right and when they are wrong, are more powerful than is commonly

---

10. K. Burk and A. Cairncross, *'Goodbye, Great Britain': The 1976 IMF Crisis* (1992), pp. 197–208. Surveys of doctrine and policy are given by N. H. Dimsdale, 'British Monetary Policy Since 1945', in N. F. R. Crafts and N. W. C. Woodward, *The British Economy since 1945* (Oxford, 1991), pp. 90–7, 129–40 and S. Howson, 'Money and Monetary Policy in Britain, 1945–1990', in Floud and McCloskey, *The Economic History of Britain. Volume 3: 1939–1992*, pp. 222–9, 242–54. See also D. Smith, *The Rise and Fall of Monetarism* (1987); J. C. R. Dow and I. D. Saville, *A Critique of Monetary Policy* (Oxford, 1990 edition).

11. For a statement from one of the converted see S. Brittan, *Second Thoughts on Full Employment Policy* (1975). The analyses of the leading advocates have not stood the test of time. See G. Maynard, *The Economy Under Mrs Thatcher* (Oxford, 1988), especially Chapter 7 which sets out the credo of Thatcherite economists, complete with confident predictions that have proved to be woefully inaccurate even by the normal standards of economic forecasting; A. P. Minford, *Unemployment: Cause and Cure* (Oxford, 1983). By contrast see R. Dornbusch and R. Layard (eds), *The Performance of the British Economy* (Oxford, 1987).

understood. ... Practical men [or women], who believe themselves to be quite exempt from any intellectual influences, are usually the slaves of some defunct economist.'[12] And in this ideological atmosphere, North Sea oil achieved an importance beyond its measurable contribution to the exchequer. It seemed to offer physical confirmation of Britain's new-found independent strength in the world economy.

Thus in the late 1970s the New Right claimed to be removing the barriers to economic progress within which Britain had become entrapped by the collectivism of the welfare state. The historical irony is that this political rhetoric was carried through into practical policy in ways that did not radically change the institutional framework within which policy was formulated and implemented. On any score the Treasury must be counted as one of the most 'ossified institutions' of the postwar period, yet at the end of the 1980s it remained as fully in control of economic policy as it had been at any time since 1945. Indeed, whilst the revenue returns from the privatization of sectors of industry and from North Sea oil allowed the government to match monetarist criteria for the level of the public sector borrowing requirement in conditions of rising unemployment, without imposing tight financial control, ultimately these criteria implied the need for more centralized control of public finance. The replacement of the ideology of Keynesianism with that of monetarism consequently did little to alter the macro-stance of economic policy. Detailed analysis of economic policy is outside the scope of this analysis, though it is important to note that monetarism, as a practical policy, had failed as early as the beginning of the 1980s and was, in effect, abandoned, not least because of the protean nature of money itself.

To aid them in their forecasts and prescriptions monetarists defined money as narrow money, subdivided into M0 and M1 and broad money, subdivided into M2, M3, M3, M4, M5.[13] But they might as well have relied on more conventional astrological tables for all the help these definitions proved to be in regulating the money supply. In a highly developed and open financial system, the forms and sources of credit are numerous and highly responsive to

---

12. J. M. Keynes, *The General Theory of Employment Interest and Money* (1936), p. 383.

13. Narrow money is defined to include (M0) notes and coins in circulation, banks' till money, balances with the Bank of England plus (to give M1) sight deposits held by the private sector with UK banks. Broad money is then successively defined to include all other forms of money and credit instruments.

demand. And whilst the government was attempting to regulate the money supply it was busily deregulating the financial system. The broader question remains, however, as to whether such changes as did occur within economic policy and performance during the period from the early 1970s amounted to an achievement matching the conditions of 'catch-up and convergence' or whether they amount to confirmation of a process of Britain's economic decline in the world.

CATCH-UP AND CONVERGENCE?

There is a broad sense in which the hypothesis of catch-up and convergence holds for the post-1945 period simply because of the interdependence of industrialized economies; an interdependence based on trade in manufactured goods, the emergence of multinational companies and the increasingly global nature of finance. Proof of the existence of these relationships was provided by the international reaction to the financial crisis of the 1970s, such that it did not lead to the kind of economic collapse and autarky which plagued the years up to the Second World War. Yet there is nothing in these conditions that guarantees a country such as Britain permanent membership of the first division of economies in the world.

More specifically, there is, to begin with, the problem of defining the critical width of the economic distance that encompasses leaders and followers, unless it is taken to cover the group of countries designated as advanced economies by the mid-nineteenth century, as measured by income per head. So far as the mechanism of catch-up is concerned, it must operate on some kind of technical change/productivity gain adjustment system that incorporates international capital flows and technical diffusion, though this has never been precisely specified. If, however, some such system is assumed, there still remains the problem of what determines its responsiveness and speed of operation. This difficulty is analogous to that affecting once-fashionable growth theory: the specification of a growth mechanism does not explain why growth rates actually differ. It does not seem that the catch-up mechanism is automatically triggered at a critical point of economic distance between a follower and the leader, since great emphasis is placed in the literature on the importance of stochastic shocks; the major cases in point being the Second World War and the oil price rises.

At best, therefore, what is offered is not a theory but a description that appears to fit a particular period as defined by rates of economic change. Moreover, as such, the analysis comes dangerously near to tautology. Given these problems, what of the case of Britain?

Britain's claims to leadership during this period are fragile.

Table 10.5 Comparative levels of GDP per worker, selected years 1913–88

	1913	1948	1973	1988	1988
	(USA = 100)				(UK = 100)
USA	100	100	100	100	132
UK	78	61	66	76	100
Netherlands	69	52	78	79	104
Denmark	58	51	64	67	88
Sweden	43	51	69	74	97
Belgium	61	49	70	87	114
France	48	37	73	90	118
Germany	49	32	68	81	107
Italy	36	31	60	75	99
Japan	18	16	56	78	103

Source: Feinstein (1994), 117 – based on Maddison (1991).

From Table 10.5 can be seen that the claim might be stretched to cover the period up to the 1970s. But at all times this still left Britain way behind the USA.[14] Furthermore, these are highly aggregated measures and reliance on them constitutes another

14. There is, furthermore, a problem with such comparisons since they are based on purchasing power parity exchange rates which are calculated to take account of price differentials between economies, but this is enormously difficult in relation to non-traded goods and services, particularly given the degree of aggregation in comparative data. The figures in the table are based on OECD expenditure data, but recent calculations based on more accurate production data yield results that show that the OECD figures result in significant overestimates of UK performance in comparison with the other major economies. I find these calculations convincing when placed in the context of overall growth rates during the past 45 years. See B. Van Ark, 'Comparative Levels of Labour Manufacturing Productivity in Europe: Measurement and Comparisons', *Oxford Bulletin of Economics and Statistics*, 52 (1990), pp. 343–74.

weakness of the catch-up and convergence model. In particular, the UK figures for the 1980s are strongly influenced by what might be viewed as the short-term effects of oil income, which also tended to push up the exchange rate, as has been noted. In the manufacturing sector, Britain had fallen behind somewhat earlier than 1970.

Table 10.6 Comparative levels of gross value added per person hour in manufacturing industry, selected years, 1951–88 (UK = 100)

	1951	1964	1973	1979	1988
UK	100	100	100	100	100
France	66	88	113	142	126
Germany	78	117	133	162	137
Netherlands	76	98	135	169	144
USA	254	253	220	226	207

Source: Van Ark (1990), 372.

The acceleration of rates of growth in the early 1980s has already been considered, and, as has been noted, the record appears less impressive when placed in the context of longer-term performance and high and rising unemployment. Altogether this hardly amounts to a convincing case of catch-up after twenty years of being overtaken.

It might be contended, nevertheless, that this was a period of adjustment and that the full effects of the catch-up mechanism will follow. Whilst this must remain largely an open question, there are grounds for scepticism. The record of capital formation is not impressive, even when allowance is made for the probability of more efficient capital use, given reduced manning levels. In only one year between 1979 and 1992 did the investment ratio reach 20 per cent and for most of the period it was significantly below that level. This performance is perhaps even more surprising given the favourable nature of company taxation. Corporation tax had been introduced in 1965 and it operated in such a way that it encouraged companies to retain profits instead of distributing them to shareholders. In this connection it has already been suggested (Chapter 7) that this system, in conjunction with the nature of

Table 10.7 UK gross domestic fixed capital formation, 1973–92 (1990 prices)

	Total (1979 = 100)	Plant & machinery (1979 = 100)	Total as a % of GDP
1979	100	100	17.5
1980	95	100	16.9
1981	86	93	15.5
1982	90	94	16.1
1983	95	98	16.3
1984	103	105	17.3
1985	108	121	17.4
1986	110	123	17.1
1987	122	130	18.0
1988	138	151	19.5
1989	146	169	20.0
1990	141	164	19.4
1991	127	152	17.9
1992	126	148	17.8

Source: *Economic Trends, Annual Supplement* (1994), 13, 63.

Table 10.8 Comparative UK gross saving as a percentage of GDP, 1974–88

	1974–79	1980–88
UK	17.0	17.0
United States	19.8	16.6
Japan	32.8	31.4
Germany	22.6	22.2
France	24.9	20.2
Italy	25.7	22.0
Canada	22.6	20.1
Total OECD	22.8	20.5

Source: OECD, *Historical Statistics* (1990), 74.

capital gains tax, was an important element in the fever of merger activity in the 1960s. In 1974 the system of corporation tax was changed and made retrospective to 1973. The initial, broad aim of the reform was to remove the discrimination in favour of retained profits, but because companies were apparently facing severe liquidity problems in 1974 a range of allowances was specified that could be set against a company's tax liability.[15]

The net result of these changes is particularly significant. Whilst the annual accounts for major companies regularly showed large profits, in many cases the actual amounts of tax paid were either little or nothing. For example, it has been shown that in 1976 British Petroleum returned profits of £1,784 million but paid no tax on this amount. Other examples are Rio Tinto Zinc £279 million (nil tax), Imperial Group £130 million (£9 million), Guest, Keen and Nettlefolds £98 million (nil) and Allied Breweries £63 million (£9 million).[16] The total of these benefits to companies during the subsequent period would seem to have been substantial, and two major points arise from this situation. First, the contrast frequently drawn between the directly subsidized nationalized industries and the private sector obviously requires modification. Secondly, taxation policy was potentially a very powerful instrument of industrial policy that was far from effectively used to achieve objectives of economic performance. The driving force of taxation policy was the fiscal requirements of macroeconomic management, and where companies were concerned the outcome was haphazard and substantially open to avoidance and abuse. There are indications that corporate taxation was an important element in comparative international economic performance. At all events, it is an area that warrants much more detailed investigation.

Whatever the achievements of the hands-off approach to industrial policy in the 1980s in terms of reducing overmanning and forcing inefficient firms out of business through a more competitive market environment, it was not matched by new growth in other sectors of the economy. It has been argued that the potential for such growth existed by the mid-eighties but that the opportunity was squandered by an overexpansionary monetary policy that resulted in an acute balance of payments problem (see

15. See for example Crafts, *Can Industrialization Seriously Damage Your Wealth?*, pp. 54 *ff.*, but also the comments on the theoretical assumptions by W. Eltis in *Economic Journal*, 104 (1994), p. 741.

16. The intricacies of the tax system are clearly analysed in J. A. Kay and M. A. King, *The British Tax System* (1978 ed.), p. 199.

Table 10.4) and undermined an exchange rate policy consistent with more solidly based expansion.[17] If this explanation of events is accepted, it implies that there was nothing automatic or inevitable about catch-up as applied to Great Britain. Apparently, the mechanism could easily be thrown out of gear. At all events, the claim of improved competitiveness in the economy is anything but self-evident. Privatization and deregulation did not reverse the process of growing concentration in British industry. By 1980 the share of output accounted for by the hundred largest firms had passed 50 per cent. The huge swing in the balance of payments in the late 1980s is hardly proof of the competitive capacity of the economy; it is a measure of the failure to compensate for sharply declining oil revenues by import substitution and with increased exports of goods and services. The degree of import penetration grew inexorably.

Recent theories of economic growth at least have the virtue of chiming more closely with historical evidence. In particular, they recognize the importance of human capital and structural factors in economic performance. Human capital is notoriously difficult to measure but studies in the field of education and training at least confirm that the gap in performance between Britain and its major competitors is substantial. Comparisons that have been made in high technology areas are particularly striking.

Table 10.9 Total of mechanical, electrical and electronic engineering qualifications awarded to craft and technician levels in Britain, France and Germany, 1975 and 1987 (000s)

	1975			*1987*		
	Britain	*France*	*Germany*	*Britain*	*France*	*Germany*
Craft	16	51	78	12	68	89
Technician	11	15	25	18	30	45
Total	27	66	103	30	98	134

Source: Steedman (1988), 67.

17. Kay and King, *The British Tax System*, (1978 ed.), p. 199.

Studies of managerial skills in relation to technical change and research and development present a similar picture.[18]

Finally in this respect, there is the role of government. Short-termism, a civil service which is inappropriately recruited and inadequately trained, the undue influence of financial interests centred on the City of London, an over-large government sector: these are among the major charges that have been regularly made against the government in relation to economic performance.[19] They remain unresolved and, as has been argued earlier, the competence of central government to manage the economy for good or ill is subject to severe restraints anyway, though politicians always promise more than they can deliver, without fully understanding the difference. But on the narrow issue of industrial policy, the record is taken by some as evidence of the inherent inability of government to operate successfully in this area, mainly because of a lack of commercial expertise and politicians' acute sensitivity to short-term political pressures and advantage.[20] Proponents of new growth economics go further, by casting doubt on one of the orthodoxies of postwar economic performance, namely, that the role of industrial policy was a powerful element in the economic success of most, if not all, of Britain's major competitors.

The nature and effectiveness of the relationship between government and industry in Western European countries and Japan is a subject of very active debate, but the evidence still points to the inferior performance of Britain in this regard. It is a mistake, nevertheless, to jump from this evidence to the conclusion that

18. See for example National Economic Development Office, *The Making of Managers* (1987); D. Finegold and D. W. Soskice, 'The Failure of Training in Britain: Analysis and Prescription', *Oxford Review of Economic Policy*, 4 (1988), pp. 21–53. S. Prais and K. Wagner, 'Some Practical Aspects of Human Capital Investment: Training Standards in Five Occupations in Britain and Germany', *National Institute Economic Review*, 105 (1983), pp. 46–65; *idem.*, 'Schooling Standards in England and Germany: Some Summary Comparisons Bearing on Economic Performance, *loc. cit.*, 112 (1985), pp. 53–76.

19. On short-termism see C. Mayer, 'Financial Systems and Corporate Investment', *Oxford Review of Economic Policy*, 3 (1987), pp. i-xvi; *idem.*, and I. Alexander, 'Banks and Securities Markets: Corporate Financing in Germany and the UK', *Centre for Economic Policy Research Discussion Paper* No. 117, 1990; J. Franks and C. Mayer, 'Capital Markets and Corporate Control. A Study of France, Germany and the UK', *Economic Policy*, 10 (1990), pp. 191–231.

20. For a survey of these views see Crafts, *Can De-Industrialization Seriously Damage Your Wealth?*, pp. 68 *ff*. Also A. Silberston, 'Industrial Policies in Britain, 1960–1980', in C. F. Carter (ed.), *Industrial Policy and Innovation* (1981), pp. 39–51.

state industry is necessarily less successful than private enterprise. As has been noted, analysis of the record of nationalized industries since 1945 does not bear this out, despite the shifts and turns of policy to which they were subjected. It is rather a case of shortcomings affecting British industry generally. Likewise, to demonstrate the incompetence of government in industrial policy does not automatically provide a case for some revised version of nineteenth-century *laissez-faire.* Government, no less than private enterprise, is open to the charge that it could do better. Whether the charge is justified it is, as yet, too soon for the historian to judge.

BRITAIN'S ECONOMIC DECLINE

As we indicated at the beginning of this chapter, the idea of decline has been a recurrent theme of both popular debate and serious analysis of Britain's political and economic position in the world since the 1960s.[21] The precise origins of the concept are complex, though on the economics side it was closely connected with the application of new techniques of growth accounting. For example, total factor productivity analysis offered a seemingly precise method of explaining why national growth rates differed. The monotonous message was that Britain was increasingly failing to hold its own in the world. As has been implied, the idea of decline was not conceived of wholly in economic terms; it went much wider to incorporate notions of Britain's political role in the world.[22] The loss of Empire has been frequently cited as an unavoidable element of decline, but for many commentators the real failure was that Britain did not adjust to this loss by adopting a more realistic view

21. A recent stimulating addition to the debate that takes a somewhat different line of argument from the one advanced here is B. Supple, 'Fear of Failing: Economic History and the Decline of Britain', *Economic History Review,* 47 (1994), pp. 441–58. G. C. Allen, *The British Disease. A Short Essay on the Nature and Causes of the Nation's Lagging Wealth* (1976). M. W. Kirby, 'Institutional Rigidities and Economic Decline: Reflections on the British Experience', *Economic History Review,* 45 (1992), pp. 637–60. See also G. Ingham, *Capitalism Divided? The City and Industry in British Social Development* (1984) and S. Newton and D. Porter, *Modernization Frustrated: The Politics of Industrial Decline in Britain Since 1900* (1988).
22. C. Barnett, *The Collapse of British Power* (1972) and *idem., The Audit of War: The Illusion and The Reality of Britain As a Great Nation* (1986). But see J. Harris, 'Enterprise and the Welfare State: A Comparative Perspective', *Transactions of the Royal Historical Society,* 40 (1990), pp. 175–95.

of where its international interests lay and by recognizing the need for corresponding social change and institutional reform. The idea of decline did not go unchallenged and the reaction became stronger towards the end of the period, as has been discussed. Whether Britain had experienced decline was, therefore, something in the eye of the beholder, and economic performance was but part of that perception. But it is still important to pose the narrower question of whether there is a practical sense in which Britain has suffered economic decline.

The definition of economic decline is not a straightforward matter of distinguishing between absolute and relative decline – relative, that is, to a given group of countries. For a start, absolute decline can be defined in different ways, depending on whether it is measured over very long periods, in terms of centuries, for example, or over relatively short periods of a decade, or less. Studies of empires in the grand mode fall into the former category, though commonly in such studies insufficient allowance is made for the fact that the economic decline of empires is not invariably accompanied by a corresponding decline in all their constituent parts.[23] Alternatively, during much shorter periods, individual countries may experience severe decline as a consequence of some economic crisis or war. But decline in these cases amounts to a setback and does not develop into a terminal state, although the temporary nature of it may not be obvious to contemporaries or to historians reflecting on it not far beyond the events. Thus the chronology of absolute economic decline, or its obverse, gives rise to conceptual problems in historical interpretation.

Whilst absolute changes in economic well-being over time have meaning it does not follow that they are always historically meaningful. In terms of quantifiable income per head, virtually every country in the world has become better off over the past century. The rise in income per head in Britain can be traced from a much earlier period. At the same time, it can be observed that countries that were once among the leaders on these terms have been outpaced by others, by so much that whilst their levels of income have risen they have become poor by the standards of the rich. In this sense, economic decline is a relative concept similar to relative deprivation as a measure of poverty. Likewise, it is meaningful because it defines standards in terms of what has

<hr/>

23. *Cf.* P. Kennedy, *The Rise and Fall of Great Powers: Economic Change And Military Conflict From 1500–2000* (1988).

actually been attained. Nations like individuals, it may be claimed, judge their comparative economic standing and performance within a time-frame of expectations. The precise length of time depends on the range and nature of expectations involved. If, for example, a family moved from middle-class to working-class status over a century, it would generally be agreed that the fortunes of the family had declined, even though it might be shown that the comparable working-class income had risen over the period to a level above that received by the middle-class family at its outset. There is an obvious and strong sense in which the same kind of relative judgement applies to nations.

In the twentieth century the rate of economic growth has become the primary measure of national economic status. The similarities between this set of values and the earlier tenets of mercantilism, in which the emphasis was on the achievement of national power through the competitive acquisition of wealth as measured by the stock of bullion, is perhaps not sufficiently recognized. Failure to match other nations becomes, in either case, a condition of economic decline. It may be countered that, in the twentieth century, to fall from grace among the rich nations but still to remain among the better off amounts to much less (and is far less important) than the now huge differences between rich and poor countries. Yet whilst this may serve as a reminder to the soul, the idea of judging success or failure, economic advance or economic decline, by the lowest standards instead of the highest hardly accords with economic realism. What is considered to be realistic is, of course, affected by the account taken of non-quantifiable elements in economic performance. Thus failure to achieve high rates of growth in gross domestic product because of an unwillingness to allow massive pollution of the environment, could hardly be counted as evidence of economic decline. But within the present context this qualification is of marginal significance because it is reasonable to assume that it applies generally and similarly to advanced economies.

A final consideration in relation to the criteria for judging economic decline concerns the data used for making international comparisons. The statistics are derived from national accounts and are mainly calculated on an aggregate basis. Even at the level of income per head it is the average that is usually measured. It is obvious that economic performance frequently affects definable and self-conscious groups in society in different ways. In other words, these average measures take no account of the distribution of economic welfare. In Chapter 2 it was pointed out that whilst it might be argued in aggregate terms that the Victorian economy failed, there were significant sections of society, especially among the upper classes, for whom the economy provided a handsome rate of return. By contrast, it can be claimed that through a process of redistributive taxation some sections of the lower reaches of society have gained disproportionately since 1945, even though this process has been reversed over the past decade or so. This, in turn, has resulted from the growing universality of expectations in modern democratic and mass-consuming societies. Thus there are complex issues of equity and the maximization of welfare that cannot be reduced to the crude calculus of national growth rates. But as with more general qualitative aspects of economic performance, it is doubtful whether these matters amount to differences between the advanced economies in the post-1945 period that are so great as to distort the general picture. Economic growth has been, moreover, the most effective solvent of the potentially conflicting demands of different groups within society since 1945.

The very broad picture of comparative economic performance among the major world economies is provided in Table 10.10. The two measures are interdependent and of equal importance. The rate of growth of GDP is a measure of economic expansion; real income per head is a measure of individual prosperity.

Long-run comparisons need to be made carefully since individual countries entered the process of industrialization at different dates. The distinctive characteristic of Britain's economic development has been its relatively low rate of growth over a long period. Its dominant position in the world economy by the end of the third quarter of the nineteenth century was the outcome of an accumulated lead built up since the late eighteenth century, whilst other countries remained largely in a pre-industrial state. In the century that followed, this gap was closed. Britain was soon overhauled by the USA and, then, in the third quarter of the twentieth century the position of the previous hundred years was reversed and Britain began to slip steadily down the league.

The process of change was by no means as even as the steady rhythm of compound rates of economic growth might suggest, since these are average rates. Two world wars and the economic catastrophe of the 1930s were, for their duration, powerful negative forces. But this fact serves to emphasize all the more the disproportionately high rates of growth subsequently achieved by a

Table 10.10 Comparative long-term rates of income growth 1870–89 (%
per year: annual averages)

(a) Real GDP

	1870–1913	1913–50	1950–73	1973–79	1870–1989
UK	1.9	1.3	3.0	2.0	1.9
USA	3.9	2.8	3.6	2.7	3.4
France	1.5	1.1	5.0	2.3	2.2
Germany	2.8	1.3	5.9	2.1	2.8
Italy	1.9	1.5	5.6	2.9	2.6
Japan	2.3	2.2	9.3	3.9	3.8

(b) Real GDP per head

	1870–1913	1913–50	1950–73	1973–79	1870–1989
UK	1.0	0.8	2.5	1.8	1.4
USA	1.8	1.6	2.2	1.6	1.8
France	1.3	1.1	4.0	1.8	1.8
Germany	1.6	0.7	4.9	2.1	2.0
Italy	1.3	0.8	5.0	2.6	2.0
Japan	1.4	0.9	8.0	3.1	2.7

Source: Maddison (1991), 49–50.

number of economies in comparison with Britain. Moreover, the
full nature of these differences is not revealed by aggregate
statistics. Economic growth was frequently concentrated in certain
sectors and/or regions of an economy with a correspondingly high
variance in growth rates. The sharp contrast between high and low
growth rates in the industrial and agricultural sectors of France,
Germany, Sweden and Japan are important cases in point. Italy
provides an example of both sectoral and regional variations. The
crucial point, however, is that unlike Britain, these were patterns of
growth that involved very rapid expansion and structural change.
The Second World War, in particular, had the effect of intensifying

these differences, as has been discussed earlier, particularly in relation to the transfer of labour.

The falling away that had occurred in Britain's position in the world economy by the 1970s was checked, though not significantly reversed, in the 1980s. Even if it is allowed that there was a degree of economic convergence among the major economies, it did not incorporate a major element of 'catch-up' by Britain. On past form there was little that was exceptional about Britain's economic performance in the 1980s. What was unusual was that the previously fast-growing economies of Western Europe and Japan slowed down and at times recorded negative growth. There is little evidence that, by the end of the period, the British economy had changed fundamentally since the 1960s in respect of the weaknesses that afflicted it. Indeed, the experience of the 1980s in some ways reflected that of the earlier period of the 1930s. Both were times of industrial decline and high unemployment combined with an improvement in productivity for those who remained in employment. In both cases, however, the real problem was not what is now defined as deindustrialization but how to generate reindustrialization based on new sectors of industry. Between the 1930s and the 1970s the economy experienced what may be described as a long period of remission, first as a consequence of the demands of war and then as it benefited from the high level of consumer demand during the long boom in the world economy. Under these conditions, newer sectors of industry expanded in the 1950s and the 1960s, but in their organization, management practices and labour relations, they inherited many of the flawed characteristics of the old industries. The motor vehicle industry is probably the example *par excellence*. Once protective measures were removed in the early 1960s the industry was driven into terminal decline by foreign competition.

The challenge of reindustrialization re-emerged in the late 1970s. But it was met by the growing conviction in government, supported among others by the claims of City institutions and a band of market economists, that the economy could almost live by services alone. At all events, the dominant belief was that the regeneration of British industry could be left to the forces of free market competition and that rising unemployment was positive proof that the process was operating successfully. The flow of North Sea oil revenues for a while sustained the fiction. The contribution of oil revenues peaked at 8.7 per cent of government receipts in 1984–85, and the average was 7.1 per cent for the period 1981–86;

thereafter the amounts declined quite sharply.[24] The falsity and damaging consequences of this dogma were painfully exposed in the economic depression of the late eighties and early nineties. Because of the decline in the industrial sector, increased productivity in the 1980s did not lead to higher output, and growth in this sector was essential for higher levels of income and employment. And despite improvements, levels of productivity of British industry remained significantly below those of its major competitors. These differences were reflected in substantially lower levels of capital investment in Britain, especially in human capital. On this count, therefore, there is at least a strong *prima facie* case that Britain remains set on a path of economic decline.

Economic decline defined as a relative concept has strong historical meaning. The drop in growth rates in competitive economies during the 1980s thus becomes an important issue. To what extent these reductions were the consequences of short-term problems in the world economy as against a more permanent shift in comparative advantage, especially in relation to newly industrializing economies, is impossible to say at this point. Even so, some commentators have gone so far as to suggest that those erstwhile thrusters and high achievers have now reached a new level of economic maturity in international terms, and will settle back into attitudes and institutional rigidity in some ways similar to those that have conditioned Britain's slower growth since the Second World War. Whether this is so must remain an open question. But as a basis for a more optimistic view of Britain's position in the world economy it is far from reassuring. Even if, for example, Britain were to sustain the margin of higher growth over OECD countries that it achieved in the 1980s, it would still take it a number of decades, up to half a century, to reach the levels of the leaders.

The thrust of our analysis is that there are few signs that Britain has reversed the condition of relative economic decline that has been endemic to its development since the late nineteenth century. Yet it is necessary to repeat that the status of nations, whether they are judged to be in the ascendant or in decline, is a matter of perception that is not restricted to economic standing and performance. But perception is so easily clouded by delusion. Thus, the prime minister who presided over Britain during the 1980s

---

24. C. Bean, 'The Impact of North Sea Oil', in Dornbusch and Layard, *The Performance of the British Economy*, pp. 64–96.

could claim that Britain's victory in the Falklands War showed that Britain was, after years of decline, restored to the path of greatness. *Plus ça change* ....[25]

25. M. Thatcher, *The Downing Street Years* (1993), p. 235.

Appendix: Statistical Sources

1. Alford, B. W. E. (1988), *British Economic Performance 1945–1975* (Cambridge).
2. Bacon, R. and Eltis, W. A. (1976), *Britain's Economic Problem: Too Few Producers.*
3. Bairoch, P. (1982), 'International Industrialization Levels From 1750 to 1980', *The Journal of European Economic History,* 11, pp. 269–333.
4. Brown, C. F. J. and Sheriff, T. D. (1979), 'De-Industrialization – A Background Paper' in Blackaby, F. T. (ed.), *De-industrialization,* pp. 233–62.
5. Cairncross, A. (1985), *Years of Recovery. British Economic Policy 1945–51.*
6. Capie, F., *Depression and Protectionism. Britain Between the Wars.*
7. Chapman, S. (1984), *The Rise of Merchant Banking.*
8. CSO, *Annual Abstract of Statistics.*
9. CSO, *Economic Trends, Annual Supplements.*
10. CSO, *National Income and Expenditure.*
11. Dow, J. C. R. (1965), *The Management of the British Economy 1945–60* (Cambridge).
12. Feinstein, C. H. (1965), *Domestic Capital Formation in the United Kingdom 1920–1938* (Cambridge).
13. *Idem.,* (1972), *National Income, Expenditure and Output of the United Kingdom 1855–1965* (Cambridge).
14. *Idem.,* (1990a), 'What Really Happened to Real Wages? Trends in Wages, Prices, and Productivity in The United Kingdom, 1880–1913', *Economic History Review,* 43, pp. 329–55.
15. *Idem.,* (1990b), 'Benefits of Backwardness and Costs of Continuity', in Graham, A. and Seldon, A. (eds), *Government and Economies in the Postwar World. Economic Policies and Comparative Performance, 1945–85,* pp. 284–93.

16.   *Idem.*, (1994), 'Success and Failure: British Economic Growth Since 1948', in Floud, R. and McCloskey, D. (eds), *The Economic History of Britain Since 1700. Volume 3: 1939–1992*.

17.   Feis, H. (1965), *Europe, The World's Banker 1870–1914* (New York).

18.   Lamartine Yates, P. (1959), *Forty Years of Foreign Trade*.

19.   Law, C. M. (1967), 'The Growth of Urban Population in England and Wales 1801–1911', *Transactions: Institute of British Geographers*, 41, pp. 125–43.

20.   Lee, C. H. (1986), *The British Economy Since 1700* (Cambridge).

21.   Lewis, W. A. (1978), *Growth and Fluctuations, 1870–1913*.

22.   Maddison, A. (1991), *Dynamic Forces in Capitalist Development. A Long-Run Comparative View* (Oxford).

23.   Maizels, A. (1963), *Industrial Growth and World Trade* (Cambridge).

24.   Matthews, R. C. O., Feinstein C. H. and Odling-Smee, J. C. (1982), *British Economic Growth 1856–1973* (Oxford).

25.   Milward, A. S. (1984), *The Reconstruction of Western Europe 1945–51*.

26.   *Idem.*, (1992), *The European Rescue of the Nation-State*.

27.   Mitchell, B. R. (1988), *British Historical Statistics* (Cambridge).

28.   OECD, (1990), *Historical Statistics*.

29.   Pollard, S. (1989), *Britain's Prime and Britain's Decline*.

30.   Prais, S. (1981), 'Vocational Qualifications of the Labour Force in Britain and Germany', *National Institute Economic Review*, 98, pp. 47–59.

31.   Saul, S. B. (1960), *Studies in British Overseas Trade 1870–1914* (Liverpool).

32.   *Idem.*, (1965), 'The Export Economy', *Yorkshire Bulletin of Economic and Social Research*, 17.

33.   Rowthorn, R. E. and Wells, J. R. (1987), *De-Industrialization and Foreign Trade* (Cambridge).

34.   Steedman, H. (1988), 'Vocational Training in France and Britain: Mechanical and Electrical Craftsmen', *National Institute Economic Review*, 126, pp. 57–70.

35.   Tew, J. H. B., 'The Bretton Woods Regime – February 1961 to March 1973', unpublished paper supplied by the author.

36.   Van Ark, B. (1990), 'Comparative Levels of Labour Manufacturing Productivity in Europe: Measurement and Comparisons', *Oxford Bulletin of Economics and Statistics*, 52, pp. 343–74.

37.   Woodruff, W. (1966), *Impact of Western Man. A Study of Europe's Role in The World Economy 1750–1850*.

Index